The Theatre of Kander and Ebb

The Theatre of Kander and Ebb

Robert Gordon

methuen | drama

LONDON · NEW YORK · OXFORD · NEW DELHI · SYDNEY

METHUEN DRAMA
Bloomsbury Publishing Plc
50 Bedford Square, London, WC1B 3DP, UK
1385 Broadway, New York, NY 10018, USA
29 Earlsfort Terrace, Dublin 2, Ireland

BLOOMSBURY, METHUEN DRAMA and the Methuen Drama logo are trademarks of
Bloomsbury Publishing Plc

First published in Great Britain 2025

A catalogue record for this book is available from the British Library.

A catalog record for this book is available from the Library of Congress.

ISBN: HB: 978-1-3501-0708-3
PB: 978-1-3501-0709-0
ePDF: 978-1-3501-0711-3
eBook: 978-1-3501-0710-6

Typeset by Deanta Global Publishing Services, Chennai, India
Printed and bound in Great Britain

For product safety related questions contact productsafety@bloomsbury.com.

To find out more about our authors and books visit www.bloomsbury.com and
sign up for our newsletters.

To O, without whom...

Contents

Figures

Introduction

Kander and Ebb in the Broadway tradition

Commercial success and artistic innovation: lowbrow/highbrow

The only scholarly monograph on Kander and Ebb's work by James Leve was published in 2009, so it is now out of date. As the monograph is written from a musicological perspective, my book aims to identify the nature of the theatrical collaboration that renders their musical dramaturgy unique, as well as to deal with all their musicals produced up to 2023.[1]

John Kander and Fred Ebb were the most artistically and commercially successful musical theatre writing team since Rodgers and Hammerstein. Their biggest hits, *Cabaret* (1966) and *Chicago* (1975), became hugely successful film musicals, but the respective revivals of *Chicago* in 1996 and *Cabaret* in 1987 and 1998, together with the numerous revivals of the latter in London[2] and on numerous European stages, made Kander and Ebb by far the most commercially successful American writers of musicals, giving *Cabaret* a combined run on Broadway of 4,112 performances and *Chicago* a total run of over 13,000 performances. At times aspiring to match Stephen Sondheim in the sophistication of their artistic approach, Kander and Ebb nevertheless aimed to appeal to a popular audience who wished to be entertained before being enlightened.[3]

Notwithstanding Sondheim's critical pre-eminence, Kander and Ebb have achieved a more effective blend of popular and 'high' art, though it must be admitted that, as in Sondheim's case, a number of their most ambitious works (*The Scottsboro Boys*, 2010; *The Visit*, 2015) while being critical successes have been box-office failures. None of the three artists was educated to view the musical's commercial imperatives as too restrictive to admit the values of high art. Sondheim, together with some of his contemporaries and successors, challenged the hierarchical distinctions of high-, low- and middle-brow art in a postmodern dispensation that has prompted the eradication of such value judgements. Indeed, Kander and Ebb's deployment of popular forms and genres is a means of creating theatre that is both commercially profitable and artistically innovative. According to lyricist Fred Ebb, 'We're looking for a new form of musical theater, one that'll break away from what's become stale and static, and self-imitative. We're looking back in time only to look forward in form.'[4]

Sondheim is still regarded by critics as the more 'serious' artist; in an interview, Kander claimed that he would be glad to have written anything of Sondheim's. In his opinion,

Steve is an extraordinary writer, and I listen to his work and admire it enormously. When something of his is new or in a workshop, I'm thrilled to be able to tell him how I feel. I remember seeing the run-through of *Sunday in the Park* when they only had the first act. I understood what he was doing, and I was very moved by it. I couldn't wait to call him.[5]

Nonetheless, the team have themselves always sought out difficult subject matter: in Ebb's words, 'the show that I like to write most . . . [is] something very unlikely, something you never imagine could be done. I'd like to prove you were wrong.'[6] Their 'landmark partnership [. . .] yielded such classics of the Broadway canon as *Zorba*, *Chicago* [. . .] *Woman of the Year*, and *Kiss of the Spider Woman* — all challenging shows which respectively deal with such difficult atypical Broadway topics as revenge killings, corrupt trials, the private life of a celebrity reporter, and prison torture.'[7]

From Broadway sound to unique sonic worlds

The critic Frank Rich has asserted that Kander and Ebb's score for *Flora the Red Menace* (1965) represents 'one of the last voices left of what the Broadway musical sounded like just before rock and roll came in'.[8] According to Kander, 'my biggest influences, if you're just thinking historically would be Jerome Kern and Marc Blitzstein . . . I'm aware sometimes of what I feel from their work.'[9] The sound of both composers can certainly be heard in *Flora*'s combination of romantic songs (especially 'It's a Quiet Thing') and the socially aware protest of the Prologue, but the pair's distinctive Broadway voice is most clearly heard in Kander's music for Ebb's insistent 'happy' lyrics in 'One Good Break' and 'Sing Happy' – the sound that would come to be indelibly associated with the star persona of Liza Minnelli.

Figure 1. John Kander and Fred Ebb. Photo: Martha Swope NYPL, Billy Rose Divi

In fact, this particular sound either blends or contrasts the urban jazz of Ebb's lyrics with the emotional intensity of Kern and Puccini, for Kander has always reminded interviewers of his abiding love of romantic opera,[10] proclaiming his musical preferences in an interview with Kristen Childs, as elsewhere, 'If you ask me overall it would be Wagner, Puccini and Mozart'.[11] As a musical technician, however, his ability to absorb a wide range of musical styles is unrivalled. Preparing for *Chicago*, he claims, 'I listened to lots and lots of jazz of the period' and his advice to new composers was 'Soak yourself in the music and forget about it'.[12] Counterbalancing Kander's love of opera and romantic music, Ebb was a huge admirer of composer-lyricist Frank Loesser, with his inventive ideas for songs, as well as the lyrical genius of Lorenz Hart.[13] The acidic quality – akin to Hart – and the wisecracking New Yorkishness, reminiscent of Loesser, gave Ebb's lyrics a vernacular comic bite that in combination with Kander's emotional intensity produced a recurring switchback of sentiment and cynicism, passion and irony that became the signature style of 'Kandernebb' ('Everything is about collaboration – everything'[14]).

According to Kander,

There has to be a kind of theatricality . . . there has to be a kind of intriguing . . . music built into it [. . .] In writing *Cabaret*, in writing *Zorba*, in writing *Kiss of the Spiderwoman* . . . any show that has a particular time or place . . . *Cabaret* was easy. I listened to lots and lots and lots of German jazz . . . and German cabaret songs of that period – not so much Kurt Weill, as a matter of fact, but songs by Friedrich Hollaender . . . a lot of people . . . The interesting thing is that I listened to everybody but Kurt Weill because I knew that was a dangerous area to be walking into. I stayed away zealously from listening to Weill at all. What I think happened is that the kind of Kurt Weill musical pieces that we hear in our heads were influenced by the same thing that I was sort of digging into. His early music and more serious music is, in many ways, in a totally different style and quite wonderful and slightly academic. When he comes to writing his musicals or operas, if you will, he's reflecting the sounds of those vaudeville houses and German jazz and that sort of sleazy world that I was trying to reflect, also . . . I didn't want to sound like second-rate Kurt Weill.[15]

Sonic worlds and dramaturgical coherence

The sonic world that seems distinctive in each of their shows from *Cabaret* (1966) to *The Visit* (2015) is the mark of 'a kind of theatricality . . . a kind of intriguing . . . music built into it',[16] which Kander considers the *sine qua non* of successful musicals. In the case of *Flora*, the failure to frame the 'Liza/Flora' voice in an appropriate sonic world of Depression-era New York is the aspect of composition that undermines the artistic coherence of the show: with a younger, less traditional book-writer/director than George Abbott, the team believe it might well have worked. If one contemplates artistically satisfying musical comedies from *Show Boat* (1927) to *Follies* (1971), one can observe how each elaborates a scheme of musical numbers that coherently and wittily evokes a 'sonic world' as a matrix for the dramaturgical style.

In fact, it was Jerome Kern's formal experimentation in *Show Boat* (1927) that, in conjunction with Hammerstein's exploration of the possibility of replacing musical comedy's 'stand-alone' songs with 'musical scenes', initiated a paradigm of musical integration for what was later named the 'golden age' musical. Employing throughout Act One a pseudo-Wagnerian technique of *Leitmotiv* that shapes a unified musical score (Act Two does not completely succeed in this respect), Kern and Hammerstein elaborated a pattern of interwoven songs rather than a random assortment of numbers, as in previous musical comedies. Possibly taking their cue from nineteenth-century melodrama, which is certainly a key element in adapting the libretto from Edna Ferber's book, Kern and Hammerstein supply underscoring of spoken passages ('melos' is the term used in melodrama), which is a virtual soundtrack to action and speech. Himself a well-schooled musician, Kern used Dvorak's 'New World' Symphony intertextually as a kind of musical reference point from which melody, harmony, rhythmic patterns and instrumentation were constructed as an aural analogue of the United States melting pot, utilizing a wide variety of contrasted European and African American musical idioms as building blocks for its musical complex. In *Can't Help Singin'*, Gerald Mast refers to the echoes and inversions of black and white music as 'musical anagrams',[17] an illuminating designation to indicate the way 'Ol Man River' and 'Cotton Blossom' are musically counterpoised to voice both the conflict between and the potential harmonization of races in *Show Boat*.

This interplay of musical styles and moods typifies key features of milieu or psychology, expressing characteristic social habits and underlying mental attitudes in vivid contradistinction – a musicalization of the different cultures that may either divide or integrate Black and white Americans. The authors even quote a popular European song of the late-nineteenth century, 'After the Ball', interpolating it in the second half of the second act to signify the precise time period of the event represented. Non-musical dramas cannot create such 'sound worlds', so are obliged to utilize the ordinary patterns of speech and rhythms of action/movement and visual spectacle to suggest a specific milieu or a particular mentality, but they cannot embody them aurally as do the immersive modes of song, dance and music.

One of the earliest musical comedies to organize its score into a scheme of songs that demonstrated the dominant 'argument' of the show was Rodgers and Hart's *On Your Toes* (1936), whose narrative structure sets a Russian ballet company against American hoofers to promote a discourse of classical (highbrow) vs. jazz/swing dance music (lowbrow). The score includes the faux-classical *Princess Zenobia* ballet composed by Rodgers in a sub-Tchaikovsky manner for the close of Act 1 and a jazz ballet in the manner of Gershwin's concert music as the eleven o'clock number.[18] In reinforcing the trope of ballet versus American hoofing, *On Your Toes* inscribes into the texture of performance American cultural anxieties concerning the inferiority of indigenous art forms by comparison with those from the 'old world'.

Through the vigorous demonstration of the virility of American song and dance as popular forms, the musical exploits the zest and spontaneity of the native form to reinforce the audience's imagined philistine prejudice against the effete elitism of Russian ballet, which is ultimately reformed when Junior composes and dances a jazz ballet that involves a fusion of the opposed forms. The sonic world of *On Your Toes* is 1930s American dance culture: while most of the musical numbers are written in a highly syncopated, up-tempo rhythm, *Too Good for the Average Man* is a *faux*-minuet, opposed to *Quiet Night* and *Glad to Be Unhappy* that represent a crossover between African American blues and European operetta, foreshadowing the impact of the show's lengthy jazz ballet.

Pal Joey (1940) develops such a scheme even more elaborately in its counterpointing of lowbrow diegetic numbers on the nightclub stage versus more sophisticated non-diegetic songs. Hart contrasted the different idioms very skilfully to produce songs that address the relationship of sex and love, with a yoking of his customary harsh wit and pervasive melancholy. The complexity of the non-diegetic songs is exemplified well by 'I Could Write a Book', with its beguiling duplicity that both reveals and conceals Joey's calculated seduction of Linda: the references to literary genres reinforce the poetic quality of the diction, yet the fact that Joey is so self-conscious about his claim of artistry as a writer – patently untrue because his literary skills are in fact primitive – also implies his feelings are being faked. 'Bewitched, Bothered and Bewildered' is genuinely literary in its self-awareness, one of the most sophisticated musical theatre songs that laments with devastating irony the humiliating consequences of sexual infatuation. The world of the nightclub and the burlesque theatre provides the ground upon which contrasts and variations are played to encompass the milieu of the show. The broad parodies of conventional nightclub numbers about love ('Plant You Now, Dig You Later' and 'The Flower Garden of My Heart') expose the ignorant affectations of performers and writers who cannot distinguish crude literary conceits from genuine poetic metaphors.

Even more ambitious in the artistic organization of its score is Weill, Gershwin and Moss Hart's *Lady in the Dark* (1941), which interpolates four mini-operas within the play. The four through-composed pieces evoke dreams disclosing the unconscious of the fashion editor Liza Elliot, framed by her sessions with the psychoanalyst who is helping her free herself from the repression preventing her from making a crucial personal decision. Ingeniously, the musical deploys the song 'My Ship', first hummed in fractured form by Liza at the beginning of the show to emblematize her frozen state as well as her ultimate victory over this inhibition when at the end of the show she manages to perform the full song, with its lyrical homage to pleasure and fulfilment. The next musical comedy to exhibit such musical coherence is Bernstein, Comden and Green's *On the Town* (1944), a musical kaleidoscope of New York City sights and sounds as encountered by three sailors on twenty-four hours' shore leave. Inspired by Jerome Robbins' sailor ballet *Fancy Free*, the musical is structured like a full-length dance piece, so that Bernstein's music aurally imitates the events and images of the day in a mode akin to programme music.[19] New York is depicted through its distinctive sound world.

Musical comedy in the 'golden age'

Written in response to Rodgers and Hammerstein's much-vaunted achievement of integrated dramaturgy with *Oklahoma!* (1943) and *Carousel* (1945), Cole Porter and Sam and Bella Spewack's musical comedy *Kiss Me, Kate!* (1948) is an attempt to achieve the narrative coherence of these paradigmatic 'musical plays' while observing the overtly *dis*integrated performance conventions of musical comedy. The show thereby elaborates a 'double economy': maintaining a carefully plotted narrative logic in which songs and dances forward the plot and/or provide character development, while at the same time, each serves to maximize the pleasure of the audience by means of sheer entertainment. The comic counterpoising of Shakespeare's *The Taming of the Shrew* against a thematically parallel framing narrative of actors presenting a production of the Shakespeare comedy wittily musicalizes the trope of demotic (lowbrow) versus artistic (highbrow) expressions of romantic love that had constituted Lorenz Hart's leitmotif from *On Your Toes* onwards, presented at its most obvious by the celebrated 'Brush up Your Shakespeare', a comic paradigm of the trope with its two gangsters showing off their surprisingly extensive knowledge of Shakespeare in broad Brooklynese. The comic point is that Shakespearean theatre has become part of popular culture so, as in *On Your Toes*, highbrow and lowbrow cultures have fused. Throughout the show, Porter exhibits a subtle mastery of both pseudo-Elizabethan and Broadway 'swing' modes of song, at times, allowing one to shade imperceptibly into the other. The sonic world is theatre – both highbrow and low.

Possibly the greatest masterpiece of Broadway musical comedy, Frank Loesser's *Guys and Dolls* (1950) brilliantly employs music to create a sonic identity for the Broadway underworld of gambling, striptease and petty crime, with the pastiche of Salvation Army marching songs balanced against and occasionally overlapping with swing and Cuban conga musical styles in a tongue-in-cheek deployment of the traditional highbrow/lowbrow trope. The exhilarating swing of the underworld and the sensuous syncopation of the conga are jokingly comprehended as the temptations of hell in contradistinction to the heavenly 'salvation' of the religious music, but a potential union of the secular and the religious is glimpsed in the gangsters' rousing rendition of their pseudo-spiritual eleven o'clock number, 'Sit Down You're Rocking the Boat' – again a concatenation of the sacred meaning of a spiritual with its African American musical form. The underworld is scenically intimated by the subterranean location of the gambling den in a sewer, while the lyrics of 'Luck Be a Lady' configure the notion of chance as personal destiny with the connected images of a refined woman (definitely *not* a doll!) as opposed to God's predetermination as destiny. The Times Square location is both musically and visually contrasted with Havana, a non-Christian Utopia in which pleasure is not a sin and where the puritanical American polarization of ethical value against having a good time does not pertain.

In some respects, *The Music Man* (1957) takes the idea of aural enactment, manifest so strikingly in *On the Town*, even further by means of Meredith Willson's use of music as descriptive sound, a type of onomatopoeic effect in which songs appear to embody their own implicit actions through sound. The climactic moment when Harold Hill gets the town's young people to hear the noise they are making on instruments they cannot play ('76 Trombones') as the music of a big brass band is the thematic key to understanding the meaning of the show; the 'soundtrack' of the real pit band mimicking the sound the children *imagine* they are making. John Kander's Broadway debut in *Gypsy* (1959) as arranger of the dance music exposed him to a sonic world of pastiche vaudeville and burlesque, its performance of onstage musical numbers spilling over into daily life to create the mindset of people who eat, sleep and dream show business.

The Broadway musical: an idea by Lehman Engel

The musical director and orchestrator Lehman Engel began to codify the principles of the 'golden age' musical in the late 1950s, publishing two books on the Broadway musical as a kind of guide for composers and librettists on writing a successful show. Needless to say, although *West Side Story* (1957) is mentioned by Engel, the conventions apply most appropriately to musical comedy written between *Annie Get Your Gun* (1946) and *Mame* (1966). His ideas on 'book' musical conventions are not entirely consistent, but many generations of budding musical theatre writers have been influenced by his concepts since he founded a regular workshop in the 1960s aimed at teaching craft skills to neophyte composers and writers. The BMI Lehman Engel workshops still run as an evening school and there has even been a musical about Engel's class, *A Class Act* (2001).

Engel categorized musical theatre songs into the following types:

- Ballads
- 'I Am'/'I Want' songs
- Comedy songs
- Charm songs
- Rhythm songs
- 'Jump' songs
- List songs
- Eleven o'clock numbers
- Reprises

He also discusses the musical scene as perfected by Hammerstein in *Oklahoma!* and *Carousel*. The types are fairly obvious, the only one needing explanation being the eleven o'clock number, which signifies the show-stopper for the star near the end of the show just before the finale. Eleven o'clock was usually just before the closing time of a Broadway show, which started at 8:30 pm and ran between two hours forty minutes and three hours. Clearly, these categories are questionable, but the typology was shared knowledge among Broadway authors, who possessed this vocabulary as an arsenal that might be deployed if necessary. In the UK or Europe, such categories have had no currency whatsoever. Kander and Ebb were *aux fait* with Lehman Engel's prescriptions for writing a successful musical, but they certainly did not follow them slavishly, if at all.

Against integration: towards a postmodern aesthetics of the musical

The drive in *Show Boat* towards 'integration' in both score and book can be construed from another perspective as promoting an alternative model of structure that tends towards ironic disjunction and separation of component parts. In 1928, a year after *Show Boat* opened on Broadway, Bertolt Brecht and Kurt Weill's *Dreigroschenoper* (*The Threepenny Opera*) made an equally significant theatrical triumph in Berlin, by comparison adopting aesthetic principles in direct opposition to those regarded as hallmarks of Kern and Hammerstein's show. Brecht and Weill championed an anti-Wagnerian separation of musical theatre elements, a kind of exaggeratedly theatrical musical comedy comprising book, lyrics, music and scenography as distinct elements whose jarring counterpoint constructed a series of ironic commentaries on one another. Interpreted through the prism of Brecht and Weill, *Show Boat*'s promiscuous accommodation of Dvorak, Italian opera, Austrian operetta, Russian Jewish klezmer, nineteenth-century Viennese waltz, vaudeville, African American jazz, 'coon' shouting, minstrelsy and Negro spiritual might alternatively be seen as a deliberate avoidance of any organicist notion of musical 'integration' in favour of a heterogeneous mix of song forms.

Over the last decade, scholars have increasingly come to question the notion of integration that has dominated earlier conceptualizations of the Broadway musical, which conventionally assume 'integration' as its chief artistic goal. Bradley Rogers' *The Song Is You*[20] is the most recent work to question the 'golden age' ideal of integration in order to characterize its dominant affect as inherently disruptive, its emphasis on performative strategies challenging earlier critical approbation for the uninterrupted flow of the linear narrative. This contemporary approach uncouples formal integration from artistic coherence, stressing the audience's desire for performers to 'break into song and dance' as the primary driver of the unique form of the musical as a heterogeneous assemblage of performative forms.

Lerner and Weill's *Love Life* (1948) prefigures the so-called concept musical of the late 1960s and 1970s. Its detachment of musical numbers from the unfolding stream of action permits the disaggregation of the performative elements from the narrative fiction. With its vaudeville songs framing the discrete historical periods to generate comparisons of different notions of marriage, the show's use of vaudeville as both structural frame and metaphor was a direct influence on Kander and Ebb, who revel in the self-reflexivity of such performative techniques in the majority of their works. Indeed, in many of their shows (*Cabaret, 70 Girls 70, Chicago, The Kiss of the Spiderwoman, Curtains* and *The Scottsboro Boys*), performance constitutes both form and subject matter. Each of these musicals maps an overtly disruptive pattern of performative moments onto a dense network of underlying tropes. By deconstructing old forms, their musicals seek to interrogate the implicit values they incarnate.

On 'Popular' and 'Mass' entertainment

From *Show Boat* to *Cabaret*, Broadway musicals have attempted to assert the seriousness of the art form by insisting on some sort of *rapprochement* between the American vernacular and European high art. Some critics and theorists of culture would challenge the very notion that such a commercial form of theatre as the musical could be regarded as art. Certain schools of sociology take the view that since the advent of wholly capitalist industrial societies, manifestations of the popular have not emanated directly from the people but have been constructed and controlled by business interests as 'mass entertainment'. In engaging with commercial artworks, a critic is obliged to formulate an appreciation that acknowledges the somewhat tricky relationship between 'popular' and 'mass' culture. Twentieth-century critiques of popular or mass entertainment have largely been informed by one of two schools of thought – the Frankfurt School of Adorno and Horkheimer, with the distinctive interventions of Walter Benjamin, or the approach of American cultural critics of the post-war period, who pursued Dwight D. Macdonald's lead in adumbrating the concept of mass culture.

Adorno was highly educated musically, so it is understandable that his attack on the inauthenticity of jazz as an exemplar of commercial 'standardisation' should have proved challenging for the criticism of musical theatre. While Adorno elevated the music of the great Western composers to an unmediated expression of genius beyond the determination of ideology, at the same time consigning popular culture to the garbage heap of inauthentic kitsch, a rival German cultural critic, Walter Benjamin, was the first Marxist theorist to consider mass art as an expression of the modern culture of the proletariat, offering an inclusive prospectus of the new opportunities of the 'art-work in the age of mechanical reproduction'. While acknowledging the 'aura' of the original artwork, he was nevertheless deeply sympathetic to the artistic ambitions of the fledgling film industry. In contrast, for instance, with the live stage production, which pre-eminently depended on the 'aura' of its unrepeatable performances, the film drama could be copied and presented millions of times around the world. For critics such as Adorno, such reproducibility implied a loss of authenticity in the mechanically replicated work. Yet for Benjamin, the notion of popularity it offered through the media of mechanical reproduction (sound recording and film) inaugurated the possibility of a kind of mass art, whose reproducibility provided the opportunity for the proletariat to encounter and appreciate complex art objects, whose lack of 'aura' was a sign of the democratic nature of their consumption.

Adopting Bernard Shaw's maxim that 'the theatre is always at a low ebb', Eric Bentley in *The Playwright as Thinker* ironically dismissed the much-touted integration of *Oklahoma!* as merely the 'ebb' of a tradition of 'theatricalism', claiming that music drama was not in itself integrated but required the director to synthesize all the artistic components in order to achieve 'integration'. Between the 1940s and 1960s, highbrow and lowbrow forms were both acceptable to critics, whereas middlebrow was judged as pretentious bourgeois kitsch. After musical plays had been denigrated by a scholar of Bentley's importance as 'middlebrow', arguments circulated about whether musicals should be affectionately championed as purely escapist lowbrow diversions – 'only entertainment' in Richard Dyer's words – or valued as highbrow artworks, increasingly the case with many of the works of Sondheim (e.g. *Sweeney Todd,* 1979; *Sunday in the Park with George*, 1984; *Passion*, 1994).

Russell Lynes' provocative article in *Harper's* (1949)[21] explained how the categories of post-war American cultural consumption underlie the hatred of highbrow cultural critics for middlebrow culture. Serious promoters and theorists of musical theatre as popular or folk art are obliged to confront the conundrum that middlebrow attitudes to art are incompatible with the forms of mass or popular entertainment, which highbrows are content to indulge.[22] Yet musicals account for the highest proportion of attendance at theatres around the world, so they demand to be studied not only by musicologists and theatre scholars but also by sociologists of popular culture and, in their cinematic form, as a species of mass entertainment. Perhaps then, it should be possible to distinguish between their economic aims and the level of artistic sophistication manifest in the many different individual variations of the mass formula. No less surprising a figure than Goebbels made careful distinctions between popular entertainment that crudely reinforced Nazi racist stereotypes and that which subtly invoked a cultural imaginary grounded in a racist Darwinian unconscious.

In 1953, Dwight Macdonald published 'A Theory of Mass Culture', in *Diogenes*.[23] Macdonald himself cited, along with Clement Greenberg, critical works on mass culture by writers associated with the Frankfurt School, including Max Horkheimer, Leo Löwenthal and Theodor Adorno, whose analysis of standardization in popular music Macdonald called 'brilliant'. The Frankfurt School combined anti-capitalist politics and modernist aesthetics. 'Folk Art was the people's own institution, their private little garden', Macdonald argued in the new essay. 'But Mass Culture breaks down the wall, integrating the masses into a debased form of High Culture and thus becoming an instrument of political domination.'[24]

What Macdonald despised most was *'l'avant-garde pompier'* – fake avant-gardism: 'There is nothing more vulgar than sophisticated *kitsch*'.[25] Macdonald eventually categorized this pseudo-avant-gardism as the culture of middlebrow aspiration – 'Midcult'. True kitsch, he believed, could be left to the masses. The real enemy was bourgeois high-mindedness in literature, music, theatre, art, and criticism, and over the next ten years, he applied his critical acumen to the task of identifying this culture, exposing its calculated banalities, often persuading his readers of its meretricious qualities. As first mooted by Bentley in his attack on Broadway theatre as 'middlebrow', the term 'Midcult' could most appropriately be applied to the golden age book musical. In different ways, Sondheim advanced the golden age musical tradition that was first formulated by Oscar Hammerstein II to create a postmodern model for the non-linear musical, while Kander and Ebb intuitively reacted to the downgrading of the golden age musical as bourgeois kitsch.

The integrated book musical and its discontents

Through the use of postmodern techniques of pastiche and deconstruction, Kander and Ebb, as much as Sondheim and his collaborators, distanced themselves from the 'mid-cult' values of integrationists by producing musical-lyrical critiques of its sentimental *Weltanschaung*. The forms they chose quoted rather than naively exploiting the conventions they inherited, interrogating its mass entertainment clichés from an ironic and somewhat unbelieving perspective that highlighted 'mid-cult' values to expose the banality of their bourgeois world view. When they wrote a conventional Lehman Engel-style ballad, its clichés were revealed by a tacit expression of its unattainable utopias. The shattering intensity of Flora's/Minnelli's 'All I Need Is One Good Break' represents a shared awareness that it is impossible to achieve the success she so forcefully demands.

In the majority of Kander and Ebb's shows, this generated a dramaturgical paradigm of self-reflection that questions the pleasures of the specularity through which the musical operates, in order to animate a dialectical discourse between musical theatre and the life it portrays, between entertainment and history, between spectacle as escapism and the brutal reality of human suffering as spectacle. Reality always betrays the desires either desperately or cynically articulated in song. Analysis of the meta-theatrical structure of *Cabaret* provides a key to comprehending Kander and Ebb's recurring deployment of modes of epistemological recursiveness, even in the shows that – unlike *Cabaret*, *Chicago* (1975) and *The Scottsboro Boys* (2010) – do not explicitly exploit popular entertainment genres as core structural devices. The photos emblematizing the photographer's fake memories in *The Happy Time* (1968), the dance marathon framing the action of *Steel Pier* (1997) or the fantasy musical movie sequences in *The Kiss of the Spiderwoman* (1993) are reminders that we are never simply watching unmediated reality on the stage, but witnessing the unfolding of narrative as an oneiric experience of dream, fantasy or memory, which foregrounds the impact of cultural forms on the construction of personal identity, be it the rules and rituals of a dance competition or the prism of an old South American film musical.

In this respect, the pastiche songs in Kander and Ebb's musicals function not merely to comment ironically on action and feeling in the narrative; they also invent a sonic world that evokes the milieu of each show. The pair's remarkable talent for musical and linguistic pastiche, initially manifested in their score for *Cabaret,* can be identified as a primary factor in their ability to intertwine escapist entertainment or fantasy with harsh reality in a way that became a definitive trope.

Sondheim told Fred Ebb that *70, Girls, 70* (1971) was 'the best entertainment show' he had ever seen. *The Musical Theatre of Kander and Ebb* will investigate the full range of the team's collaboration from the pure comic entertainment of *70, Girls, 70* (1971) and *Curtains* (2006) to more overtly serious musicals such as *The Kiss of the Spiderwoman* (1992), *The Scottsboro Boys* (2010) and *The Visit* (2015), which were less commercially successful precisely because they addressed disturbing subjects. It will explore how difficult material inspired beautiful scores whose ironic counterpointing of lusciously romantic or raucously jazzy music with satirical and demotic lyrics makes complex demands of a Broadway audience, challenging its desire for escapist entertainment devoid of critical self-reflection, to become sophisticated yet popular masterpieces of the genre.

The ironic relationship of words and music in a song was first exemplified by Brecht and Weill in their 'gestic' music, in which music and lyrics did not combine in a Wagnerian union of words and music but *commented* on each other, prompting an audience to notice the complexity of songs in a dialectic of confrontation between emotion (music) and thought (lyrics). Paradoxically, while the première productions of *A Funny Thing Happened on the Way to the Forum* (1962), *Company* (1970), *A Little Night Music* (1973) and *Into the Woods* (1987) turned a profit, none of Sondheim's other Broadway shows earned back their investment. Rather than proclaiming himself an avatar of high culture, the pair's closest contemporary – and a friend of John Kander's since *West Side Story* (1957) – always maintained that he regarded success on Broadway as his primary aim.

Increasingly, after 1973, however, Sondheim moved away from Broadway models towards the avant-garde, while Kander and Ebb continued to locate their projects in a nexus between art and commercial entertainment. One might describe the aesthetics of Kander and Ebb as the art of the popular. Two of the shows produced well after Ebb's death in 2004, *The Visit* and the new, wholly rewritten stage version of *New York, New York* (2023), with additional lyrics by Lin-Manuel Miranda, demonstrate their range, the first being almost a contemporary opera while the latter is sheer Broadway musical comedy razzle-dazzle. Rather than exploring a more avant-garde musical vocabulary, their works sought to recycle and deconstruct popular forms in a process of exposing their ideological basis in capitalism or even fascism. However 'difficult' the subject matter of musicals like *Kiss of the Spiderwoman* and *The Scottsboro Boys* may have been, both utilized familiar types of music in ways that *Passion* or *Pacific Overtures* (1976) did not.

The content and artistic values of the team's shows were challenging, yet their intention was always to exploit popular entertainment forms rather than avant-garde musical and dramaturgical techniques. This has helped them communicate uncomfortable truths in a musical and theatrical language easily embraced by Broadway audiences. Richard Watts Jr. observed in the *New York Post* that *Cabaret* 'can upset you while it gives theatrical satisfaction. It is disturbing, provocative, meaningful, believable and highly entertaining'.[26] Although its use of a traditional narrative structure may on the surface appear to compromise the authorial team's more radical intentions, the experimental nature of its form can be construed as a complex deconstruction of the 'golden age' musical paradigm, whose clichés are subverted by their ironic framing within the disorienting montage of diegetic cabaret routines. The pleasure promised to and enjoyed by a Broadway audience is exposed as popular entertainment's escapist lie.

Notes

1. The stage version of *New York, New York* ran on Broadway from 24 March to 30 July 2023 and a national tour is promised in 2025.
2. The starry revival in London that opened to rave reviews in 2021 is being reproduced in New York in 2024.
3. Sondheim himself always regarded box-office profit on Broadway as the mark of a show's success, though the premiere of *Sunday in the Park with George* off-Broadway may have signalled a change in his attitude.
4. Ebb, quoted in James Leve, *Kander and Ebb,* New Haven: Yale University Press, 2009, 35.
5. Kirsten Childs, Interview with John Kander, How Music Shapes Us, https://www.youtube.com /watch?v=HmJ3gMEVkXE. Accessed 14 July 2023.
6. *Kander and Ebb - Great Performances*. (https://www.youtube.com/ watch?v=vDIRejHmwyU https:// www.youtube.com/watch?v= vDIRejHmwyU. Accessed 15 July 2023.
7. Kander and Ebb - Great Performances, as above.
8. Kander and Ebb - Great Performances, as above.
9. Childs, Interview with John Kander, as above.
10. 'It's [my music] almost all classical . . . I do remember seeing the first opera I ever saw . . . in Kansas City . . . when I was ten . . . a company came through and they did *Aida* . . . I was kind of overwhelmed by it . . . And the next day they were doing *Madame Butterfly* and I pestered her . . . and my aunt took me. (Childs, Interview with John Kander, as above.)
11. See *Kander and Ebb – Great Performances*.
12. Childs, Interview with John Kander, as above.
13. See Fred Ebb in Al Kasha and Joel Hirschhorn (eds.), *Notes on Broadway*, New York: Simon and Schuster, 1987, 98-9.
14. Interview with Terry Gross, https://freshairarchive.org/segments/kander-and-ebb-musical-theater-songwriting-team.
15. Interview with Terry Gross, as above.
16. Childs, Interview with John Kander, as above.
17. Gerald Mast, *Can't Help Singin'*, New York: Overlook Press, 1987, 61–4.
18. The 'eleven o'clock number' is a term used by Broadway insiders: it dates from the time when musicals began at 8:30 pm, so that the show-stopping eleven o'clock number occurred towards the end of the show, exciting audiences before the denouement.
19. A descriptive form of art music that evokes images or illustrates a story in aural terms.

20. Bradley Rogers, *The Song Is You*, Iowa City: University of Iowa Press, 2020

21. Russell Lynes, 'Highbrow, Lowbrow, Middlebrow' in *Harper's,* 11 April 1949, reprinted in *The Wilson Quarterly*, Vol. 1, No. 1 (Autumn 1976): 146–58, https://www.jstor.org/stable/40255171, accessed 3 June 2020.

22. This debate was concurrent with Benjamin and Adorno's influential argument about the aura of the high art object versus the worthlessness of mass art in the era of mechanical reproduction. For an interesting and succinct analysis of this debate, see Alex Ross, 'The Naysayers: Walter Benjamin, Theodor Adorno, and the Critique of Pop Culture', *The New Yorker*, 15 September, 2014, https://www.newyorker.com/magazine/2014/09/15/naysayers, accessed 3 June 2020.

23. Louis Menard, 'Browbeaten: Dwight Macdonald's War on Midcult', *The New Yorker*, 12 August 2011, https://www.newyorker.com/magazine/2011/09/05/browbeaten, accessed 15 April 2020.

24. Dwight Macdonald, 'A Theory of Mass Culture', in Bernard Rosenberg and Manning White (eds.), *Mass Culture*, New York: The Free Press, 1957, 59–73.

25. Macdonald, 'A Theory of Mass Culture'.

26. Richard Watts, Jr, *New York Post*, 1966, Quoted in Broadwayworld, https://www. broadway world.com/article/From-the-Berlin-Stories-to-Cabaret-20140610.

1 'Sing Happy'

Flora the Red Menace (1965) and the invention of the Liza persona

Flora marked the team's first collaboration with Harold Prince. Kander's association with Prince had begun with *A Family Affair*, for which he had acted both as producer and replacement director. In retrospect, it can be seen as unfortunate that Prince, as producer of *Flora*, allowed the legendary George Abbott to both co-write the book and direct the show. What might have become the first successful instance of a fruitful collaboration instead turned out to be a Broadway flop with a winning star performance. As with many of his innovative productions, the initial idea to musicalize Lester Atwell's novel, *Love Is Just Around the Corner* (1962), was Prince's:

> Hal had brought the rights to [. . .] *Love Is Just Around the Corner* [. . .] based on . . . [Atwell's] memories of the early thirties, and the Communist Party and life in New York – a beautiful, funny, touching story. Hal [. . .] immediately thought of it as a musical. In those days he hadn't really started directing yet. He had directed *A Family Affair* in less than ten days, and that was his first directing experience on Broadway [. . .] Hal produced [. . . *Flora*] for Abbott, who was probably the wrong person to direct that show [. . .] he really didn't have any affinity with the material.[1]

When Kander and Ebb played Abbott the score of *Golden Gate*, their first (unproduced) show he was so impressed that he insisted they write the score for *Flora* – and most probably resolved to direct it himself. Prince later concurred with Kander that Abbott was the wrong choice as the director of the musical. In his book *Contradictions: Notes on Twenty-six Years in the Theatre*, Prince gives his own candid account of what went wrong in the genesis of *Flora the Red Menace*:

> [It] was the last of the plays I produced that I didn't direct [. . .] I wanted to direct that show. Of all the shows I have done which didn't work, I regret the failure of *Flora* most especially. What it could have been! And it was the perfect time for it. Joe McCarthy was dead. I gave it [the novel] to Kander and Ebb to read [. . .] They agreed to compose some songs on spec.[2]

The first draft of the book by Robert Russell (rewritten by George Abbott) is closely based on Atwell's novel. Set in the Depression, the novel is a comic *bildungsroman*, representing a year in the life of Flora Meszaros, during which the would-be fashion illustrator progresses from naïve idealism to a more clear-headed, yet still determinedly optimistic, maturity. Prince's first impulse in securing the rights to musicalize the novel clearly anticipated his contribution to *Cabaret*. The reference to the infamous Senator McCarthy implies a revisionist attitude to the history of the period that had just begun to make its impact on Broadway theatre. As in almost all the musicals he directed, including those of Sondheim and Lloyd-Webber, Prince saw that the political and social environment of the novel was the key to shaping the material for the stage:

> I understood the milieu. I understood the characters. My wife's family had been victims of the blacklist, and I knew full well how idealistic and naïve and innocent so many of the people who were pilloried really were, and I wanted the show to be about that.[3]

Prince's first choice as book-writer, Garson Kanin, turned the job down, but he recommended screenplay writer Robert Russell, who had personal experience with the Young Communist League and commenced work with Barbra Streisand in mind as Flora.

In retrospect, Prince considered that Russell's own experience of the failure of American Communist ideals and the subsequent attacks on former Communists by Senator Joe McCarthy and the HUAC[4] may have made him cynical about the 1930s and inflexible as a collaborator. In addition, he needed assistance with the craft of the professional Broadway musical theatre writer, so Prince believed his own mentor, George Abbott, would be the ideal person to guide Russell in adapting the novel for the stage. Prince remembered that,

> Abbott liked the novel, some of Russell's dialogue, and while he found Kander and Ebb's songs brilliant, he quarrelled with the best of them on the grounds that they were overemotional, even turgid. The title, which was Russell's, perfectly set the tone of the show [. . . yet unlike many,] Abbott [. . . had] predicted the Crash and was out of the market six months before it happened.[5]

Although the decision to employ Abbott as director and co-writer delayed the songwriting team's collaboration with Prince as director, it did ensure that he would choose them to write *Cabaret*.

A highly proficient craftsman, Abbott was known for rationalizing musical comedy as entertainment rather than experimenting with the musical as an art form. Yet the legendary 'Abbott touch' was not the approach Prince, Kander and Ebb had envisaged for *Flora*. In Prince's opinion, 'He brought to *Flora* no clear attitude about the Party. His Communists were cartoon characters, some of them farcical, others evil.'[6] Since Abbott's first draft of the book utilized little of Russell's work, Prince realized that there was now a stylistic mismatch between the book and Kander and Ebb's songs. Abbott, who was spending winter in Florida, suggested that the songwriters visit him:

> I assumed they would stay about ten days, and during that time could persuade him to put the emotion back in the show. More specifically, to clarify our attitudes about radicals in that period. They arrived in Florida one day, they were back in New York twenty-four hours later. Abbott had conducted his characteristically terse session: Had they understood what he wanted? Did they agree with him? (Apparently they gave him that impression.) [. . .] Abbott's granite-like stability tranquilised them. More appropriately, they were intoxicated, and this pattern prevailed.[7]

At seventy-eight years old, 'Mister' Abbott was a veteran of the Broadway theatre with 104 directing credits to his name. He naturally wielded more power than any of the other collaborators. A successful writer of crime dramas and farces,[8] he had authored the books of numerous musical comedies.

From the 1930s, his approach to the form of musical comedy had been dominant on Broadway. Abbott was regarded as a master in plotting the arc of a musical that ensured songs and dance numbers were located at key moments when the narrative demanded some sort of heightening or exclamation and was famous for his slick editing of the narrative material that ensured no superfluous interruption of its smooth flow. Characters and situations were expected to be clear and simple so that the action was straightforwardly presented to make immediate sense. There was no time for complicated self-reflection, subtle nuances of characterization or philosophical debate. Situation, song and dance were structured so as to engage and excite the audience, provoke laughter and progress the narrative swiftly. Although it established the pattern of the shows Lehman Engel would later extol, it was the opposite of the neo-naturalistic approach Rodgers and Hammerstein made famous in *Oklahoma!*

Before *Cabaret* enabled Kander and Ebb to conceive particular strategies of meta-theatre as their signature approach to musical theatre dramaturgy, the team's score for *Flora* succeeded in voicing an emotional attitude that would shape a musical identity for the persona of 'Liza with a Z'. Not yet entirely coherent as a sonic world for the historical milieu of an individual show, the most successful songs in *Flora* nevertheless contained elements with which both artists could identify. Perhaps the limitation in the score is a result of the contradictory attitudes towards the Depression manifested by the various creatives, whose widely differing experiences of the 1930s may have undermined their attempts to assume sufficient distance from the period to achieve a distinctive style for the show. Kander partly explains the lack of historical distance as follows: 'I didn't have to do any research for Flora because I was there [. . .] I was very young, but I remember the sounds well.'[9]

One of the few reviews of Atwell's novel, which was published during a newspaper strike in New York, suggests that Flora is a born loser:

> If ever a character validated the loser-winner theory of human endeavour, it's Miss Flora Meszaros, the lovable nincompoop of Mr Atwell's Depression novel. She is a loser extraordinaire who, within the course of a single year, loses her job as a commercial artist (she can draw neither hands nor feet), botches up a Herculean store mural (she draws a horizontal mural vertically and drips a great deal), gets expelled from the Communist party [. . .] and loses a stammering lover.[10]

It may have been that Abbott simply could not accept the notion of an idealistic and talented young individualist like Flora as a loser, not only to the Communist Party but also to the capitalist bosses of a department store. Kander believed that,

> Mr Abbott didn't want to see Liza do anything ugly or unseemly at all. The one thing that became very clear to us toward the end was that he couldn't bear the idea that Flora would be seriously in love with a Communist, because of his own political feelings.[11]

Whatever the case, the urgency and intensity that the nineteen-year-old Minnelli brought to the role translated Flora from the 'loser extraordinaire' of the novel into a feisty optimist, with the force of personality to view failure as merely a momentary obstacle to be overcome. Although he had taken a great deal of convincing by Kander, Ebb and producer Harold

Prince to cast her, Abbott was soon won over by Liza's charm and ability as a performer, and it was she who garnered most of the praise received by the show, in the process cementing a creative relationship between performer and writers that was to last until Fred Ebb's death in 2004.

By all accounts, Abbott's unsympathetic view of Depression-era Communism, reinforced by his platonic love affair with Minnelli, led him during rehearsals and out-of-town tryouts to revise what was intended as a more complex exploration of a group of naïve idealists in a left-wing, bohemian milieu so that it became a quirky musical comedy with a star-making role for Liza. In some respects, David Thompson, who collaborated with the songwriters to produce a new version of *Flora* that ran off-Broadway in 1987, restored many of the early ideas of Prince, Kander, Ebb and Robert Russell, thereby exposing some of the problems with Abbott's libretto.

In the interests of speed and clarity, Abbott had simplified the action, cut a major dance number and a few songs and repositioned others, reshaping the book to emphasize its musical comedy elements at the expense of a more complex and emotionally engaged exploration of its thirties milieu. The loss of both the 'Tree of Life' ballet and the 'Blood on 42nd Street' number, a sustained parody of thirties agitprop theatre performed as an epic ballad in the manner of 'The Saga of Jenny' (Weill/Gershwin) and 'Dr Crippen' (Weill/Nash), hugely diminished the moments of dance and musical staging, leaving *Flora* more intimate but less varied than had been planned. Intended as performances to entertain the comrades at the Communist Party meetings, their loss effectively reduced the time allocated to the Communist characters. The length of 'Blood on 42nd Street' may have been a factor in Abbott's decision to cut it, but the fact that it had been praised by reviewers in New Haven and Boston suggests that Abbott removed it to downplay a substantial element of left-wing thought rather than because it was slowing down the pace of the action.

The avoidance of intended references to the Roosevelt government's social welfare programmes (the 'New Deal') in Abbott's book involved the simplification of a more complex dramatic scheme opposing the values of collectivism against the ethos of altruism and independence represented by Flora and the artists who work in her studio. In one early sketch for the libretto, an idea for 'The Forgotten Man', a politically themed song intended for Harry to sing at his first meeting with Flora, is described:

> Harry leads, and Flora is impressed with his idealism, with his goodness, and she is excited by his radical appeal for all Forgotten Men to stand together, march together, etc. The pattern of the song can come from the questions on the employment application, all of which Harry manages to convert into propaganda: *job application* is a place a man can take to build a better world; *salary desired* is a living wage, with security etc; *recommendations* come from Tom Paine, John Henry, Joe Hill and other Forgotten Men, heroes of the folk-singing left wing; [. . .] Flora is so inspired that she falls for Harry.[12]

The conceit of the song as a series of classic left-wing answers to the application form is clever, and its outline implies that it would have amplified the political debate in an entertaining manner. James Leve points out that in an early draft by Russell, the initial scene in Flora's studio was to have included a song called 'Strive and Succeed':[13]

> This is the other side of the social picture of the Depression – the 'Self-Help' bunch with old-fashioned virtues of independence and struggle. They are not taking the Depression

lying down, no sir! They are fighting to get ahead; they are full of Horatio Alger zeal. Each foolish optimist has his bit . . . It is all proud and sad because we all know that, two years hence, they will all be on the W.P.A.[14]

What remained in the show that opened on Broadway were fragments of the original conception, chiefly in the musical numbers, wedded to a somewhat off-beat musical comedy book. The brief sung Prologue retains the score's evocation of the harsh struggle to survive during the Depression. With its minor key refrains, the opening boldly sets the scene in a grey, cold New York street in 1933, indicating the poverty that has driven these people to become panhandlers:

Actor 1.
Apples.
Actor 2.
Pencils

Actor 1/Actor 2.
Only a nickel, mister.
Waiting all day
Waiting in line
Just for a bowl of soup.

Waiting all day
Waiting in line
Just for a heel of bread.[15]

One of the choruses of the song is later intercalated between various scenes, with occasional variations on the lyrics, as for example,

Keep your fancy penthouse
High above the park
Mister just give me a job.[16]

Music and lyrics here echo Marc Blitzstein's *The Cradle Will Rock* (1935),[17] a left-wing exposé of the corrupt nature of the capitalist system. Yet the song switches a few times from its slow, sombre opening to a fast-paced and bouncing metre that evokes the apple-pic optimism of Americans before the crash:

I used to be a salesman
Travelling on the big highway;
I used to be a broker
Sitting at a desk all day.[18]

The songwriters are unable to resist a reference to popular entertainment of the period:

I used to have a house on Murray Hill.
I used to juggle in vaudeville.[19]

Such an antithetical pairing of sadness and regret with optimism and pleasure constitutes a leitmotif threading through Kander and Ebb's work. This jaunty section was removed from the 1987 version of the show, suggesting that it was originally written at Abbott's request to ensure the number did not stray too far from musical comedy conventions. Nevertheless, it does reveal the songwriters' facility in exploiting the quick switchback between fun and pathos in an ironic manner that would have supported Prince's original artistic aims. What becomes intrusive in Abbott's book is its insistent jokiness, with comic schtick substituted for character development and political argument.

The generic Broadway musical comedy craft with which Abbott shaped *Flora* precluded the team's best attempts to create a sound world that would suggest the moods of left-wing victims and protesters on the streets of New York during the Great Depression. Rather than a realistic comedy about the Depression with a musical language that ironized Flora's optimism, what remained was an oddball musical comedy with fragments of the musical Prince might have directed, by taking poverty and suffering seriously while framing Flora's 'can-do' naivety in a harsher, more ironic narrative of social failure. What remained possible was for Kander and Ebb to write for the youthful Minnelli and with Minnelli in mind – and while some material was written before she became attached to the production – they did this brilliantly, creating for her a tough yet tender New York mode of musical comedy belt with enough irony, spunk and self-awareness to obviate excessive sentimentality. The scene in New York's High School of Commercial Art introduces Flora Meszaros, whose speech as valedictorian on behalf of the graduating class swiftly segues into a marching song ('Unafraid') which gives Liza an opportunity to show off her bold belt.

Some of the lines present Depression tropes, somewhat too intense for a conventional high school graduation ceremony, yet reinforcing Prince's initial conception:

> Bruised and battered
> But we will be unbowed
> Clouds may gather and swarm
> Yet, this promise is made
> We will weather the storm
> Uniformly unafraid. (14)[20]

The song evokes political anthems and slogans, foreshadowing Flora's ambivalent involvement with the Communist Party.

In the third scene at Garret and Mellick's department store, Flora meets the nervous and eccentric Harry Toukarian while making an application for the job of fashion illustrator. The dialogue of the 1987 version is more overtly political, and the writers have re-inserted 'The Kid Herself' rather than retaining Abbott's choice to bring 'All I Need (Is One Good Break)' forward from Scene 4 to Scene 2. Flora's sarcastic humour and her positive 'can-do' attitude are evident in both versions of the scene, but Abbott's positioning of 'All I Need (Is One Good Break)' so early in the show as an urgent and self-defining 'I Want' song for Flora was a choice that reinforced her centrality in motivating the arc of the plot. Although supported by the chorus of other artists who are waiting to submit their portfolios to Garret and Mellick, the song is upbeat and assertive, exploiting the individualistic drive of *Funny Girl*'s 'The Greatest Star' in the previous Broadway season as a trope expressing Flora's optimism in hard times.

The number Kander and Ebb had intended for Scene 2, 'The Kid Herself', is a comic 'I Am' song. Its tongue-in-cheek boastfulness demonstrates the contradiction between Flora's bold optimism and her self-deprecating honesty:

Step right up
And you will answer 'yes';
The wonders of the world are really eight not seven.
On the list
Beside that pyramid
You gotta put
The kid herself. (18)

The first of a number of veiled references to Liza's parentage occurs later in the number:

Artists.
Away out west
At MGM,
Louis B. Mayer's on the phone

Flora.
Louis B. Mayer's on the phone
To holler, 'Flora dear,
Please hurry up out here,

Artists.
We want to star the kid herself

Flora.
With Gable.' (20)

In comparison, 'All I Need' is neither ironic nor comic in any way: its lively and upbeat style taps into the Broadway 'I Want' number tradition of no-holds-barred ambition, its driving rhythm expressing the strength of Flora's resolve to succeed. When positioned in Scene 4, the song had been intended to be delivered by a group of aspiring artists working in her studio who were to sing to Flora and Harry, whom she brings home. Brought forward to Scene 2, it became part of Flora's job application, the chorus of job-seekers merely there to back her up vocally:

Flora.
All I need is one good break
Just one good break
Then Mister watch my speed
One substantial break is all I need.
One substantial break is all I need
To make them all stand up and cheer
Set the world of art right on its ear.

Gimme gimme a chance
I don't want any handout;
Gimme gimme a boost
Cause I got it all planned out.
Gimme gimme a lift
And I'll bet ya they'll stand outside my door
All begging for a chance to study my sketches.[21]

Figure 2. Liza Minnelli as Flora. Photo: Friedman-Abeles, NYPL, Billy Rose *Division.*

The new version authorized in the currently published playscript presumably corresponds to Kander and Ebb's first idea, in which the number is more fully developed with additional lyrics to particularize the different ways in which each artist at Flora's studio hopes to succeed. Very little of this, however, survived in the Broadway production, in which Flora sings the verse introduction, which enacts her filling out the job application aloud before launching into the first sections of the refrain with a lively attack that began to typify Minnelli's approach to an up-tempo number. The song is shorter than the first version, many of the lyrics are cut and those that remain generalize Flora's situation (e.g. 'Hey, New York, I'm gonna get you yet'), representing an all-purpose demonstration of guts and nerve rather than exploring the character's career plans in any detail.

Her confidence is spelt out through the recurring lyric exhortations, an insistent rhythmic force created by the staccato effect of the repeated, 'All I need is one good break' and 'Gimme, gimme', reinforced by the emphatic insertion of 'just one' twice in the second half of the song ('All I need is one good break, just one good break'). The Horatio Alger-type egotism of the number is very different from its original aim of Flora calling for a little help (Roosevelt's 'New Deal'), which then progressively built a sense of how one individual artist's aim was echoed by another's until they merged harmonically and progressed in the form of a fugue to construct a musical manifestation of the solidarity of creative bohemians in the kind of supportive self-help community that Flora envisaged. This was an antithetical yet complementary concept to the Communist Party's doctrine of slavish collectivism: the version that was performed on opening night was a paean to the conventional trope of individual success as an emblem of 'the American Dream'.

In both versions of the libretto, long-standing musical comedy conventions shape the presentation of the romance between Flora and Harry. His stammer is a sign of the underlying anxiety caused by the conflict between his earnest wish to be faithful to Communist Party dogma and his sexual desires. Finding Flora's bold flirtatiousness both attractive and threatening, Harry becomes progressively more conflicted – a major source of comedy in the musical. Later that day, Harry's ambivalence is succinctly portrayed in the verse of 'It's Not Every Day of the Week', with its repeated parentheses and the stuttering effect created by the deliberate effort of cramming too many syllables of speech into its rhythmic structure:

> **Harry.**
> You're very aggressive
> (In the nicest way possible)
> I mean that you're pushy
> (That is to say bold).
> I feel like I've been run over
> (In the nicest way possible)
> And believe me whatever you're selling,
> I'm sold. (30–1)

Flora's sung response to Harry is characteristically honest,

> You're very peculiar
> (In the nicest way possible)
> I'm mean you're unusual,
> That is to say strange,
> You're a horse of another color
> (In the nicest way possible)
> It's refreshing to meet someone odd
> For a change. (31)

In turn, Harry warms up to Flora's offer of free space to work in her studio and ends up singing in chorus with her. The charm of this song resides in the unexpectedness of its variations on the stock love ballad of musical comedy. The two characters' unequivocal acknowledgement of their eccentricities and defects as potential lovers renders the song almost parodic. Flora unashamedly sings that she is 'someone whose charms could be somewhat greater', while her recognition of the need to make compromises in order to seize whatever opportunities are presented portrays her attitude to the circumstances of the Depression:

> I must make the most of the moment that's here
> On account of it's not every day of the week
> And honestly not every week of the month,
> And certainly not every month of the year! (32)

Notwithstanding the celebratory mood of the music (the up-tempo drive of the chorus is particularly apt for Flora's determinedly optimistic pragmatism), the positive determination of certain lyrics alternates with hesitancy and ruefulness, creating the kind of ironic tension between music and lyrics that became a Kander and Ebb trademark. Here the team's talent for setting the rhythms of everyday speech to music is fully apparent. Not only does the number wittily characterize both Harry's stammering outbursts and Flora's garrulous enthusiasm, it does so in a vernacular that is natural, concise and appropriate to the situation. Kander and Ebb brilliantly demonstrate in the crafting of this song that simple, idiomatic diction does not in any way need to result in simplistic songwriting. Just as Sondheim had shown in *West Side Story* (1957) and *Gypsy* (1959), a musical theatre song written in an idiolect appropriate to the characters constitutes a small drama that can fully be comprehended only within its dramaturgical context.

An even more complex song that did remain in the show was the next duet in which – out of the blue – Harry declares that he is a Communist. At this point, Flora has realized she is attracted to Harry, allowing Kander and Ebb to exploit her astonishment for comic effect in 'Sign Here'. Ebb believed that the number 'may be the best musical comedy song I ever wrote, because it's smart and it's deep, and it's important, and it meant a lot to me, and I think he [Abbott] just played it for laughs.'[22] In Harry's unexpected attempt to manipulate Flora into joining the Communist Party, he announces his political principles for the first time. 'Sign Here' remains one of the most unusual and complex songs in the show, indicating the effect of comedy interwoven with political reflection initially envisaged by Prince. Having stolen some cheese sandwiches for lunch from a Macy's 'cooking with cheese' demonstration, Flora is startled by Harry's blunt declaration:

Harry.
Flora – there's s-something I just gotta tell you.
Flora.
You hate cheese! (*She gathers up the cheese.*)
Harry.
No. I'm a Communist.
Flora.
Huh!?
Harry.
And I took the liberty of bringing you an application to j-join the party. (*He gets out an application.*)
Flora.
Oh.
Harry.
Look at it this way, Flora

Are you in favor of democracy?
You must be in favor of democracy.
Well since you're in favour of democracy
Here sign, sign here.

[. . .]

The rights of man
Democracy
Then it's clear! It's clear!
You're a Communist
Sign here. (33–4)

From this point on, the lyrics specify an epic range of political aims, with somewhat helpless spoken interjections by Flora, who, for the first time in the show, seems lost for words. The repeated choruses are varied slightly by the incremental piling up of topics – 'everlasting peace', 'free milk for kids', 'security', the draft, 'jobs for everyone', 'the filthy rich', doing away with slums and 'saving America'. As the benefits of most of these ideals appear to be self-evident, Harry's preaching of Communist Party doctrine becomes comic through its blind assumption that all decent political values are associated with Communism. Abbott may have 'played it for laughs' but 'Sign Here' also functions ironically to suggest that everything the Communist Party proposes in the era of the Depression is no more than that which every fair-minded American has actually always desired:

> **Harry.**
> America
> Away with slums
> No filthy rich
> No unemployed
> Protect our youth?
> Security?
> Free milk for kids
> A lasting peace?
> The rights of man?
> Democracy?
> Then it's clear! It's clear!
> Find that dotted line
> Here . . . (*He kisses her. She signs.*)
> Sign. (34)

By the end of a proposal of love that takes the place of a mock declaration of political affiliation, Flora has abandoned all attempts to resist and signs the membership form.

The only Communist Party meeting that remained in the show when it opened on Broadway in 1965 was treated as a joke. As sung by the fanatical Comrade Ada, 'The Flame' is a pastiche of a Russian 'Kamarinskaya' dance, with an apparently endless list of heroic revolutionary clichés:

> **Ada.**
> On Monday I put pickets on twenty-seven lines
> I also started riots at B. Altman's, Saks and Kleins.
> I broke three Woolworth windows, destroyed an automat;
> You'd think I'd be entitled to a breather after that.
> (*The crowd rumbles. They agree. She looks up at them and they all stop.*) [45]

It is funny not only because Ada's numerous attempts at bringing the capitalist system to a halt appear eccentric and even ridiculous in a city as large as New York, but her wild enthusiasm appears absurdly anachronistic to an audience whose collective memory of the American Communist Party is filtered through the prism of the McCarthy witch-hunts:

> But then I felt the flame,
> I felt it burn inside me
> Like a glowing torch to light my way;

Although my shoulders drooped
And I was plenty pooped,
I heard a little voice within me say,

[. . .]

Ada's hypocritically faux self-deprecation of herself as merely a cog in the collective party machine, in comparison to the revolutionary 'flame' burning within, seems as inappropriate as Flora's hopeless fantasy of transforming herself into a successful fashion designer by wishful singing:

You must do more
You must do much more,
Until you've lit the flame
In every single heart. (45–6)

At Flora's studio, The Lady and Bronco Smallwood rehearse for Major Bowes' Amateur Hour, singing a rather broad parody of a cowboy song called 'Palomino Pal'. A much more entertaining tap dance routine – 'Keeping It Hot' – replaced this rather weak number in David Thompson's 1987 version. The remainder of the first act includes two very good numbers for Flora: one further idiosyncratic comic song. 'A Quiet Thing' is one of the great American musical theatre songs. Perfectly capturing the feeling and mood of the situation, it reveals the songwriting team's complete mastery of their medium, characterizing Flora's sensitivity in counterpoint to her brash social image.

The verse provides an opportunity for the actress to express the thrill Flora feels at having been offered a job as a fashion illustrator at Garret and Mellick's. Her amazement is demonstrated by the fact that at first she merely repeats the offer she has just been made:

Flora.
Whaddya call a job with Garret and Mellick's?
Whaddya call fashion illustrator?
[................]
Whaddya call thirty dollars a week? (43)

Then she verbalizes in song the kind of emotions a young person imagines they ought to feel at such exciting moments in their lives, trying out various histrionic possibilities such as running and screaming before stopping herself ('No I don't') when she realizes she just wants to sit down:

I don't hear anything.
You're supposed to hear bells, drums, trumpets;
I don't hear anything.
Do you hear anything ? No?
Well whaddya know? (43)

The deliberate gesture of eschewing the clichéd images of joy that are ubiquitous in popular songs ('bells, drums, trumpets')[23] allows Ebb to clear the ground in lyric terms to prepare the audience for an unadulterated expression of Flora's pure joy. The simplicity is earned by its contrasting context. Although the rhetorical strategy is sophisticated, the lyric itself is entirely consonant with Flora's obsessive self-questioning throughout the action; the gentle effect of the last slow and softly vocalized line of the verse is almost like a lullaby, which soothes Flora, allowing her to calm down and experience her genuine feelings rather than to theatricalize them in her usual fashion.

By using a fairly extended verse that includes three false starts where the first chorus might have begun, the songwriters delay its introduction to heighten the audience's anticipation so that when the moment finally arrives, it generates unalloyed pleasure:

> When it all comes true
> Just the way you've planned
> It's funny but the bells don't ring
> It's a quiet thing. (44)

The many elongated vowels in the first three lines are sung by Minnelli with a legato effect, the sustained vocal notes enhancing the mellifluous conjunction of words and music until the flow of sound is abruptly broken by the rhythmically jagged cluster of consonants in the fourth line. Strongly onomatopoeic impressions are created by many of the lyric images introduced merely so their putative effects can be denied – 'a choir sing', 'exploding fireworks', 'roaring of the crowds'. The stillness and inward quality of the true emotion are evoked by a few metaphors that in context attain a poetic beauty: 'When you hold the world/ In your trembling hand' and 'Happiness comes in on tip-toe' are especially memorable. By providing a glimpse of the intense feelings below Flora's brash mask, the song allows the expression of an interiority at odds with the more superficial style of Abbott's musical comedy book. As the one moment of unmitigated happiness in the musical, it interrupts the broad comedy, the political skirmish and the competitive struggle for survival that dominate the surrounding action. The only comparable moment in the 1965 production was 'Sing Happy'.

The next scene and song return to Abbott's conventional musical comedy format. Imitating the ancient Greek orator Demosthenes by putting marbles in his mouth while practising a speech he has been asked to deliver on the picket line, Harry pleads with Flora to go to bed with him, while she resists.

Flora.
I know about the waves already,
I've heard about Demosthenes too.
Something else is on your mind
When you talk to me this way.
Go on, get it off your chest,
Say what you really want to say.

All right, even with the pebbles in your mouth!

'Hello Waves' comically expresses both Harry's sexual frustration and Flora's ability to cope with his speech impediment by 'translating' and speaking for both of them:

Harry.
Mm Mm Mm Mm Mm Mm

Flora.
I feel the same way too

Harry.
Mm Mm Mm Mm Mm,

Flora.
Yes I agree with you.

After he goes back home alone rather than spending the evening of Valentine's Day with her, Flora reconsiders her refusal to oblige Harry in the waltz 'Dear Love'. The number starts slowly as she carefully considers her feelings about Harry's proposition. At the end of the first chorus, she breaks into speech to signal her change of heart: 'I know. I'll go over to his apartment. It's February 14th. It's Valentine's Day. It's also HIGH time! (*She grabs her coat and the box of candy.*) You want to F-F-Foxtrot Harry? I'll show you how to Foxtrot' (62).

At the end of the verse, she walks from her apartment to the street en route to Harry's. The slow waltz has sped up to a galloping tempo as Flora becomes more animated and joyous. After the powerful emotion of 'A Quiet Thing' and the strong implications of Harry's suppressed desire in 'Hello Waves', the audience is primed to share the empathy that enables Flora to equate a dedicated Communist's joy in celebrating May Day with the thrill of realizing she is truly in love. Marking a turning point in their relationship, the number is fittingly placed at the end of Act 1 for maximum dramatic effect.

With the loss of some Communist Party scenes in Act 2, Abbott must have felt obliged to employ Charlotte's rivalry over Harry as the key to plot complication and denouement. In a comic scene that includes the song 'Express Yourself', the sexually assertive Comrade Charlotte attempts to seduce Harry in order to liberate him from his repressions; although nothing much has happened, they are discovered together in Harry's flat by Flora at the crucial moment when she arrives to tell him she has decided they should consummate their relationship. To compensate for cut songs and scenes, an entirely redundant and rather far-fetched romantic entanglement between Bronco Smallwood (the Cowboy) and Comrade Ada is added. The old-fashioned vaudeville schtick of their rather silly duet, 'Knock Knock', does not contribute in any way to the plot. Abbott's script resolves the love triangle rather too arbitrarily by having Charlotte maliciously plant copies of the Communist *Daily Worker* in Flora's locker at work, obliging her to admit that she is a member of the Party, which results in her losing her job. This is the moment when Flora is most alone. Betrayed by Charlotte and under the impression she has been rejected not only by the Party but also by Harry, she performs the eleven o'clock number, 'Sing Happy', perhaps the most powerful moment in the show.

Unbeknownst to Flora, however, Harry has phoned Garrett and Mellick's in an attempt to exonerate her of having brought a Communist newspaper to work. In the novel, Harry is an entirely selfish character who ends up leaving Flora on her own by marrying Charlotte, but Abbott made him more likeable to accommodate the musical comedy form and style he envisaged. In the musical, he proposes marriage to Flora, but although touched, she believes they are too different and refuses, handing him back her Party membership card. A few minutes later, her boss, Mr Stanley, arrives to comfort her and explain that the call, which established her innocence, was from someone who stammered. The ending is softened by the presence of Mr Stanley who offers to arrange an interview for her with a new employer.

Although confused, Flora, supported by the older Mr Weiss and her other friends at the studio, resolves in 'You Are You' to go on without Harry – a final celebration of the individual's freedom to define one's own identity as opposed to collectivist dogma.

In the new 1987 version, Kander, Ebb and Thompson place 'You Are You' earlier in Act 2, just after Flora learns that the rally planned to be held outside Garrett and Mellick's is to become a picket line, forcing Flora to cross it if she wishes to turn in her artwork to the store on time. In trying to convince her that she should have crossed the picket line rather than sending her friend Willy to deliver the design work, Mr Weiss and Elsa sing 'You Are You', joined midway through by Flora. At this juncture, the number helps to promote Flora's self-realization, permitting the audience to observe a transitional phase in her growing maturity as she begins to perceive the difference between her own equivocal attitude to the Communist Party and Harry's fanaticism. As it occurs in the middle of a bewildering series of plot complications, it is an assertion of Weiss and Elsa's beliefs rather than constituting the conclusive statement it does as the show's final number. For Flora, it is an opportunity to test and explore a different identity in song:

> **Flora.**
> I am me?
> I am not someone else;
> Someone else is someone else
> I am me.
> I am sick of all the strain
> [...............]
> And the movies that they show where they force you to go,
> Like who else do you know who has seen 'Potemkin' thirty-seven times? (82)

Once more, there is a veiled reference to the Hollywood 'heritage' with which Minnelli is associated in Flora's lines:

> I am me,
> I am not Myrna Loy;
> Myrna Loy is Myrna Loy.
> I am me. (82)

Deliberately intended to provide a reference to the era of the thirties, these lines inevitably acquire a further association when sung by Liza.[24] One of the two entirely new songs written for the 1987 revival of *Flora* (the other was 'Keeping It Hot') is 'The Joke', an emotive, political song sung by Harry after he has been mocked in the street for his inadequate delivery of the speech Charlotte has written for him.

Apparently, Kander, Ebb and Thompson wished to restore some of the balance between the positive representation of American individualism and the first version's aim of taking Depression-era Communism seriously. Typically, Kander and Ebb's solution was to employ irony to turn Abbott's repeated joke at the expense of the Communist Party against itself:

> **Harry.**
> I don't blame you for laughing.
> When I speak I'm a joke,

I know.
There are people out there
With no shoes on their feet,
Who find shelter in doorways
From the snow and the sleet;
And they search through the garbage
To find something to eat,
And that's no joke.
[…………………………..]

We can right what is wrong
Our oppressors will know
From the words of our song
That the joke is on them. (85–6)

This is a bold and clever way of reinstating some aspects of the political debate lost when Abbott cut songs and scenes at Communist Party meetings, and it helps to make the character of Harry less of a comic stereotype, thereby enhancing what is at stake in the drama. Thompson's conceit that the show is being put on as part of the Federal Theatre Project[25] introduces a framing device for the new book in line with the many meta-theatrical devices Kander and Ebb have deployed throughout their joint career. With Willy addressing the audience directly at the start and end of the performance and at certain moments throughout, the effect is to justify any of the musical comedy conventions that might have appeared clumsy or dated twenty-two years after the musical had premiered. It repeatedly reminds the audience that the musical is actually an entertainment of the type that was devised as part of a state-sponsored welfare programme, which provided unemployed actors with work during the Depression. The self-reflexivity engendered by this Brechtian strategy encourages the spectators to judge the performance as an interpretation of history rather than an attempt at a straightforward retelling of events from the Depression.

The moment of narrative closure also creates a more moving drama by suggesting that Flora has become an adult with the grit and resilience to stand up for her own aims and values. Paradoxically, the intensity of Minnelli's performance may have convinced Kander and Ebb that it would make the most powerful impression at the end of the show. The fact that she interpreted the song with such a raw emotional quality would unintentionally have enhanced the incoherence of what must have appeared in 1965 to be a musical comedy with an unusually sour twist at the end. In 'Sing Happy', Minnelli's irrepressible assertion of talent as a performer can only act as assurance that Flora's future will be happy/successful. Abbott's emphasis on Liza as a star in the making may have been his attempt to mitigate the potential bleakness of the musical's conclusion, which leaves Flora unemployed and single at the show's conclusion, albeit cheered on by her friends and fellow artists. By contrast, 'You Are You', as the moment of narrative closure, actually recognizes the failure of individual ambition during the Depression rather than reinforcing the overcoming of such failure.

Probably inspired as much by the performer's nascent 'gamine' persona as by the professionally crafted identity for Flora, Liza and Flora began during rehearsals to seem a perfect match. From 'One Good Break' to 'Sing Happy', Fred Ebb and John Kander provided lyrics and music that would exploit Minnelli's instinctive drive and plucky power as a belter as well as the overwhelming poignancy that she is able to bring to lyrical moments of sadness and pain. Her distinctive talent is to bring these two moods together to enact the defiance of a person picking herself up from the floor to overlook past failures and overcome future obstacles. It was 'Sing Happy' that defined this complex mix of strength and vulnerability.

Although they had started writing the score for *Flora* before Minnelli was cast, 'Sing Happy' was written at the request of George Abbott during the out-of-town tryout. If there is no sonic world created for the overall milieu of the Depression, a distinctive Kander-and-Ebb attitude nevertheless emerges in the score that over time became identified with the 'Liza' persona fashioned by Minnelli and Fred Ebb for her concerts. Based on the tension between Kander's fusion of romanticism (vulnerability) and Broadway swing (guts), the attitude is both complemented and ironized by the faux-sophistication of Ebb's depiction of the switchback of reckless optimism and hard-bitten self-awareness. The team, in writing a vehicle for Minnelli, also managed to pattern a series of songs that clearly contrasted her musical idiom with the other characters' attitudes and manners, which are written more in the vein of comic stereotype. So the score, while failing to develop a sonic world that might fully evoke the environment of the Depression, does succeed in suggesting how the destructive forces of repression and rejection are defeated in the blossoming of a 'winner' from the failure that should logically have been her destiny. An emblem of the triumph of tremulous passion and determined optimism over reality, the latter motif became the essence of 'Liza':

> No need reminding me that it all fell apart,
> I need no lyric of stormy weather;
> There's quite enough around me that's breaking my heart.
> Sing happy! (94–5)

In Kander's words, '"Sing Happy" was the story of a woman who is literally having a nervous breakdown, whose world has collapsed around her, so that it was really screaming at somebody. The right way to do the song is in the context of the show.' [26]

The number does not celebrate happiness in song but represents an angry demand for what, under the circumstances of the Depression, is impossible. In dramaturgical terms, 'Sing Happy' anticipates the function of Sally Bowles' 'Cabaret' number: in both, the heroine wilfully refuses to face the dark or depressing realities of the world at large, preferring to 'Sing Happy' or 'Come to the cabaret' Instead. The many reiterations of 'Sing Happy' or 'Keep It Happy' provide an edge of desperate defiance in ironic contrast with the stock imagery of popular song such as 'robins in Spring', 'catching the ring', 'peaches and cream', 'clouds lined with a silver lining' and 'trips to the moon'. It is only the singer's forceful rendition and determined attitude that gradually insist on building an optimistic attitude out of the experience of disaster.

With its deliberate variations on her mother's signature song 'Get Happy' by Arlen and Koehler, 'Sing Happy' transforms Garland's teasingly ironic dismissal of her own sadness in the faux-spiritual genre of her song into an insistent anthem of hope and wilful determination. It is Minnelli's ability to express the coexistence of despair and optimism that renders the Kander and Ebb song electrifying in its dramaturgical context. Yet 'Sing Happy' was not only a perfect vehicle for Liza/Flora, it was a paradigmatic 'Kandernebb' song. [27] Its knowing and occasionally ironic references to other emblematic 'Garland numbers' such as 'Stormy Weather', 'Over the Rainbow' ('rainbows blending' [45]), 'When You're Smiling' and 'Look for the Silver Lining' compete with more general allusions to popular sixties song lyrics ('Fly Me To the Moon', 'The Impossible Dream'),[28] employing a sophisticated strategy of intertextuality that rejects pastiche in the creation of an identity for Liza/Flora as survivor that absorbs Garland's pathos while replacing her vulnerability with naively confident resilience.

At one and the same time, the team had found their own distinctive voice as theatrical songwriters and collaborated in the invention of a singular style and unique performing identity that would transform Judy Garland's talented daughter into a star in her own right. Norman Nadel put this point bluntly in *The New York World Telegram*, 'Miss Minnelli [. . .] is herself and no second edition Judy . . . Liza is this year's Liza – individual, unduplicated and electrifying – and she will be a star on her own terms for [. . .] many years . . . ' The Tony Award and rave reviews she garnered attest not only to her unique identity as a stage performer but also to the fine match of Minnelli with her material. The *Time* magazine critic opined, 'Liza Minnelli is a star to be, a performer of arresting presence who does not merely occupy the stage but fills it', while Whitney Bolton was more detailed in his analysis of her particular qualities:

> [Liza] is the most promising youngster that has come along in years. She can belt out a tune or whisper it, give it a sizzling coalition of sex and/or scorn, or make it so tender you want to cry with her [. . .] and she knows that you don't parrot lyrics, you make them poetry and give them life [. . .] Liza Minnelli is a winner, a fine singer, an excellent singer, and she can control her voice in a remarkable way for one so young and not yet richly experienced. [29]

Flora, the Red Menace was therefore responsible for one of Kander and Ebb's most important and long-standing collaborative relationships.

By identifying the climax of the show as the conflict between Flora's desolate situation and her attitude of defiance, Abbott not only preserved a note of American optimism to offset the gloom of the Depression but ensured that the narrative would be dominated by Minnelli's own tremulous intensity as a performer. Most of his decisions to delete musical numbers for characters other than Flora made the show into a star vehicle for Minnelli. What Abbott failed to do as a director was to establish a range of voices from the world of the 1930s to counterbalance the interiority so powerfully evinced in Flora/Minnelli's songs. In some ways, this may be connected with the fact that, unlike the show's producer, Harold Prince, he may not have actually 'heard' a difference between the musical comedy vocabulary in which he came to maturity as director and book-writer and the newer languages of 1960s theatre.

The musical's Depression environment of the 1930s, with its characters battling to survive extreme poverty, echoed the experience of the writers' childhoods, but the tension between Ebb's hard-bitten New York humour and Kander's romanticism motivates a series of definitive 'Kandernebb' songs that maintain an ironic counterpoise between representation of the harshness of social reality and the corresponding urge to defy it. Prince, Ebb and Kander together identified their work as belonging to a progressive theatre, indicating the potential for future collaborations by agreeing to meet a day after the show closed. Within a year, the trio had created *Cabaret* (1966), followed in 1968 by *Zorba*.

Notes

1. John Kander, Fred Ebb and Greg Lawrence, *Colored Lights*, New York: Faber, 2003, 38–9.
2. Harold Prince, *Contradictions: Notes on Twenty-six Years in the Theatre*, New York: Dodd, Mead and Co., 1974, 117.
3. *Colored Lights*, 50.
4. House Un-American Affairs Committee.
5. *Contradictions*, 118.
6. *Contradictions*, 118.
7. *Contradictions*, 119.
8. His most successful farces were *The Fall Guy* (1925), *Love 'Em and Leave 'Em* (1926) and *Three Men on a Horse* (1935).
9. John Kander, *Notes on Broadway*, New York: Simon and Schuster, 1987, 195.
10. Review of Lester Atwell's *Love Is Just around the Corner*, in Kirkus Reviews: https://www.kirk usreviews.com/book-reviews/a/lester-atwell/love-is-just-around-the-corner/Atwell novel.
11. In *Colored Lights*, 49–50.
12. Quoted James Leve, *Kander and Ebb*, New Haven: Yale University Press, 2009, 178.
13. *Strive and Succeed* (1872) is the title of a novel by Horatio Alger, who was widely known in the late nineteenth century for his many novels in which poor boys overcome obstacles with pluck and perseverance to succeed in life as men.
14. Quoted Leve, *Kander and Ebb*, 179.
15. These lines are transposed from the original cast recording of the show (1965), RCA, B000003F51.
16. Transposed from original cast recording.
17. In a television interview with Kristen Childs, Kander identified Marc Blitzstein as one of the two chief musical theatre influences on his work as a composer.
18. Transposed from the original cast recording.
19. Transposed from the original cast recording.
20. All page numbers are from David Thompson's revised version of the show (1988).
21. Transposed from the original cast recording.
22. Quoted in Leve, *Kander and Ebb*, 176.
23. 'If I Were a Bell', 'Bells Are Ringing', 'Before the Parade Passes By', 'Don't Rain on My Parade', 'There Won't Be Trumpets' et al.
24. Garland herself made the connection somewhat bitchily when she told Fred Ebb after the show, 'Listen, I have a suggestion for that song. "You are not Judy Garland. Judy Garland is Judy Garland. You are you!" That's what it should be' (*Colored Lights*, 46).
25. As part of his 'New Deal' designed to mitigate the worst effects of the Depression, the Works Progress Administration (WPA) funded the Federal Theatre Project as a means of keeping theatre people employed.
26. *Colored Lights*, 44.
27. 'Kandernebb' is the term Kander has jokingly used to refer to the closeness of the writing partnership. See Isa Goldberg in https://theaterlife.com/john-kander/ for a reference to the term.
28. *The Man of la Mancha* opened a few months after *Flora*, but it is very likely that Ebb had already heard 'The Impossible Dream' while writing the lyric for the out-of-town tryout.
29. *Morning Telegraph*, 3 June 1965. Quoted in CD liner notes, original cast recording.

2 The art of *Cabaret (1966)*

A classic in the making

Over a period of almost sixty years, *Cabaret* has become a classic. In a process that resembles the way several texts of Shakespeare's plays have, throughout their history been reconfigured for performance, being radically cut and reshaped to suit the changing aesthetic and ethical values of different sociocultural contexts, every new staging of *Cabaret* has been a unique version.[1] While the central tropes in its first stage production have remained a hermeneutic key to all subsequent interpretations, the high-profile success of Bob Fosse's very different cinematic version[2] has led, since 1987 to the regular inclusion in stage productions of 'Mein Herr' and 'Maybe this Time'[3] from the film, as well as its new 'Money' song performed by both Sally and the Emcee to replace the Emcee's original 'Sitting Pretty'. Since the 1990s, the piecemeal restoration of a few songs cut from the show before it opened on Broadway (e.g. 'I Don't Care Much') and the cutting of Herr Schultz's 'Meeskite' after the London premiere (1968) have also contributed to significant variations in emphasis and affect from one production to another.

Beyond the Broadway tradition: Harold Prince

Prince had been inculcated in the golden age tradition of musicals since working as an assistant stage manager to the legendary playwright/director George Abbott in 1950. In 1954, he became Abbott's co-producer on *The Pajama Game* and began his directing career with the Kander/Goldman brothers' *A Family Affair* in 1962. As producer of *Fiddler on the Roof* (1964), Prince could not have failed to grasp how Jerome Robbins' stylization of traditional European Jewish folkloric rituals and dances transformed Boris Aronson's haunting scenographic evocation of the mythic Russian *shtetl* of Marc Chagall's paintings into a vibrant symbol of nineteenth-century Yiddish culture. Employing Aronson as the designer of *Cabaret*, Prince was well situated to exploit the cabaret locale as an emblem of pre-Hitler Berlin, but the daring development of the cabaret's function as both symbol and framing device heralded a new approach to the organization of narrative, song and image to form a 'concept musical'. It was as though Jerome Robbins had used Aronson's Chagallesque designs for *Fiddler* as the conceptual principle for shaping that show. As both producer and director of *Cabaret*, Prince in effect shared authorship with Kander and Ebb, whom he engaged to write music and lyrics, as well as Joe Masteroff, who was commissioned to write the book.[4]

Flora the Red Menace adheres to the standard Broadway musical theatre format of the 'golden age' (1943–65), which assumed the non-diegetic convention by which characters sing and dance for spectators who nevertheless accept such performativity as a transparent form of 'speaking from the heart' – a simple heightening of the pseudo-naturalistic style. Classic examples of how this was first technically achieved by Rodgers and Hammerstein can be seen in 'The Surrey with the Fringe on the Top' in *Oklahoma!* and the 'bench' scene ('If I Loved You') in *Carousel*. These are 'sung scenes' in which dialogue and lyrics are craftily interwoven. In aesthetic terms, the Rodgers and Hammerstein model offered the equivalent in musical theatre terms of stage naturalism; in sociocultural terms, they constructed a theatrical vehicle resembling the classic realism of cinema, an expression of mid-century American exceptionalism at its most unselfconsciously optimistic and – subliminally – imperialistic.[5]

In the typical golden age musical, men are masculine and women are feminine and happy to be so.[6] Even after asserting her independence from men for more than half of the film musical *Calamity Jane* (1953), it becomes apparent that Calamity unconsciously desires to be 'tamed' by Wild Bill Hickok. Fifties Broadway musicals unashamedly sell consumerism as the true pathway to the American Dream. The freedom of the frontiersman to create a new state in *Oklahoma!* had by the time of *The Pajama Game* (1954) become the right to a consumer lifestyle. By the mid-1960s, however, the paradigmatic musical comedy ending, in which heterosexual marriage was an emblem of social harmony (the nuclear family as norm), was an utterly inappropriate means of representing a deeply uncertain and conflicted society.

While teasingly undermining the heteronormative romantic narrative that typified golden age musical comedy, *Flora* only went part of the way to challenging the manner in which a conventional happy ending celebrated heterosexist norms. The affectionately satirical representation of Communist ideology in *Flora* is ultimately compromised by the implicitly capitalist celebration of Flora's grit and talent as a would-be star fashion illustrator, while the not-so-happy ending leaves the heteronormative musical comedy paradigm intact. Flora still believes she will find the right job *and* the right husband.

In their very different ways, *Cabaret* (1966) and *Hair* (1967) heralded a revolution in Broadway musical theatre. The apotheosis of the traditional Broadway musical tradition, *Fiddler on the Roof* (1964), was only midway through its six-year run when the two shows opened. Prince was the producer of *Fiddler on the Roof*; Jerome Robbins was its director-choreographer. It was to be Robbins' last new musical on Broadway. Taken together, the new shows rendered the paradigm of the golden age book musical obsolete. After these shows, musicals that did not question or challenge the old linear narrative model would appear formulaic. So while a hit such as *Promises, Promises* (1968) was perfectly viable as a fashionably styled musical comedy with 1960s pop songs especially written by Bacharach and David, it was not innovative in form but merely updated the musical comedy style and format familiar since *Pal Joey* (1940). As a result of reviewer Martin Gottfried's apt formulation of the term 'concept musical' to indicate the significance of Hal Prince's directorial concept in shaping the book and score for *Zorba* (Kander, Ebb and Joseph Stein, 1968), the new kind of non-linear musical acquired the status of a distinct sub-genre. In retrospect, *Cabaret* and *Hair* could be called concept musicals.[7]

From their experience on *Flora the Red Menace*, Prince, Kander and Ebb had learned the danger of following Broadway convention in adapting a novel or story into a musical. Without the kind of restrictions imposed by the old-school director George Abbott, Prince was both more experimental and more directive in working on *Cabaret*. Not content with following John van Druten's rather tame adaptation of Christopher Isherwood's *The Berlin Stories* (1945) into the well-made play *I Am a Camera* (1951),[8] Prince and his collaborators were responding to the startlingly theatrical impact of Joan Littlewood's radical *Oh What a Lovely War!* (1963). In addition, Prince, on a visit to Moscow in 1966, had been hugely impressed by the traces of Meyerhold's aesthetic praxis in the Taganka Theatre's revue, *Ten Days That Shook the World*.[9] Exposure to such potent anti-naturalistic styles of staging in work that utilized a range of revue techniques to represent and critique historical events encouraged him to be more artistically adventurous.

Inventing the metaphor: from *I Am a Camera* to *Cabaret*

A comparison of the stage play *I Am a Camera* (1951) with the original Broadway production of *Cabaret* reveals how completely Prince's collaborative team transformed the style and point of view of John van Druten's stage play – and subsequently John Collier's film adaptation – of Christopher Isherwood's *The Berlin Stories* (1945). The main plot of *I Am a Camera* involves a straightforward dramatization of the relationship between Christopher Isherwood and Sally Bowles, complicated by Sally's opportunistic affair with the wealthy American Clive Mortimer while presenting the romance between Christopher's student Fritz Wendel and the Jewish heiress Natalia Landauer as a subplot. The action takes place entirely in Christopher's room in the anti-Semitic Fraulein Schneider's Berlin flat. Although both the play and film do expose Christopher's gradual disillusionment with the blind and self-serving escapism of Sally and others, his growing awareness that the moral implications of Nazism make it untenable for him to go on living in Germany does not by the end of the play or film, resolve the implied tension between the view of the writer's function as merely that of a camera truthfully recording the Berlin milieu, and that of an engaged citizen-artist who must exercise ethical responsibility by means of direct political engagement.

In the film version of *I Am a Camera* (1955), Sally meets Christopher in the Lady Windermere nightclub, but the venue merely serves the function of allowing the audience to see Sally perform 'I Saw Him in a Café in Berlin', the kind of song an amateur might have performed in imitation of a second-rate Marlene Dietrich. With her bolero pantsuit, long cigarette holder and monocle, Julie Harris appears eccentric rather than decadent, while the nightclub is merely a background for the action. It has no aura and no metaphorical significance. The venue reveals nothing of the libertarian ethos of Berlin during the Weimar Republic, nor does it expose the escapist mentality that one might conceive as a response to the material poverty and spiritual desperation of the majority of Germans after the First World War and during the Depression. Sally's wilful escapism remains peculiar to her, being an aspect of her ignorant and self-deluded bohemianism, which is by turns infuriating and endearing.

Unlike the stage play or the musical, the film of *I Am a Camera* is told in the form of an extended flashback from the present moment of a London publisher's party, in which

Christopher's somewhat ambivalent memories of Sally, Fritz and Natasha are set against his encounter with the real Sally, who has become older without really changing. This framing of the past by the present meeting of the two characters somewhat diminishes the political implications of Christopher's *bildungsroman*, ending the film on a wistful note of nostalgia for the infuriating charm of Sally Bowles, rather than in confrontation with the horrifying reality of the historical events that succeeded the period fictionalized in Isherwood's *Berlin Stories*.

Although *Cabaret* retains much of van Druten's Chris-Sally plot, it substitutes the bittersweet story of the wooing of the (no-longer anti-Semitic) landlady Fraulein Schneider by the Jewish grocer Herr Schulz in place of van Druten's subplot of Clive Mortimer, Fritz Wendel and Natalia Landauer. *Cabaret* starts with the ubiquitous 'Wilkommen', a pastiche Berlin cabaret number, before it initiates a pattern of intercutting the narrative of Cliff's arrival and experience of the Berlin *demi-monde* with numbers from the cabaret, which begin to acquire a metaphorical significance as the musical continues. The score functions effectively to support and amplify the conventional 'book' musical as well as to develop the metaphor of Berlin as represented through the prism of the somewhat surreal cabaret. This self-reflexive tendency has wide-ranging implications for the developing dramaturgical form of the mainstream Broadway musical, which was soon to be even more directly challenged by the direct address to the audience in *Hair*'s songs.

The backstage musical and the changing social landscape

The setting of large parts of *Cabaret* as a show within a musical was not by any means a new convention at the time; the backstage musical has been a staple of film musicals since the start of 'talking pictures', while the sophisticated thematic exploitation of meta-theatrical devices in presenting 'book' scenes was central to the dramaturgy of musicals at least as early as *Show Boat* (1927). The startling originality of *Cabaret*'s exploitation of the Kit Kat Klub locale as both emblem and framing device becomes apparent, however, if one compares the show to Rodgers and Hart's recognized classic, *Pal Joey* (1940) – also set largely onstage or backstage of a nightclub. The key venues in the show are a second-rate nightclub in Chicago and a more up-market one in the second act called Chez Joey, in which a series of pastiche song-and-dance numbers, rehearsals and offstage scenes are presented. As in *Cabaret*, some non-diegetic songs and scenes happen outside the nightclub, but the milieu of the club is pervasive. The chief difference between the two shows is that the nightclub in *Pal Joey* has no metaphorical significance.

Cabaret's innovative collaborators were undoubtedly aware of the extent to which the conventions of mainstream Broadway musical theatre no longer expressed the structure of feeling[10] of contemporary sociocultural realities.[11] The dramaturgical model of a romantic love story with narrative complications being overcome to culminate in marriage reflected a univocal social discourse that bore no resemblance to the fractured society exposed in the mid-sixties. *Cabaret* establishes a double perspective on the more naturalistic milieu of Isherwood's stories. By 1966, the clearly ghettoized and embattled American society plainly visible to all was, in cultural terms, obscured by the multiplicity of popular representations that presented love as a universal panacea and replaced social conflict with utopian visions of personal happiness and social integration in the American melting pot.

Such social fault lines had already been manifest culturally in the creation of 'off-Broadway' as an alternative to and protest against the theatre of the white middle-aged middle class; in the rock 'n roll and rock music that had come to emblematize the emergent youth culture; in the gathering momentum of the Black civil rights movement that was beginning to articulate a new identity for African Americans and in the nascent awareness among women and homosexuals of the necessity for a liberationist politics of identity that would cumulatively maintain its impact on Western society and culture from the late 1960s to the present day. This political fragmentation provided Prince with a strong impetus for the innovations of *Cabaret*, which represents a challenge to the linear narrative model expressive of the univocal social discourse of mainstream post-war sociocultural consensus.[12] The creative chaos of the Weimar Republic became Prince's emblem of the 1960s USA.

The pleasures of the musical and the dialectics of escape

Cabaret broadens the stage musical's customarily narrow focus on the temperamental disposition of individual characters to offer a metaphor for an entire society in crisis, locating Sally's desperate hedonism as one of a number of alternative responses to the tumultuous social and political conflicts provoked by the disintegration of the inter-war German economy. In *I Am a Camera*, Van Druten maintained the passive observer's neutrality implied in the title he took from Isherwood's narrator, who insists on preserving his detachment from what he observes around him in Berlin: 'I am a camera with its shutter open, quite passive, recording, not thinking. Recording the man shaving at the window opposite and the woman in the kimono washing her hair. Some day, all this will have to be developed, carefully printed, fixed.'[13]

Figure 3. Joel Grey and company sing 'Wilkommen' in *Cabaret*. Note the tilted mirror at the back. Photo: Friedman-Abeles, NYPL, Billy Rose Division.

Cabaret, by contrast, subjects the act of looking or observing to scrutiny, so that the theatregoer's usual passivity becomes problematic in the very act of viewing the events and performances of *Cabaret*. The musical's manner of deploying the meta-theatrical frame of the backstage musical is radically unconventional. The tilted mirror confronting members of the audience when they entered the auditorium of the Broadhurst Theatre with the *Cabaret* sign in neon made spectators acutely conscious of their own act of viewing.[14] With this innovation, Prince and Aronson initiated a deconstruction of the formulae of the backstage musical on screen and on stage.[15] By means of this self-reflexive representation of the Berlin-cabaret-within-a-Broadway-stage-show, producer-director and designer directed the historical representation of the libertarian behaviour of Weimar Germany directly at their Broadway audience,[16] thereby invoking the more complex and ambivalent attitude articulated in Isherwood's own subsequent critique of his narrator's *faux* moralism in *Mr Norris Changes Trains*:

> What repels me now about *Mr Norris* is its heartlessness. It is a heartless fairy-story about a real city in which human beings were suffering the miseries of political violence and near-starvation. The 'wickedness' of Berlin's night-life was of the most pitiful kind; the kisses and embraces, as always, had price-tags attached to them, but here the prices were drastically reduced in the cut-throat competition of an over-crowded market [. . .] The only genuine monster was the young foreigner who passed gaily through these scenes of desolation, misinterpreting them to suit his childish fantasy.[17]

Watching themselves in the tilted mirror in the act of watching the opening of the show, spectators are obliged to problematize their role as consumers of entertainment and question not only the nature of theatrical representation but their own identity as spectators. Throughout the performance, multiple possibilities of *looking* are offered to the spectator: the role of voyeur, escapist, willing participant, responsible confidant, hedonistic Broadway consumer, guilty onlooker or reluctant bystander. As the show unfolds, each spectator experiences the interrogation of their role as a member of a Broadway audience in the form of a drama analogous to the clash of conflicting (and internally conflicted) roles in the fictional representation – and by extension, contemporary New York. The crisis of spectatorship tests the audience's responses to the nature of every character's attitudes to the politics of living in Germany in 1929–30, implicating them in the ethical dilemmas as witnesses. The question confronting each member of the audience is given voice in Fraulein Schneider's trenchant challenge to Cliff in her final song, 'What would you do/ If you were me?' (453).[18] As a subtext to the entire performance, the notion of guilt and responsibility for terrible crimes that include the barbarity of the Holocaust inevitably plays itself out at a deeply personal level in the imagination of each spectator; this subtext surely acquired peculiar intensity on Broadway where a large percentage of the audience was Jewish. [19]

Another way of emphasizing the combination of self-reflexiveness and historical perspective in the show was the use of the iron staircase:

> Boris [Aronson] designed an iron staircase typical of those backstage in nightclubs and he put it in the limbo area of the stage [. . .] and I placed ladies of the chorus on it, observing the realistic scenes of the play. Their indifference generated a curious dynamic in the scenes. They become the surrogate German population.[20]

With the score of *Cabaret*, Kander and Ebb evince for the first time their remarkable facility in elaborating a scheme of musical theatre dramaturgy that fashions the contradictions between dramatic context and song content into an intentional pattern of ironies, so that songs must be comprehended contextually rather than as straightforward generators of affect. From this point in their career, the meaning of most songs in their *oeuvre* requires unravelling to detect the complicated process whereby the singer is ignorant of the full implications that the dramaturgical scheme or the wider historical context supplies.

On the other hand, the performer, in singing a number, may ironically adopt a pose in clear opposition to their character's genuine feelings/intentions. These various gaps and contradictions in and between the attitudes and perceptions of various *dramatis personae* promote a hermeneutic game experienced as a chain of meanings accumulated sequentially in the dialectical progress of the show. Ebb's lyrics match the pastiche music unobtrusively, adopting either the naughty, teasing style of comic German cabaret and *Varieté* speciality numbers or the more romantic mode of period ballads in a relatively simple idiolect to suggest the quotidian thought/feeling patterns of the characters. Unlike the wit and humour of the pastiche subsequently displayed in *Chicago*, the brilliance of *Cabaret*'s lyrics is manifest in the subtle character delineation of the non-diegetic songs and the astonishing ironies of the diegetic show numbers. While the linguistic expression in songs may on a literal level be (deliberately) simple and the style or form of the accompanying music (intentionally) conventional, the contradictions between music, lyrics, staging and dramatic context complicate and enrich the play of meanings activated by the overall ensemble of heterogeneous components.

'Wilkommen': establishing the tone and style

Eschewing the usual Broadway 'medley' overture, the isolated drumroll and cymbal crash in the dark presage the sinister undertones of the show. This musical effect precedes a trademark Kander vamp, which forms a musical trope persisting throughout the show. James Leve has demonstrated its thematic function as a musical motive:

> It contains the seeds of the rest of the score. The opening chord, a tonic chord with an added sixth, and repeated eighth notes on the offbeats encapsulate the naughty burlesque milieu. The vamp recurs throughout the opening scene, underscoring the Emcee's salacious remarks to the audience [. . .] Kander sneaked it into the end of 'Don't Tell Mama' [. . .] and also employed a tightly wound version in the minor key at the opening of 'Cabaret', as an allusion to the ultimately sad outcome of Sally's decision to have an abortion.[21]

In 'Wilkommen' Joel Grey's arch and roguish manner both titillates and mocks the naivety of spectators who cannot fail to notice the disparity between the pretension to glamour and the licentious display of flesh actually present, upon which their gaze is nevertheless riveted. Staring unblinkingly into the eyes of the audience, the Emcee casts them in the role of patrons of the Kit Kat Klub on New Year's Eve 1929 – accomplices in the tired escapism the production number ironically vaunts.

In Harold Prince's production, 'Wilkommen' was a tease and Joel Grey's Emcee a puzzle. On stage, the spectacle initially appeared eccentric and naughty rather than sinister. Wryly weaving in and out of the dance, prodding the girls lasciviously and leering at the boys, his performance self-consciously nudged the audience to view the spectacle as a show about showing:

> Wilkommen, Bienvenue, Welcome!
> Fremde, Etranger, Stranger,
> Glucklich zu sehen, je suis enchante,
> Happy to see you, bleibe, reste, stay!
> Wilkommen, Bienvenue, Welcome!
> Im Kabaret, to Cabaret, au Cabaret. (415)

The Emcee stresses the exotic quality of the spectacle by addressing the audience in German, French and English as strangers, immediately putting their status as spectators into question, as if they were all foreign tourists searching Berlin for some kind of companionship.

The stark contrast between the world outside and the onstage reality of the Kit Kat Klub was stressed in the Emcee's address to the audience: 'Leave your troubles outside . . . So – life is disappointing? Forget it! In here life is beautiful . . . The girls are beautiful . . . Even the orchestra is beautiful!' (415). One look at the ageing and corpulent female orchestra is enough to tell that he is lying, but the licentious mythologizing of the cabaret as a safe retreat from the harshness of life in the streets outside ('outside it is winter, but here it is so hot we have to fight to keep the girls from taking off all their clothing') (415) is firmly established, so theatre audiences can conceive of the offstage reality as considerably more threatening than what they are actually watching in the cabaret.

The effectiveness of *Cabaret* as art inheres in the very vulgarity of the form it both celebrates and deconstructs.[22] In order to evoke the momentousness of the rise to power of the Nazis, the authors keep actual historical events in the wings, never attempting a direct representation of their enormity on stage. By illustrating precisely how people habitually avoid direct confrontation with an unpalatable reality, *Cabaret* artfully suggests its historical magnitude while at the same time avoiding melodramatic clichés. The one respect in which Prince and his collaborators did compromise with audience taste was in following the closeted (at the time he wrote the stories) Isherwood in skirting around Christopher/Cliff's homosexuality.[23]

Although Prince subsequently criticized his 1966 production as 'soft at the centre' believing he could 'only go so far with a Nazi musical' at that time, thus compromising the material 'with my eyes wide open', the show written by Masteroff, Kander and Ebb was to establish the central trope that gives coherent meaning to almost all the pair's subsequent shows, a trope inherent in *Oh What a Lovely War* – the exploitation of popular entertainment to whitewash unpalatable truths. Foster Hirsch's view is that 'in making Isherwood's characters at home on the musical-comedy stage – the world in which the characters are "having a good time" is closer to George Abbott than to a reflection of Berlin before the Third Reich – Prince is [therefore] in danger of making Fascism attractive.'[24] The key point of the show is that the Nazis *made* fascism attractive to the majority of Germans. In fact, by omitting a direct presentation of their most didactic political sloganeering, Prince and his collaborators were better able to pose disturbing questions about how and why this occurred without resorting to emotionally manipulative representations of violence or Nazi atrocities. Prince was later to observe 'Along with *Evita*, *Cabaret* is my sexiest show [. . .] sexy in the sense of seductive, not pin-ups',[25] a perceptive analysis of its attractiveness to audiences.

As Emcee, Joel Grey's knowing posture of camp seemed an acknowledgement of the vulgarity of the show-within-the-musical: 'We are all slumming it', he seemed to say. Certainly, the girls lying on their backs at the front of the stage, crossing and uncrossing their legs in the air were far removed from the chic glamour of the previous year's Tony-award-winning musical, *Mame*. In *Cabaret*, show business is sleazy, the Kit Kat Klub more reminiscent of a burlesque show than a Broadway musical. The first 'book' scene of Cliff's arrival in Berlin by train is framed by the Emcee's performance as he repeats Ernst Ludwig's 'Welcome to Berlin' as part of a ghostly reprise of 'Wilkommen' to provide a bridge into the scene of Cliff's meeting with his new landlady Fraulein Schneider in Scene 3 (416).

Prince recollected in 1987 that all those who saw the 1966 production recalled the mirror and the neon sign, but there were also 'trolley-car cables and globe street lamps which went upstage diminishing in size to give a sense of distance. It was strong and abstract and definitely Berlin pre-war.'[26] Ultimately the separation between the cabaret and the life outside starts to blur as the metaphor for the Berlin ethos begins to contaminate the entire action of the play, while conversely, the libertarian values of showbiz escapism themselves are corroded by the gradual ascendancy of the hostile Nazis. Although often assumed to be 'epic' in the manner of Brecht/Weill's *The Threepenny Opera*, the dramaturgy of *Cabaret* (1966) employs a mode of conscious stylization more reminiscent of the grotesque defamiliarization techniques of Meyerhold to affect its radical deconstruction of the integrated forms of musical play and musical comedy dominant on Broadway since the mid-forties.

By comparison with the positioning of songs in *The Threepenny Opera* outside the flow of the narrative, Kander and Ebb's songs always function to extend the dramatic presentation of the narrative by being sung *in character* and wholly within the logic of the dramatic moment.[27] *Cabaret* might in one respect, however, be considered Brechtian: in the dialectical nature of the relationships between the questions addressed by the characters in the song and the ethical and political issues raised by the surrounding narrative. Whether the songs are diegetically presented as musical numbers performed in the cabaret or sung in non-diegetic contexts as part of the older conventions of the integrated book musical, the thematic trope that persists throughout *Cabaret* comprises a dialectical confrontation between the necessity of accepting and confronting reality and the opposed impulse to escape from its harshness. That this dialectical discourse both exploits and mocks the escapist conventions of Broadway musical comedy remains not only a significant irony but has also heightened *Cabaret's* remarkable power and ongoing appeal. Reviewing the show in the *New York Post* in November 1966, Richard Watts Jr. reflects on this paradoxical duality of grim reality and escapist entertainment: 'It is the glory of *Cabaret* that it can upset you while it gives theatrical satisfaction. It is disturbing, provocative, meaningful, believable and highly entertaining.'[28]

While critics have found *Cabaret* aesthetically sophisticated and historically resonant, its enormous popularity, as evidenced by the Bob Fosse film and by innumerable revivals around the world, attests to its status as commercial entertainment rather than high artwork.[29] Indeed its power as art inheres in the very vulgarity of the form it both celebrates and deconstructs.[30] Right from its opening in 1966, the contrast between the old-fashioned musical comedy conventions of the book and the emblematic moments of cabaret performance was noticed by reviewers of the premiere production. Martin Gottfried thought 'the differences between the cabaret and the plot halves [of the show] could not be more striking. On the one hand there are unique ideas, striking use of lighting and movement, a sense of the bizarre. And on the other the same old romance, secondary romance and sketched-in complications.'[31]

One of the design features that had astonished Prince at the Taganka was 'the curtain of light', which had effected smooth scene changes by blinding the audience in order to permit the equivalent of cinematic dissolves from one image to another. He urged the innovative lighting designer Jean Rosenthal to reproduce this effect for *Cabaret*, but the architecture of Broadway theatres presented a serious challenge to her ingenuity. Notwithstanding the difficulties, Rosenthal found a solution that involved a lighting trough, which could not only be electronically raised above or lowered beneath the stage but also angled at various degrees to produce very different effects: 'Downstage at 45 degrees we momentarily blinded the audience. And at 90 degrees straight up into the flies we made a curtain of dust'. Lighting could therefore divide the stage into two areas – 'an area to represent the REAL WORLD, the vestibule in Sally's rooming house, her bedroom, the train, the cabaret; and an area to represent the MIND'.[32] Prince called the latter 'limbo', which presented metaphorical numbers in contrast to the diegetic routines represented literally on the nightclub stage.

Non-diegetic songs and rhetorical questions

The humorous and poignant presentation of the middle-aged romance between the landlady and the Jewish greengrocer Herr Schultz does not appear in Isherwood's stories nor in either version of *I Am a Camera*. It is clearly derivative of the comic love stories that constitute the conventional subplot of a golden age musical. Although such a traditional use of linear narrative may seem to betray the authorial team's more radical intentions, clichés are subverted by the disorienting effect of the intercalated cabaret routines. As played by the redoubtable Lotte Lenya, Fraulein Schneider's battle to survive under difficult and changing circumstances became a vehicle for portraying the impact of the Nazis' rise to power on the lives of ordinary German citizens, her eventual decision to end the relationship with Herr Schultz demonstrating the insecurity generated by institutionalized anti-Semitism.[33]

The casting of the iconic Lenya was, of course, ironic for a number of reasons: not only was she Kurt Weill's widow, but, like him, she had been forced to flee from the Nazis in 1933, ending up in New York in 1935. At the same time as her presence in the show validated its authenticity, she was a refugee playing the role of a person who was justifying her reasons for burying her head in the sand and rejecting the possibility of escape. Kander's music, although it contains the occasional homage to Kurt Weill (the first chorus of 'Wilkommen', for instance, echoes that of 'Mack the Knife'), is more akin to Friedrich Hollaender and other popular Berlin songwriters of the 1920s, many of them Jewish.[34]

Although the opening and the third number both occur as routines onstage at the cabaret, marking the musical as very different from either the stage or screen versions of *I Am a Camera*,[35] the 'golden age' convention of non-diegetic song is employed in Fraulein Schneider's 'So What', which is the first of a series of songs that asks a rhetorical question, this time rationalizing the need to accommodate the harsh realities of the economic Depression:

> So once I was rich
> And now all my fortune is gone,
> So what?
> And love disappeared
> And only the memory lives on,
> So what?
> If I've lived through all that,
> And I've lived through all that,
> Fifty marks doesn't mean a lot.
> If I like that you're here,
> And I like that you're here,
> Happy New Year, my dear,
> So what? (419)

The rhythm of the song evokes the sound of a revolving fairground carousel, the music enacting a cyclical notion of time that is amplified by the repetition of the rhetorical question, 'so what' in the lyrics. Fraulein Schneider's rationalization of the need to compromise under adverse conditions not only delineates her character but also initiates a broad thematic motif that is subject to variations in the particular viewpoints of other characters. Fraulein Schneider's surrender to the rollercoaster movement of history ('It'll all go on if we're here or not') involves rejecting the existentialist ideal of actively shaping one's future in favour of a homespun philosophy of survival that accepts chance as a governing principle. A number of other songs constitute tacit responses to the question of how best to survive difficult conditions, offering variations on the notion of pragmatism or hedonism as a means of escape from harsh reality.

The second non-diegetic number is the 'Telephone Song', one of two numbers sung in the cabaret environment but not performed diegetically as part of the onstage entertainment. Invariably cut in later productions, the number does help to depict the decadence of the Kit Kat Klub as a milieu in which the boys and girls offer themselves more or less interchangeably to the clientele. Every table has a telephone, which lights up as a girl or boy rings a potential client:

> CLIFF: Hello?
> GIRL ON PHONE: (*singing*)
> Hello.
> Sitting all alone like that,
> You happened to catch my eye.
> Would you like to buy a girl a drink?
> CLIFF: Sorry.
> GIRL ON PHONE: Ach! Goodbye. (425)

At the end of the number, the homosexuality of a certain section of the nightclub audience is acknowledged:

ALL:
Sitting all alone like that,
You happened to catch my eye
GIRLS:
Would you like to buy a girl a drink?
BOYS:
Would you like to buy a man a drink?
ALL:
Would you like to buy a boy a drink?

(They dance, and from different parts of the stage – right, center, left – the dancers alternately say 'You will,' 'Why not?' Goodbye'.) (426)

Character as performance

In the diegetic 'Don't Tell Mama', performed on stage at the Kit Kat Klub, Sally enacts the role of a naughty schoolgirl who has tricked her mother into believing she is staying in 'a secluded little convent in the southern part of France' when she is actually 'singing in a nightclub in a pair of lacy pants' (421). By identifying with the role of the decadent reprobate she plays on stage, Sally characterizes herself as a wilfully amoral vamp. The relish with which schoolgirl/ Sally identifies the various relatives (father, uncle, brother) who secretly come to watch her at the club implicates members of the theatre audience as spectators of the cabaret show.

The second scene in Cliff's room reveals Sally charming the young writer into allowing her to share his lodgings, her scheme coming to a head when she sings the third of the show's non-diegetic songs, 'Perfectly Marvellous'. The rhetorical structure of the song demonstrates Sally's deft use of role-playing to manipulate Cliff, but by glamourizing her sexual promiscuity, she also betrays her own naïve belief in the fast-living image she has cultivated to impress others. Exploiting the pose of sexual libertinism invoked in 'Don't Tell Mama', Sally employs in both dialogue and song a typically British upper middle-class speech register – its insouciance intended to convey a bohemian disregard for conventional morality:

So if anyone should ask about you and me, you have two alternatives: you can either say 'Oh yes, it's true we're living in delicious sin' or you can simply tell the truth and say,

I met this perfectly marvellous girl
In this perfectly wonderful place
As I lifted a glass
To the start of a marvellous year. (429)

By voicing the words she would like Cliff to use, Sally conjures up the scenario she has imagined as an idealized vision of an unorthodox affair with a novelist:

But since my stay in Berlin
Was to force creation,

Figure 4. Judi Dench in 'Don't Tell Mama'. Photo: David Magnus, Arenapal.

What luck to fall on a fabulous
Source of stimulation. (430)

Yet when he protests that he cannot let her stay, her mask slips to betray the reality of her homeless situation as she pleads to stay for 'a day or two'. Once he gives in, Sally resumes her romantic scenario:

CLIFF. Besides, I've only got one narrow bed.
SALLY. We'll think of something . . . (430)

Cabaret performance as Brechtian commentary

The action segues to the cabaret show as the Emcee announces a thematic connection between the non-diegetic number and 'Two Ladies', reinforcing the motif of pleasure as a means of escape: 'So you see everyone in Berlin has a perfectly marvellous roommate. Some people have two people' (431). The song-and-dance routine titillatingly represents a sexual *ménage a trois*, inviting the Broadway audience to identify with the voyeuristic Berlin spectators. The Emcee's gleeful pleasure in having 'two ladies' in his bed while being 'the only man' is in direct opposition to Cliff's reluctant agreement to share a bed with Sally in the previous scene:

> EMCEE.
> We switch partners daily
> To play as we please;
>
> GIRLS.
> Twosies beats onesies
>
> EMCEE.
> But nothing beats threes.
> I sleep in the middle
>
> GIRL 1.
> I'm left
>
> GIRL 2
> And I'm right –
>
> EMCEE.
> But there's room on the bottom
> If you drop in some night. (433)

The lyric implicates spectators in a prurient fantasy of becoming participants in the sexual romp, an amplification of the open sexual soliciting of the 'Telephone Song'. The reckless embrace of hedonism by the Berlin *demi-monde* portrayed in the majority of cabaret numbers is ironically juxtaposed throughout the show with grim hints concerning the rise of the Nazis, thereby constituting a dialectical pattern in which this persistent escapism is tested against the reality of intensifying political turmoil. A few other songs either satirize the political situation directly or articulate deeply emotional responses to the dangers it portends.

Contradictory visions of the future

In sharp contrast, the succeeding duet 'It Couldn't Please Me More,' illustrates the genteel courtship of Fraulein Schneider by Herr Schultz. The sweetly sentimental wooing by means of the gift of a pineapple from his store is presented in romantic musical clichés as a comic Hawaiian fantasy. Although the odd choice of a pineapple might seem unromantic, the historical context of the extreme devaluation of the German currency in the late 1920s would have made this somewhat exotic fruit a genuine luxury at the time:

> FRAULEIN SCHNEIDER:
> If you brought me diamonds
> If you brought me pearls,

If you brought me roses
Like some other men
Might bring to other girls;
It wouldn't please me more
Than the gift I see,
A pineapple for me. (435)

In Act 2, the couple's illusion that they can avoid the terrible truth of the Nazi threat is shattered. When, at their engagement party, the Nazi Ernst Ludwig exposes their planned wedding as an impossible dream, Fraulein Schneider is made aware of the dangerous consequences of being married to a Jew. Yet another escapist fantasy is shockingly undermined.

An insight into how the Nazis exploited pastoral images to romanticize their battle for power is manifest in the haunting 'Tomorrow Belongs to Me', a pastiche of an anthemic German folk song sung by off-duty waiters at the Kit Kat Klub:

The sun on the meadow is summery warm,
The stag in the forest runs free;
But gather together to greet the storm.
Tomorrow belongs to me. (437)

The notion of greeting 'the storm' hints at a nationalistic desire to embrace the myth of Aryan domination, but the benefit of hindsight affords the image uncanny intimations of the destruction precipitated by the Third Reich. While its patriotic exhortation is at first ambiguously figured in 'nature' imagery, the Emcee joins the waiters for the final chorus, which is more sinister in voicing the Nazi view of German destiny:

Oh Fatherland, Fatherland show us the sign
Your children have waited to see;
The morning will come when the world is mine,
Tomorrow belongs to me. (437)

The song is highly allusive, appealing to irrational impulses and instinctive feelings in the way that effective propaganda functions. The repetition of 'Tomorrow belongs to me' accumulates an unsettling force as the audience observes the waiters' blind mouthing of fascist ideology in the mistaken belief that they will be its beneficiaries. So convincing is Kander and Ebb's pastiche that various people have insisted they did not compose the song but merely quoted an authentic Nazi anthem.[36] Its persuasive power resides in the exultation of the typical fascist psychology that offers a revivification of national pride as a compensation for the suffering of poverty and the humiliation of defeat. In a grotesque distortion of Fraulein Schneider's pragmatic philosophy of chance ('So I'll shrug and I'll say, so what?') the waiters' song transmutes what is actually an abandonment of moral values into a teleological process of nature that merely requires acquiescence to the predestined triumph of the fatherland.

Prince used visual effects in varied ways to communicate meaning, with the conclusion of this number being one of the most striking:

Working on the button for [the waiters' song . . .] 'I want a count of four followed by a black-out. I want the singers to disappear into *total* blackness: that's the point. Then we have the blinder lights, which have to blind.' [. . .] the song ends,, the actors turn upstage into a black abyss as the blinders at the foot of the stage light up – the moment is a startling visual premonition of the darkness that is to envelop Germany.[37]

This is a pivotal moment for audiences in emblematizing the way ordinary working people succumbed to the political machinations of the Nazis. Set entirely apart from action and dialogue, the song projects a hallucinatory indication of the belief in Aryan superiority, the right of Germans to rule over those deemed inferior, which was soon to infiltrate the collective unconscious of the nation.

Pleasure and self-deception

The song's dark foreboding infects the following scene, subverting Cliff's defiant assertion of the right to indulge in careless pleasure:

> I said it was *possible* I was sleepwalking. And – if I am – who cares? What's the point in opening my eyes?
>
> (*He sings.*)
>
> Why should I wake up?
> This dream is going so well.
> When you're enchanted,
> Why break the spell? (438)

Cliff's references to living in Berlin with Sally as a kind of enchantment elaborate the central trope of escapist activity, yet by activating the subliminal historical consciousness shared by members of the theatre audience, 'Tomorrow Belongs to Me' contaminates Cliff's set of questions in 'Why Should I Wake up' with the ironic apprehension that in this historical context, blind avoidance of social responsibility in the pursuit of personal gratification might ultimately be tainted by the potential guilt of Nazi collaboration. Indeed, later Cliff's eyes are opened to the fact that Sally has manipulated him into unknowingly smuggling for Ernst, a Nazi from whom he needs to disentangle himself.

In this way, the audience is constantly reminded of the fact that even small decisions made by ordinary German citizens in their everyday existence might have considerable ethical significance. Prince was very aware of the danger of overstating the Nazi presence in the early parts of the show. In 1987, he said:

> [T]here's a trap in *Cabaret*'. If you have Nazis on stage right at the start [. . .] where is your trajectory? In Act 1 I want to indicate these are people trying to have a good time; they're coping. I want to show that 'just folks' became Nazis. I like the character of Fraulein Kost [the prostitute]; she's a fun-loving woman who got caught up in the Nazi groundswell because it brought her money and nice clothes – and there she was.[38]

At the point in the narrative when Cliff celebrates his overcoming of his habitual emotional reticence, his language sounds unexpectedly insecure, the recognition that he may be 'lonely again' is out of keeping with the mood of joy:

Don't I adore you
And aren't you mine?
Maybe I'll someday be lonely again,
But why should I wake up till then? (438–9)

This may relate to the often-remarked problem of Cliff's unconvincing characterization in the musical as heterosexual, which perhaps reflects the reticence of the narrative voice in the *Berlin Stories* (Christopher Isherwood, gay but still in the closet in 1966). With the character's orientation – bisexual in the 1972 film, and changed to homosexual in stage productions since 1987 – his nervous and repressed response to seduction by Sally is far more understandable and the song represents social attitudes of the 1930s far more powerfully. In Joe Masteroff's words:

> In the original production, Cliff was totally sexless. you couldn't have a gay leading man in those days. In the movie, he was bisexual. In the 1987 revival, as we travelled around the country, he was sort of bisexual. When we got to New York, we said, what the hell, let's make him a homosexual?[39]

As a heterosexual man, Cliff is a mere cipher whose passivity does not justify the only song he ended up with in the 1966 production. As a queer man, the character is far more vivid, his drama more poignant and conflicted as he struggles to repress his homosexuality by launching determinedly into a relationship with Sally. In this scenario, 'Why Should I Wake up' makes the sense Kander and Ebb may initially have intended it to. James Leve examines a number of songs the pair wrote as duets for Cliff and Sally, many of which represent responses to the news that Sally is pregnant. When Sally admits to Cliff that she is pregnant in Scene 10, they discuss whether she should have an abortion. Typically, Sally's attitude towards her pregnancy is fraught with deception and ambivalence. When Cliff realizes it isn't the first time she's had an abortion, she attempts to reassert her dizzy, careless manner:

> Oh, Cliff – remember – you mustn't ever ask me questions. The truth is I should never have told you about the baby. But I thought – if you didn't mind, perhaps I wouldn't mind. It might even have been rather – nice. But now we know where we stand, the subject is closed. (439)

The 'Man in the Mirror', which is modelled on the twin soliloquies in *South Pacific*, suggests an interior life for the characters, the verses for Sally, in Leve's opinion, unconvincingly articulating a desire for domesticity:

> See that girl in the mirror
> Well that girl's on her way out.
> [.............]
>
> She'll be wildly adorable
> As she's pushing the pram.
> Though her past was deplorable
> Now, she's meek as a lamb. (65)

The lyrics for Cliff, on the other hand, might be effective if the character were convincingly bi- or homosexual; like many gay men in the period, Cliff would be trying to believe he could change his sexual orientation by marrying and fathering children:

> CLIFF
> Maybe we can make it work
> SALLY
> Maybe we can make it work
> CLIFF
> All we have to do is change
> SALLY
> All we have to do is change. (64)

Cliff does begin to romanticize the notion that he might be a father and considers getting a job, thereby offering Sally a chance to have the baby ('This might be the best thing that ever happened to me', he says), precipitating her automatic, cynical reaction, 'And I'll go back to the Kit Kat Klub!'

Money and power

At this moment, fortuitously it seems, Ernst Ludwig enters to deliver a somewhat shady 'business' proposition whereby Cliff would receive seventy-five marks in return for travelling to an address in Paris that he will be given:

> ERNST
> [Y]ou pick up a small briefcase – you bring it back to Berlin . . . And I promise you are giving help to a very good cause.
>
> CLIFF
> Well, whatever it is, please don't tell me. I don't want to know. (440)

Here, Cliff deliberately avoids precise knowledge of the machinations involved in furthering Ernst's 'very good cause', preferring to ignore his own potential complicity in corruption and treachery for the sake of earning money he desperately needs.

'Sitting Pretty', the Emcee's next cabaret number, situates the couple's concern over their financial difficulties within the general context of the Depression. The duo's first attempt at writing a 'money' song was 'A Mark in Your Pocket', a Brechtian reflection on the usefulness of money in hard times:

> They take you in front of the judge
> You wish that he weren't so honest
> You'll find that he isn't so honest
> But first put a mark in your pocket[40]

In order to enhance the force of the satire, Kander and Ebb wrote the first version of 'Sitting Pretty':

> The grocer needs money
> The baker wants money

They tell me my rent's overdue
But me, I'm sitting pretty
Life is pretty sitting with you.[41]

Even this was not explicit enough, so Ebb rewrote the lyric to exaggerate the Emcee's ruthlessness. Descending the spiral staircase in expensive attire, his exultation in the disparity between his own wealth and the poverty of his relatives is a cruel and ostentatious display of *Schadenfreude*:

My father needs money,
My uncle needs money,
My mother is thin as a reed.
But me, I'm sitting pretty
I've got all the money I need. (440)

The mention of 'four starving children' and the nasty joke, 'And my sister and my brother/ Took to hocking one another, too', not only evokes the misery of ordinary Germans in this period but is a mocking reminder that very rich people supported the Nazis in order to make huge profits. There follows a kitsch song-and-dance routine in which the Emcee presents a series of showgirls from Russia, Japan, France, the United States and Germany, each in turn exhibiting coins of the appropriate currency on strategic parts of her body:

But I'm not a nincompoop,
I've got an income you
Put in the bank to accrue. (441)

The rattling rhythm of the Emcee's fast-paced delivery mimics the jingling of metal coins as he shows off the money he earns from being a pimp. Sex and money are revealed as instruments of barter in a corrupt economy of illicit pleasures, further complicating the underlying trope of hedonism.

Marriage as utopia

In sharp contrast, Herr Schultz and Fraulein Schneider's succeeding duet envisages their prospective marriage as a utopian existence in which quotidian circumstances are transformed into a blissful idyll. Left alone in the living room when Fraulein Schneider goes into her bedroom after having promised to consider his offer of marriage, Herr Schultz voices his private thoughts optimistically:

SCHULTZ.
How the world can change,
It can change like that,
Due to one little word –
Married.

See a palace rise
From a two-room flat
Due to one little word –
Married. (443)

The song becomes a musical scene as Fraulein Schneider, sitting on the bed in her own room, repeats the two choruses while contemplating his offer.

The dramaturgical device whereby the pair vocalize the same song in separate rooms allows the authors to reveal each character privately contemplating the prospect of marriage over a brief passage of time, coming at last to the same conclusion in the repeated chorus:

> FRAULEIN SCHNEIDER.
> And the old despair that was often there
> Suddenly ceases to be,
>
> SCHULTZ and FRAULEIN SCHNEIDER.
> For you wake one day, look around and say,
>
> SCHULTZ.
> Somebody wonderful
>
> FRAULEIN SCHNEIDER.
> Somebody wonderful
>
> SCHULTZ and FRAULEIN SCHNEIDER.
> Married me. (443–4)

Once again, the musical directly explores the possibility of escape from the harsh realities of the political situation by a retreat into the private sphere. At the end of the song, Fraulein Schneider returns to the living room and agrees to the proposal. When Herr Schultz excitedly shouts out the good news, Sally enters and promises to throw an engagement party, but Schultz insists that he will host the party in his fruit shop.

Anti-Semitism on stage

When Cliff arrives at the party on his return from Paris, he looks for Ernst, who is not yet there, in order to get rid of the briefcase full of money as quickly as possible. Fraulein Kost arrives with a bunch of sailors (her 'cousins'), one of whom invites Fraulein Schneider to dance. As Ernst arrives and takes the briefcase from him, Cliff spots his swastika armband and then attempts to refuse the money, but Sally unhesitatingly grabs it instead.

Unaware of this tense atmosphere, Herr Schultz is embarrassed when he notices two young men dancing together, so, apparently in order to prevent an incident, he asks everyone to stop dancing and sit down while he entertains them with a comic song. First, he explains that 'the only word you have to know to understand my little song is the Yiddish word: "meeskite." "Meeskite" means ugly, funny-looking' (446). The song tells the story of an ugly baby who, in his adolescence falls in love with Pearl, a girl who is an even worse meeskite than he is. A year after they are married, she gives birth to a beautiful child:

> Gorgeous, gorgeous,
> They produced a baby that was gorgeous, gorgeous;
> Crowding round the cradle all the relatives aahed and oohed,
> 'He ought to pose for a baby food'. (447)

According to Herr Schultz, the extended fable contains a moral, which he explicates directly:

> Moral, moral,
> Yes indeed, the story has a moral, moral,
> Though you're not a beauty it is nevertheless quite true
> There may be beautiful things in you.
>
> Meeskite, meeskite,
> Listen to the fable of the meeskite, meeskite,
> Anyone responsible for loveliness, large or small,
> Is not a meeskite
> At all. (447–8)

'Meeskite' anticipates the Emcee's 'If You Could See Her', the anti-Semitic number with a gorilla performed in the club in Act 2. In both numbers, being different is hailed as a potential source of beauty – albeit ironically in the Emcee's later number. Paradoxically, the gorilla that looks like a Jewess yet appears attractive to her lover is comparable to the two ugly parents capable of producing a 'gorgeous' child.[42]

Ernst takes Fraulein Schneider aside to urge her to break off her engagement to the Jewish greengrocer. When Cliff overhears the conversation, he defends Herr Schultz's rights as a German citizen, which precipitates Ernst's threat to leave because the engagement of a German woman to a Jew offends him. The prostitute Fraulein Kost persuades him to stay by rendering a bellicose reprise of 'Tomorrow Belongs to Me' with slight changes to the lyrics that include more overt references to Nazi dogma. First, Ernst joins her in singing a rewritten chorus of 'Tomorrow Belongs to Me' before most of the guests take up the song, 'their voices growing louder and louder, even rather frightening' (448) in proclaiming the future triumph of the Third Reich.

In lieu of an overture, *Cabaret* has a raucous entr'acte featuring a medley of numbers from the show, its jazzy style obliterating any memory of the sombre ending of Act 1 in favour of a gleeful recapitulation of its carnivalesque qualities as entertainment. The fun-loving mood is both continued and undermined by the goose-stepping kickline of girls led by the Emcee in drag, which is followed by the melancholy scene in which Fraulein Schneider explains to Herr Schultz why she must break off their engagement. During their conversation, her reasons for doing so are apparently reinforced by someone throwing a brick that shatters the window of his fruit shop.

Returning to the stage of the Kit Kat Klub, the Emcee's 'If You Could See Her' begins as a grotesque masquerade in which he appears to plead for the tolerance of otherness:

> I know what you're thinking.
> You wonder why I chose her
> Out of all the ladies in the world
> [...................................]
> If you knew her like I do
> It would change your point of view. (451)

The Emcee ironically debases the *laissez-faire* attitude towards alternative lifestyles by making his love object a gorilla:

I understand your objections,
I grant you the problem's not small
But if you could see her through my eyes,
She wouldn't look Jewish at all. (451)

The final line explodes by invoking the disgusting racist caricatures of Jews, the ugliness of the meeskite prompting an association with Nazi genetic theory, which categorized Jews, Romany and Black people as sub-human in order to justify their genocide as a method of preserving the purity of the allegedly superior Aryan race. The cabaret routine also demeans the foregoing representation of the older couple's wooing, snidely juxtaposing their romance against an illicit affair between the Emcee and a gorilla.

The number involves a further elaboration of the trope of *looking*, the difference between the supposedly righteous 'point of view' of a spectator and the love-stricken perception of the Emcee being emphasized in the constantly repeated line 'if you could see her through my eyes'. The Emcee takes for granted the anti-Semitic views of the cabaret spectators – and, by extension, the theatre audience – his ironic degradation of their identity as detached onlookers to that of leering racists, making them uncomfortably aware of their potential guilt as passive bystanders. When in 1966, the punchline, 'She wouldn't look Jewish at all', proved offensive to a number of Jewish groups and individuals, Prince reluctantly decided to replace it with, 'She isn't a meeskite at all', establishing a direct connection with Herr Schultz's genuine argument for the acceptance of difference, in an effort to avoid the shock of the baldly racist line. The original punchline was restored in Bob Fosse's film version (1972) and has remained in all subsequent revivals, thereby restoring the shock value of the number.

Personal and political: what would you do?

The following scene in Cliff and Sally's room foregrounds their disagreement over the political situation:

CLIFF
Someday I've simply got to sit you down and read you the newspapers. You'll be amazed by what's going on.

SALLY
You mean – politics? What has *that* to do with us?

CLIFF
[....................................]
Sally, can't you see – if you're not against all this you're for it. Or you might as well be. (452)

Fraulein Schneider's arrival a few minutes later intensifies the darkening atmosphere. As a result of her breaking off the engagement, Fraulein Schneider feels obliged to return Sally and Cliff's gift of a crystal fruit bowl. When Cliff urges her not to give in to the racist propaganda of the Nazis, she retorts:

That is easy to say! Easy for you, fight!

(*Music starts*)

And if you fail – what does it matter – you pack your belonings. You move to Paris. It is easy for you. But if you were me? (452)

Her rationalization for the decision not to marry is articulated in a song that is funereal in its fearful prefiguration of the inevitable Nazi victory. Its unique power resides in the synthesis of the repeatedly dissonant pitches of the music, reinforced for once by Ebb's stark reiteration of the rhetorical question, 'What would you do?' which the landlady flings in the faces of Cliff, Sally and by extension the theatre audience. The defiant recklessness of Fraulein Schneider's rhetorical 'So What?' has been inverted to signal a resignation to her personal tragedy, which resonates as an emblem of the crisis of an entire generation, trapped in a historic catastrophe. The potency of the lyric can be perceived in the way it utilizes simple language to create images that simultaneously invoke particular and common experience:

> With time rushing by
> What would you do?
>
> With the clock running down
> What would you do? (452)

In this moment, Fraulein Schneider identifies her personal experience of growing older as part of the historic destiny that was leading inexorably to catastrophe. The accusatory gesture of the rhetorical question is linked to the slowing of the tempo to create a rhythm that mimics the fatal arrest of historical time, the entropic undermining of historical progress. In its dramaturgical context, the excruciating tempo of the song enacts a frozen moment to provoke a self-reflexive motif of *looking*, whereby the quality of the onlooker's engagement is interrogated in the relationship between characters and audience shaped by both mise-en-scène and score:

> Go on, tell me,
> I will listen.
>
> What would you do
> If you were me? (453)

The final lines of the lyric challenge the audience as much as Cliff and Sally, activating the trope introduced at the start by Aronson's tilted mirror. By directly challenging Cliff and Sally to put themselves in her place, Fraulein Schneider demands that each member of the theatre audience consciously examine their own repressed conscience concerning those who suffer while they prosper. The relentless struggle to survive is evinced in Fraulein Schneider's stark account of her existence:

> I have battled alone, and I have survived. There was a war – and I survived. There was a revolution – and I survived. There was an inflation [. . .] but I survived! And if the Nazis come – I will survive. [. . .] For, in the end, what other choice have I? This is my world. (453)

After Fraulein Schneider leaves, Sally and Cliff continue to argue about whether she should accept the offer to work at the Kit Kat Klub again, with Cliff insisting that she should leave Berlin to go back to America with him: 'Sally, wake up! The party in Berlin is *over*! It was lots of fun, but it's over! And what is Berlin doing *now*? Vomiting in the streets' (454). At the end of the scene, Sally has a silent moment when she appears to be making a decision, grabs her fur coat and rushes out. Evidently, she has resolved to have an abortion.

That evening, Cliff meets Sally in the bar of the Kit Kat Klub and attempts to disabuse her of her delusions regarding herself as an indispensable fixture at the club:

> CLIFF
> When are you going to realise, the only way you got this job was by sleeping with somebody?
> SALLY
> That's not true.
> CLIFF
> And the only way you'll get a job in New York or Paris or London is by sleeping with someone else. But you're sleeping with *me* these days. (455)

When she exits to change for her performance, Cliff receives a telephone call at his table from Ernst, who is sitting in another part of the club. Now Ernst offers to pay 150 marks to Cliff for taking a briefcase to Paris, raising the amount to 200 when Cliff seems hesitant. As Cliff makes to leave, there is an altercation:

> ERNST
> But what is wrong with you? I don't understand!
> CLIFF
> Take your hands off me!
>
> (He does.)
>
> ERNST
> Clifford – I know you need the money. So why won't you go? It is because of that Jew at the party? (455)

Cliff punches Ernst, provoking a brutal counterattack by his two Nazi bodyguards, who beat him senseless. As they drag Cliff out of the club, the Emcee enters, laughing hysterically – 'as if the fight were part of the floor show', (455) to announce Sally.

The ultimate illusion: life is a cabaret

On the surface, her song 'Cabaret' is a jazzy exaltation of escapist fun, an extension of the trope begun in her first number. Yet its strategic juxtaposition against a portent of Nazi barbarism focusses the jarring irony of Sally's defiant salute to ceaseless revelry (the underlying theme of the onstage entertainment) as a blaring crescendo. Reiterating the interrogative pattern of many other lyrics in the show, 'Cabaret' begins with a rhetorical question to the audience:

Start by admitting from cradle to tomb
Isn't that long a stay.
Life is a cabaret, old chum.
Come to the cabaret. (456)

The most self-referential number in the entire show, Sally's perverse glorification of pure entertainment as an escape from the dullness of everyday reality, is meta-theatrical: her delivery of 'Cabaret' *becomes* the very act of denying the ominous forebodings of historical reality. By addressing each member of the audience with the supposed familiarity of an 'old chum', Sally treats them as habitual partygoers who share her devotion to merrymaking. The lyrics indicate the actual sound of the orchestra ('Come hear the band'), this particular performance-within-the-show illustrating the metaphorical significance of the milieu on display. The lines, 'Come blow your horn,/Start celebrating', (456) ingeniously cast members of the theatre audience in the role of guests at the 'party' while the pun on the idiomatic expression 'blowing your own trumpet (horn)' and its literal meaning implicate each as a decadent spectator of a 1930s Berlin cabaret. The more a spectator enjoys the most popular and best-known number in the show, the more deeply they are drawn to identify with its values. At its most fundamental level of signification, the cabaret symbolizes the way the Broadway musical itself has typically refrained from confronting the conflicted reality of its own dysfunctional society.

'Cabaret' makes a surprising use of meta-performance. The account of the singer's flatmate in Chelsea is a brief narrative verse within the song, while her memory of the neighbours who used to snicker 'Well that's what comes from too much pills and liquor', (456) complicates the layers of self-reflexive performance even further. Yet the singer/Sally contradicts their *Schadenfreude* by applauding Elsie's carelessly hedonistic attitude, 'She was the happiest corpse I'd ever seen' before pointing out the moral of her tale by boasting of how she has adopted her friend's philosophy a few choruses later, 'I made my mind up back in Chelsea/ When I go, I'm going like Elsie' (456). In her lead-in to the penultimate chorus, the singer/Sally reveals that she learned the tag line she sings five times in the number from Elsie, so even this maxim is a quotation: 'I think of Elsie to this very day. I remember how she'd turn to me and say, "What good is . . . "' (456) Sally's unexpected oxymoron 'happiest corpse' inverts the moral of the traditional cautionary tale, to praise rather than censure or punish Elsie's unfettered pursuit of pleasure.

The recurrent repetition of the metaphor of cabaret as life involves a generalization that goes beyond any other lyric in the show in emphasizing its universal validity. The last chorus not only reiterates the cabaret 'hook' three times but repeats the expression 'old chum' from the opening lyric twice more. Ironically, in admonishing spectators to heed her maxim before it's too late, Sally's final lines surprisingly exploit the form of a *memento mori*:

Start by admitting from cradle to tomb
Isn't that long a stay.
Life is a cabaret, old chum,
Only a cabaret, old chum,
And I love a cabaret. (456–7)

The linguistic generality of this chorus permits multiple different interpretive approaches to playing Sally – as will be shown later in a comparison of the various performers who have famously played the role. While the underlying import of Sally's simplistic outlook remains consistent, the character's specific attitude and motivation in singing the song can vary according to each actor's innate vocal qualities, histrionic personality or conscious choice.

The following day, while Cliff is packing to leave Germany, Herr Schultz arrives bearing a parcel of fruit as a farewell gift for Sally and Cliff. Although he claims to be moving to the other side of Nollendorfplatz because 'it is easier for *her*', he still believes the disturbances caused by the Nazis will die down: 'I *know* I am right – because I understand the Germans . . . After all, what am I? A German' (457). Sally enters, looking pale and insists on a gin as soon as he leaves. When Cliff asks why she is not wearing her coat, she makes evasive small talk until she euphemistically informs him she has had an abortion: 'My one regret is I honestly believe you would have been a wonderful father. And I'm sure someday you will be. Oh yes, and I've another regret: that greedy doctor! I'm going to miss my fur coat' (458).

When Cliff slaps her, she babbles on incoherently, the stale clichés about her bohemian life as 'a strange and extraordinary person', (458) now exposed as a pathetic sham. After Cliff sorrowfully hands her a railway ticket before leaving to catch the train to Paris, Sally picks up her long cigarette holder in a vain attempt to resume her pose as a fun-loving sophisticate, but she cannot sustain the illusion so she lowers it and turns to the door while the lights fade very slowly. In the dark, the audience hears the loudspeaker announcement of the train's imminent departure. When the lights come up, they reveal Cliff seated in his compartment as two customs officers enter to check his passport. Cliff's negative reply to a question as to whether he will return to Germany soon elicits a somewhat surprised response from the officer:

You did not find our country beautiful?

CLIFF
(*tonelessly*)
Yes, I found it – beautiful. (459)

The reiteration of the word 'beautiful' echoes the equivocal comment the Emcee has repeatedly made in describing the louche and buxom cabaret girls; in this context, his sardonic misuse of the word undermines the apparent guilelessness of the customs officer's question while reinforcing Cliff's equivocal use of it.

When the officers leave, he returns to writing on his notepad before reading what is apparently the beginning of an autobiographical novel:

'There was a cabaret and there was a master of ceremonies and there was a city called Berlin in a country called Germany – It was the end of the world –

(*Music plays*)

– I was dancing with Sally Bowles – and we were both half-asleep . . .' (459)

Cliff's reversion to the cabaret as the key to his memories of Berlin triggers a phantasmagoria of images. As he sings the opening lines of the show, 'Wilkommen, Bien venue, Welcome',

(459) the Emcee appears and mimics Cliff by moving his lips soundlessly, before accompanying him in song, taking over from him as the train glides to the rear of the stage into darkness.

As the Kit Kat Klub rematerializes, the Emcee's perfunctory reprise of his salutation to the audience is resoundingly hollow: 'Where are your troubles now? Forgotten. I told you so. We have no troubles here. Here life is beautiful – the girls are beautiful – even the orchestra is beautiful' (459). The spectral atmosphere is enhanced when the all-female band appears out of the darkness on a sliding platform in an ironic contradiction of his remarks: 'The girls are not as pretty, German uniforms and swastika armbands are now apparent', while their music has a dissonant sound. Sally is then 'lifted high on a chair' to reprise, 'I made my mind up back in Chelsea/When I go I'm going like Elsie' (460). According to Keith Garebian,

> Prince developed an almost hallucinatory vocal and musical kaleidoscope as Schultz, Fraulein Schneider and Sally reappeared within a moving crowd and repeated words from the earlier scenes in a montage. Sally had one more passage from the title song, before she vanished into the darkness [. . .] leaving the Emcee alone onstage for the wrap-up.[43]

This ghostly audiovisual mosaic dissolves the strict sense of historical verisimilitude by representing Berlin in 1930 as an expressionistic patchwork of reconfigured memories. After singing part of the final line, 'Auf Wiedersehen! A bientot!' he disappears before he can sing the final 'Good night!' (460)[44] Instead the performance breaks off abruptly with a drumroll, then a cymbal crash, leaving the members of the audience to trawl the collective memory for a convincing narrative conclusion.

Notes

1. In some respects, the existence in print of two – and occasionally three – different versions of Shakespeare's plays (Quarto and Folio versions) and the scholarly supposition that his company probably abbreviated written texts for performance, challenge the idea of a definitive text just as much as the relatively brief production history of *Cabaret* does.
2. The screenplay was written by Jay Presson Allen.
3. 'Maybe This Time' was actually performed by Liza Minnelli in her nightclub act and recorded in 1965, long before she was cast as Sally Bowles.
4. According to John Kander, '*Cabaret* evolved from Hal Prince's concept . . . The director, writer and composer sit in a room together and imagine the characters and the elements of the story. That's an area where Hal's strength as a leader of collaboration shone through . . . It was . . . the ideal way for collaborators to work on a piece' (John Kander, Fred Ebb and Greg Lawrence, *Colored Lights*, New York: Faber, 2003, 60, 61).
5. The transformation of Indian Territory by white settlers into the new state of Oklahoma disguises the theft of the land and the further marginalization of indigenous Americans as nation-building, an example of the imperialism that characterized the United States' international politics after the Second World War.
6. In this context, Hammerstein's lyric in *Flower Drum Song*, 'I Enjoy Being a Girl' is not only typical but normative. (Think John Raitt, Howard Keel, Ezio Pinza, Gordon Macrae and Mary Martin, Kathryn Grayson, Jane Powell, Jennifer Jones).

7. While the label has become ubiquitous, it is somewhat problematic and was rejected by Sondheim.

8. In 1955, the play was adapted into a film of the same name.

9. The revue was adapted from John Reed's novel of the same name.

10. This is a term coined by Raymond Williams, the British Marxian cultural critic, to indicate the ideological (aesthetic) manifestation of socio-economic circumstances.

11. Ironically, not all critics in 1966 fully comprehended the new approach to dramaturgical structure. A reviewer of the Boston tryout, Steven Landrigan, while praising a number of the show's features, censured the book for failing to live up to the narrative coherence of its sources: 'Unfortunately, in Joe Masteroff's book for "Cabaret," the characters and plot merely float about for two and a half acts before they settle into any realistic and understandable form. The trouble stems partly from the constant interspersing of cabaret acts between scenes, thus shattering the play's unity'.

12. Prince's stated intention was to confront affluent white Americans with the 'invisible' injustice and inequality suffered by Black Americans as a consequence of the innate racism of a materialistic society indifferent or blind to the poverty of contemporary urban ghettoes.

13. Weeks before the Broadway opening, Prince wrote to Isherwood to explain why he had transformed the stories he himself admired so radically for the musical.

14. Both the name of the show and the neon sign were book-writer Joe Masteroff's ideas.

15. Prince credits Boris Aronson with conceiving the idea of the tilted mirror. (See Harold Prince, *Sense of Occasion*, Milwaukee: Applause Books, 2017, 132).

16. In 1966, Harold Prince believed *Cabaret* would challenge Broadway audiences with the question, 'Are you doing anything more to help African Americans than the average German did to help Jews and other persecuted minorities in the Third Reich?'

17. Quoted in Jonathan Fryer, *Isherwood: A Biography*, New York: Doubleday, 1977.

18. All quotations from the show refer to Joe Masteroff, John Kander and Fred Ebb, *Cabaret*, New York: Random House, 1967.

19. See Foster Hirsch, *Harold Prince and the American Musical Theatre*, revised and expanded edition, New York: Applause Books, 2005, 40–1 for an explanation of Prince's view of the show's contemporary relevance.

20. Prince, *Sense of Occasion*, 132.

21. James Leve, *Kander and Ebb*, New Haven: Yale University Press, 2009, 53.

22. Note the comments by Kander and Ebb about writing a Broadway 'entertainment' in *Colored Lights* (128) and Prince's comments in Hirsch, *Harold Prince and the American Musical Theatre*, 5.

23. 'Were I to do *Cabaret* now, I would take the opportunity, as Fosse did in the film, to restore the original gay sub-plot. Cliff was gay and there was no future for him and Sally. But putting Nazis on the stage in a musical seemed a big enough step at the time' (Prince, *Sense of Occasion*, 138).

24. Hirsch, *Harold Prince and the American Musical Theatre*, 1.

25. Prince, *Sense of Occasion*, 134.

26. Carol Ilson, *Harold Prince: from Pajama Game to Phantom of the Opera*, Ann Arbor: University of Michigan Press, 1989.

27. In a stage direction in *The Threepenny Opera*, Brecht explains the convention thus: 'Mr and Mrs Peachum step in front of the curtain and sing. Song illumination: a golden light. The organ is lit up. Three lights come down on a bar from above, and on the board is written: The I for One

song' (Bertolt Brecht and Kurt Weill, trans. Ralph Manheim and John Willet, *The Threepenny Opera*, London: Methuen, 1976, 13).

28. *Colored Lights*, 128.

29. As well as the film version in 1972, *Cabaret* has had three major Broadway productions and five in London; in the theatre season of 1993–4 there were twelve new productions of *Cabaret* in Germany alone.

30. Note the comments by Kander and Ebb about writing a Broadway 'entertainment' in *Colored Lights* (128).

31. Martin Gottfried, *Women's Wear Daily*, quoted in Keith Garebian, *The Making of Cabaret*, New York: Oxford University Press, 2011, 122–3.

32. Harold Prince, *Contradictions*, New York: Dodd, Mead and Co., 1974, 130–1.

33. In Fosse's film, she plays a minor role as an anti-Semitic landlady, as in the stories.

34. In various interviews, Kander has stated that he did his best to steer clear of Weill's influence:

> I got all the recordings I could of Berlin jazz and Berlin vaudeville songs [. . .] I was very careful not to listen to . . . [Weill's] work for obvious reasons. I wanted to have as much of Berlin's popular music running through my head and then put that away and start writing [. . .] I said to [Lotte Lenya], 'I'm sure that some critics would say this is watered-down Kurt Weil'. She took my head in her hands and said. 'No, this is not Kurt, it's Berlin, and when I'm on that stage I'm singing Berlin' (file:///Interview%20with%20Composer,%20John%20 Kander.webarchive).

35. The stage play by Van Druten takes place entirely in Cliff's room at Fraulein Schneider's boarding house, while the film has one scene in the cabaret.

36. Garebian, *The Making of Cabaret*, 82–3.

37. Hirsch, *Harold Prince and the American Musical Theatre*, 49.

38. Quoted in Hirsch, *Harold Prince and the American Musical Theatre*, 42.

39. Quoted in Hirsch, *Harold Prince and the American Musical Theatre*, 66.

40. Quoted in Leve, *Kander and Ebb*, 59.

41. Quoted in Leve, *Kander and Ebb*, 59–60.

42. Also in 1987, Prince decided to drop Schultz's somewhat meandering song near the close of Act 1. The number had been perfect for the beguiling comedian Jack Gilford. Although it added to the sweetly sentimental image of the Jewish character, it was unlikely that a German Jew would have spoken Yiddish, and it would be difficult for any other actor to equal Gilford's charming and gentle performance in the first production.

43. Garebian, *The Making of Cabaret*, 123.

44. This is how the musical ends in the 1966 script; on the original cast recording, Joel Gray does sing the final 'Good night'.

3   (Re)visions of *Cabaret*

Bob Fosse's film and after

A casual reading of reviews of each of the many variant productions and versions of Kander and Ebb's *Cabaret* reveals a critical tendency to regard the original script in an Aristotelian manner as the immanent germ of a perfect performance as if some inexplicable teleological process from conception to performance might eventually generate an ideal production. David Spencer's review of Sam Mendes' New York production for the Roundabout Theatre in 1998 is typical in this respect: 'It is only now . . . that Sam Mendes and the authors have taken the musical to the next and, possibly, ultimate, level of its journey [. . .] Never has *Cabaret* been closer to its ideal than at the Kit Kat Club, never more effective as a warning, and never more relentlessly theatrical.'[1] The truth is that, situated in a specific historical context, each revisal of any 'classic' tells us as much about an audience in a particular sociocultural moment as it does about an individual directorial vision. Rather than seeking to establish a teleological hierarchy of more and less ideal productions actuated from an immanent ur-text, a comparison of various versions might more productively reveal the ways in which each version/production riffs off the original text, thereby constructing a new cultural moment from the auteur's personal response to their society's values.

Bob Fosse's film

Bob Fosse's 1972 film of *Cabaret* was a fairly radical revision of the 1966 stage show, which was a major reason for its unqualified success in a period when the movie musical as a genre was in a state of crisis. The film maintains and elaborates the idea of the cabaret as both social milieu and metaphor, even using a few specific pieces of staging from Prince's stage production, but Fosse's fundamental decision to fully exploit the unique properties of film as a medium required him to cut all non-diegetic songs and ground the form of his *Cabaret* in a system of film montage that utilized a technique of rapid cuts between diegetic cabaret performance and *verismo* representation of the 'real world', thereby enabling the cabaret numbers to form a continuous commentary on the characters' attitudes and actions. This artistic strategy can be identified from the earliest sequence of shots on screen, which in the middle of the final note of the Emcee's second chorus ('cabare-e-et') on the cabaret stage, jump cuts to a shot of a train arriving at Berlin Anhalter railway station, with Michael York looking optimistic as he walks along a platform beside it. Once this choice was made to interpolate or even collide images of social life and onstage performance, much of what followed was simply logical, although naturally, Fosse expressed his own artistic and personal identity in creating every shot and editing them as he does.

The removal of the subplot of Fraulein Schneider and Herr Schultz's relationship is a logical second step, as their romance is expressed in musical comedy terms and Fosse was clearly aware of the contemporary moviegoing public's distaste for the convention of non-diegetic singing on film – witness the commercial failure of his recent *Sweet Charity* on film (1969). In fact, Cliff's landlady in Isherwood's stories and Van Druten's play is a rabid anti-Semite, nothing like the tough but likeable survivor of the stage musical – and the figure of Herr Schultz does not exist in Isherwood. So Fosse and his screenwriter Jay Presson Allen return to the more complicated plot and subplot of the film version of *I Am a Camera* – derived from the stories – and import the characters of Fritz Wendel, Natalia Landauer and Clive Mortimer (translated into Maximilien in *Cabaret*) from it. The change nonetheless still features the theme of Nazi anti-Semitism, although this is more subtle and complex because Fritz is a closeted Jew and Natalia Landauer is a Jewish heiress, while Maximilian is aristocratic, wealthy, married and bisexual. Ernst Ludwig does not appear in the film version.

The next major change of approach concerns Fosse's representation of the central characters' sexuality. The rather primly heterosexual Chris/Cliff of all earlier versions now becomes the bisexual Brian – a significant and necessary change in the post-hippy/post-Stonewall era of fashionable androgynity and sexual liberation.[2] Cliff's sexuality had been a problem from the stage version of *I Am a Camera* onwards because Christopher Isherwood, the implied first-person narrator of *Goodbye to Berlin*, had in fact travelled to Berlin in the late 1920s to enjoy what he and his gay friend Auden regarded as 'the bugger's daydream'[3] so John van Druten's representation of Chris/Cliff had involved an act of censorship at a time when Isherwood himself was obliged to conceal his own homosexual identity. The repressed trope of sexual liberation in all the previous versions is suddenly permitted to appear fully, with Sally as its icon. By entirely removing the Schneider/Schultz subplot with its four major songs, the screenplay transforms Liza Minnelli's Sally into its central character – the only one with an 'offstage' life who sings. From this perspective, Fosse's premeditated display of the process whereby a recognizable film and stage performer transforms herself on screen into a genuine star embeds Minnelli's personal qualities in the part just as she herself introjects the 'Sally' persona to make performer and role indistinguishable. Ironically of course the ultimate proof of Liza's star power – the film's final number, 'Cabaret' – manifests Sally's egotistical existential demonstration that pure entertainment has the power to annihilate all concern for Nazi barbarism. Once again Fosse embodies in the film his own obsessive theme: show biz celebrates the delusion that 'real' life, no matter how terrible, can be replaced by sheer escapism.[4]

Visual qualities of the film

The startling originality of Fosse's film, however, is inherent not merely in his dramaturgical innovations but in his mastery of mise-en-scène and editing. Composing shots with the skill of a painter, he pays homage to the art of the Weimar Republic from the outset of 'Wilkommen'. In her astonishingly perceptive review, Pauline Kael both anticipates and invalidates the subsequent clichéd readings of the film as a cautionary tale of the decadence various critics believe paved the way for the eventual triumph of the Nazis:

> Here in a prodigious balancing act, Bob Fosse [. . .] keeps this period [. . .] at a cool distance. We see the decadence as garish and sleazy, and yet we see the animal energy in it, and the people are driven to endure. The movie does not explain decadence; rather, it gives it its due. The reminiscences of Brecht and Kurt Weill in [. . .] 'Wilkommen' and of *The Blue Angel* in [. . .] 'Mein Herr,' help us to get our bearings: reminiscence is part of the texture.[5]

Close analysis of the opening sequence of the film serves to highlight the wide-ranging intertextuality of these 'reminiscences', revealing the intricately detailed historicity of Fosse's 'cool distance':

> The whory chorus girls displaying the piquant flesh around their garters, the Max Beckman angles and the Edvard Munch hollows are part of the texture too. *Cabaret* does not merely suggest Egon Schiele's moribund erotic figures and the rictus smiles and rotting flesh in the paintings and graphics of artists such as James Ensor and George Grosz but captures the same macabre spirit – and *sustains* it. What makes the art of such men powerful is that they help us recognise the sensual strength of decadence. The grotesque immorality in *Cabaret* is frightening, not because it's weak, but because it's intensely, obscenely alive.[6]

The opening credits are played in silence – white against a black background, which blurs into a monochromatic but uneven silver/grey mirror that slowly begins to reflect movement as the faint sounds of a band swell to accompany the slow saturation of the screen with colour as Joel Grey/the Emcee pops up at an odd angle at the side of the frame to sing 'Wilkommen' as he stares knowingly into the camera. The famous vamp begins as Grey smiles unctuously at the camera, a gleefully teasing pierrot face suspended in a fauvist painting until he walks towards the right of the screen using a bamboo cane to point his way to a sudden explosion of red, in fact, a velvet curtain above and behind him. This is the first visual indication of the show-within-the-film, producing a devilish tinge to the proceedings, the Emcee's naughty relish contradicted by the blank monocled stare of a figure posed to resemble Otto Dix's 'Portrait of the Journalist Sylvia von Harden' (albeit with a different dress on), a reminder that we are witnessing the nightclub audience seen through the eyes of Dix and his contemporaries as enumerated above by Kael. As the Emcee walks back left, the spectator can recognize the mirror as an object behind him, acquiring a clearer view of the cabaret stage before the jump cut to the train, then to the interior of a compartment with the face of Michael York with two other faces around him before a return to the cabaret with the camera opening out to show Grey moving across the mirror to the right as the mirror rises upwards, to expose more of the theatrical machinery, until the image of the Emcee cross-cuts to another painterly quotation of a bored bourgeois couple and a waiter at a dinner table, followed by the profile of a thin bald man in the audience, behind whom a waiter surreptitiously brushes his own hair in preparation for his 'role play' as a waiter.

Fosse now switches from the self-consciously composed montage of quoted paintings to a shot of a large dark-haired man donning a large blonde woman's wig to complete his drag: this image locates us clearly in the backstage world of the Kit Kat Klub, introducing the trope of the human persona as a theatrically constructed self. The whole sequence presents an extremely concise montage, interrogating the various forms of representation the film is utilizing – the pseudo-documentary recording of material/historical reality (the railway station), and the manifold illusions of the cabaret performance/milieu as rendered by performers (Joel Grey as ghost-like Emcee), paintings and the camera as 'spy' (the casual observation of a man assuming the drag appearance of a woman who will later proposition members of the cabaret audience). As the Emcee cynically praises the cabaret world as 'beautiful' ('Even the orchestra is beautiful')[7] the all-female band is initially romanticized by a translucent curtain and shiny lights, which suffuse their silhouettes in a luminous blue, before changing to reveal their ageing, fleshy bodies being lasciviously goosed by the Emcee.

The subsequent mocking introduction of the louche cabaret girls – 'each and every one a virgin' – to the laughter of disbelief by the nightclub clientele, who make the assumption that they are close to being whores, reveals the cynical complicity of the onscreen audience in the Emcee's game of illusions. This charade is immediately followed by the introduction of the speciality performers, brilliantly shot through a choreographed flurry of arms and legs that obscure the faces and body parts of those being named. After the Emcee peers at the camera lewdly through the bowed legs of a chorus girl, Sally Bowles is shown from the shoulders down, her bright red long dress sandwiched between the backsides of two dancers bent over to stare through their legs at the camera. When he does name Sally, we see her bowing and smiling, followed by a juxtaposed image of the tall blonde drag queen bowing – a visual contrast of naïve optimism and jaded disillusionment. The sequence has formulated a significant question for the spectator: What is real and what is illusion? Already we have caught a glimpse of Sally's deluded notion of being a star.

'Divine decadence': Weimar and the rise of the Nazis

One of the aspects of the *Cabaret* film that is easy to mistake or misrepresent in criticism is the extent to which an audience is asked to view the spectacle of Weimar decadence as directly responsible for the rise of the Nazis and the triumph of the Third Reich. James Leve echoes the opinions of a number of commentators who equate the sexual libertarianism of the Weimar period with the moral decadence of the Third Reich. His discussion of camp as an expression of homosexual culture involves some oversimplification of its strategies and significance.[8] Quoting Al Lavalley's aphorism, 'camp is a gay version of "irony and critical distance,"'[9] he identifies Liza Minnelli's performance in Fosse's film of *Cabaret* as 'the heart and soul of camp performance' and describes the Emcee as 'camp personified'.[10]

In my view, such a reading leads Leve and others to a simplistic identification of the artifice of camp with the theatricalized representation of Nazi power in the quasi-expressionistic staging of rallies and processions: 'By conveying the mixed theatricality and hysteria of such orchestrated events, Isherwood draws attention to the role of artifice, fantasy and spectacle during the creeping totalitarian policies of the Nazis'.[11] Leve quotes Joseph Bristow's evaluation of Isherwood's *The Last of Mr Norris* as '"a camp comedic romp through contemporary Berlin starring a dandy-aesthete with [. . .] a penchant for S&M." The narrator takes in the "sexually perverse culture."'[12] To draw parallels between the use of spectacle in the real clubs that may have been models for the Kit Kat Klub and the aesthetics of Nazi self-presentation is to conflate camp with kitsch. The Nazi aesthetic possessed none of the self-awareness of camp; it was kitsch in its heightened use of artifice to romanticize the ideals of the Reich and to provide dark forebodings of terror to those who refused to succumb to its spell.

Notwithstanding the above distinction, there is a deep-rooted tradition of Puritanism in Western culture that conceives sensuality and pleasure as inherently debased and potentially vicious hedonism. The danger of such moralistic simplification is not so great in the stage version, but it is this tradition that Bob Fosse plays with in his 1972 film, testing the limits of his viewers' tolerance and sophistication as ethical observers.

One must question whether the film insists on this equation or merely puts it into play as a potential response to the spectacle of the cabaret:

> Expanding upon Prince's innovative technique, Fosse used the eye of the camera to engender cultural critique, slicing unexpectedly between the real and the imaginary and blurring the space between the two. The parallel editing, which has been called 'a sort of shock editing', provides a disturbing disjunction between the eerie unreality of cabaret culture and the grim reality of political life. [. . .] On a literal level, the film seems to draw a causal relationship between decadence and fascism, suggesting that Weimar culture allowed, through indifference, neglect, or complicity, the development of a politically oppressive regime.[13]

Ironically, 'many of the most important figures in the Weimar cultural scene, such as Jews, African Americans, homosexuals, and Communists, among others, were persecuted under the Nazi regime' so that the Puritan interpretation does not account for the progressive social reality and experimental cultures of Weimar Germany just before 1933. In fact, the level of tolerance and liberal thinking in Weimar Germany was truly advanced, and the very clubs that championed such libertarianism were most at threat from the Nazis, who attacked the LGBTQ culture that had thrived in Weimar Germany with the same ruthlessness they applied to the persecution of Jews, Communists and Romany people. Most of the clubs were apolitical, although there were a few that espoused left-wing satire of conservative politics. But after the purging of Rohm's SA in 1933, Hitler and his supporters were extremely homophobic and sought to cleanse the Reich of what they considered moral decadence. So the film challenges its viewers' unthinking association of hedonism, sexual/artistic decadence and barbarity while observing at the same time the ostrich-like nature of its onscreen escapists as an avoidance of social responsibility.

Although the art direction and editing at times create grotesquely stylized effects, this approach allows the film to utilize the camera as an omnipresent eye, observing and recording events as though they were actually happening in Berlin in 1931. The only two songs that are not presented as part of the cabaret performance are nevertheless diegetically presented – 'Married' is played on a gramophone and 'Tomorrow Belongs to Me' is sung by a blond member of the Hitler Youth as a spontaneous outburst of nationalistic fervour on a sunny afternoon.

The casting of Liza Minnelli as Sally Bowles ensured that the role would have an emotional intensity and complexity that would effectively compensate for the loss of Lotte Lenya's emotionally charged Fraulein Schneider. But this creates a new problem. Once Minnelli is playing her, Sally must become a good singer rather than the second-rate dilettante of Isherwood's stories. The transformation of Sally Bowles into a star role for Minnelli reinforces the moulding of the central narrative strands into a story of libertinism expressive of the values of the contemporary sexual liberation movement: Isherwood's thirties bohemian becomes an icon of seventies hedonism. No longer eccentric or immoral, she acts as a modern young woman asserting her right to free love. In sexual terms, the American Sally becomes normative, while the English Brian Roberts (the new name for Cliff Bradshaw) appears unworldly. Michael York's slightly fey British public school manner signifies sexual repression to an American viewer. Significantly, Sally is introduced as a character at the same time as Brian when she answers the door in lieu of Fraulein Schneider and shows him the room to let. In a fairly extended sequence, Sally's *faux-naif* style and her selfish but charming materialism are revealed, indicating her temperament before the viewer sees her in performance.

In its presentation of Sally (the only performer in the cabaret to be shown outside it), the film adheres to the conventional motif of the backstage musical, depicting the contrast between her role as a cabaret performer and the pleasure and pain of her personal life. Minnelli's interpretation of Sally enhances Fosse's treatment of the subject matter. She is beguiling – lusty, sybaritic, exhibitionistic, funny, physically healthy but emotionally needy. Her pathological ambition to be a film star distinguishes her from the Sally of the play and the stage musical and re-positions her in narrative terms. No longer entirely self-deluded, Minnelli's Sally is deluded about the *world*, her blind desire to succeed emblematizing a

Figure 5. Helmut Griem, Michael York and Liza Minnelli as Maximillien, Brian and Sally in a ménage a trois from the film *Cabaret*.

belief in what Fosse exposes in all his mature work as the lie that show business triumph brings personal happiness. Presented with Sally as an American in a film by Americans for Americans, the viewer is torn between identification with her fashionable seventies hedonism and Brian's old-fashioned 'Englishness'. The attractiveness of Sally's personality and her powerful aura as a performer seduce the viewer into sympathy with her attitudes, at least for part of the film, so that when she sings 'Cabaret' at its climax, the ironic tension between the spectator's desire for Minnelli/Sally to succeed as a star and the ruthless selfishness of the sentiments the song represents in context is overwhelming.

The replacement of 'Don't Tell Mama' with 'Mein Herr', crafted to show off Minnelli's singing and dancing skills, reveals Sally's stage persona as louche in the manner of Lola/Marlene Dietrich from *The Blue Angel*, rather than naively naughty as she is in van Druten's play. In the words of Pauline Kael, 'When there is nothing to believe in but survival and pleasure, gaiety has a ghastly, desperate edge, but the way people still seek pleasure is testimony to something both base and fascinating. Everything seems to become sexualised'.[14] Fosse's choreographing of the chorus girls' legs and the deployment of bentwood chairs as part of the dance illustrates Kael's point, its objectification of the women's bodies so lacking in sensuality they almost become props – a garish cartoon of the sex act with the life drained from it. The camera focusses briefly on a plump old man ogling Sally, juxtaposed with a shot of the large blonde transvestite in the audience ogling Brian. When Sally introduces Fritz to Brian as a potential pupil, the old man summons her over to his table, their interaction implying that she will supply him with sexual services later.

Sally seems oblivious to political events from which the club insulates her, continuing to flirt as Fosse presents a sequence of shots of debased women performers mudwrestling. Then a young Nazi with a swastika comes into view for the first time. As the women humiliate themselves for the pleasure of the Kit Kat Klub clientele, they are replaced by a kickline of cabaret girls dressed as German soldiers. The Nazi is thrown out of the club while the Emcee paints his top lip with mud to suggest a Hitler moustache as the spectator witnesses the club proprietor being brutally assaulted by Hitler Youth in retaliation for his expulsion of their associate. This is the first overt reference to the rise of the Nazis, which the Emcee seems merely to mock with amoral relish.

In Minnelli's portrayal, the psychodynamics of Sally's interior life are suggested in her self-aggrandising fantasies. She clearly romanticizes her father as 'practically an ambassador' in conversation with Brian and others, while she sentimentalises the idea of being discovered 'in a dump' by a famous producer from Ufa. In a scene with Brian in a café, Minnelli evokes Sally's underlying hysteria as she screams while a train passes overhead. In a style redolent of the later performances of her mother Judy Garland, Minnelli convincingly exploits this dramatic release of tension – almost mimicking a sexual climax – in contrast to Brian's repressed Englishness. Minnelli/Garland's manifestation of being 'on the edge' is often utilized in their performances to imbue the drama with a quality of psychic disturbance that verges on the pathological. In this context, the Sally of the film acquires an interior self that transcends the character in all previous versions, a quality imitated in several, but not all, later stage versions. Sally's pent-up hysteria becomes an emblem of the inchoate fear experienced by inhabitants of an increasingly dangerous Berlin in the following scene near a railway arch when Sally coaches Brian in screaming: just before she and Brian actually scream, Fosse jump cuts to a man being beaten and bloodied by Nazis, after which the

Emcee dressed in lederhosen takes up the motif of sadomasochistic violence, laughing as if the incident is merely entertainment. This is followed by the suggestive slapping actions of a traditional *Schuplattler* on stage with the chorus girls dressed as men. Violence is here presented as a spectator sport, its sadistic pleasures signalling the desensitizing of the Kit Kat Klub patrons. Although the art direction and editing at times create grotesquely stylized effects, Fosse's split approach contrasts the stylization of the Kit Kat Klub performances with the verismo representation of the 'real world' outside the club, which allows him to utilize the camera as an omnipresent eye, observing and recording events as though they were actually happening in Berlin in 1930.

The greater openness of the movie to the presentation of sex and sexuality is evidenced in the new narrative material involving Brian's relationship with Sally and later the ménage a trois of Sally, Brian and Maximilien. Sally recommends Brian to Herr Ludwig as a translator of his novel, which turns out to be hardcore porn entitled *Kleo the Whip Lady*. One day, while she is lying beside Brian on top of his bed, she kisses him and he freezes so she gets her gramophone and dances seductively to a jazz record (actually the deleted 'Pineapple Song' from the stage show). He watches her intently as she half-jokingly teases, 'Doesn't my body drive you wild with desire?' When he fails to react, she opines. 'Maybe you just don't sleep with girls?' to which Brian retorts, 'The word for my sex life now is nil' soon admitting that he has tried three times with girls but only his homosexual experiences have been pleasurable. When Sally manages to arouse him, she says, 'Maybe they were just the wrong three girls' and they laughingly proceed to have sex as Fosse intercuts her torch song 'Maybe This Time' at the Klub within a sequence of shots that charts the progress of their romance. During the montage, Fosse films Michael York as a sex object from the viewpoint of Sally's *female* gaze. As the bisexual Brian playfully assumes the traditional feminine role of 'being looked at' the character borrows Sally's line to flirt with her, 'Doesn't my body drive you wild with desire?' The sequence shows them both in a moment of genuine happiness, but in the overall context of the drama, it is only an illusion.

Soon Fosse cuts entirely to Sally onstage, and the line between joy/pleasure and show business success is blurred. 'Everybody loves a winner/So nobody loved me', presages Sally's increasingly desperate desire to be a star at the end of the film: 'Maybe this time/ I'll win'. Her belief in this illusion is directly undermined as she bows to a virtually empty auditorium of two depressed and bored faces, with a shot of the Emcee grinning devilishly. The intensity of the number is very different from the wry teasing of the non-diegetic 'Perfectly Marvellous' in which Sally in the stage version inveigles her way into Cliff's room (and bed).

The extension of Sally and Brian's affair to include the Baron (Maximilien), whom Sally meets in a laundry, makes the sexual *ménage a trois* the chief centre of narrative interest outside of the cabaret, while Brian's English pupil, Fritz, initiates a subplot with his apparently unrequited love for the heiress, Natalia Landauer who he informs Brian comes from a family of 'enormous rich Jews'. Fritz claims to be a gigolo ('I should make a pass after her') but later falls deeply in love with Natalia, who Sally tutors in the art of 'pouncing'. Eventually, Fritz reveals himself to be Jewish and marries Natalia.

There is a new piece of dialogue inserted into the Emcee's 'If They Could See Her Through My Eyes'; in confessing to a bizarre infatuation with a gorilla, he mockingly tests the prejudices of the 1972 audience as he sings and dances with her before making an exaggeratedly sentimental appeal for them to overcome moralistic attitudes:

Meine Damen und Herren, Mesdames et Monsieurs, Ladies and Gentlemen – is it a crime to fall in love? Can one ever tell where the heart truly leads us? All we are asking is *ein bischen verstendnis* [*sic*] – a little understanding – Why can't the world *leben und leben lassen* – live and let live?

In the film, Fosse reverts to the original last line, 'She wouldn't look Jewish at all' a shock effect no longer muted by euphemism.

In a scene in a car driving to Max's castle home, it becomes clear that Sally is being used by Max to 'buy' Brian's favours. Max repeatedly gives Brian a gold cigarette case, which he repeatedly returns. After the drunken trio dance together closely, Brian succumbs to Max's sexual flirtation. On one of the trips in Max's car, they stop for a drink at a beer garden where a blond boy wearing a swastika armband sings 'Tomorrow Belongs to Me', joined in incremental steps by all the revellers, who stand and sing with increasing aggression. Only a puzzled and sad old man does not join in. As Brian and Max leave with Sally asleep in the car, Brian asks, 'Do you still think you can control them?' The image cuts to the leering face of the Emcee announcing 'Money'.

The Emcee's 'Sitting Pretty' on stage is replaced by a new song, 'Money Money' which forms a darkly funny commentary on the temptations to which both Sally and Fritz have succumbed in bartering sex for financial rewards. Its cynical and sexually stimulating exultation of greed proves more sinister than the stage number, giving Sally another song that connects her to the increasingly Mephistophelean figure of the Emcee in which the deadly sins of lust and greed are linked in an orgy of hedonistic abandon. As Sally and the Emcee dance lasciviously offstage, the silhouette of an act involving girls whipping someone in a harem adds S & M to the catalogue of illicit pleasures being enjoyed by the audience. The deadpan faces of the ventriloquist and Emcee are shown watching Sally, who in turn sees them. Sally wears an expensive fur coat that Max had bought her during a scene in a high-class restaurant where her hysterical demand for the conspicuous consumption of huge quantities of caviar climaxes in her shrieks of laughter as she describes an incident she and Maximilien witnessed – 'you should have been there' – preceding a startling jump cut to the silent, frozen image of a dead man in the street. Fosse's technique of alternating between the cabaret and the socio-political reality presaging the Nazis' increasing power is by now overtly apparent.

The impact of both the film and stage show proceeds from their animation of a dialectical discourse between musical theatre and the life it portrays, between entertainment and history, between spectacle as escapism and the brutal reality of human degradation as spectacle – a self-reflexive questioning of the pleasures of specularity. Are viewers, while watching *Cabaret* as liberal spectators, endorsing the hedonism we applaud and laugh at as earnest of our political freedom and moral tolerance, or are we indulging it as mere escapism?

The lives of Sally Bowles: Judi Dench

Harold Prince's London transfer production with Judi Dench has fairly recently become available on CD, but video excerpts of Dench performing 'Don't Tell Mama' convey a fuller impression of her performance. Understanding the lyrics of Sally's final song in purely aural terms involves not only a response to melody, rhythm and harmonic development but also a reaction to the idiosyncratic tone and timbre of Dench's singing voice. When perceived in isolation from the visual and kinetic context of performance, small details of voice and musicality assume a great intensity in constituting the full effect of her portrayal. Dench's husky and cracked chest belt creates a mocking and sensuous growl that serves to detach the singing from both the pert-looking yet aloof Dench and from the content of lyrics whose gestic attitude Brecht and Weill would consider to be defined by being half-sung, half-shouted. The ironic placement of the 'Cabaret' song seven minutes before the end of a 150-minute narrative that has repeatedly and with accumulating force invoked the audience's retrospective knowledge of the reality of the Third Reich locates the thirty-year-old Dench's distinctive representation of Sally's reckless escapism within history's grim narrative, thereby implicating the English Sally as one who failed to assume moral responsibility for acting against the growing evil of Nazi crimes. In this context, her singing actually *sounds* sinister.

Comparison with Minnelli

Liza Minnelli's performance of the last moments of the song creates a very different experience of its meaning. It is noticeable how the grain of the voice (its timbre and tone), together with the jazzy rhythmic variations and the many more subtle jazz singer's transitions from singing to whispering and shouting, creates a very different sound texture and a more varied temporal dynamic. The performer's intense identification with the lyrics transforms their dramatic significance. Dench's apparent detachment from the sentiment of the song implies that its careless decadence has, for the character become something of a sham – a party-girl posture she adopts to rationalise both her lack of talent and the spiritual poverty of her existence. But Minnelli sings as if her life depends on it, her manic investment in its cheap showbiz philosophy exemplifying the classic syndrome of the performer who believes that becoming a star will heal the scars of a loveless childhood. During the few minutes leading up to the song in the film, the audience has witnessed Sally's reaction to what we gather to be her father's indifference towards her, her announcement that she has just aborted the child she was to have by her boyfriend, and Brian's decision to leave Berlin.

The intensity and power of her performance is exhilarating but unsettling. On the one hand, Sally is acting out the psychodrama of her conflicted personality. Initially hiding her private unhappiness under the performer's mask of exaggerated gaiety, the feeling of potency conferred by her talent as a singer gradually blurs the line between Sally as victim and exploiter as she is herself seduced by the show business clichés she is selling. On reflection, the performance we feel impelled to applaud appears as both an act of psychological repression or denial and as a celebration of the ruthless ambition of the collaborator who wilfully ignores the political corruption and brutality around her in order to promote her own career. The genuine pleasure given by the performance is paradoxically exposed as a lie, the garish make-up that earlier in the film had glamourized Sally's 'divine decadence' as exotic now being lit and photographed in such a way as to echo the lurid clown mask of the Emcee. Her final exit into backstage darkness becomes a sign of her retreat into his Mephistophelian world. Even though we are not watching a live performance, the song is filmed in a way that constructs a theatricalized aura for Minnelli as a stage star in order to coax the spectator into cheering an act which their comprehension of the accumulated significance of the film's faux-historical narrative demands that it rejects. In a historical context, to view the 1972 film is to reexperience the Germans' collective failure to confront the dangers of Nazi ambition.

While afficionados of the first stage productions of *Cabaret* believed that Liza Minnelli was too talented a singer to be convincing as the dilettantish Sally Bowles depicted in Isherwood's *The Berlin Stories*, memories of the film have remained so powerful that while some British film reviewers initially compared Minnelli's interpretation unfavourably with that of Judi Dench, commentators now regularly compare new portrayals of Sally Bowles unfavourably with the mythic memory of Minnelli. Ironically, the Broadway and West End productions had deliberately cast actresses with little or no professional singing experience – Jill Haworth and Judi Dench. In the event, Haworth's performance was regarded as rather bland. Walter Kerr of the *New York Times* maintained that Haworth was 'trim but neutral, a profile, rather than a person, and given the difficult things *Cabaret* is trying to do, she is a damaging presence, worth no more to the show than her weight in mascara.' In his opinion, Prince revealed 'a totally uncharacteristic lapse of judgment'.[15]

Although Dench's sophisticated acting and unconventional but bold belting earned accolades from London critics eighteen months later, the subsequent belief that her performance was universally admired for its authenticity is itself a myth. Writing in *Plays and Players* (May 1968), Frank Marcus expressed the dissenting view of an Isherwood devotee,

> It is almost beyond belief that artists of the calibre of Harold Prince (producer) and Joe Masteroff (author) should have seen fit to reduce the brother-and-sister relationship of Isherwood and Sally to that of a boring and commonplace *affaire*. . . It is all the more disappointing (and wasteful) because in Judi Dench they have an actress more than capable of playing the original Sally . . . She sings well . . . She isn't really the right build for the flapper period [. . .] and she lacks the frenetic gaiety. Towards the end she communicates disillusionment and pain most movingly. My own feeling is that she should be more, not less, frenetically gay at the end . . . . On the whole Judi Dench has too much warmth and intelligence for the Sally of *Cabaret*.[16]

Although Prince refused to consider Minnelli for the role on Broadway, Kander and Ebb always had her in mind while writing the score, and it seems logical that Bob Fosse chose an alternative approach to the character in shaping his innovative screen version. The film was so influential that stage revivals since 1986 began replacing 'Hush Up Don't Tell Mama' with the more forceful and German-sounding 'Mein Herr' from the movie, 'Sitting Pretty' with the ubiquitous 'Money Money' and adding 'Maybe This Time', a Kander and Ebb number recorded by Minnelli some while before the show was written. In doing so, the role acquired a new emotional intensity, and Minnelli/Sally was able to project the aura of 'divine decadence' that shaped the fascination with alternative sexualities in the glam rock era. The collective memory of the film has caused directors of major stage revivals to revise the original libretto to incorporate some or all of these new songs, to foreground the show's depiction of alternative sexualities by making Cliff bisexual or (more recently) gay and to include an homage to Fosse's choreography by increasing the burlesque sexualization of the dancing in various ways. By 1972, Fosse's signature choreographic style of ironized bump-and-grind was recognisable to audiences on stage and film[17] but the wit of his self-referential style is here deployed grotesquely to expose the dancers' flaws, while Minnelli's irrepressible *joie de vivre* stands out as hopelessly naïve within this compromised and tawdry milieu.

Other Sally's in other productions

All productions since 1972 have exploited the detached hyper-sexuality that characterized Fosse's style to devise stagings whose obsession with sex and sexuality reflects modern Western culture's voyeurism. In 1986, the original stage version of *Cabaret*, including Herr Schulz's 'Meeskite' – never used again – as well as 'Maybe This Time' from the film, was directed by Jerome Savary in Paris and Dusseldorf, starring the new sensation, Ute Lemper. At the end of the show, the provocative Emcee placed his top hat downstage to be crushed by the falling curtain, the first production to suggest that the cabaret performers themselves would become victims of the Nazis. In 1987, Prince revived his own production with Joel Grey on a tour culminating in a Broadway run; during this revival, Cliff at first became bisexual and eventually gay, while Sam Mendes directed a revisal of the show at the Donmar in London in 1993, with Alan Cumming as a decidedly queer Emcee and Jane Horrocks as a consciously role-playing Sally. With the permission of the authors, this rewritten version formed the basis of a highly sexualized production, choreographed and co-directed by Rob Marshall, which ran from 1998 to 2003 at Studio 54 in New York, initially starring Cumming and Natasha Richardson; the production was revived for a year in 2014.

The inventive staging of the show in 1998 by Sam Mendes and Rob Marshall as an environmental piece within a cabaret-type venue ran far longer than the original production, demonstrating the continuing appeal of a show that is now as inextricably connected to the film as to the original stage version. Cumming and Richardson were deemed by many critics to have banished the abiding images of Joel Grey and Minnelli in the roles, with Cumming bringing a louche yet cupid-like relish of pansexuality to the Emcee and Richardson interpreting Sally as a progressively drug-addicted failure whose rendition of 'Cabaret' became an unwitting enactment of her own nervous breakdown. The 2014 revival of Mendes' production provoked a large number of criticisms of Michelle Williams, which compared her unfavourably to Minnelli: for example, 'Her mannerisms have been practically copied from Liza's (and honestly who can blame her?)'[18]

In a much-admired performance, Natasha Richardson stepped out of the shadow of Minnelli by suggesting Sally was a privileged party girl whose life of pleasure had spiralled by the time of her final number to a state of alcoholic desperation masked by hysterical *joie de vivre* – as though she were struggling to convince herself during the number that her story would end happily. Roger Copeland described her performance of the song as 'a ritual of self-hypnosis' until at the end she knocked over the microphone stand and stumbled offstage. Mendes' revisal was the first to use immersive staging. He put tables onstage at the Donmar, with its small three-sided auditorium to create the feeling that the audience was in the Kit Kat Klub; this immersive effect was greatly enhanced at Studio 54. Spectators could buy drinks and small food platters, in this respect pre-dating the current London production by twenty-four years. Cumming erased memories of Joel Grey by presenting a much more human figure, hyper-sexualized, a kind of pornographic, androgynous cupid, flirting with the audience and even inviting men up on stage to dance with him. At the end of Act 1, he exposed his buttocks to reveal a swastika ironically tattooed on it; at the end of Act 2, he was dressed in a concentration camp uniform, wearing both a pink triangle and a yellow star. The mock Nazi supporter had become a victim of the Nazis.

Rufus Norris' brilliant historically distanced reinterpretation of the show as a phantasmagoria of images seen through the eye of a writer was first presented in the West End in 2006 with James Dreyfus as an aloof and manipulative Emcee, Anna Maxwell Martin as a drug-addicted Sally and Sheila Hancock as a worldly but ultimately tragic Fraulein Schneider. The locations outside the Kit Kat Klub were set as if they were in the wings adjacent to the stage, enhancing Cliff's experience of Berlin as an oneiric recreation of everything he saw in 1930 – as if it were all being recorded through a camera lens. A major trope was the body, with the chorus often dressed in revealing black leather costumes, the choreography by Javier de Frutos not titillating but cold and stylized, making use of S & M references to the body as a source of power, as well as contrasting Leni Riefensthal's fascist idealization of the strength of the nude Aryan body at the end of Act 1 with the abjection of the body, as naked inmates stand at the end of Act 2 outside a smoke-filled evocation of a gas chamber.

Both the leather Kit Kat Klub costumes and Javier de Frutos' postmodern choreographic approach alluded directly to S & M, going beyond Fosse's teasingly lewd choreography by literalizing the sexual references and introducing moments of full-frontal nudity. Although many critics invoked the spectre of the Fosse film: '[T]he revival proves no match for the famous film version in which Liza Minnelli incarnated Sally Bowles' (Nicholas de Jongh, *Evening Standard* 11 October, 2006), I believe Norris' interpretation progressed beyond both the film and Mendes' stage version by mixing the onstage and backstage worlds of the Kit Kat Klub to evoke, in an expressionistic mode, the hallucinatory character of a Berlin encountered by Cliff/Isherwood as an oneiric experience rather than material reality. Norris appeared to have taken Cliff's originally rather awkwardly motivated song 'Why Should I Wake up?' as a cue to represent the mindscape of Berlin in 1930. One location dissolved into another as Cliff seemed to drift onstage and backstage and away from the Kit Kat Klub to the Freudian stage of phantasy.

The Emcee was played by TV star James Dreyfus as a somewhat boorish would-be Nazi collaborator, and he was later succeeded in the role by the tall and improbably butch-looking queer comedian Julian Clary; the role was somewhat reinvented in 2012 by Will Young as a bored and nasty toy-boy with cupid lips, dressed in lederhosen. Anna Maxwell Martin echoed Natasha Richardson in representing Sally as a good-time girl who gradually succumbed to drug addiction. While a few critics actually complained that her singing lacked distinction (by comparison with Minnelli's, of course), she actually proved a far more proficient singer than Judi Dench:

I surrendered my heart to Liza Minnelli's Sally Bowles when I saw Bob Fosse's film version of *Cabaret* as a susceptible adolescent. She was funny and sexy and vulnerable as hell, and no one has ever . . . torn a torch song to tatters with more feeling . . . But Anna Maxwell Martin won my heart all over again in Rufus Norris's dangerously dark, disturbingly depraved and, yes, divinely decadent new stage production [. . .] and she couldn't be more different from La Minnelli. Blonde rather than dark, and with a face that suggests an Angela Brazil schoolgirl heroine gone to the bad [. . .] she is far closer to the character in Christopher Isherwood [. . .] What Maxwell Martin captures, heart-stoppingly, is the emotional neediness [. . .] and the sense of damage that lies at the very heart of the character . . . And the desperate hope with which she sings 'Maybe This Time' is almost unbearable, because we know that everything will come to grief for her yet again.[19]

After some decades of exposure to successive variations on themes from the original production, one begins to perceive the notion of authenticity as itself a myth, with memories of previous productions becoming layered as a palimpsest that each generation reacts to both in relation to its collective memory and to the values and styles of contemporary society and culture. Prince himself had initially responded most directly to the race riots of the 1960s, Fosse to the hedonistic individualism that expressed the ethos of the anti-Vietnam generation of the early 1970s, and Sam Mendes to the sexualized consumer culture of the postmodern epoch in which fascist iconography became fashionably kinky. Rufus Norris was commenting on a post-Abu Ghraib *Zeitgeist*[20] which has conceived the body as the only reality, the site of pleasure and pain on which authority is enacted through the privileging of the perfect/strong body and the exclusion of the weak/abject body. What was entertainment in Mendes' production became, in 2006 a depiction of the reality of power that characterizes the 2000s as completely as it defined the values of the Third Reich.

The latest West End production (opening November 2021) caused a sensation not only for its movie star casting of Eddie Redmayne and Jessica Buckley but also because of its much-vaunted 'immersive' staging. On the one hand, the production invited a voyeuristic audience to 'come to the cabaret' as pleasure-seeking participants and observe decadence live and up close in an atmospheric 'pre-show' in the theatre's luridly lit art-deco style foyers and bars. On the other hand, the promise of 'inclusivity' was compromised by a pricing policy, which had the effect of limiting access to the elite few. The challenge set by director Rebecca Frecknall was to engage the audience in new ways by transforming a 56-year-old classic into a fresh and pertinent experience rather than a form of titillation for jaded theatregoers. David Benedict precisely describes the major features of the design:

> [The Playhouse] is now a dimly lit Art Nouveau palace of faded grandeur, with the audience on two sides wrapped around and focusing in on a tiny, bare circular stage from which the dancers can tease and toy with audience members. [. . .] For once the overworked term 'immersive' is entirely justified and the mood feeds the interpretation.[21]

Patrick Marmion actually boasts about the way the conspicuous consumption of privileged members of the audience was built into the redesign of the auditorium:

> [Tom] Scutt's refurb goes right down into the woodwork, with seats in the stalls fitted with ledges for all important 'refreshments'. That also means more leg room. . . it's like travelling business class, danke schon![22]

Although the production proved hugely successful with both critics and the public, I found it both opportunistic and incoherent.[23] Just whose decadence were we witnessing? The public is directed through a maze of corridors backstage, where each was given a glass of schnapps before moving through the pre-show to drink in one of two bars where costumed musicians played while dancers in gossamer-thin costumes performed slightly grotesque and mildly sexualized postmodern dance moves. Once you entered the auditorium the pre-show continued with some members of the band playing while, in Marmion's words, 'dancers twerk on a balcony or grind hips on a marble bar'.[24] The problem is that for anyone *au fait* with avant-garde theatre techniques since the 1960s, it was all rather tame. No genuine eroticism, no shocks, no confrontations with members of the public, no nudity – and most importantly – no sense of history. The mismatch between the environment with which we are presented and the seedy atmosphere of a Berlin nightclub in 1929/30 does not help to make the audience genuinely complicit in what happens on stage. The more the performers confront spectators, the further the historical period of *Cabaret* recedes as the audience is caught up in a game being played in the present. Any sense of a Berlin audience, poor and desperate for escapist pleasures, dissolves in the very different spectacle of contemporary inequality. When, during the interval, members of the audience were prompted by performers to clap and sing along, the aim of the production to shock and involve was lost.

The aggressive tone of the performance suggested more than anything else that the director was anxious to distinguish her interpretation from preceding versions. Productions of *Cabaret* adopt either a distanced historical perspective, with the audience gradually seduced by the songs and action into identifying with the complicity of the more ambivalent characters, or they cast the audience in the role of spectators at the Kit Kat Klub. In an apparent effort to startle, the sneering tone of Frecknal's production is first apparent in Redmayne's Emcee – a bizarre figure who snarled his 'Wilkommen' at the audience. Rather than being progressively seduced by the cabaret, which in earlier productions was only gradually revealed as corrupt, the aggression towards the audience, in this case, signalled a directorial judgement on the two main characters at the outset, thereby ignoring the unsettling process whereby the audience is increasingly made to feel complicit in ignoring the rise of the Nazis by its unthinking acquiescence in the perverse debasement of common decency as the cabaret performance promotes blind escapism and moments of anti-Semitism.

Redmayne did not so much portray a human being as a shape-shifter of grotesque figures, at first a red-haired gnome in postmodern leather *culottes*, a crocheted vest, a green party hat and large black leather gloves. He looked totally androgynous, his body contorting into various poses as he sarcastically spat out songs and comments, contemptuous of the audience. During the performance, his costume changed from eccentric partygoer to a pierrot, to a kind of Mephistophelian black and gold devil with claws in Act 2, before ending up as a conformist in a modern beige suit. There was little to link one image to another. By fragmenting the identity of the Emcee, the character was totally dehumanized. Unlike Joel Grey, who presented an evil genius who guided the audience through the show, apparently knowing more than he let on, or Alan Cumming, who revelled in the decadence of which he became part until he ultimately became a victim of those at whom he was poking fun, Redmayne stood apart from the show. Rather than actually presiding over the mayhem, the Emcee commented on it but his emblematic significance as the 'soul' of Berlin was not effectively integrated with his role as a character, for example in 'Two Ladies' or 'If You Could See Her'.

In 'Don't Tell Mama', Jessie Buckley, dressed as a schoolgirl but wearing Doc Martens, screamed at the audience; the song, originally conceived to be 'naughty but nice', here carried overtones of anarchic disobedience. Buckley is an extremely talented singer and a skilled actress, yet the hesitancy of her fractured and tomboyish performance as Sally seemed to stem from decisions made by the director rather than the character's own ambivalence. Sarah Crompton's view was that,

> There's something already disappointed about Buckley's Sally when we first meet her [. . .] she conveys Sally's journey from brittle belief to disenchanted clinging-on. [. . .] Her final 'Cabaret' changes the song from a show-stopper to one that freezes the blood, powered with fury and unbearable self-knowledge, screaming at herself and at the world. At the close she drops into the depths of the stage, as if vanishing into her own moral void.[25]

In my view, this latest production was fraught with contradictions. Determined to be different from its British and Broadway predecessors, it appears confused. The sound was so loud the effect was that the actors were treating the audience to a rock concert. The impact of fascism was rather obviously signposted midway through Act 2 by the cast changing from an array of individualistic garments into identical men's suits, somewhat devoid of colour, but this 'fading to beige' was a contemporary reference to conformism with no relevance to historical reality. Given the exorbitant prices, the sense of being a real audience at the Kit Kat Klub was a pale echo of what Mendes had achieved at Studio 54. In contradiction to the teasing fun of its pre-show, most of this performance was confrontational. The much-vaunted immersiveness of the production did not help audiences engage with the musical or grasp its relevance to the danger of proto-fascist governments and political parties today. The production's huge commercial success was more a result of celebrity casting than a new approach to Kander and Ebb's classic.[26]

The impact of both the both film and stage show proceeded from their animation of a dialectical discourse between musical theatre and the life it portrays, between entertainment and history, between spectacle as escapism and the brutal reality of human degradation as spectacle – a self-reflexive questioning of the pleasures of specularity. In a good production, the question remains: Are audiences, while watching *Cabaret* as liberal spectators, endorsing the hedonism they applaud and laugh at as earnest of their political freedom and moral tolerance, or are they indulging in it as mere escapism? What responsibility does an individual have as a spectator – a witness? From what spectacles does one avert one's gaze? At what jokes does one desist from laughing?

Notes

1. David Spencer, *Aisle Say* review of the Roundabout Theatre production at the converted Club Expo on West 43rd Street, once the Henry Miller Theatre, but renamed The Kit Kat Klub for the duration of the production, www.aislesay.com/NY-CABARET.html, accessed 10 August 2023.
2. David Bowie, Marc Bolan and exemplars of the Glam Rock style were the most obvious icons of this new fascination with androgynity.

3. W.H. Auden to Christopher Isherwood, quoted in *The Guardian*, https://www.theguardian.com/books/2014/nov/07/the-rise-and-rise-of-sexology-wellcome, accessed 10 August 2023.

4. The theme is most fully elaborated in Fosse's film musical *All That Jazz*, which reveals the dead director (a surrogate Fosse) being wheeled out of the operating theatre to the strains of Ethel Merman belting, 'There's No business like Show Business'.

5. Pauline Kael, *Deeper into Movies*, London: Calder and Boyars, 1975, 410.

6. Kael, *Deeper into Movies*, 410.

7. All quotations from the film, *Cabaret*, W3-9ZNB-M7FE, ASIN B0002K10XY.

8. James Leve, *Kander and Ebb*, New Haven: Yale University Press, 2009, 44–9.

9. Leve, *Kander and Ebb*, 44.

10. Leve, *Kander and Ebb*, 44.

11. Leve, *Kander and Ebb*, 48.

12. Leve, *Kander and Ebb*, 47, quoting Joseph Bristow, '"I Am with You, Little Minority Sister": Isherwood's Queer Sixties', in Patricia Juliana Smith (ed.), *The Queer Sixties*, New York: Routledge, 1999, 147.

13. Terri J. Gordon, 'Film in the Second Degree: *Cabaret* and the Dark Side of Laughter', *Proceedings of the American Philosophical Society*, Vol. 152, No. 4 (2008): 448.

14. Kael, *Deeper into Movies*, 410.

15. *The New York Times*, 1966.

16. *Plays and Players*, May 1968, 14–17, 64.

17. *The Pyjama Game* (1957), *Damn Yankees* (1958), *How to Succeed in Business Without Really Trying* (1967), *Sweet Charity* (1969).

18. Jose, http://coulsdonfilmnathaniel.blogspot.com, accessed 10 March 2022.

19. Charles Spencer, *The Daily Telegraph*, 11 October 2006, https://www.londontheatre.co.uk/reviews/cabaret, accessed 12 March 2022.

20. Abu Ghraib prison was a site of torture by American solders and CIA officers who during the Iraq War in 2004 arbitrarily demonstrated their power by sexual humiliation and rape of prisoners.

21. David Benedict, https://variety.com/2021/legit/reviews/cabaret-review-eddie-redmayne-1235131905/#:, accessed 12 March 2022.

22. Patrick Marmion, *The Daily Mail*, 13 December 2021, https://www.dailymail.co.uk/tvshowbiz/article-10302945/At-Eddies-Cabaret-sets-wunderbar-PATRICK-MARMION-reviews-Cabaret.html. Accessed 12 March 2022.

23. The production transferred to Broadway in the spring of 2024.

24. Marmion, *The Daily Mail*.

25. *Whatsonstage*, 13 December 2021, https://www.whatsonstage.com/news/?categories=reviews, accessed 11 August 2022.

26. The production was not nearly as well received in New York as in London.

4 Self-reflexive storytelling

The Happy Time (1968) and *Zorba* (1968)

Both *The Happy Time* and *Zorba* experiment with modes of self-reflexive storytelling that test or challenge the limits of the linear narrative or 'book' musical, which had by 1964 begun to seem dated. David Merrick had initially acquired the rights to musicalise Samuel Taylor's *The Happy Time* (1950), about a French Canadian family, which had run on Broadway for 614 performances. The play had been based on a popular novel by Robert Fontaine, inspired by his experiences of growing up in Ottawa, Canada. At first, Nash had declined Merrick's offer to write the book for the show, but while they were in London for the opening of *110 in the Shade*, produced by Merrick with a book by Nash, the producer approached the writer once more. Nash objected to the sentimentality of the material:

> However, he did suggest an idea for a musical based upon an original story of his own, which he thought held more promise. It concerned a small-town Midwestern photographer who returned home every four or five years only to ruin his family's serenity. Eventually his father compels him to face the truth concerning the glamorous life he supposedly has led: that he is a liar and a failure who, because he has never found himself, has hung at the brink of dishonesty most of his life.[1]

Nash 'made him a photographer because I wanted to find an artist who could go either way, towards art or commercialism'.[2] (In the original script, Jacques was actually a photographer of shoes.) Eventually, Merrick managed to persuade the writer to include the French Canadian location of St Pierre and the family from the novel. Many of the characters were simply taken over from the sources, but Nash transformed the travelling salesman, Uncle Desmonde, into the central character of the musical: Jacques Bonnard is a photographer who is the charming but wayward uncle of Bibi, the teenage hero of the original *Bildungsroman*. By importing the themes of honesty, deception and self-deception from his own story, Nash shifted the primary focus from the teenager to the uncle, adopting a less sentimental attitude towards the narrative material while still satisfying Merrick's interest in representing the French Canadian milieu.

When the original songwriting team, Cy Coleman and Dorothy Fields, withdrew, Merrick offered the job to Kander and Ebb, both of whom were sympathetic not only to Nash's conception but initially also to the idea of using the new IMAX system of back projection, which Gower Champion had discovered at the Montreal World Fair. It is ironic that Merrick engaged Champion as director and choreographer of this particular show. Champion had achieved universal acclaim for staging *Hello, Dolly!* so his reputation rested on having helmed one of the two most commercially successful of the 'golden age' musicals of the

1960s. To compound the irony, Champion's arresting montages of photographs and film were conceived as a meta-theatrical amplification and interrogation of the narrative, yet the expensive and complicated deployment of new IMAX technology may well have been a major reason why *The Happy Time* lost money on Broadway.

Champion envisaged the musical as a memory play. The various montages of photographs projected on huge screens were a way of theatricalizing the moments of memory captured in snapshots, in order to question the reliability or veracity of Jacques' memories. Complementing the innovative high-tech visual montages, Champion devised various elaborate dance numbers in order to provide the spectacle that Nash's book conspicuously appeared to lack. The thematization of the notion of memory offered by Champion's filmic device certainly enhanced the dramaturgical complexity of the musical, but the size of the screens dwarfed the actors and rendered conventional scene changes difficult. Instead of the usual set pieces being flown in vertically or trucked horizontally, designer Peter Wexler left the stage bare, constructing a three-tiered revolve mechanism that unobtrusively delivered props and furniture to the stage without any interruption of the action, achieving a cinematic quality, as befits the stream of images in memory.

With an enormous cast of forty-five, the small-scale narrative musical inevitably became a lavishly staged spectacle: clearly, Champion was aiming to live up to his reputation by using innovative techniques to represent the family conflict as a more archetypal tale of small-town values versus a cosmopolitan career of success and pleasure. The production was perfectly suited to the vast size of the Ahmanson Theatre, in Los Angeles but the Broadway theatre was one of the few New York playhouses with a stage large enough to accommodate the back projections. So, what had originally been written as an intense drama of family reunion and personal self-discovery was, during rehearsals transformed into a large-scale Broadway show by cutting much of Nash's book and four of the songs to make room for some delightful ensemble dance numbers, which, however, did very little to develop the plot or deepen the characters.

John Kander explained:

During our collaboration [. . .] the concept of the show changed in a way that disappointed us when we were in Los Angeles [. . .] Gower Champion lost confidence in what the story was about, and Dick Nash had written a beautiful script. But we changed the show out of town in ways that we didn't like.[3]

According to Ebb, *The Happy Time* was 'a tough little libretto, and rightly so, reminiscent of *The Rainmaker*[4] in that the story essentially involved fraud, but with much warmth and humour.'[5]

Champion's initial interpretation of Nash's piece was at fault: it was the fact that, in 1967, the technology was not sufficiently advanced to permit the projection of smaller images in a more intimate space that did not require a long distance between the rear of the stage and the screen. His need for critical approval was certainly a factor in amplifying the show to fairly epic proportions, allowing Champion the opportunity to exhibit his legendary expertise in staging musical numbers. Bibi's song 'Without Me', for instance, was a choreographic tour-de-force, illustrating the boy's delight at becoming his uncle's photographic assistant by showing a photomontage of Bibi's bad pictures that gradually filled the entire screen, fading as he began singing to leave 'only their outline as a Mondrian-like backing for the number' in the school gym (191), as

> [. . .] each member of the boys' chorus went to an assigned place [. . .] and proceeded to work out on a particular piece of equipment in time with the music. After sliding down boards, climbing up ropes and swinging out over the audience from the bars of the jungle gym, the boys joined [. . . Bibi] in a series of semaphore like movements. For the climax, [. . . Bibi] perched himself on the uppermost rung of the jungle gym to take final shots of the boys that flashed on the screen as they tumbled out of a pyramidal formation and went sprawling in several directions at once until they collapsed, totally spent, upon the floor.[6]

It is easy to understand why this number became the highlight of Act 1, but it must also be supposed that an audience would then have expected further production numbers in Act 2 to equal or outdo the impact of such a show-stopper. Champion devised two numbers intended to rival the gym routine, also conceiving Jacques' song 'Being Alive',[7] as a spectacular multimedia finale, designed to conclude the narrative with a prospective view of Bibi's progress to adulthood. The school gym was utilized again as the setting for an inventive production number 'The Life of the Party', which changed the tone and pace of the musical early in Act 2 from the contemplative interiority of 'Among My Yesterdays' to the kind of brassy show business exuberance so often associated with Kander and Ebb.

Grandpere decides to give himself a 'surprise' birthday party. With the utmost economy of means, Champion seated two schoolboys at a lavender piano, which circled slowly around a tall ladder in the centre. When David Wayne (Grandpere) ascended the ladder as he began to sing, the stage gradually filled with boys who climbed poles and rope ladders to hang party decorations all around the gym while they sang one of Kander's typical vamps ('Boom, boom, boom, boom'), until at the climax Grandpere slowly descended the ladder wearing a red coat and red paper top hat. This simple yet breathtaking routine was inserted just before the Broadway opening as a replacement for the less effective 'I'm Getting Younger Every Year'. The 'Chase Ballet' later in Act 2 enacted Bibi's attempt to retrieve the naughty pictures that he had stolen from Grandpere and pasted up around the school to impress his classmates. The ballet incorporated several musical motifs from Kander's score, but the dance music arranger Marvin Laird also added some new musical material to accompany the sequence. The ballet involved a series of 'catching, running, chasing [movements] and finally tossing a great spray of pictures into the air'[8] Although the number added more thrilling kinetic energy, there was no dramaturgical necessity to illustrate the incident in such detail.

In composition and orchestration (by Don Walker), the score did not attempt a slavish imitation of the musical styles prevalent in French-speaking Canada in the late 1920s, the period when the story is set. Rather, its retro approach impressionistically conjured up the 'old-world' atmosphere of a very small French town[9] at that time. If the score contains any genuine pastiche, it is noticeable in the French music hall style of 'Catch My Garter' and 'The Life of the Party', as well as the anthem 'St Pierre', sung by children at Bibi's school. 'Jeanne Marie', cut before the Los Angeles premiére, was reminiscent of old French folk songs. Other musical numbers reference ballads or ragtime tunes (e.g. 'A Certain Girl') of the kind that might have been played and sung at home until it became normal for most households to possess a radio receiver in the 1930s.

Figure 6. Mike Rupert as Bibi, Robert Goulet as Jacques and David Wayne as Grandpere in *The Happy Time*. Photo: Friedman-Abeles, NYPL, Billy Rose Division.

Several of the songs articulate the motif of the subjective quality of individual perception and memory. At the beginning of the show, the title number initiates a discourse on the reliability of memory. Jacques introduces 'The Happy Time' to the audience by means of a prologue: the direct address contains a warning regarding how memory can distort the past:

> You know, it's a very strange thing, but the memory plays tricks. Perhaps home is only a memory. Ah, but what a pleasant place! What a happy time! Come back with me, would you mind – and remember![10]

With the repeated exhortation in the song to 'remember' Jacques summons commonplace images – 'pale, pink sky', 'a Christmas morning long ago', 'frosted glass', 'dancing snow', 'the chocolate kiss', 'the painted horse, the carousel', 'your first Easter hat' – thereby provoking a stream of associations typical of an idealized domestic existence. Yet Jacques subverts the direct correlation of images in memory with real events by singing:

> I'm longing to see you smile
> And hear you laugh
> So I can have the photograph,
> And remember you remembering
> The happy time.

A photograph is not a complete and objective record of a moment of reality: it may later becomes a cue to the activity of memory, but the image has been deliberately composed and will also require interpretation by the viewer. Repeated a few times in the song, the words 'remember you remembering', emphasize the phenomenon by which a person compounds memories by recalling themselves or others in the process of reconstituting a memory. In Jacques' depiction of memory, the 'truth' of the original event or object is relative because a new 'happy time' is generated in each act of remembering by the operation of nostalgia, which continuously reshapes the past according to the demands of the present. He thereby maintains a selectively positive point of view that gradually becomes undermined by the conflicts occurring during the remaining action.

Another dimension of the theme of differing memories is the opposition of two attitudes to life, initially signified by the next song for the family, 'He's Back'. This articulates the anxiety of Jacques' father (Grandpere) and other relatives about the trouble his visits always cause ('If memory serves, / He'll shatter the nerves'). The threat posed to the bourgeois respectability of the family by Jacques' libertarian attitudes is demonstrated when he persuades his willing father and his curious nephew Bibi to attend a French music hall performance by the Six Angels, a group of female dancers ('Catch My Garter'). Both Jacques and Grandpere stand against the small-town repressiveness of Jacques' brother Philippe, as is shown by 'Tomorrow Morning' a high-stepping march, during which the two reprobates are joined by Bibi and the Six Angels in celebrating the pleasures of wine, women and song.

When they return late that night, Bibi tries to persuade his uncle to 'Please Stay', in a number that wittily expresses Bibi's fantasies concerning Jacques' travels. In the language of a tourist brochure, the boy imagines how wonderful the great cities of the world are while at the same time ironically pleading with Jacques to remain in provincial St Pierre. A concisely phrased representation of the tension between the love and security represented by 'home' and the need for the adventure of 'abroad', the song reveals not only how Bibi idolizes his uncle but also, in coming to comprehend the conflict Jacques has struggled with during the past two decades, recognizes his own ambivalent attitude to the comparative merits of small-town and cosmopolitan lifestyles:

BIBI.
> I mean with Paris, Rome, Lisbon and Venice, why would anyone want to stay in St Pierre?
> [...........................]

> > And Venice takes your breath away,
> > They say.
> > Stay!

> > It's dumb to be in St Pierre
> > When you can be in Rome;
> > Please stay home!
> > [. . .]

> > I know you'll never do it,
> > But I'm asking anyway,
> > Please, please stay!

> Isn't it funny, Uncle Jacques? I mean terrible, Uncle Jacques,

> > The saddest story
> > That you ever knew.

                    I haven't said I love you
                    In all these many years,
               But, Uncle Jacques –

JACQUES.
          Yes.
BIBI. I love you.

The motif of memory is amplified when, in 'I Don't Remember You', Jacques compares a
photographic image of the young Laurie Mannon with the respectable schoolmistress she
has now become:

    That was another girl.
    You're not all like her,
    Though for an instant
    When I saw you,
    I believed you were.

Jacques asserts the power of memory to remake the past as he rejects the image of his
first sweetheart:

    But I was wrong,
    This moment is new,
    Because I can't, I won't,
    I don't remember you.

Interwoven with the last part of the song is the French town anthem 'St Pierre'. As he arrives
at the school to visit the sweetheart of his youth, Jacques' singing is gradually overtaken
until he finally joins in the rendition by the school glee club under Laurie's direction – for a
moment apparently in harmony with the local community.
    At the beginning of Act 2, as he develops and prints old photographs in his former studio,
Jacques is prompted to sing the fullest and most sceptical exploration of the gulf between
past and present in the score, 'Among My Yesterdays':

    Was it really
    All that sweet,
    In that house
    And along that street?

    Memory clouds
    In a thousand ways,
    Walking among
    My yesterdays.

    Did it happen?
    Was it real?
    Eyes can see
    What the heart can feel.

When the photographs are flashed upon the screen, the audience is invited to question their value as records while Jacques ruminates on how memory has transformed the meaning of the images:

> One more trick
> That the camera plays,
> Walking among
> My yesterdays.

'Seeing Things' represents the final revelation of a truth concerning Jacques' character and status that has been masked by his inner conflict and self-deception. When Jacques sings the refrain of the song, he uses a metaphor of visual perception to express the opposition between his and Laurie's individual perspectives:

> You and I
> Have a way of
> Seeing things,
> A different way of
> Seeing things,
> I'd say.
>
> Paint your truth
> With my illusion;
> Please consider
> Seeing things
> My way.

In response to Jacques' invitation to enter into a permanent relationship, Laurie repeats the metaphor of different visual perspectives, but this time the words become a method of rejecting his proposal:

> I'm of the earth
> And you're of the sky.
> I love you very much,
> I love you very much,
> Goodbye.
> [.......................]
>
> I need more than love,
> I need someone I'm certain of;
> And when I reach for him,
> He must be there.

Laurie has realized that Jacques will never completely adapt to life in a small town, so as much as she loves him, their attitudes are incompatible. The duet makes ingenious use of simple lyrics sung to music that is operatic in its melodic intensity, in order to honestly articulate the complexity of a declaration of love that becomes, at the same time, a recognition of the impossibility of a union.

The use of a large Los Angeles theatre with up-to-the-minute technical facilities for a pre-Broadway tryout did not help preserve the integrity of the book. A major example of how Champion was affected by opening at the Ahmanson in Los Angeles in November 1967 was his vulnerability to the pressure of what Fred Ebb later recognized as 'real Hollywood advice'[11]. Champion's friends persuaded him not to allow Jacques' illusions concerning his successful career to be exposed as a sham because they felt Robert Goulet was too good-looking a man to play the role of a failure. So the harsher implications of Nash's representation of sham and self-deception were softened to make Jacques more likeable. When the expensive and visually beautiful 'Being Alive' montage arrived during the Los Angeles run, the seven-minute sequence proved to not only be technically over-complicated but also to completely undermine the impact of Goulet's performance. Reluctantly, Champion was forced to cut Jacques' depiction of Bibi's growth to maturity that ended with a triumphant shot of the young man in midair. In its stead, an epilogue was added for the Broadway production in which Jacques speaks of finally achieving success as a photographer and being happily married to Laurie – in direct contradiction of the resolution of the earlier 'Seeing Things'. The 'Finale' comprised a reprise of 'St Pierre' sung at the high school graduation by the full company, followed by Jacques' words:

> Yes, I never will forget St Pierre. And you know, I never did take the perfect picture. But then, perfect pictures, they're never in the camera but in the memory. So let us remember them . . .
> (*Sings*)
> > The reason I tell you this is that
> > I'm longing to see you smile
> > And hear you laugh
> > So I can have the photograph.

At this point, Jacques was joined by the company in a reprise of 'The Happy Time' that concludes the show.

Despite universally poor reviews in Los Angeles, audiences warmed to the show: the sold-out run at the Ahmanson convinced Champion to go ahead with a Broadway run. When Nash confronted the director a few days after the opening, Champion reminded him of the reviewers' universally negative criticism of the book, using this to justify the alterations he was continuing to make. This was the last straw for Nash, who had been obliged during rehearsals to accept wholesale deletions and changes to his book that destroyed its dramaturgical logic. Ironically, most of the reviewers in Los Angeles had praised the musical staging and the system of projections while dismissing what was left of the book as slight and sentimental.

On Broadway, the musical received mixed reviews, many of which once more praised the performances and the production while commenting negatively on the book. A number of critics, however, blamed Champion for submerging what they believed was a weak book under an overblown production. Fred Ebb has said that the production was like seeing *The Glass Menagerie* at Radio City Music Hall. In 1969, William Goldman summed up the consensus view:

> What Champion tried to do was to recreate the *Dolly* experience. The projections – the razzmatazz part of the show – stayed, because that was the part [. . .] that was

working. The part that wasn't working – the part involving characters – Champion tried to brighten up.[12]

This resulted in a 'soft, gooey, marshmallow-cored' show. Interviewed in 1992, Fred Ebb explained:

> [Champion's] concern was that he maintain his reputation and his status in the theatre, which were enormously high [. . .] Gower wanted [. . .] approval, and had every right to want it. He had gotten it fairly consistently and was now this highly successful and very rich fellow [. . .] And he did the very best he could on every show in the way that he was able to do it – as a showman.[13]

The Happy Time achieved a run of 286 performances and 23 previews. Despite earning a Tony Award for Robert Goulet and two Tonys for Champion for Best Direction and Best Choreography, the production lost an estimated $375,000.[14] In time, Kander, Ebb and Nash came to believe the book and score had been poorly served by Champion's lavish production. For a revival of the show at the Goodspeed Opera House in 1980, the team restored much of the original book intended for its 'tryout' at the Ahmanson as well as four songs added in rehearsal and subsequently cut. Kander and Ebb helped out with a production at the University of Niagara in 2002 and helped to reconstruct what they regarded as a definitive version of the musical. A new song 'Running' was added to replace the deleted 'Being Alive' montage by way of explaining Jacques' eventual self-realization as well as motivating his decision to leave St Pierre for the last time.

In 'Being Alive', Jacques had attempted to convince Bibi of the need to be open to the new opportunities offered by the wide world beyond St Pierre:

> I'm not wise, Bibi
> Everyone tells me so
> But I have eyes and ears
> And I know
>
> Being alive
> While you're alive
> That's what matters.
>
> Open your eyes, Bibi
> Open your mind, Bibi
> Keep it alive as long as you live.[15]

In the new song, Jacques has achieved a greater degree of self-knowledge, forcing Bibi to see him without illusions, acknowledging that he was wrong to escape St Pierre at the age of sixteen and urging his nephew not to make the same mistake.

> So you think you've found the answer
> Running,
> Some wonderful solution
> Running,
> You're prepared to travel light
>
> And to vanish in the night
> And the life will be all right?

Wrong!

[. . .]

Look at me,
I've been running all my life,
Looking for a chance to stop,
All runners do.

Look at me,
Bibi now I'm running scared,
Maybe time is running out?
That's true,
But just for me.
Not for you.[16]

After this version of *The Happy Time* was given a reading in New York in 2007, it became the basis for a new professional production, which opened in April 2008 on the 120-seater Ark stage at the Signature Theatre in Arlington, Virginia. This staging illustrated how effective *The Happy Time* could be when performed as a chamber musical. The *Theatre Mania* reviewer hailed the revival in the following way:

> Forty years after failing on Broadway, this rarely staged show [. . .] may finally be able to claim its rightful place in the duo's rich legacy. [. . .] the show generates quietly powerful sentiment with the fleeting moment it captures. Director Michael Unger, aided by composer John Kander has stripped away the Broadway trappings to reveal a quaint but emotionally intense chamber musical.[17]

Michael Unger's production utilized small-scale projections of photographs, which unobtrusively highlighted the musical's interrogation of memory, enabling a fresh approach to the confrontation between Jacques' unreliable memories of the past and the reality of facing his family in the present moment. In this revival, the mechanics of the projection system did not threaten to obscure the precise focus on the intricate web of family relationships. A review for *BroadwayWorld* emphasized the revelatory quality of Signature's production:

> [. . .] one of the most dazzling jewels of the season [. . .] definitely a fresh look at an overlooked jewel of a show. [. . .] *The Happy Time* will certainly cause (and rightly so) historians to re-evaluate what is certainly a deeply heartfelt and charming show.[18]

In this revival, the affect of the score in expressing the emotional lives of the characters and evoking the way recollections of the past question its reality was palpable. Whether or not the success of this revival will encourage other small-scale revivals of the work is a moot point. Nevertheless, the production remains as testimony to the expert work of Nash, Kander and Ebb in locating a subtle drama of relationships within an epistemological frame that problematises the role of memory in fashioning the past.

During their stay in Los Angeles for the pre-production period of *The Happy Time*, Kander and Ebb were persuaded by Harold Prince via the telephone to make a musical from Nikos Kazantzakis' renowned novel *Zorba the Greek* (1946). Although Fred Ebb claimed the book was 'a tome',[19] the duo was charmed by Prince's description of the way in which he conceived the theatrical form of *Zorba* as a stage musical. Despite the dark and often disturbing elements of the novel, Prince's vision of the piece as a story told by a chorus, commenting on the action in song as in an ancient Greek tragedy, provided the impetus for Joseph Stein, the book-writer of *Fiddler on the Roof,* to shape the narrative of a vast novel into an intelligible plot for a musical in which the sung chorus sections have multiple functions. The reviewer Jesse Green believed that 'in its darkness, high concept, and superb Kander and Ebb score [*Zorba*] represented a high-water mark of late–Golden Age musical storytelling'.[20]

Too grim in its depiction of suffering and despair for the average member of a Broadway audience, *Zorba* was nevertheless highly adventurous in its deployment of musical and dramaturgical techniques. Letters praising the musical over a period of thirty-five years reinforced Prince's own view that Zorba was 'something of a masterwork'.[21] The journey of Nikos to his ancestral Crete to reopen an abandoned coal mine he has inherited leads to a friendship with the peasant Zorba, whom he met en route in Piraeus. Zorba advises Nikos on mining but, more importantly, their conversations throughout the musical initiate an ongoing philosophical argument about the best way to live. Steering clear of the film *Zorba the Greek* (1964), partly because Prince did not have the rights to adapt it, Stein, Kander and Ebb's sources were the novel and some letters to Kazantzakis written by the person on whom Zorba was actually based. Paradoxically, the musical's attempted fidelity to the world of 1920s Crete, together with the particular circumstances of the central characters, only made the show more alien to a Broadway audience, who could not relate the fiction to cultural memory, as, for example, a large part of such an audience could do with *Fiddler on the Roof* or *Cabaret*. Nonetheless, the skill and ingenuity of Harold Prince's mise-en-scène combined with the startlingly effective score to create a milieu in which the incidents of the narrative seemed credible while generating an emotional effect at once both shocking and deeply moving in performance.

Musically and structurally, *Zorba* explores new ways of telling a complex story in musical theatre terms. Martin Gottfried, noting the impact of the director's staging idea, was prompted to use the term 'concept musical' to categorize Harold Prince's approach to staging the narrative. In keeping with the idea of the show as a tale told by a chorus of storytellers, it was Prince's theatrical conceit to begin *Zorba* with a stage on which there was nothing but a semicircle of musicians and a chorus seated in two rows, which he called a 'bouzouki circle'. There were thirty-eight performers on stage, half of whom accompanied the singing and dancing of the chorus. In this present-day prologue to the action, figures on stage argue about whether they should sing or tell a story. Having settled on the 'Zorba story', the discussion becomes a debate on how stories express 'what life is' before several people begin to sing variations on 'Life is . . . ' only to be interrupted by the leader of the chorus:

> Wait!
> [. . . . .]
> Wait! I will tell you. Listen . . . (*She moves to the center of the stage They all sit watching her as she sings.*)
> Life is what you do while you're waiting to die.
> Life is how the time goes by . . . (6)

This Beckettian trope is quite possibly the bleakest lyric ever sung in the opening song of a musical – so much so that when *Zorba* was revived in 1983, it was changed to 'Life is what you do till the moment you die'. The lyric certainly indicates the harshness of the environment in which the characters exist, but the staging draws attention to the means of recounting the story, analogous to the many autobiographical tales told by Zorba in the novel. By distancing the audience from mundane reality, Prince sought to create a Brechtian effect that would render the unfamiliar quality of the social environment comprehensible to audiences that might find the events of the narrative entirely alien to their own experience of the world.

In order to enhance this Brechtian effect, Boris Aronson's set utilized the shape of an ancient Greek amphitheatre, but instead of spectators seated on the levels where the Athenian audience would have sat, he placed fragments of scenery, gradually adding new pieces to them to suggest the component parts of a typical Cretan village. According to Prince, these included,

> an olive tree, the entrance to a church, a restaurant, a store, a balcony – and by the third scene in the play we'd constructed a realistic village in Crete, made of molded Styrofoam, and climbing the side of the hill. By then the company was realistically costumed.[22]

In 1974, Prince reflected that the production became too realistic after Scene 3, but in 2017 he reconsidered this view, opining, 'I disagree with my appraisal of our "realistic" production. It wasn't. Boris's set, far from being realistic, delivered an entire Greek village on a mountainside. Amazing!'[23]

The presence of several members of the chorus watching the action unfold from the periphery of the stage elaborated a staging idea first explored in *Cabaret*. By placing observers on stage, Prince undermined any tendency the audience might have had to construe the events being represented according to naturalistic conventions, again utilizing epic theatre techniques to *show* the process of enacting a story rather than creating the pretence that the audience is actually watching the order of events occurring in time. Neither Stein's book nor Ebb's lyrics attempted to shy away from the brutality of the life depicted in the novel:

> Having if you're lucky.
> Wanting if you're not
> Looking for the ruby
> Underneath the rot;
> [………………..]
> Life is where you stand just before you are flat.
> Life is only that, mister,
> Life is simply that, mister,
> That and nothing more than that! (6)

The art of these lyrics resides in the combination of their colloquial simplicity with subtle rhetorical effects. The many repetitions of 'Life is' suggest the unschooled philosophy that has been distilled into a kind of folk wisdom, while the repetition with slight variations of 'only that, mister', 'simply that, mister' together with the repetition of 'that' in the last line creates a powerful emphasis without drawing attention to its technique. The nihilism of the lyrics could be devastating, but the blending of these words with the sound of zestful dance music produces a more complex effect – as though the body takes pleasure in living even when the mind comprehends the narrow limits of the human condition. The impact is preserved in the sequence presented at the 1969 Tony Awards, in which the overwhelming effect of the number with its full-throated singing and vigorous dance steps is exhilaration. The performers wear smart modern clothes as if dressed for a concert, and soloists step up to one of the three microphones to sing.

Having established a storytelling convention in the opening scene, the following scene exploits the idea of performers acting out the narrative by revealing the chorus members arranging tables and chairs and putting on bits of makeshift costumes to become customers at a seafront cafe in Piraeus forty years previously. At this point, some members of the cast use their musical instruments to evoke wind and sea sounds. When Zorba enters and swiftly attaches himself to Nikos, who is seated alone at a table, the 'Zorba story' promised in the first scene begins. Zorba's forceful and eccentric way of presenting himself involves a type of performance by which he insinuates himself into the company of the reserved Nikos:

ZORBA Travelling? Where to?

NIKOS I'm going to Crete. Why do you ask?

ZORBA Taking me with you?

NIKOS (*Intrigued*) I don't understand. Do you know me?

ZORBA Not yet. But I would like to – why not? I have nothing
    against you.

NIKOS And you approach a complete stranger and say 'Take me
    with you.' I don't understand.

ZORBA (*Exasperated*) I don't understand! I don't understand! We
are strangers because we don't know each other. If I go with
you, we will know each other and we will stop being strangers.
(9)

After probing Nikos in the manner of an interviewer in order to elicit information about his life, Zorba expresses his philosophy in a song, a self-reflection performed publicly, without regard to Nikos' apparent indifference to hearing it:

You think too much. I believe in grabbing at life. Every minute is a
new minute. Every second is a new second. It never happened
before.

> I hear a bouzouki;
> You can't imagine how often I've heard a bouzouki.
> But each time is the first time! (13)

Zorba's awareness of his own social behaviour as a performance is indicated later in the song when he says to Nikos, 'Like for instance, I came up and talked to you. Look how interesting I am.' Again the storytelling trope is alluded to when he asks 'Do you want to hear a story?' (14)

Before Nikos has a chance to resist, Zorba launches into a new section of the song, in which he tells of his meeting with a Turk, who, for lack of a common language, communicated with Zorba by means of dance. This separate 'story' section of the number, in the style of a patter song, is a musical motif repeated similarly on two other occasions, a rhetorical ploy by means of which Zorba illustrates his philosophy. The storytelling mode changes to enactment when a chorus member impersonates the Turk so that Zorba can interpret his steps to Nikos before returning to the refrain of the song, 'The First Time'. Only at the very end of the scene does Zorba tell Nikos his name.

The exterior of a café in Crete in the following scene is the first full location to appear complete at the end of a set change that occurs during a blackout. From now on, the cast will no longer manage the setting of props and scenery, but the narrative mode of the representation is maintained through the interventions of the chorus who observe and help to motivate the action. The change from Scene 3 to Scene 4 is effected during the next number, which begins as a trio consisting of the chorus leader and two men who appear to encourage Zorba on his path to the house of the French woman Hortense, where he and Nikos have chosen to lodge:

> Zorba! Zorba! Zorba! Zorba!
> There's a house at the top of the hill where
> someone's waiting for you,
> Waiting for you!
>
> There's a room in the house at the top of the hill where
> someone's waiting for you,
> Waiting for you! (24)

The details of the scene accumulate from one stanza to the next, increasing the sense of anticipation and painting a mental picture of the succeeding scene, which eventually includes 'a door to the room', 'a woman at the door', a red roof, white walls and descriptions of the ouzo, the veal, the bed, the bread and the wine. The style of the verbal scene painting is surreal in its fragmentation of the individual scenic components into a series of objects the audience is required to reassemble in order to construct in imagination the house of Madame Hortense.

The many repetitions of 'someone's waiting for you' as well as 'a woman at the door' function as an intimation of the future, with a sense of foreboding in the meeting of Hortense and Zorba that stimulates speculation about how she will receive him. As in ancient Greek tragedy, the chorus is often used to prompt questions about the possible outcome of the narrative as well as to identify the probable motives and feelings of central characters. Before Madame Hortense has appeared, the song has established a 'horizon of expectation' that generates not only curiosity but also suspense.

Hortense is, in fact, a fading courtesan who, in a series of reminiscences about 'the old days' claims to have been a cabaret star. Zorba flirts with her outrageously, putting his arm around her and kissing her on the cheek at one point. Although Hortense willingly drinks the wine Zorba keeps pouring, she affects a coy demeanour while clearly enjoying the attention. Her reply to Nikos' questions about how she ended up in Crete is at last articulated in the song, 'No Boom, Boom':

> Crete was in a state of revolution, and the fleets of four great powers anchored here. So I anchored here. Four great powers, four admirals . . . Ah, you should have seen them . . .
> (*The four ADMIRALS have appeared at the side of the stage, observing the scene*) (33)

While up to this point the songs have delineated a world view or probed the outcome of a future event in such a way as to create suspense, Hortense's elaborate number is a false memory of a past event that she has mythicized in order to interpolate herself into the broader panorama of Cretan history:

> They were just about to fire on Crete
> When on my knees in a pink chemise,
> I distracted them, *toute suite,* by saying . . .
> Please sir, little admiral, no boom boom.
> Please sir, pretty admiral, no boom boom.
>
> This evening when it's dark
> I'll let you come to my room.
> But first you have to promise, no boom boom. (33–4)

In the style of a song-and-dance routine from a French revue, the appearance in memory of a quartet of admirals as Hortense's 'back-up' singers not only complicates the staging but also draws attention to the theatricality of this fanciful enactment of the past, thereby questioning the reliability of the narrator's account of events:

> And so, my dear
> If Crete's still here,
> It's all because of me. (35)

Hortense's tears at the apparent failure of the King of Greece to acknowledge her part in preventing the bombing of Crete lead Zorba and Nikos to cheer her up by joining the singing and the scene concludes on a joyous note with Zorba lifting Hortense and taking her into the house while Nikos exits to the cottage. During the scene change to Hortense's bedroom, the admirals and chorus move to the front of the stage to sing 'Vive la Différence', which becomes the song Hortense is playing on an old phonograph and which accompanies and interrupts Zorba's attempt to seduce her during Scene 5.

Figure 7. Lila Kedrova and Anthony Quinn in *Zorba*. Photo: Martha Swope, NYPL, Billy Rose Division.

After Nikos protects a young Widow from mockery and abuse by several of the villagers in Scene 6, Zorba urges Nikos to pursue her on the assumption that she will favour him in appreciation of his gallantry. Clearly, Nikos finds the Widow attractive, but he cannot follow Zorba's exhortation to act on animal instinct: 'Maybe sometime I'll be able, as you say, to move. But not too soon. Not too fast' (48). This reply to Zorba cues the next song, in which the observing chorus advises Nikos to follow the natural process, in response to which he sings the story of 'The Butterfly', a cautionary tale concerning the dangers of trying to force growth instead of allowing nature to take its course. The choric convention of commenting in song motivates the chorus to spell out the wisdom inherent in Nikos' tale:

> Not too fast!
> Not too fast!
> Let it grow!
> Let it last!
> Nature knows when and why . . . (48)

This becomes a refrain that is repeated a few times by the chorus leader and the Widow, joined finally by Nikos and the whole chorus. The reference to the life cycle of the butterfly constructs a metaphor that is explicitly applied by Nikos as the moral of his own situation:

> Every man has a moment,
> And I'm waiting for mine, when I'm finally free.
> But I mustn't be hurried.
> Give me light, give me time
> Like the butterfly. (50)

At the same time as clarifying what Nikos is feeling at this point, the song creates an expectation that some kind of relationship between him and the Widow is imminent, establishing a comparison between Zorba's opportunistic wooing of Hortense and Nikos' tentative steps towards greater intimacy with the Widow. In a startling comic contrast, Zorba's farewell to Hortense as he departs to buy equipment for the mine is acted out as a duet in which he plays the role of Hortense's Italian general Canovaro. Any potential romantic declaration is undermined by the scepticism of her repeatedly sung phrase, 'Don't forget me', which turns the whole song into a quarrel in which Zorba has to constantly reassure Hortense he won't forget her while away in the town of Khania for three days. After his exit, she sings to Nikos, 'They always do . . .' but confesses that 'until they do . . . it's very nice' (58). The duet adds a further layer to the characterization of Hortense in its implication that she is fully aware that Zorba's courtship is a game that will end in failure as all her earlier romantic affairs have done.

The letter Nikos receives in Scene 8 to explain Zorba's delay in returning is played out as a rather complicated sequence, which changes from narration to action and back again. Nikos begins by reading the letter, illuminated by a single spotlight before the 'flashback' enactment begins with Zorba throwing money at an attractive belly dancer during a somewhat desultory routine she performs in a café. When the dancer's rival calls Zorba 'grandpapa', Zorba sings another song to protect his reputation: 'Grandpapa! I'll show her who's grandpapa!' While Zorba speaks his letter directly to Nikos, the action in the café freezes. As he has done previously, Zorba asks, 'Do you want to hear a story? Then I'll tell you' before beginning a song about his youthful cruelty towards his grandmama, who mistakenly thought the boys that came regularly to serenade a pretty young girl across the way were singing to her. The song gives way to the speaking/reading of the letter before the frozen stage action is unfrozen to reveal events occurring in a highly condensed time sequence on stage.

Zorba, it transpires, has lived with the belly dancer for a few days, but when she departs with a young man, leaving him alone on stage, the chorus taunts him by singing 'Grandpapa'.

> Look at that! Look at that!
> Poor old man is weak and fat!
> [....................]
> Look at that! Poor Zorba.
> Old and feeble grandpapa. (62–3)

After Zorba concludes the number with a dance, Hortense and Nikos discuss the contents of the letter. Nikos, in order to punish Zorba for wasting his money on the belly dancer, pretends that he has especially remembered Hortense and bought her a ring. This lie provokes a rapturous response from the old woman and prompts her haunting song 'Only Love', a brief but soaring ballad with Ebb's simple lyrics set to one of Kander's most beautiful melodies. Hortense celebrates traditional wisdom in a manner that counters Zorba's masculinist philosophy of the pleasure of grabbing every opportunity with, 'Give me love, / Only love, /That's everything'. On her exit, the music swells to a poignant climax before it segues into 'The Bend of the Road', a variation of 'The Top of the Hill', which had in Scene 3 announced the appearance of Hortense.

At this point, the chorus sings the song in order to persuade Nikos of the Widow's desire for his visit,

> There's a girl in a room in a house at the bend
>   of the road and she is waiting for you.
> Waiting for you.
>
> There's a girl on a bed!
> There's a girl on a bed!
> There's a girl on a bed! (67)

The number functions as a kind of challenge to Nikos, as though the chorus were a voice in his head, depicting the Widow's loneliness in simple but vivid images that goad him to take the next step in their relationship. During the scene change to her home, the orchestra plays a musical motif from 'Only Love', the music reinforcing the thematic parallel between Hortense's dream of married bliss and the Widow's yearning for a relationship with Nikos.

As the chorus leader watches the Widow and Nikos' long embrace, she ends the act with a short refrain from Hortense's song: 'For after all, /After love, /What else is there?' The interweaving of 'The Bend in the Road' and 'Only Love' promotes a heightened anticipation of romantically satisfying endings to both the story of Hortense and that of the Widow, although an audience may at this midpoint in the show have doubts about the potential outcome of Hortense's plan.

The storytelling motif is again signalled at the start of the second act by the image of the chorus seated in a semicircle in the village square. Much of the music in the act is motivated by ritual. The 'Bell Dance' is interrupted by the sound of a mourning song coming from the church at the rear of the stage, followed by a ceremonial procession with the dead body of Pavli, who has apparently drowned himself after witnessing Nikos kissing the Widow, with whom Pavli was hopelessly in love. The mourners make their way down the church steps in a straight line downstage and exit, followed by the chorus, 'leaving the village square empty' (71).

When Zorba returns from Khania, he is trapped into an engagement with Hortense, another ritual celebrated by a choral dance to the spirited music of 'Y'assou', joyously if somewhat inappropriately sung and danced by the chorus, Hortense, Zorba and Nikos in celebration of the 'restoration' of Hortense's virginity and Zorba's innocence. Here the time-honoured ritual becomes an elaborate game played by Zorba and Nikos to make Hortense believe Zorba will marry her. While both Zorba and Hortense are perhaps over-expressive, making declarations of love which are either exaggerated or false, Act 2 Scene 3 reveals the Widow by contrast as having powerful feelings she is unable to verbalize, while Nikos is, for the first time, haltingly yet persistently talking to elicit a response from the silent woman as they walk along a country road. The song 'Why Can't I Speak?' presents a kind of internal monologue in which the Widow sings about her inability to talk directly to Nikos as a series of questions to herself. A girl who emerges from the chorus voices the Widow's deepest feelings in song:

> Nikos, I want you.
> Nikos, I'll say it.
> Nikos, I feel that I'm living at last.
> [...............]
> Nikos, my moments of silence have past. (84)

Following the fatal stabbing of the Widow by Mavrodani in Scene 4, and a blackout of the lights on Nikos kneeling over her lifeless body, a religious chant sung by monks is heard in the darkness, echoing the ritual of mourning for Pavli, though ironically this chant is to bless the opening of the mine, which the villagers celebrate by dancing. As an extension of the ritual motif in the transition to Scene 6, four men and the chorus leader emerge from the dark wearing black shrouds to sing 'The Crow', a lament for the dying Hortense. It is a grotesque song of keening that mimics the cawing sounds of a crow, with the men imitating the four women who are seated around Hortense's bedroom, waiting for her to die so they can grab gloves, a scarf, spoons, feathers and other possessions.

When Zorba and Nikos arrive at the bedside to pay their last respects to Hortense, the chorus comes forward again to reprise 'The Crow', this time with the four old women who have come to take whatever they can get as soon as she is dead.[24] The chorus leader sings,

> Soon
> We'll see the crow
> Circle and dive, flutter and climb.
>
> Then
> Someone in bed,
> Barely alive, knows it's the time. (104)

At this moment, the old 'crows' rush to the bed, thinking Hortense has died. Other old women arrive to scavenge possessions from the house, but Hortense rises suddenly and, supported by Zorba, begins to reminisce about her youth as the other characters freeze:

> My mother dressed me in a white organdy gown, and she said, 'Ladies and Gentlemen, my beautiful daughter . . . it's her birthday . . . She's sixteen years old . . .' and my mother said, 'You will dance through life. You will dance all through life'. (105)

Hortense's memory triggers a flashback to her girlhood when her mother promised her the future would bring her a lifetime of love. She walks downstage to face the audience directly while she sings 'Happy Birthday'; the sweetness of the child's birthday song is in stark contrast to the surrounding gloom. Together with the ironic contradiction between the child's hopes for the future and Hortense's adult life as a courtesan, the various emotions generated by the old woman singing as if she were a young girl generate a complex and overwhelming affect:

> She [mother] envies me the love I'm just about to see.

> But she was yesterday
> And I'm tomorrow.
> Happy birthday to me! (106)

In the middle of the number, Hortense dances before returning to bed where she sings 'Don't forget me' to Zorba/Canovaro as she closes her eyes. The re-enactment of past hopes in song at the moment of death is a daring dramaturgical device[25] to represent how Hortense has held on to her youthful dreams in spite of the repeated experience of disillusionment in romance. Zorba's simple announcement, 'She has left us, boss' (108), prompts the women immediately to start pilfering her belongings. Instead of funeral rites, the scavenging women empty the room while they murmur their prayers, finally leaving Zorba and Nikos alone with the body of Hortense. After a long silence, Nikos starts to dance clumsily, revealing the influence of Zorba on his changed attitude towards life. After watching for a while, Zorba joins him and the two men dance with increasing momentum and intensity to a finale 'when they collapse in relief' (108).

Once again the chorus is utilized to effect the transition to the next scene as two of its members come on stage to give the two men their coats and luggage. Zorba and Nikos remain in position as the scene changes around them to a road leading out of the village. When Nikos contemplates accompanying Zorba on his wanderings, Zorba predicts that Nikos will not have the 'touch of folly' to do that: 'Your head's a careful little shopkeeper. It won't let you risk . . . everything' (110). By comparison, Zorba represents in song his own freedom to choose whatever he pleases. He asserts his freedom by living as if he would die any minute, seizing whatever experience offers itself at every moment. As Zorba and Nikos say farewell in a long embrace, the lights fade slowly, to return to the image that opened Act 1 – the whole company seated in a semicircle. Zorba and Nikos seat themselves as part of the semicircle for the reprise of 'Life Is', ending the show in the same storytelling mode as it began.

Kander's score, with its brilliant orchestrations by Don Walker, constructs a sonic world uncanny in its evocation of Greek folk music, yet without ever seeming to be a pastiche of

Mikis Theodorakis' ubiquitous 'Zorba's Dance' from the Michael Cacoyannis film. According to Jesse Green, the overall coherence of the various aspects of the story is created by the music:

> This is mostly the magic of Kander's exceptionally fluid and varied score, in which an idea of Greek music is so thoroughly absorbed into the Broadway palette that the songs all seem 'found', almost geological in their layered rightness.[26]

As with *Cabaret*, John Kander's compositional method involved familiarizing himself with the authentic music of the period and place:

> The first thing that happened is that I listened to lots and lots and lots of Greek music. And then I forgot about it [. . .] I made the assumption that I would just write with that influence in the back of my head. I do know that the very first notes I wrote for *Zorba* were the opening vamp to 'Life Is.'[27]

In addition to the ethnic instruments onstage (bouzoukis, oud, doumbek), most of the strings in the original Broadway pit doubled on mandolins and mandolas, but in preparation for the national tour in 1970 with John Raitt as Zorba and Chita Rivera as the leader, the musical arrangement was simplified by orchestrator Don Walker. In Kander's opinion,

> That was necessary. The interesting thing is that the final version of the show happened with the tour. There was something musically not quite complete about the version that was on Broadway. When we sent it out on tour, we had a chance to write some new things. [28]

The new material included 'That's a Beginning' which was added for Nikos as a sung response to the Widow's 'Why Can't I Speak?' A new song for Zorba, 'Woman', was included in the 1983 revival, directed by Cacayonnis as a vehicle for the film's stars, Anthony Quinn and Lila Kedrova. Although the revival was a commercial success on Broadway and on tour, both Kander and Ebb regarded the directorial approach as unimaginative and crude.

The most problematic aspect of the musical is not so much that it purports to illuminate the possibility of joy within lives of hardship and even misery, but that the conception of narrative and character is unacceptably sexist. In reviewing the *Encores!* revival that ran for seven performances in May 2015, David Rooney suggests why it is unlikely that *Zorba* will ever be revived in a full staging:[29]

> [I]t's the dated aspects of the work as drama that really hold it back [. . .] The life-affirming title character – with his voracious appetite for women, booze and conversation, and his fearless acknowledgement of death – is a tired archetype. And the treatment of the female characters now seems hopelessly retrograde.[30]

No doubt the novel's attitude to gender is consonant with the dominant ideology of Cretans and Greeks before the Second World War, yet in a post-1970s culture, the sixty-year-old Zorba appears as a patriarchal dinosaur, his belief in savouring every moment of life to the full being played out in the narrative as a relentless series of sexual conquests of willing or desperate women.

Even if a director attempts to historicize the piece, audiences are expected to celebrate the triumph of Zorba's philosophy over the more repressed world view of the writer, whose conventional book learning has taught him to suppress his natural instincts and who, therefore, finds it difficult to be with a woman he does not love. In the film, Basil (played by Alan Bates) is of Greek extraction, but his sophistication has been cultivated by means of an English upbringing. In the musical, Nikos is a Greek-American, but his scholarly education has made him effete by comparison with the outrageously instinctive Alexis Zorba. When Nikos sleeps with the young widow and begins to fall in love with her, the event is intended to be a sign of the liberation of his instinctive self.

There are other aspects of human nature to which Nikos ultimately has his eyes opened. Nikos' hope of finding good among ordinary peasants is mocked by his witnessing of the savage vengefulness manifest in the killing of the widow by Mavrodani in order to punish her for the suicide of his son Pavli, who felt rejected by her (Act 2 Scene 4). When he is finally forced to watch Madame Hortense's few worldly possessions snatched from her house by peasant women literally crowing as she dies, any illusions he may have had about the magnanimity of the human spirit are shattered.

Despite Zorba's infidelity to Hortense with the belly dancer in Khania, the power of his personality and his blunt admission of his own weakness are meant to portray him as a lovable rogue: 'I'm sorry about that, boss, honest. But man is weak and I'm a man . . . And I'm going to make it up to you, every drachma' (73). His response to Nikos' accusation that he has betrayed Hortense is risible: 'Don't worry. I'll give her a slap on the behind and she'll be fine' (73). Although Nikos demonstrates his anger by pretending to Hortense that Zorba wrote from Khania to say he wanted to marry her (74), the sexism inherent in Zorba's demeaning attitude to women is never directly challenged.

While the score remains one of the greatest achievements of Broadway theatre in the 1960s and the storytelling device invented by Prince motivates what is possibly the most progressive experiment in musical theatre dramaturgy until *Company* (1970), aspects of the book and characterization would have to be altered to guarantee that any future production of the musical does not seem to be celebrating sexism.

Notes

1. John Gilvey, *Before the Parade Passes By*, New York: St Martin's Press, 2005, 183.
2. Gilvey, *Before the Parade Passes By*, 183.
3. John Kander, Fred Ebb and Greg Lawrence, *Colored Lights*, New York: Faber, 2003, 75.
4. *The Rainmaker* was a successful play on Broadway, written by Nash.
5. *Colored Lights*, 75.
6. Gilvey, *Before the Parade Passes By*, 191.
7. This song was written two years before the Sondheim number in *Company*!
8. *The Happy Time*, *Dance Magazine*, April 1968, 27, quoted in Gilvey, *Before the Parade Passes By*, 192.
9. St Pierre is a very small town on the island of Newfoundland, which legally belongs to France, not Canada.
10. All dialogue and lyrics are transcribed from the original cast recording, RCA Victor Broadway, 1968.
11. Interview with John Kander and Fred Ebb, December 12, 1992, https://av.lib.umd.edu/media_objects/c247ds68c. Accessed 14 May, 2020.
12. William Goldman, *The Season: A Candid Look at Broadway*, New York: Limelight, 200.

13. Interview with John Kander and Fred Ebb, December 12, 1992. Acceesed 14 May, 2020.

14. See *Ovrtur*, on *Variety* estimate, https://ovrtur.com/show/119775. Accessed 22 May 2020.

15. James Leve, *Kander and Ebb*, New Haven: Yale University Press, 2009, 192–3.

16. Leve, *Kander and Ebb*, 192–3.

17. *Theatre Mania.* https://www.theatermania.com/news/the-happy-time_13459/.

18. https://www.broadwayworld.com/shows/The-Happy-Time-311618.html. Accessed 3 April, 2021.

19. *Colored Lights*, 86.

20. Jesse Green in *Vulture*, May 2015.

21. *Colored Lights*, 92.

22. Harold Prince, *Sense of Occasion*, Milwaukee: Applause Books, 2017, 141–2.

23. Prince, *Sense of Occasion*, 144.

24. '"The Crow" was another rich moment [. . .] and Hal staged that beautifully' (*Colored Lights*, 88).

25. Fred Ebb described the moment as 'one of the best realized musical moments in our careers' and as 'breathtaking' (*Colored Lights*, 87).

26. Jesse Green in *Vulture*, May 2015, https://www.vulture.com/2015/05/theater-review-zorba-at-encores.html.

27. *Playbill*, Interview with John Kander, May 2015.

28. *Playbill*, May 2015.

29. From May 7th to 10th 2015, there was a partly staged *Encores* revival, which ran for seven performances at the City Center Theatre with John Turturro, Zoe Wanamaker and Marin Mazzie as the Leader.

30. David Rooney, *The Hollywood Reporter*, 7 May 2015, https://www.hollywoodreporter.com/lifestyle/lifestyle-news/john-turturro-zorba-theater-review-794201/. Accessed 3 May, 2021.

5 Meta-theatrical crime stories

70, Girls, 70 (1971) and *Curtains* (2004)

Vaudeville as structure

Cabaret and *Zorba* had demonstrated the talent for pastiche that underpinned Kander and Ebb's extraordinary ability to create meta-theatre deploying musical and theatrical idioms of past times and different cultures to represent milieus with which a Broadway audience would be unfamiliar. Two shows that exploit the penchant for pastiche and meta-theatre consistently are *70, Girls, 70* and *Curtains*: these musicals offer alternative approaches to the presentation of crime stories in musical theatre form. By means of its vaudeville pastiche, *70, Girls, 70* anticipates Ebb's framing of the action of *Chicago* within a vaudeville show, as well as looking forward to the deconstruction of B-movies in *Kiss of the Spider Woman* and the startling deployment of the minstrel show format in *The Scottsboro Boys*.

While *Curtains* is an hilarious backstage detective story, whose mingling of fiction and reality doubles the solution of the whodunnit with a comic critique of the dramaturgical principles of musical theatre itself to resolve the structure of the musical-within-the-show, *70, Girls, 70* is paradoxically more obvious and more ambitious in its dramaturgy. Kander and Ebb had wished to adapt the British film *Make Mine Mink* (1960) into a stage musical. Unable to secure the rights, they turned instead to its source play, Peter Coke's *Breath of Spring* (1958), a spoof crime thriller that had been successful on the London stage and has subsequently been beloved by amateur dramatic societies. Ebb and fellow book-writer Norman L. Martin understandably transformed the English country house setting to the Sussex Arms Hotel on Manhattan's Upper West Side, exploiting the core of the plot concerning an old woman's theft of jewellery into a narrative that would conveniently motivate the frame of showbiz with which they were familiar.

Having used an onstage storytelling convention in *Zorba* three years earlier, Kander and Ebb elaborate on this in a Pirandellian fashion to present the narrative of *70, Girls, 70*. After the opening number, 'Old Folks', which is sung directly to the audience by the characters/ actors, Melba, a Black waitress, addresses the audience, reinforcing the 'open-stage' technique of direct address as part of an armoury of non-naturalistic conventions:

> I guess you wonder why I'm talking to you. Well you better get used to it, honey.
> We'll be doing it all night long. We talk when we want to, sing when we want to,
> use Lorraine when we want to. And all the while we'll be telling you a story. So, if you
> don't want to get confused. Pay attention. [. . .] All right. Let the play begin. (1)[1]

Opening a few weeks later than *Follies* with which it shared the meta-theatrical approach to the presentation of narrative material, it was in some ways the polar opposite of Sondheim and Goldman's show.[2] Where *Follies* is a bitter reflection on America's broken dreams and failed hopes focused through the disappointment of its central pair of middle-aged couples, *70, Girls, 70* is an optimistic crime caper that involves a number of robberies at various stores by a bunch of septuagenarians, who illustrate the stories in song and dance performances that at times directly or at others only vaguely connect with the actual situation. The pastiche of old show numbers in the two musicals is used to opposite ends – in *70, Girls, 70* to invigorate the present with the force of pleasant and positive old memories that characterize the age and milieu of its characters, while in the Sondheim show to generate a complex and ambivalent nostalgia for a period thirty or forty years prior when life seemed simpler and the characters' ideals more attainable. In *Follies* these songs contrast with a series of contemporary hymns of regret for 'the road not taken'.[3]

Although reviews for *Follies* were by no means universally positive,[4] there is no doubt that the high-profile reception of the show (cover stories in *Time, Life, Look, After Dark, Show, Forbes* and *Theatre Crafts* magazines as well as ninety minutes on David Frost's TV talk show)[5] overshadowed the Kander and Ebb show and made this second musical about old stagers more difficult to market. In Fred Ebb's opinion,

> It never occurred to me that the audience would hate it until Sondheim's *Follies* opened about three weeks before us. [. . .] That show was just breathtakingly brilliant. But then it occurred to me that show was also about getting old and dealing with it [. . .] I wondered if that would hurt us. Then I became convinced that it would.[6]

Critics were extremely negative about *70, Girls, 70,* although at first, audiences loved it. Sondheim was one of those who enjoyed the show and included 'Home' as one of the hundred 'Songs I Wished I'd Written at Least in Part'.[7] Ebb remembered his praise for the show as follows: 'It was one of the only times Stephen Sondheim ever complimented me. [. . .] As he was leaving he called my name [. . .] and he said, "This is the best audience show I've seen in years. Everybody loves it! Congratulations!"'[8]

Only entertainment?

Word of mouth seems not to have been sufficient to overcome poor reviews, and the show closed after thirty-five performances and nine previews. Part of the problem was the fact that the double structure of the book never made complete sense. Many of the songs – 'Old Folks' is a good example – were sung by the actors who were putting on a show at the Broadhurst (the actual theatre where *70, Girls, 70* was playing!) rather than by the elderly characters in the crime story who discover they will be homeless as a result of the proposed sale of the Sussex Arms. The deliberately retro form of the show is reminiscent of the Broadway musical comedy of the 1920s when songs and speciality numbers were inserted merely to entertain. The performer of the role of Melba herself confessed that the delightfully jazzy 'charm' song 'Coffee in a Cardboard Cup', which she sang with the actor who played Fritzi, has no dramaturgical function: like a number of others, it was there to cover a scene change. The comic song 'You and I, Love' about watching television on a

TV set that doesn't work was a non-diegetic number taking place in the Sussex Arms but, apart from generating comedy, it is there merely to provide a bridge to Ida's return and the group's reactions after the unexpected accidents that occur while returning a stolen fur to Sadie (they are determined only to steal from large businesses who can afford to lose expensive items). During their final heist, while the gang is offstage trying to escape from the cold storage vault by blowing it up, Sadie and Eddie, a bellhop from the hotel, perform a song-and-dance number, 'Go Visit Your Grandmother', which has no relation to the crime fiction but is inserted to cover another scene change.

One of the highlights of the show is the up-tempo 'Broadway, My Street', which has it both ways by parodying as well as eulogizing the classic no-business-like-show-business anthem:

> How many times have you heard the performer say,
> 'Gee but it's great to be back here on old Broadway!'
> That's such a worn and a boring cliché,
> Well steal yourself, you're just about to hear it again.[9]

Although structured as a zany entertainment about old performers acting out the story of a gang of elderly thieves, the show deliberately challenges ageism. Many of its numbers genuinely explore the problems of ageing and celebrate those who choose to welcome the experience of getting older by accepting its compromises and creatively embracing new possibilities. The difficulty that audiences had with the 1971 version is that the Pirandellian frame, although clearly intended as a didactic exposition by the *actors* of the theme of growing older inherent in the fiction, did not operate consistently but was speciously 'justified' by *characters* who occasionally stepped out of the action to explain that a song is merely a 'cross-over'.

When a revised version of the show (1989) with a new book by David Thompson was performed at the Chichester Festival (1990) before transferring to London in 1991 with the British star Dora Bryan[10] as Ida, it notched up little more than 120 performances, but critics were more enthusiastic. By making most of the characters themselves retired vaudevillians whose interviews in a police station initiated the narration of the heist at the beginning, the show was more plausibly set entirely on a bare stage, eliminating the elaborate scene changes and removing the double structure so that it was justifiable for the characters (rather than the actors) to alternate plot-driven with self-referential showbiz songs. The new version removed a few supplementary characters and dropped Ida's 'The Elephant Song' about death, which, eccentric and charming as it was, slowed down the action just before the eleven o'clock number, 'Yes'. The more melodic 'Well Laid Plans' replaced 'The Caper,' a new song was added for Harry and Walter – 'I Can't Do That Anymore' – while Ida took the place of Sadie in 'Go Visit Your Grandmother'.[11] The show ended optimistically with the number, 'Yes':

> Say yes.
> [……………………..]
> Yes I'll try, yes I'll dare,
> Ye-es I'll fly, ye-es I I'll share;
> And yes I am, and yes I'll be
> And yes I'll go.
> Oh yes!
> Yes.[12]

Figure 8. Mildred Natwick and company in 'Yes' from *70, Girls, 70*. Photo: Martha Swope, NYPL, Billy Rose Division.

Although the show ran so briefly on Broadway, 'Yes' found a wide audience on television a year later as the opening number of *Liza with a Z* (1972); here the defiant anthem of gritty optimism was used to introduce Fred Ebb's characterization of the Liza persona.[13] With *Chicago* (1975), Ebb and Bob Fosse – credited as co-writer of the book – achieved the most perfect integration of book and score that the team had managed up to this point in their career. Here, the vaudeville pastiche became the spine of a performance that absorbed the fictional narrative into a metaphorical dramatization of the events of the narrative *as* vaudeville turns. There was no longer any fiction outside the vaudeville stage because the putative reality being represented was itself a series of staged performances.

Backstage detective story

As early as the mid-1980s, the team began working on book-writer Peter Stone's idea for *Who Killed David Merrick?* the original title of what eventually became *Curtains*. Kander and Ebb proposed that they use *Tango Mogador*, their own spoof of desert films for which they had written a complete score in 1971, as the musical-within-the-detective-play, which they intended to call *Sand*. Working on and off until the book-writer's death in 2003, Ebb and Stone changed *Sand* to create *Harlequinade*, which complicated the Pirandellian form of meta-theatre to an improbable degree; they gradually rid the show of its references to real theatre personalities and cut the direct parodies of actual musicals. Replacing Stone, Rupert Holmes substituted a burlesque Western musical called *Robbin' Hood* for the earlier shows-within-the-show, thereby simplifying the meta-theatrical games, as well as changing the title to *Curtains*. The opening number, 'Wide Open Spaces', is a delightful parody that mocks the optimistic clichés of 'Western' musicals like *Calamity Jane*, *Seven Brides for Seven Brothers* and *Destry Rides Again*, positioning the audience backstage at the Colonial Theatre in Boston in 1959, to view the finale of *Robbin' Hood*'s final preview performance.

As the cast takes their bows the supremely untalented leading lady Jessica Cranshaw exits into the wings, only to crumple to the ground as though mortally wounded. As Jessica dies, the curtain of the historic Colonial Theatre comes down to the applause of the audience-within-*Curtains*. It opens again to reveal four characters on an empty stage, behind newspapers, which each is reading as the orchestra plays a sinister vamp: the implication in their grim tones is that these four characters are reading Jessica's obituaries. They are, in fact, scanning reviews that ring the death knell for the show prior to a Broadway run. The wisecracking dialogue sets the sarcastic tone. The wry, tongue-in-cheek humour of *Curtains* treats the audience as Broadway insiders, making them complicit in the cynicism of experienced show people. Self-mocking wisecracks pepper the dialogue as when a number of the creatives read out bits of various reviews:

GEORGIA:
Holy shit!

AARON:
Holy mother in Heaven!

OSCAR:
The reviews aren't good? What don't they like?'

CARMEN:
That we put on a show.

AARON:
The *Boston Globe* says,
'If you loved Oklahoma!', stay there as long as 'Robbin' Hood' is running in Boston!'

CARMEN:
Critics! Who'd make a living out of killing other people's dreams? I mean
[. . .]

(*sung*)
What kind of putz would squeeze your nuts like that
Who could be prick enough

ALL:
Mentally sick enough
Who'd want to grow to be
Everyone's enemy
Critics are hated and
So excoriated tell me
What kind of man
Would want a job like that?[14]

A typically comic payoff comes in the hypocritical switch of the group's exaggerated contempt to praise for reviewers the minute they come across the only good review in the newspapers:

OSCAR (spoken):
Hey, hey, hey, get a load of this. *The Cambridge Patriot* says, 'Considering the talent
and experience of the veterans involved, 'Robbin' Hood' is sure to be a huge Broadway
smash.'

ALL:
What kind of genius has a mind like that
So perspicacious, wise and kind like that
Far from his mother's knee,
She must be thrilled to see
How he grew up to be
Such brilliant company.

The darkly satirical song about the *Schadenfreude* that motivates theatre critics, 'What
Kinda Man?' ('Critics! What kind of person makes a living by killing other people's dreams?')
is interspersed with quotations from a slew of negative reviews. The deliberate mismatch of
music and lyrics creates a wonderful irony as the characters believe the critics are trying to
'kill' their show: they sing with aggressive energy in a hopeless but hilarious protest against
the destructiveness of theatre reviewers, the music itself suggesting that in spite of their
protests, the show is doomed. The overt self-reflexiveness of this anti-show business lament
maps the mental world of cynically wisecracking Broadway show people, trapped in the hell
of a bad tryout, taking the injury of an incompetent star in stride, yet mourning for a show
that might close on the road. The sonic world constructed in *Curtains* is a generic pastiche
of 'golden age' musical comedy from *Annie Get Your Gun* (1946) to *Mame* (1966), the big
show business anthems and ballads musically undercut by funereal tones.

The self-reflexiveness about show biz is surprisingly amplified by the entrance at the start
of the next scene of Lieutenant Frank Cioffi, a chatty detective, swiftly identifying himself
as a theatre buff who spends each summer vacation as an actor with an amateur theatre
group. Although he seems to be more interested in helping rescue the new show before its
Broadway debut, Cioffi quarantines the cast and crew inside the theatre while he searches
for clues to what is soon revealed to be Jessica's poisoning. His forensic skills and passion
for theatre are equally clearly demonstrated in his ingenious unravelling of a mystery that
becomes progressively more complicated, as well as in his detailed suggestions for revising
the musical-within-the-whodunnit for Broadway – a witty doubling of the plot that teasingly
equates the challenge of solving a crime with the problems of rewriting a poorly constructed
musical. Jessica Cranshaw turns out to have been universally disliked so almost everyone
involved in *Robbin' Hood* becomes a potential suspect.

Pastiche, Parody and burlesque

Broadway reviews were grudgingly mixed in 2007. Ben Brantley (*New York Times*)
captured the faint praise most reviewers accorded the show: '"Curtains" lies on stage like
a promisingly gaudy string of firecrackers waiting in vain for that vital, necessary spark to
set it off'.[15] It may have been the case that with the hilarious but overpraised *The Producers*
(2001) and the innovative *Avenue Q* (2003), Broadway insiders had been over-exposed to

this kind of burlesque of old musical theatre conventions, but it appears that most critics overlooked or took for granted the markedly superior craft skills evinced by *Curtains*. By comparison with *Chicago* or *Cabaret,* the new show lacked a 'tough' or socially significant subject, the satire of Broadway insiders being too generic to elicit shock or surprise. A few years later, the overwhelming critical acclaim for *The Book of Mormon* (2011) shows the kind of postmodern musical comedy the theatre community may have been searching for, but that show typifies the kind of outrageous broad-brush parody that subsequently replaced an older, more thoroughly informed burlesque of the Broadway traditions. Yet the show has been popular beyond Broadway. Having successfully previewed in Los Angeles in 2006, there was a US tour in 2010, followed by productions in Prague, Visby, Coburg, Toronto, Abu Dhabi, Melbourne, Pforzheim, a fringe production in London (2012), a West End production (2019) and a major UK tour (2019–20).

It must be said that the stylistic virtuosity exhibited in *Curtains* is superior to the craftsmanship of any of the three more 'modern' shows (*The Producers, Avenue Q* or *The Book of Mormon*). Kander and Ebb's score segues effortlessly between the hard-bitten sentimentalism that typifies their 'Broadway' show tunes and the parodic musical comedy songs of *Robbin' Hood*. Each style is entirely consistent, so the direct counterpointing of the two illustrates the difference between sophisticated songs, written as straightforward pastiches of golden age conventions, and clichéd Broadway numbers for *Robbin' Hood*, composed as comic parodies. In addition, the 'backstage' songs from the putatively 'real' world of the Colonial Theatre are highly self-reflexive, offering a hilariously *ad hominem* critical commentary on critics ('What Kind of Man'), a rudely satirical review of untalented leading ladies ('The Woman's Dead') and an ironic, faux-naïve paean to show business ('Show People'). 'I Miss the Music', one of three gentle but deeply affecting ballads ('Thinking of Him' and 'Coffee Shop Nights' are the others), offers the audience a brief lesson in songwriting.

At director Christopher Belling's request, Georgia sings Jessica's opening number ('Thinking of Him') beautifully, exposing her sadness at her failed marriage to Aaron, who joins her in song until her new lover, Bobby, cuts him off to complete the number with her – the way it should be sung in *Robbin' Hood*. As in *Kiss Me Kate* (1948), the conceit at this moment demonstrates the parallel between the narrative of the musical-within-the-show and the framing action, the actors projecting their real feelings onto the fictional characters.

After Carmen enters with confirmation of Jessica's death, the cast performs an ironic eulogy; it is clear that no one is sorry to see their leading lady gone:

CARMEN (spoken):
Jessica Cranshaw will never be better than she was this evening.

BOBBY:
But she was horrible.

CARMEN:
I know. But she'll never be better. She's dead. That was the hospital on the phone. In terms of future performances, Jessica Cranshaw now has a conflict.

GEORGIA:
Chris, do you want to say something to the company about Jessica?

CHRIS:
Shall we all observe a moment of silence? To match the audience's response to Jessica's first number?
[. . .]

The tongue-in-cheek dialogue mocks the clichéd show biz lingo of the *Robbin' Hood* performers, while the song itself is a hilarious comic parody of a funeral hymn, with the congregation's true thoughts being verbalized rather than the conventionally false eulogizing typical of such situations. Beginning with choral humming, the song continues funereally:

ALL:
The woman's dead
The woman's dead

BAMBI:
She was a bitch

CHRIS:
And under pitch

BAMBI:
And now she's dead
ALL:
Our star is dead

AARON:
She had no voice

OSCAR:
She had no wits

CARMEN:
She had no brains
She just had tits

AARON AND CARMEN:
And now she's dead

ALL:
Can't blow her nose
Can't shake her head
See for yourself
It's like I said
The woman's definitely
Positively

CIOFFI (spoken):
Excuse me, I'm Lt. Frank Cioffi of the greater Boston Police. I'm assigned to the homicide division and, oh, it's an honor to be standing on the same stage with each and every one of you!

ALL: (sung):
Dead! Dead!

As soon as they learn that Jessica was murdered by cyanide poisoning, members of the ensemble decide to quit the show, prompting Carmen to manipulate them to stay on the basis of the hoary showbiz cliché that 'the show must go on', which quickly degenerates into a sung union dispute in which Carmen threatens to sue the performers for breach of contract. Once again, Kander and Ebb's joke about the cynicism of stage performers is both sharp and funny: what actually motivates 'show people' is their own personal gain.

CARMEN: (sung)
I got a contract
You signed a contract
Go read your contract
And I will count to ten
And then I'll sue you
Ah, yes, I'll sue you
And when I sue you
You'll never work again

It is a double irony, then, that the detective is the person who sings the hymn celebrating 'Show People' *a la* 'There's No Business Like Show Business' in order to remind the performers of the nobility of their calling.

The detective, played on Broadway by *Frasier* star David Hyde Pierce, was praised by the *New York Times* critic for being 'a soft-sell star in a hard-sell world. He uses this incongruity to make Cioffi a surrogate for everyone in the audience who has had fantasies about appearing in a big Broadway musical.'[16]

CIOFFI: (spoken) I can't believe I'm hearing this. I won't believe it. Putting on a musical
has gotta be the most fulfilling thing a person could ever hope to do. You people you're
all heroes to me.
(*sung*)
You're a special kind of people known as show people,
You live in a world of your own;
[.........
.........]
Did you know your dentist longs to be in show business
Your window washer wants to be a star
[.................
...................]

Some policemen and detectives dream of show business;
They can't get arrested, but still
They sit around the station and fancy this life.
They jeer Sherlock Holmes
And cheer Mack the Knife
[.................
.................]

Figure 9. Jason Manford as Cioffi in London production of *Curtains*. 'Photo: Richard Davenport'

In time-honoured Broadway fashion, the act of singing the song restores the company's faith in show biz!

COMPANY:
It's an honor and a joy to be in show business
I feel that spotlight hit me and I'm gone
At the last curtain call
I'm the envy of all
So I know the show must

CARMEN: (*sung*)
Go on!
[..........
..........]

COMPANY:
So thrilling that show people
EVERYBODY:
Go on!

Ebb develops the dramatic situation throughout the song in textbook fashion, with first Carmen, then Oscar, Christopher, Georgia and finally the whole company joining in as they become convinced by Cioffi's enthusiasm. As Cioffi believes Jessica's killer is one of the company, he won't let anyone leave the building, so they have nothing to do but go on reworking the show.

Charmed by young Niki, the detective confides in her about his lonely life, consumed by police work in the gently ambivalent 'Coffee Shop Nights'. When the author of the savage review in *The Boston Globe*, Darryl Grady, arrives, he is invited to re-review the show with Georgia in the leading role. Cioffi's suggestion that Niki, Georgia and Bambi's song, 'In the

Same Boat', now being re-rehearsed by Chris, needs to be totally rewritten gives him the opportunity to learn about the compositional process from Aaron. 'I Miss the Music' echoes 'Thinking of Him' in expressing Aaron's nostalgia for the happy work relationship with his former writing partner Georgia. Kander is here, in reality, expressing his grief for the loss of friend and co-writer Fred Ebb, an ironic case of life mimicking art.

Georgia's dress rehearsal of the saloon hall production number 'Thataway!' proves her talent as a performer, so everyone believes the show now has a chance of success. Again, the number manifests Kander and Ebb's subtlety in parodying a big Wild West song and dance number: the song is not *bad*, just overwritten and overproduced in a way that renders its exaggerated high energy as camp. As soon as Cioffi reveals that Carmen's husband, Sidney Bernstein, has been blackmailing every cast and crew member into working on the show, the curtain descends as, simultaneously, Sidney ascends with the curtain rope tied around his neck, ending Act 1 on a proverbial cliffhanger – in a number of senses!

Act 2 opening: 'He Did It'

Sasha, the conductor, turns to the audience to reveal that Sidney's hanging was fatal ('The Man Is Dead'). A makeshift dormitory has been set up on the stage of the still-sequestered Colonial Theatre. Each member of the company suspects the others. In the middle of the night Cioffi returns from the coroner's office and tells everyone that Sidney was knocked out before being tied to the rope, so everyone is still a suspect, but he focuses more on whether the show will be ready for its reopening. When a death threat for Sidney is found, stating he will die unless he closes the show, Oscar reveals Sidney died for nothing as he was going to comply. He even gave Oscar back the last cheque he made out. Carmen takes it back, saying she is going to keep the show open. Aaron previews his new version of 'In the Same Boat' featuring Bobby, Randy and Harv ('In the Same Boat #2'). Cioffi is not yet satisfied with the production and has other advice for the show's creators.

Bambi asks that a pas de deux be added for herself and Bobby. Carmen agrees, but she is no stage mother; her duty is to the box office, as she points out in the hilarious but scathing 'It's a Business':

> It's time for you to know
> Why I really backed this show.
>
> You asked me for my motives,
> Well you needn't be so smart;
> It's a business.[17]

Carmen exposes her philistine ignorance of classical theatre in the song:

> Shaw and Ibsen, take them away,
> And don't bother me with Moliere,
> Those Russians never pay.[18]

The number is a comic highlight of the show – not only a cynical anti-showbiz anthem but also a comic expression of Ebb and Kander's view that, no matter how serious, a Broadway musical must be commercial entertainment. While exposing the grossly commercial motives of Carmen, it also reveals her erudition as someone who can joke about losing money on productions of Samuel Beckett, Eugene O'Neill and Gorki yet knows how to make a profit by clever programming:

> I do the Kama Sutra
> With a Richard Rodgers score;
> That's good business.[19]

This number flaunts its meta-theatricality in offering a sung discourse by Carmen on the pros and cons of introducing a pas de deux into *Robbin' Hood* by parodying Irving Berlin's 'There's No Business Like Show Business' as the basis for rationalizing the principles behind Carmen's production.

Daryl Grady then comes in and tells everyone that he's taking interviews from the cast in the Green Room. 'Kansasland' is a parody of the kind of number celebrating a state (the most popular being 'Oklahoma!'), also referencing *The Wizard of Oz* in its allusion to the idealization of a rural home: 'So let's follow the yellow brick road backwards in the wrong direction all the way to Kansasland.'[20] At the start, Bambi does well in rehearsing the re-staged square dance number; however, towards the end of the dance, a shot rings out from offstage; Bobby is wounded in the arm. Cioffi soon figures out that Carmen was actually the target of the shot. Niki comes forward with the gun, and the company immediately jumps to the conclusion that she is guilty – 'She Did It (Reprise)'. She says that she innocently found the gun backstage and hands it over, albeit after she accidentally pulls the trigger and almost kills Cioffi.

As Cioffi works on solving the case, he tells Aaron, Georgia and Bobby that Sidney had nothing on them and yet they were still working for very little money. Georgia then quotes a death threat which Cioffi hadn't read out loud. Cioffi is about to arrest her when Aaron attempts to take the blame for her, reviving their romance. In 'Thinking of Him/I Miss the Music', a reprise of 'Thinking of Him' from Act 1, Kander clearly channels his feelings about the loss of his friend Fred Ebb to motivate some additional lyrics:

> I missed the music,
> I missed my friend
> [. . .]
> I choose the music,
> I make with you.
> I love the music
> I make with you.[21]

After Aaron leaves, it is revealed that it was all an act and that Bobby had only been pretending to be Georgia's boyfriend so that she could see if she could stir anything in them. When Georgia leaves, Bobby confesses that he does love Georgia and that he would do anything for her, even commit murder. Niki laments how love makes people feel bad, but Cioffi begins flirting with her and reminisces about the first time he saw her on stage and how he thought that he could be her perfect partner. Soon, they have an elaborate fantasy sequence in which they become a couple in a musical, 'A Tough Act to Follow'. 'Choreographed as a dexterous blend of sendup and valentine by Mr [Rob] Ashford, the number expresses the sheer, lightheaded love of that silly and sublime form, the musical that is what "Curtains" is meant to be about.'[22]

Cioffi tells Niki that some cast members were using certain people to get higher ratings, and in Sidney's book, where he had coded memos for the cast's blackmails, there was a black zero next to her name. Stage manager Johnny knows the secret but won't tell the detective what it is. He is shot and killed before he can reveal any more. He tears out a page from his notebook saying, 'Drop in Planet Earth'. Cioffi takes Niki and Belling up to the theatre's catwalk high above the stage as the cast rehearses a third version of 'In the Same Boat' below. While searching for messages on the back of the drops, he announces that he's solved the mystery. Left alone, he is hit with a sandbag and is sent tumbling down. He narrowly escapes death by clutching onto a prop, which lowers him to safety. When on the ground, he exclaims that he has solved it – he knows how to best stage 'In the Same Boat'. Putting together all of the versions, the cast is able to sing a show-stopping number.

With the number completed, Cioffi tells Niki he has a plan to solve the murder before announcing over the theatre's public address system that he is engaged to Niki. He then asks the cast to re-stage the bows, when Jessica was murdered and they notice that Georgia is only being offered one bouquet, not two. Cioffi figures out that the murderer, disguised as an usher, hid a gun pellet with a poison capsule inside a bouquet and killed Jessica with it. Bobby suddenly comes on stage with a bloody head and collapses, and everyone realizes that the masked Rob Hood standing on stage is a fake.

Cioffi then announces that the zero and the 'Drop in Planet Earth' both represented a globe: *The Boston Globe*. He finally solves the case: the murderer is the *Boston Globe* critic, Daryl Grady. Grady then takes off the mask and reveals that he is in love with Niki and does not want her to move to New York, so he decided he would try and close the show. Grady then holds a knife to Niki's neck, threatening to kill her to prevent her from marrying Cioffi. He demands Cioffi's gun, but when he tries to shoot the detective, he realizes it has no bullets. He is foiled when Cioffi takes another gun from his jacket and Carmen pulls the trapdoor on Grady. Detective O'Farrell takes Grady into custody, and the cast of the production is relieved that the murder is finally solved.

After the cast returns backstage to prepare for the reopening, Cioffi privately confronts Carmen, who confesses that she killed Sidney. Carmen has been secretly acting on behalf of Bambi while pretending to be unsupportive so Bambi would have to work to get ahead rather than rely on nepotism. She has belittled Bambi in public so nobody would know how much she was actually helping her succeed. She wanted her daughter to move to Broadway, but Sidney was intending to close the show. Cioffi agrees to allow her to wait until the show's Broadway opening to turn herself in: with the right lawyer, he believes she would be acquitted of justifiable homicide. Carmen tells Cioffi that he's one of them ('Show People [Reprise]'). Belling comes on and tells them that with Bobby's injury, he may not be ready for the performance.

When the show reopens, Georgia plays Madame Marian, while Cioffi replaces Bobby as Rob Hood and 'Tough Act to Follow' has become the new finale of the show. *Curtains* finally interweaves offstage reality with onstage performance, so that the detective's new role as the hero of the stage performance represents his success both in solving the murder and fixing the show.

Notes

1. All page references are to the libretto for online rental by Concord Theatricals, https://shop.concordtheatricals.com/customer/digital-file/11484648.
2. Serendipitously, Sondheim and Goldman had begun work on *The Girls Upstairs*, the original title of *Follies*, as a thriller, more a 'Who will do it?' than a 'Whodunnit'.
3. Robert Frost's poem 'The Road Not Taken' seems unquestionably to have inspired the song 'The Road You Didn't Take' in *Follies*.
4. Clive Barnes' crucial *New York Times* (5 April 1971) and Walter Kerr's *New York Sunday Times* (11 April 1971) reviews were negative.
5. See Ted Chapin, *Everything Was Possible: The Birth of the Musical Follies,* New York: Applause, 2004), 301.
6. John Kander, Fred Ebb and Greg Lawrence, *Colored Lights,* New York: Faber and Faber, 2003, 104.
7. In Marc Eden Horowitz, *Sondheim on Music: Minor Details and Major Decisions*, Lanham: Scarecrow, 2003, 171.
8. *Colored Lights,* 103–4.
9. Lyrics transcribed from CD *70, Girls, 70*, Sony Broadway, SK 30589, 1992.
10. Between the mid-1950s and 2005, Dora Bryan was something of a British institution. Starting as a juvenile performer in pantomime during the war, Bryan played roles in numerous films (most notably a 'serious' role in *A Taste of Honey,* 1960), later onstage in numerous revues and musicals and finally on television. One of the memorable moments of her stage career was following Mary Martin as Dolly Levi at the Theatre Royal Drury Lane between 1966 and 1968.
11. In the West End, most of the fur thefts were changed to jewellery heists in anticipation of complaints by animal rights activists.
12. Lyrics quoted at https://songmeanings.com/songs/view/3530822107858936491/, accessed 2 October 2023.
13. 'Sometimes I Think I'm a Figment of Fred Ebb's Imagination', Liza Minnelli quoted by John Kander in *Colored Lights,* 112.
14. Lyrics from *Curtains*, quoted from All Lyrics at https://www.allmusicals.com/c/curtains.htm, accessed 2 October 2023.
15. Ben Brantley, *New York Times*, 23 March 2007, Section E, 1.
16. *New York Times*, as above.
17. https://www.allmusicals.com/lyrics/curtains/itsabusiness.htm, accessed 25 August, 2023.
18. https://www.allmusicals.com/lyrics/curtains/itsabusiness.htm, accessed 25 August, 2023.
19. Lyrics at https://www.allmusicals.com/c/curtains.htm, accessed 25 August, 2023.
20. Lyrics at https://www.allmusicals.com/c/curtains.htm, accessed 25 August, 2023.
21. Lyrics at https://www.allmusicals.com/c/curtains.htm, accessed 25 August, 2023.
22. *New York Times*, as above.

6   *Liza with a Z (1972)*, Barbra and the art of collaboration

Liza Minnelli has joked many times in interviews and concerts that Kander and Ebb created the persona of Liza with a Z: in an interview in *The Guardian*, she claimed, 'Fred Ebb invented me'.[1] They greatly admired her performance in *Flora the Red Menace*, which, while the show was not conceived with her in mind, may well have been influenced by her personality once she was cast. Following its short run, the pair started to create special material for her concerts and Fred Ebb subsequently 'wrote' all her US concerts and television specials until *Minnelli on Minnelli* in 1999.[2] They supplied a new opening number for *Liza's Back* in 2003. John Kander has stated: 'One of the nice things about writing for Liza is you don't have to write for Liza. She can do anything. You know that whatever you do write, she's going to deliver it exactly the way you intended it.'

Fred Ebb, who himself loved performing, had a unique connection with Minnelli, at times regarding her almost as an alter ego. He contributed to the invention of a performance persona for 'Liza with a Z' that may have ventriloquized some of his own contradictory attitudes. At once a cynic and a sentimental showbiz aficionado, he drew as well on selected elements of Minnelli's own history and personal identity, so that the lyrics he wrote especially for her combined his sophisticated, self-referential camp with her apparently innocent optimism, his unqualified love of show business mythology with her grit and determination and his rather repressed passions with her nakedly volatile emotions.

Onstage, Liza was *faux-naif*, a spontaneous sixties child with the polished veneer of a hard-bitten seventies pro. It appears that in working to construct the Liza persona, Ebb and Minnelli were resolved to forge a public persona that belied comparison with her mother – a gutsy, wacky, more overtly sexual 1970s icon. Yet the predetermined mother/daughter script of gossip columnists prevailed. While Garland had been ironically or ruefully self-deprecating onstage and in interviews, Minnelli was breathlessly enthusiastic or over-emphatic in her sincerity. In fact, Garland concealed the drive, guts and guile that enabled her to overcome illnesses, addiction and private sadness to perform with winsome charm. By comparison, Minnelli always appeared to be defiantly camping it up, her affectation of utter sincerity with a corresponding spontaneity somewhat overwhelming even when her spoken concert material was pre-scripted by Ebb.

In spite of the many differences between mother and daughter, throughout Minnelli's career, journalists have remained fixated on the following presumed parallels: Judy and Liza were both alcoholics (Judy was not; Liza is). Liza and Judy were both drug addicts (Liza has occasionally been addicted to prescription medication but also used cocaine between 1977 and 1985; Judy became addicted to sleeping tablets and 'uppers' prescribed by MGM doctors to keep her awake for as many working hours as possible, leaving her with severe insomnia. In spite of a number of attempts to cure herself of the addiction in hospitals, she was never able to do so. Minnelli has regularly publicized her spells in rehab and her membership of AA; Garland never publicly admitted her drug problem.

It would appear that after her mother's death in 1969, Liza felt free to express her own attitudes, while her performance as Sally Bowles added another layer to the public's comprehension of her persona, allowing her to be seen as 'divinely decadent' rather than as mama's girl. At very few moments in television or in newspaper and magazine interviews can one sense a level-headed intelligence that belies the 'Liza with a Z' construction, but it appears that she usually masks this to present the persona that the public has paid to see. One of Minnelli and Ebb's fundamental aims was to build a recognizable identity that explicitly erased the 'Judy's daughter' scenario the press latched on to in the early 1960s and has continued to exploit until the present day. A great number of reviews of Scorsese's *New York, New York*, for instance, purport to notice uncanny echoes of Judy's portrayal of Esther Blodgett in *A Star Is Born* (1954) in Minnelli's characterization of Francine Evans.

While Scorsese consciously paralleled the 'Happy Endings' musical montage with the famous 'Born in a Trunk' sequence in *A Star Is Born*, there is very little overlap between the characterization of former child performer Esther and usherette Francine. As Francine, Minnelli is slick and unctuous, seemingly sceptical of showbiz 'happy endings', while Garland/Esther's tremulous passion to succeed climaxes in the authentic relish with which she appears to perform 'Swanee' as the climax of her success story. While 'Born in a Trunk' teasingly references Garland's own rise to stardom, there is no echo of Minnelli's life

Figure 10. Liza Minnelli and Robert De Niro in *New York, New York*, 1977. Photo: United Artists Corporation.

in the *New York, New York* sequence. Scorsese's construct is quadruply self-reflexive, the sequence being framed as an artificial flashback montage being watched by a producer in a cinema, in turn, viewed by De Niro's character, Jimmy Doyle, in a cinema, while the real movie audience watches it in a cinema. Earl Rauch's screenplay for *New York, New York* ends with Francine and Jimmy finally walking side by side out of the cabaret venue she has just performed in, whereas Scorsese filmed it far more bleakly, without a sense of any kind of rapprochement.

A television discussion soon after her one-month concert at the Winter Garden in 1974 illustrates the incredible rapport between the performer and her favourite songwriters. Kander tells Liza, 'I have never written a song that I have really liked, that I wouldn't rather hear you sing than anybody in the whole world.'[3] In the interview, both songwriters talk about the need for good collaboration in musical theatre writing. 'In learning to create musicals', Kander asserts, 'What needs to be taught [. . .] is how to collaborate'.

Ebb:	Collaboration, exactly.
Kander:	Writing can be taught, but collaboration is . . .
Minnelli:	And this is something I understand as a singer [. . .]
Ebb:	You're the best at it.[4]

The trio agrees that one of the reasons their collaborations work well is that the inventiveness of one constantly impresses the others. Kander admits that he is always astounded by Ebb's ability to improvise in rhyme and metre, while the lyricist avers that he is always impressed by his composer's compendious knowledge of opera, even though he himself does not like the genre. Ebb claims that Minnelli regularly surprises him with the fresh details she invents in performance, while Liza asserts that she is often astonished by the ingenuity of new songs that they play for her. Interestingly Ebb suggests that Liza has changed in the last five years from someone who simply listened and absorbed their ideas to someone whose views they listen to and whose instincts they trust completely.

The interview ends with the three agreeing to explore Liza's innately feminist notion of a concert dedicated to songs that voice the inner lives of conventional women who feel ashamed of admitting their genuine desires and fantasies, a reflection of her love of French *chansons*, in particular the repertoire of Charles Aznavour. All three assert their desire to create songs that speak directly to the individual lives of audience members, reassuring one other that they are not alone in their private world. Kander teasingly suggests that he writes for ordinary people rather than to impress other songwriters and theatre experts, a principle that has guaranteed much of their work huge appeal on Broadway and internationally.

It was Barbra Streisand who approached the duo at the beginning of her career to ask if she could record 'My Coloring Book' as a single in 1962. The single did not sell well, but when the song was included alongside the duo's 'I Don't Care Much' on *The Second Barbra Streisand Album* (1963), it became enduringly popular. 'I Don't Care Much' was later proposed to be sung by a prostitute in *Cabaret* before Sam Mendes gave it to the Emcee to perform just before Cabaret. Their songs for Streisand's *Funny Lady* (1974) were highly effective, even though the film was a critical failure. No doubt, their high profile as a result of the huge success of 'Cabaret' and *Liza with a Z* prompted Streisand to employ the team to create a few new songs for the sequel to Jule Styne/Bob Merrill's *Funny Girl* (1964). The veteran critic Pauline Kael identified one of the film's major artistic problems.

> Streisand is in beautiful voice, and her singing is terrific – too terrific. It's no longer singing, it's something else – that strident overdramatization that turns a song into a big number. The audience's attention is directed away from the music and onto the star's feat in charging it with false energy. Streisand is out to knock you cold, and you get cold, all right.[5]

Evidently, providing songs for Streisand was merely a professional job for the team, whereas voicing Liza with a Z was a central strand of their artistic expression. Liza was as 'hot' as Barbra was cool. Kander has suggested that the team worked merely as 'a gun for hire' on *Funny Lady* (1974), which wasn't a happy experience:

> There was a song called 'Isn't It Better?' that we wrote for her Fanny Brice character in the movie. What Barbra was singing with that number and what they were arranging were so far away from the song that I could hardly believe it. It soon became clear that I was unhappy, and I remember the musical director, Peter Matz, trying to calm me down. Finally it boiled down to an exasperated Barbra saying, 'Well, what did you write in the first place?' So I said, 'This is what we wrote,' and I played her the song. She said, 'Oh well, that's nice'. Then she recorded the song the way we wrote it [. . .] She liked all the songs, which was practically historic, but when I went to the Coast, I found they'd meddled with them without checking with me. You feel you're working for her, not with her.'[6]

To some extent, Kander and Ebb's new numbers – many others were genuine 1930s songs shoehorned into the movie – are brilliant examples of the kind of period pastiche in which they excelled. These were commissioned to illuminate particular moments in the narrative. The film begins with Fanny singing 'How Lucky Can You Get', a belting song more reminiscent of one of Liza's 'screamers' than anything from *Funny Girl*. It is an 'I Am (Now)' song – an angry assertion of identity comparable to 'I'm the Greatest Star' from the earlier show, its bittersweet proclamation of Fanny's star status revealing the difficulties of the mature Fanny, who has already achieved stardom. 'Isn't It Better?' is a quiet love song reminiscent of 'Who Are You Now?' from the stage version of the musical, while the lyrics of 'Blind Date' written in the style of Fanny Brice's comic songs, resemble 'Exactly Like You', performed in Liza's 1974 concert. 'Blind Date' is a story song, funnier than any of the comic numbers in *Funny Girl*, yet because cinema audiences had seen Streisand do precisely this kind of schtick in the earlier movie, it appears stale.

'Let's Hear It for Me' near the close of the film is an obvious attempt to outdo 'Don't Rain on My Parade'. Whereas the Jule Styne/ Bob Merrill song is a perfect example of a show-stopper to end Act 1, the new number intended to showcase Fanny's defiance of adversity is guilty of overkill. The tugboat of the earlier film is here replaced by her driving in a silver Rolls Royce and then flying in a bright yellow biplane to surprise her husband Billy Rose. Kander and Ebb themselves noted that 'the arrangement and staging of "Let's Hear It for Me" mimicked that of "Don't Rain on My Parade" [. . .] "There was Barbra on her way somewhere", Ebb said.'[7] A potentially wonderful 'screamer', the song's placement is a mistake because its loudly optimistic egotism neither elaborates the voice developed for

Fanny in the film nor does it relate to her decision to try and get Billy Rose back, rendering the lyrics generic.

Out of context, the lyrics are highly effective, but rather than narrating the travel sequence, they wittily portray the theatrical milieu of a Broadway star:

> For this overwhelming sensation
> I could stand a standing ovation
> Give my entrance cue to the band
> Give the little lady a great big hand
> Slide the trombone
> Let it swell out
> This performance is a sell out
> And the critics and the public agree
> I'm the number one attraction to see
> So applaud it and cheer it
> Come on now let's hear it for me[8]

This lack of dramatic motivation leaves it exposed as an exaggerated imitation of its predecessor, while Fanny's discovery of Billy in bed with another woman provides bathos rather than the appropriate shock, as it directly follows the triumphant number. The coda of the film, years later in a radio studio in Hollywood where Fanny and Billy meet again, is a further example of anticlimactic dramaturgy. In viewing Kander and Ebb's work for both stars, what is most apparent is the high professional standard of their craftsmanship. Writing for Minnelli was not merely a professional chore, however; it was a process of constructing their own/Liza's voice.

Notes

1. Susie Boyt in 'Secrets and Liza', *The Guardian*, 12 November 2006, https://www.theguardian.com/music/2006/nov/12/popandrock12.
2. *Liza* (1970) w Newley et al; *Liza with a Z* (1973); *Liza* (1974); *Baryshnikov on Broadway* (1980); *Liza Live in New Orleans* (1982); *Goldie and Liza* (1982); *Liza in London* (1986); *Liza at Carnegie Hall* (1987); *Liza: Stepping Out* (1990); *Minnelli on Minnelli* (1999).
3. 'The Creative Process: Liza Minnelli, John Kander and Fred Ebb', PBS, 1974, Minnelli/https://www.youtube.com/watch?v=ENpVm1XRaog. Accessed 27 June, 2022.
4. 'The Creative Process'.
5. Pauline Kael, 'The Current Cinema', *The New Yorker*, 17 March 1975, 112–14.
6. 'Barbra, and John Kander and Fred Ebb', https://www.tapatalk.com/groups/ thebarbrastreis andforum89123/barbra-john-kander-and-fred-ebb-t22905.html.
7. From 'The Barbra Archives', https://www.barbra-archives.info/funny_lady_ overview.
8. Lyrics from https://www.azlyrics.com/lyrics/barbrastreisand/letshearitforme.html.

7 All that jazz

Chicago on stage and screen

Chicago is at one and the same time a paradigmatic instance of how collaboration can complement, even enhance, the expression of individual talent. All theatre involves acts of collaboration, but no form more so than the musical. The primary act of collaboration is that between creators/performers and audience: scholars refer to this as reception, but it seems to me that in the production of new musicals, with their very long gestation through workshops, tryouts and previews, audience involvement becomes far more significant than in the writing of plays or the composition of concert music. All producers have been determined to 'road-test' musicals before allowing Broadway critics to review them; until 1975, almost all musicals had one or more out-of-town tryouts, most commonly in Boston, Washington DC or Philadelphia. After that date, musicals were increasingly tried out in previews on Broadway, the longest-running of these being the *Spiderman* musical, which ran a few years without ever having an official press night. In this context, the audience is a primary collaborator in the creation of a musical.

The major difference between the production of a 'straight' drama and a musical is that play-texts are usually the creation of a single author, whereas the construction of a musical more closely resembles that of an industrial production (a Hollywood film is the closest equivalent). Traditionally, there are three primary functions in the writing of a musical – musical composition, book-writing and lyric-writing, with various combinations of these three being shared among two or three people, although there have rarely been musicals written by one person only.[1] In commercial theatre, the producer is often a further significant contributor, as is the director, who often requires changes to be made to the script and score right up to the opening night – and even beyond it. But musical theatre collaboration can also include material by artists who have created works in other genres or media that have provided the source material or inspiration for the new work.

As has been observed in the chapter on *Cabaret*, Harold Prince as both producer and director had as much, if not more to do with the structure of that show than the book-writer, composer and lyricist. Although it was Masteroff's idea to call it *Cabaret*, the idea for the nightclub setting came from Prince, as did so many details of the show's style and content. Although traditionally the producer has the power to make decisions on the form of the show that opens on Broadway, ultimate control will rest with the individual who has the ability to attract an audience. So in reality, no decision would have been made on *Woman of the Year* if Lauren Bacall had not sanctioned it, while in 1975 Gwen had unprecedented legal rights over *Chicago*, even though it was almost certainly Bob Fosse who exercised ultimate control over the aesthetic aspects of the show.

Gwen Verdon's role in the production was ubiquitous. Surprisingly, the idea for *Chicago* originated with its star. Ever since seeing the film *Roxie Hart* (1942)[2] starring Ginger Rogers on television in the late 1950s, Verdon had considered Roxie a role that could be tailored to suit her own unique talents as a superb dancer who could act (well) and sing (passably well). After more than a decade of trying, she finally managed in 1969 to purchase the rights from the estate of journalist Maurine Dallas Watkins to the source play of 1926. Verdon's contract guaranteed her extraordinary power: she was given,

> [A] nice piece of the profits; a strictly limited pre-Broadway run; and star billing, with her name as large and prominent as the show's title on posters and promotional materials (all subject to her approval). She also had approval of all creative elements, including but not limited to *Chicago*'s principal cast; scenic, lighting, and costume designers; their designs; her own clothes; the show's composer and compositions; orchestrator and orchestrations; librettist and libretto; dance music and dance orchestrations; and any of her understudies – whatever Lola wants.[3]

Even for a genre that demands collaboration at many stages and levels of its conception and production, *Chicago* offers a surprising example of the process. This was possible because its principal collaborators (Verdon, Fosse, Kander, Ebb and designer Tony Walton) had all worked together before – and some many times.[4] Also the rights and responsibilities of the production were intermeshed among the personnel in unusual ways: Fosse had co-credit with Fred Ebb as book writer; he was, of course, both director and choreographer, while, unusually, Ebb was writing lyrics but also co-writing the book with the director. Although *Chicago* was fairly well received by a number of critics at its premiere, any chance of real box-office success was trumped by the critical triumph of *A Chorus Line* a few weeks earlier. *A Chorus Line*'s run of 6,137 performances made it the longest-running musical in the history of Broadway. At the time, people thought that *Chicago* was too dark, too cynical and too vulgar to rival the soft-centred *A Chorus Line*. The show was in danger of closing after a few months when Gwen Verdon was hospitalized soon after the opening with a throat injury. At this point, another intervention by a performer saved the show. Liza Minnelli agreed to take over from Gwen Verdon for five weeks as Roxie; although unadvertised, word of mouth spread like wildfire and fans clamoured to buy tickets to see Minnelli, then at the height of her international celebrity as the star of Bob Fosse's film of *Cabaret*, from 8 August 1975. The resulting publicity, including a number of positive new reviews, allowed the show to run for over 936 performances – respectable if not record-breaking.

With hindsight, however, *Chicago*, not *A Chorus Line*, has turned out to be the show that was ahead of its time. The transfer to Broadway of the *Encores* production in 1996 has ended up making the show the longest-running American musical on Broadway (well over 11,000 performances) as well as the longest-running Broadway musical (6,016 performances) in the West End (1997). The extraordinary afterlife of this show illustrates the complex weave of intertextual and collaborative processes that impact the production and reception of a musical. A different sociocultural context gave new urgency to the theme and subject of *Chicago* in the

1990s. Audiences of over 35,000 across the United States, the United Kingdom, Germany, Austria, Korea, Australia, Japan, the Czech Republic, as well as cinema audiences globally, have responded positively to a show that has become an iconic expression of the postmodern moment. While almost forgotten for twenty years, its mass circulation since 1996 has made it a significant part of social/cultural discourse in the new millennium.

Fosse, Ebb and Kander

Fosse had promised to direct the show but had been extremely busy with projects that were self-evidently more rewarding – the film of *Sweet Charity* (1969), the Oscar-winning film of *Cabaret* (1972), the long-running stage musical *Pippin* (1972) and the high-profile television special, *Liza with a Z* (1973). Work on *Chicago* was something of a chore for Fosse – it was a payback he felt he owed his wife Gwen Verdon, who had endured his philandering for over a decade while remaining a loyal and extremely helpful advocate and workmate. After a fraught relationship with Roger O. Hirson, the book writer of *Pippin*, whose book he had felt obliged to revise and at times parody, he was determined to maintain legal control over the adaptation of the original stage play, so he insisted on a co-credit with lyricist Fred Ebb as the author of *Chicago*'s book. Although it was Ebb's idea to dramatize the story in the form of a vaudeville show in order to suggest the milieu of the Prohibition as well as to create the metaphor of show business as life, Fosse had become obsessed with this idea since filming *Cabaret*. In the event, he was to prove gratuitously unkind to Ebb, a rather sensitive man who often felt obliged to oppose the unrelenting cynicism with which Fosse wished to imbue the musical.

During the first week of rehearsals for the show in 1975, Fosse was rushed to the hospital suffering from severe chest pains: it was discovered that he had almost had a heart attack and required open-heart surgery. Rather than engage another director, it was decided by the producers to close rehearsals down until Fosse recuperated; it was a tribute both to the cast's admiration for Fosse and Verdon's diplomatic mothering that the whole company remained committed to the production until his return. This episode is represented in Fosse's autobiographical film masterpiece *All That Jazz* (1979); in any event, his near-death experience is said to have transformed Fosse's already cynical attitude into a view of life that was unrelentingly harsh, colouring his whole approach to *Chicago*. Others involved were shocked and did not entirely approve of Fosse's dark vision,[5] but such was his power in the industry at that time (in 1973, he had won an Oscar, a Tony and an Emmy) that no one could deny his right to put his own stamp on the material, in spite of any differences of opinion on the part of collaborators.

In ironic counterpoint to its vaudeville format, Fosse darkened every element of the show and his co-collaborators had a difficult time restraining him from over-emphasizing the moral point of the narrative: ultimately the entertainingly tongue-in-cheek quality of its satire of the judicial system would become a sardonic exposé of the American Dream as a capitalist nightmare, but the witty pastiche songs and the mocking sensuality of the dances permitted a comic expression of social critique through the nostalgic prism of popular entertainment. Although it was nominated for eleven Tonys and is now regarded as a musical theatre masterpiece, it was the only one of Fosse's shows as director-choreographer not to garner a single award, being beaten in every category by the sentimentally life-affirming *A Chorus Line* (1975).

Significantly, Fosse, while having no conventional academic or artistic education, had much admired a production of *The Resistible Rise of Arturo Ui* in New York in 1963, which, with its fable-like device of enacting the rise of Hitler as a Chicago gangster, must have offered him a model for the doubleness that layers *Chicago* with irony and self-reflexiveness. Similarly to the technique of Brecht in *Arturo Ui*, the vaudeville conceit reduces the portentous subjects of human cupidity and social corruption to a mock-vaudeville show as savagely satirical as *Dreigroschenoper* (1928) and *Arturo Ui*. A few reviewers and critics have noted the inspiration of Brecht and Weill's *Dreigroschenoper* on Fosse as well as Kander and Ebb.[6]

By appearing to reduce content to form, the musical implies what Billy Flynn the lawyer says in the lead-in to his appearance as ringmaster in a court represented as a circus ('Razzle Dazzle'): 'These trials . . . the whole world . . . show business'. The vaudeville show that constitutes a frame for the narrative is a metaphor for the fact that in an entirely mediatized society, everything is a performance. The forms of justice and government – in fact, the whole social and political order – are a pretence. The only reality beneath the lies being spoken and enacted is what we literally see onstage: the power of bodies writhing in orgiastic pleasure at ill-gotten gains. The meta-theatrical trope of life as show business is suggested in the original play *Chicago*, yet the structure of Watkins' play was a straightforward dramatization of the trial, which utilized real events she had reported in the Chicago press. Beulah Annan had been acquitted of murder with the aid of two clever lawyers (William Scott Stewart and W. W. O'Brien) who exploited her feminine charm to manipulate the jury's sympathies. The savagely comic exposure of legal corruption is present in Watkins' forensically detailed play, which includes a number of female killers, chief among them, Beulah ('the most beautiful')[7] and, to a lesser degree, cabaret singer, Belva Gaertner ('the most stylish')[8] as well as the chief supporting characters (Billy Flynn, Amos Hart, Mary Sunshine, Matron Morton, Hunyak) who appear in Kander, Ebb and Fosse's show.

The original play is transformed by Fosse and Ebb from an acerbic, journalistic account of Roxie's case that exploits Watkins' first-hand experience of legal corruption in Chicago into a meta-theatrical emblem of human greed, lust and corruption validated by American capitalism. Most of Kander and Ebb's shows deploy meta-theatre, from *Cabaret* (1966) to *The Scottsboro Boys* (2011). Even those shows that do not literally require the audience to view their narratives through the prism of a popular entertainment form – such as *The Happy Time* (1968), *Zorba* (1969), *All about Us/Over and Over* (1999) and *The Visit* (2007) – do incorporate some form of epistemological distancing device that obliges a spectator to conceive the action as self-conscious artifice. The photographs emblematizing the photographer's fake memories in *The Happy Time*, the dance marathon that frames the action of *Steel Pier* or the continual interventions by the stage manager and other characters in *All about Us/Over and Over* are self-referential reminders that we are not watching unmediated reality on the stage (as in naturalism), but seeing the action unfold through a representation of oneiric experience (dream or memory), the replay of a competitive ritual or the telling of a self-consciously fashioned tale.

What Fosse introduced to the partnership's previously elaborated artistic attitude was the sleaziness of his own adolescent experience as a dancer in risqué nightclub entertainments and burlesque shows and his now-unshakeable belief in the ideology of show business as the hellish punishment of damaged narcissists by ruthlessly egoistical exploiters. The producers objected to the moments of simulated copulation between dancers at the sides of the proscenium during 'Razzle Dazzle'; eventually, Jerry Orbach managed to persuade Fosse that it would undermine the Brechtian conception of the number, an example of an actor's intervention in the collaborative process. Kander and Ebb always explore serious and potentially dark subject matter, but most of their musicals embrace such dark material without insisting that the characters can have no possible alternative destiny.

Initially, Fosse had been close to Ebb and invited him to co-author the book as well as write the lyrics. In fact, Ebb wrote the entire book himself,[9] as Fosse more or less admitted soon after *Chicago* opened: 'I'm very good at seeing what's wrong, at fixing scenes and dialogue. As a writer, I'm more of a fixer than I am a fellow who comes up with original ideas.'[10] Much of the rewriting that occurred in Philadelphia was the subject of unpleasant rows and desperate last-minute changes. Although in many ways, the talents of Fosse, Kander and Ebb were entirely complementary, the songwriting team found work on the production extremely unpleasant.[11] After Fosse's return from the hospital, they felt manipulated and bullied by him and during the tryout period, Kander suggested to Ebb, who was bearing the brunt of Fosse's anger and suspicion, that they return home to New York.[12] 'No show is worth dying for.[13] Nonetheless, Fred Ebb believed that:

> For all the difficulty working with him, and that was enormous, I always thought it was worth it . . . [in my] opinion [he] is a bona fide genius. But at the same time, he showed discernable signs of being a detestable bully . . . [nevertheless] I made peace in my mind with all the contradictions and allowed my own love of the work on *Chicago* to supersede everything.[14]

In many respects, the dramaturgical form of *Chicago* was determined by Ebb, who stated:

> [. . .] I made it a vaudeville based on the idea that the characters are performers. Every musical moment in the show was loosely modeled on someone else. Roxie was Helen Morgan, Velma was Texas Guinan, Billy Flynn was Ted Lewis, Mama Morton was Sophie Tucker.[15]

Ebb came up with the idea of deploying the epic theatre technique of captioning each scene before it occurred, a device that was eventually replaced by the parallel one involving the announcement by the conductor of each vaudeville 'number' from his position on a round cylindrical drum on stage, which suggested the bandstand of a large dance hall lit by garish coloured neon lights. The Brechtian distancing achieved by these 'headlines' before each number prevented the audience from being wholly seduced by the sexualized dancing, being prompted instead in the words of 'Razzle Dazzle' to view it as 'just disgusting'.

Embracing Brecht/Weill's 'gestic music' aesthetic

In my opinion, Kander and Ebb's work on the score of *Chicago* represents the epitome of their craftsmanship. Perfectly evincing Brecht and Weill's notion of gestic music[16], the ironic commentary of music on lyrics and vice versa pervades the entire score. Kander explained that the pair 'always write the first song first. I don't think it's necessarily the most important song, but the opening of a show tells you something about what you're going to do.'

James Leve points out that:

> The jazzy style of the score provides a metaphor for the corruption on display as well as creates a sense of time and place. A few musical features in particular suggest the 1920s: 'blue' notes, minor mode inflections, melodies centering on the 6th scale degree, and syncopated rhythms . . . . Over half of the seventeen songs in *Chicago* – as well as most of the cut-out songs and the numbers written for the film – either are in a minor key or incorporate pitches from the blues scale or minor scale.[17]

Although the tempi vary from the syncopated up-tempo 'Looping the Loop' (Overture) to the slow and dirty burlesque vamp of 'All That Jazz', the ubiquitous minor key in the numbers provides a lugubrious contrast to the upbeat 'Jazz Age' smart talk of the lyrics, the clash functioning as a 'gestic' effect.

In complete silence at the start of the show, the band leader addresses the audience: 'Welcome. Ladies and Gentlemen, you are about to see a story of murder, greed, corruption, violence, exploitation, adultery and treachery – all those things we all hold so near and dear to our hearts. Thank you' (9).[18] The overture consists of the music from the deleted 'Looping the Loop', a frenetic dance tune at first intended as Roxie and Velma's final vaudeville number, which segues into one of Kander's famous vamps, as Velma Kelly rises on an elevator in the central drum of Tony Walton's set to sing a song ubiquitous on Broadway during the last half-century, 'All That Jazz'. Directly addressing an onstage audience of dancers and, by implication, the whole theatre audience, she sings:

> Come on, babe,
> Why don't we paint the town?
> And all that jazz.
>
> I'm gonna rouge my knees
> And roll my stockings down
> And all that jazz. (9)

The number starts the show with a panoramic evocation of the milieu of Prohibition Chicago – its pleasure-loving milieu of illicit sex and illegal liquor consumption, depicted in a metonymic stream of period details. The sheer relish Velma seems to take in her use of the 1920s idiomatic slang delights modern audiences while vividly depicting the lifestyle of the *demi-monde* via its own peculiar argot. The relentlessly repeated hook 'all that jazz' is drawn from both its literal reference to music and its continuing use as an indexical idiom, a synonym for 'etcetera'. In the 1920s, the term 'jazz' itself still had undertones of sex,[19] so 'All That Jazz' has multifarious connotations of lascivious fun:

> Start the car
> I know a whoopee spot
> Where the gin is cold
> But the piano's hot

It's just a noisy hall
Where there's a nightly brawl
And all that jazz! (9–10)

The perfect rhythmic placement of lyrics on syncopated music and the succinct wordplay with its effectively simple rhymes – 'gin is cold' against 'piano's hot'; 'noisy hall' against 'nightly brawl' – places this in the top drawer of Broadway songwriting. Not even Stephen Sondheim has bettered such idiomatically witty and concisely interrelated music and lyrics in his work. Every image supplies an effective sketch of behaviour in this particular social stratum during the 1920s, and the virtuoso number quickly becomes an ear-worm emblematic of the musical. References to dancing such as the 'Bunny Hug', a popular contemporary dance, 'Shimmy Shake', which depicted the shaking movement of an iconic dance, illustrate the obsession with modernity characteristic of the period, while garters breaking was presumably a common occurrence when women danced with a wild lack of restraint. 'Playing fast and loose' creates a pun on gambling and being sexually libertine, while 'Lucky Lindy' was the nickname of Charles Lindbergh, who famously crossed the Atlantic for the first time. 'Sheba' was a name for a voluptuous and sexually adventurous woman, derived from the apocryphal Queen of Sheba.

Fosse's choreography itself not only mimics parts of the dances referred to but also develops a vocabulary of gestures by fingers, wrists, heads, hips, shoulders and feet that mime parts of the action as well as conjuring the spasms of desire, twitches of spontaneous exhilaration and involuntary corporeal reactions that to him signify the state of being alive. More than in any other show, Fosse's musical staging of *Chicago* has become an aspect of the performance so fundamentally embedded in the musical numbers, that it appears to be an integral part of the fabric of the 'writing'. In 'All That Jazz', interpolations of action and dialogue create the impression that all the action is simply part of the vaudeville show, a highly original exploitation of the 'sung scene'. The first action is introduced after nine choruses of the number as a drunken Roxie brings home Fred Casely. When in reply to his anxious question, 'Listen, uh, your husband ain't home, is he?' Roxie shakes her head, and Velma acts as onstage narrator: 'No her husband is not at home' (11).

As the two disappear inside the centre drum under the bandsta, Velma continues the song for a few minutes until the drum doors part again to reveal Roxie sprawled out on a bed in short pyjamas as Fred takes off his trousers and climbs under the sheets with her to perform a very mechanical sex act before getting dressed to leave. Velma and the company continue to perform repeated choruses in counterpoint until Roxie interrupts as Fred puts on his jacket to leave: 'So that's final, huh Fred?' before pulling a gun from under the pillow and shooting him, '*Nobody* walks out on me'. (13) The 'girls' of the company tauntingly voice what Fred hears before Roxie's line ('Oh Fred'), echoing Velma's earlier choric intervention, a further indication of the action as part of the scene that the song amplifies with comment. The tension is disrupted by Roxie's hysterical reaction 'Oh, I gotta pee', after which Velma cynically frames the episode with a celebratory chorus of praise for *un*married life:

Oh I'm no one's wife
But oh I love my life
And all that jazz!
COMPANY.
That jazz! (13)

Life as performance: the vaudeville structure

Although the narrative is divided into a series of vaudeville numbers suggesting the fragmentation of the 'concept' musical, which was still a new format for musicals in 1975, the dramaturgy of *Chicago* is not non-linear as the story is still laid out chronologically. Extending the pattern established in 'All That Jazz', 'Funny Honey' is intercalated into the action of Scene 2, which starts as a very brief dialogue exchange between Amos and Sergeant Fogarty in the bedroom Roxie has vacated three hours previously. It is soon obvious that Roxie's husband, Amos, has agreed to confess that he killed Casely, believing him to be a burglar. The vaudeville conceit continues as Roxie enters atop an upright piano 'a la Helen Morgan' (14), being announced as a singer by the onstage band leader: 'For her first number, Miss Roxie Hart would like to sing a song of love and devotion dedicated to her dear husband Amos.' (14) The irony in this sentimental introduction is obvious in that the audience has just witnessed her act of adultery with the man she has murdered.

For the second time, the intertwining of action, dialogue and song constitutes a vaudeville turn that exhibits duplicitous behaviour as an 'act' or performance designed to manipulate public sympathy. As the scene unfolds in conjunction with the pastiche torch song, it gradually becomes apparent to the uxorious Amos that he was duped by his wife: 'Fred Casely. *How could he be a burglar? My wife knows him. He sold us our furniture!* [. . .] She lied to me. She told me he was a burglar' (15).

At the conclusion of the scene, the conductor announces cheerfully, 'And now the six merry murderesses of the Cook County jail in their rendition of the Cell Block Tango.' (17) Another virtuoso musical scene, the sequence is a complex interweaving of song, dialogue, music and dance, beginning with a series of onomatopoeic sounds and words repeated four times to conjure key moments from each of the six women's narration of her killing:

FIRST GIRL (LIZ)
Pop

SECOND GIRL (ANNIE)
Six

THIRD GIRL (JUNE)
Squish.

FOURTH GIRL (HUNYAK)
Uh Uh.

FIFTH GIRL (VELMA)
Cicero.

SIXTH GIRL (MONA)
Lipschitz. (17–18)

The music begins in a minor key, with simple and repetitive chorus lyrics:

He had it coming
He had it coming

He only had himself to blame
If you'd have been there
If you'd have seen it
I betcha you would have done the same! (19)

Set to a tango rhythm, with harmonies alternating between major and minor, the number is aggressively belted, the gestic effect created by the deliberate contradiction between its passionate tango style and the facetious insistence of the female killers that they are justified in getting away with murder: 'I didn't do it/But if I'd done it/How could you tell me that I was wrong' (22). In the next section, every killer professes her innocence in a short monologue enacted to the others' hushed counterpoint of the chorus. Every specious account provided by the women is so obviously a travesty of events that it implicates her further ('It was a murder/But not a crime', 20), as in: 'He was crazy. And he kept on screamin': 'You been screwin' the milkman.' And then he ran into my knife. He ran into my knife ten times.' (21) or Velma's disingenuous claim to have 'completely blacked out': 'I can't remember a thing. It wasn't until later when I was washing the blood off my hands, I even knew they were dead.' (22)

Even the Hungarian Hyunak has a monologue (in Hungarian!) but has obviously been coached to deny her guilt ('Uh Uh. Not guilty.' [21]) in English. The comic vulgarity of the women's slang reaches a bathetic climax with, 'The dirty bum, bum, bum, bum, bum, / The dirty bum, bum, bum, bum, bum' (22–3), after which the ritualistic repetition of seven exclamations introduced at the start of the number builds to all the women belting the final line, 'I betcha you would have done the same' (23). One of the highlights of the first act, 'The Cell Block Tango' laconically discloses the spurious defences audaciously proffered by these manifestly guilty women in their attempt to 'act' their way out of gaol. The cumulative effect of the successive revelations progressively generalises the corruption inherent in the Illinois justice system.

'When You're Good to Mama' maintains the trope of corruption by elucidating in several startling images the proverb, 'you scratch my back and I'll scratch yours'. The pastiche Sophie Tucker number[20] is introduced by the band leader thus: 'And now, Ladies and Gentlemen, the Keeper of the Keys, the Countess of the Clink, the Mistress of Murderer's Row, Matron "Mama" Morton' (24). Mama Morton is a butch lesbian, who gleefully illustrates her system of 'reciprocity' in song:

Got a a little motto
Always sees me through,
When you're good to Mama
Mama's good to you (24)

The predominantly minor key music is juxtaposed with lyrics replete with sexual innuendo, which reiterates the notion of bribery as the means of advancement in the prison:

Let's all stroke together
Like the Princeton crew,
When you're strokin' Mama
Mama's strokin' you (26)

As the musical progresses, its delineation of Chicago as a milieu comes to resemble more and more the microcosm of a world in which being virtuous is merely a form of naivety.

When in Scene 5, Roxie, now in prison, asks a somewhat hostile Velma for advice, Matron Morton and Velma give her a crash course on how to 'play' the legal system. To Roxie's admission that she has no lawyer, Velma responds, '[Y]ou are shit out of luck' (28), but the Matron reassures her, 'In this town, murder is a form of entertainment. Besides [. . .] Cook County ain't never hung a woman yet' (28), and advises Roxie to pay her $100 to telephone the lawyer Billy Flynn, who will defend her for $5,000. Scene 6 is announced by the band leader as 'a tap dance' (30), which is performed by four male dancers in the background, while Roxie figuratively dances her way around Amos, in order to persuade him to find her the $5,000 fee for Flynn. 'All I Care about Is Love' (Scene 7) heralds the entrance of Billy, who arrives in the prison to meet Roxie at Mama Morton's request.

Around him, chorus girls, who have invoked his entrance in song, ('We want Billy . . . He's our kind of a guy' [31]), perform a fan dance reminiscent of the most famous fan dancer in burlesque, Sally Rand, who between the 1920s and the 1950s performed a dance involving the twirling of ostrich-feathered fans around her body to both conceal and reveal her supposed nudity. The elaborate charade evokes not only Sally Rand and her imitators but also pays homage to popular bandleader Ted Lewis and the style of crooner Rudy Vallee. Billy welcomes the audience with catchphrases reminiscent of Lewis ('Is everybody here? Is everybody ready?'[21] [31]), as the girls flutter their fans around him to conceal every part of his body except his face, the lyrics highlighting his generous persona as a woman's best friend, while he strips down to his underwear to reveal the not very pleasant truth of his cupidity. Jerry Orbach was over 6 feet 1 inches, with a no-nonsense attitude and a face that, while not entirely unprepossessing, was in no way suggestive of movie star glamour so that the number's exposure of Billy's sleazy hypocrisy was not merely funny but subversive, his idealization as 'lover' being revealed as over-exaggerated in the plain light of the morning after.

In Scene 8, the undressed Billy is being measured for a suit while Amos apologizes for only having raised $2,000 of Billy's $5,000 fee, but Billy explains that the rest of the money can be acquired by auctioning Roxie's possessions: whether she wins her case or hangs, her celebrity as the 'hottest little jazz slayer since Velma Kelly' (35) will guarantee they fetch at least three times their current value.[22] After Amos exits, Flynn explains the strategy for ensuring her acquittal to Roxie. In attracting sympathy from the press, the lawyer will begin by interesting the sob sister Mary Sunshine ('. . . *we hear a coloratura trill*');[23] in her case. Flynn suggests, 'I don't figure we'll have any trouble with her (*Another trill*.) She'll swallow hook, line and sinker. Because it's what she wants' (35–6).

Summoned onto the bandstand by Billy, Miss Sunshine sings the preposterously sentimental paean to the inherent goodness of human nature, 'A Little Bit of Good' to an onstage audience of Roxie and Billy, her song in some ways a burlesque of the relentless optimism of Kern and Da Sylva's 'Look for the Silver Lining',[24] made famous by Ziegfield soprano Marilyn Miller:

> Yes, there's a little bit of good
> In everyone
> Though many times, it doesn't show
> [. . . . .]

Although you meet rats,
They're not complete rats,
So try to find that little bit of good. (36–7)

When all the reporters, including Mary Sunshine, enter, Roxie's assumed Southern accent cannot disguise her vulgarity ('I guess you wanna know why I shot the bastard'), so Flynn forces her to sit on his knee like a ventriloquist's dummy as the bandleader announces: 'Mr Billy Flynn sings the "Press Conference Rag" – notice how his mouth never moves – almost' (37). Billy manipulates the press with a story of the orphaned Roxie eloping from a convent with Amos, who 'stole my heart away' (39). While ventriloquizing Roxie's voice, Billy admits that she was wrong to pursue an adulterous affair with Fred Casely, but claims that he was 'like a madman' when Roxie started to walk out on him, so she killed him in self-defence:

BILLY.
He had strength and she had none

BILLY. (Roxie.)
And yet we both reached for the gun. (40)

The sob sister editorializes in song that Roxie's action was 'perfectly understandable' after which the number becomes more frenetic with multiple staccato repetitions of 'the gun'.

The celebrity criminal as vaudeville star

In the following scene played at first against a newspaper backdrop, the reporters telephone their sympathetic reports of the events narrated by Roxie/Billy: 'Roxie sobs, I'd give anything to· bring him back.' After the reporters exit, Roxie enters with a newspaper bearing the headline, 'Roxie Rocks Chicago'. She then embarks on a monologue in which she addresses the audience directly: 'Look, I'm gonna tell you the truth. Not that the truth really matters, but I'm gonna tell you anyway' (44). Roxie's speech is a hilarious exposé of her clichéd ambition to become a star dancer in vaudeville.

It was one big world full of 'No' [. . .] I gave up the vaudeville idea, because after all those years . . . well, you sort of figure opportunity just passed you by. (*Sings*) Oh but it ain't. Oh no, no, no, no, it ain't. (*Speaks*) If this Flynn guy gets me off, and with all this publicity [. . .] I could still have my own act. Now I got me a world full of 'Yes'. (*Sings*)

The name on everybody's lips
Is gonna be Roxie.' (44)

Gwen Verdon's age (50) and her husky voice with its querulous vibrato undermined the positive spin of the 'Roxie' number; she sang it rather slowly in a deadpan manner, thereby tingeing its optimism with rueful ambivalence. Just like all other scenes in *Chicago*, the monologue is a vaudeville turn as much as the succeeding musical number, a routine in which Roxie plans and rehearses her future act with a 'whole bunch of boys' (45). Her lyric, 'Who says that murder's not an art?' wittily asserts that crime becomes show business in a world dominated by cheap journalism. A typical Fosse truism is demonstrated as part of the routine as she and the boys speak cynically about the star's desperate need for the love of an audience ('And that's because none of us got enough love in our childhood [. . .] And that's show biz, kid' [46].) Roxie betrays her innate vulgarity as the song reaches its climax:

> And Sophie Tucker'll shit I know
> To see her name yet billed below.
> ALL.
> Foxy, Roxie Hart (47)

Learning from Mama Morton in Scene 10 that Roxie's huge celebrity has shattered her own chances of a vaudeville career, Velma decides to tempt her rival with the idea of reviving her old sister act. Baldly announced as 'Miss Velma Kelly in an act of desperation,' (48) she bows and immediately sings to Roxie, who is seated in her own cell. 'I Can't Do It Alone' is a virtuoso song-and-dance speciality act designed to show off Chita Rivera's triple-threat talent. In it, she illustrates the lyrics by recreating the steps she and Veronica used to perform:

> First I'd . . .
> Then she'd . . .
> Then we'd . . .
> But I can't do it alone! (49)

Roxie is not interested in working with Velma: 'I'm a big star *single*. [. . .] Nothin' personal you understand' (50).

After Velma dejectedly does a final chorus on her own, the bandleader becomes a radio broadcaster facilitating the segue to Mama's bedroom, where she is listening to 'Chicago after Midnight' on the radio while talking directly to the audience (another 'act') about the latest news of an heiress, Kitty Katz, who is then displayed on stage murdering her boyfriend Harry as well as the two women she has discovered in bed with him. As they die in slow motion, the bandleader calmly says, 'Goodnight, folks' (52). Billy appears with a straitjacketed 'Go-to-Hell Kitty' in prison in Scene 13, which reveals Roxie to be ignored by Mary Sunshine who, like other reporters, is trying to prise a story from Kitty. When both Velma and Roxie are brushed aside by Billy Flynn, each recognizes she is completely on her own: 'And now Miss Roxie Hart and Miss Velma Kelly sing a song of unrelenting determination and unmitigated ego' (54).

The brilliant conceit of 'My Own Best Friend' is to have the duet sung by the two women as a kind of round, with Velma a beat behind Roxie:

> ROXIE AND VELMA.
> One thing I know
> ROXIE.
> And I've always known
> VELMA.
> I've always known
> ROXIE.
> I am my own best friend.

VELMA.
I am my own best friend. (54)

Not only is this a clever *Verfremdungseffekt*[25] (defamiliarization device), which functions to undermine the intensity of Roxie's powerful belting, it reinforces the parallel delusions of Roxie and Velma concerning the chimera of easy celebrity:

ROXIE.
And trusting to luck
VELMA.
And trusting to luck
ROXIE.
That's only for fools
VELMA.
Only for fools. (55)

This slow torch song is an 'I Am' number, with the two women sounding as though they are in competition to outdo each other in the desperate assertion of selfishness in hard times. As Velma takes a bow at the end, Roxie faints. Calling Flynn and the reporters from her prone position, she announces, 'Oh, don't worry about me. It's just that I'm going to have a baby' (56). As the reporters crowd around her, Velma closes the act by singing sarcastically to the audience: 'And all that Jazz!' (57)

The star system: winners and losers

Before Act 2 begins, the band plays a raucous 'hot jazz' *entr'acte*, which cues the second act as a continuation of the vaudeville. After this, Velma walks onto the bandstand and greets the audience with Texas Guinan's famous line, 'Hello suckers . . .' before commenting on her rival's audacious duplicity in song while reporters snap photos of Roxie:

VELMA.
Do you believe it?
I mean, Do you believe it?

ROXIE.
My dear little baby
VELMA. (*Sung, mocking Roxie*)
My dear little baby
ROXIE.
My sweet little baby
VELMA.
My sweet little baby (60)

As Velma ends and exits, Roxie takes over with a vigorous song-and-dance, 'clapping her hands like [Eddie] Cantor' (61). While she dances, Mary Sunshine and Billy speak sympathetically, while the gullible Amos exclaims, 'Hey, everybody. I'm the father! I'm the father!' (61). Roxie continues the song, interpolated by Mama Morton's words of approval and Billy's new scheme: 'I'm gonna get Amos to divorce you. That way all the sympathy will go to you – not him' (62). At this juncture, Roxie's boys re-enter dressed *as babies [in diapers] in the form of an old vaudeville routine.'* (62)

When Amos enters again, excitedly proclaiming himself to the audience as the father, a chorus girl enters, helping him dress in a clown/hobo costume. As he *'continues speaking to the audience [. . .] his speech becomes noticeably slower and more like Bert Williams.'*[26] That's the story of my life. Nobody listens to me. [. . .] Nobody (63). In a typical vaudeville clown act, Amos characterizes himself thus:

> I tell ya
> Cellophane,
> Mr Cellophane
> Should have been my name,
> Mr Cellophane,
> 'Cos you can look right through me,
> Walk right by me
> And never know I'm there. (64)

Not only is the pastiche of Bert Williams' 'Nobody' highly effective, but Ebb's images supply an ingenious variation on the old lyric in his vaudeville incarnation of the invisible Amos as 'Mr Cellophane'. This is an extremely suggestive evocation of the way Amos is either consistently ignored or treated as a mere pawn in the elaboration of the plot. After the verse and two choruses, Amos has a scene with Billy in which he learns that the baby could not possibly be his, whereupon the lawyer plants the idea that he should divorce Roxie. Amos responds, *'I'll divorce her . . . (To audience*[. . .]) She probably won't even notice' (65). 'Mr Cellophane' begins again, and after building to a bold climax with a long note held on 'know' Amos, left alone, adds a spoken coda, 'Hope I didn't take up too much of your time' (66) as the lights dim.

Act 2 Scene 3, announced by the bandleader as 'the poker game' and accompanied by an underscore that highlights its quality as performance, commences with Velma, Mama and two other prisoners playing poker; all of them are shown to be cheating. When Billy enters to see Roxie, he informs Velma that her court appearance has been delayed so that Roxie can take her trial date. Velma, accompanied by four boys with megaphones, demonstrates in song and dance the kind of act she plans to 'perform' in court. Choreographed on and around a chair, 'When Velma Takes the Stand' deconstructs the way she might attempt to elicit sympathy from judge and jury in a kind of self-referential number that illustrates the way Fosse himself has conceived most of the routines in *Chicago* as expositions of the use of show business as a self-presentational strategy. The theatrical moment offers a kind of *mise-en-abyme*, the illusion of an infinite series of self-reflections on life as a performance that bridges the gap between the authors' creative process and the character's onstage act of conception and execution. As Velma concludes by asking the band for 'my exit music, please', singing and dancing her way off-stage with her male quartet, the exit applause is both for Velma and the performer Chita Rivera: theatre and life have become indistinguishable as performances.

This series of meta-theatrical reflections is followed by the spectacle of Billy and Roxie arguing about how to construct her trial 'performance'. The compounding of fictions in the previous episode is 'reverse engineered' by Billy, who now tells Roxie the plain truth:

ROXIE. Ya treat me like dirt, Billy Flynn. You treat me like some dumb, common criminal.
BILLY. But you *are* some dumb, common criminal! [. . .] You're a phony celebrity, kid. [. . .] In a couple of weeks, nobody'll even know who you are. That's Chicago. (71)

In Scene 4, when Hunyak is coached by her lawyer, the Matron translates with the aid of a Hungarian-English dictionary, 'She says Uncle Sam is just and fair and he wouldn't put her into jail because she is innocent. Aaron, I think she's telling the truth' (71).[27] Her trial is announced by Morton, 'And now, Ladies and Gentlemen, for your pleasure and entertainment – we proudly present . . . the one . . . the only Katalyn Hunyak and her famous Hungarian rope trick' (72). A drum roll and cymbal crash are succeeded by the bandleader's voice, 'After 47 years a Cook County precedent has been shattered. Katalyn Hunyak was hanged tonight for the brutal axe murder of her husband . . . [Her] last words were "Not Guilty"'(73).

During the next scene, Roxie is arguing with Billy about her dress for the trial ('I look like a Woolworth's lampshade.') while he tries to re-rehearse parts of their 'act'. As he ruffles his hair and rumples his shirt and suspenders to look like the heroic defence lawyer Clarence Darrow, he addresses Roxie and the audience: 'It's all a circus, kid. These trials – the whole world – all show business. But kid, you're working with a star, the biggest!' (75) 'Razzle Dazzle' has become iconic. A darkly cynical version of the show business anthems that have echoed Irving Berlin's 'There's No Business Like Show Business'[28] its slow, fairground-style tempo and its tinny orchestration mythicizes a world of tinsel and sequins to conjure a child's vision of show business magic. The metaphor casts Billy as the illusionist who conjures up a blinding smoke screen that will bamboozle the audience into believing his pretences, enabling him to disguise the ugly reality beneath the glitter:

What if your hinges all are rusting?
What if, in fact, you're just disgusting?
Razzle dazzle 'em
And they'll never catch wise. (75–6)

As the performers dance in slow motion, Billy self-reflexively indicates his philosophy of perpetual deception: 'How can they hear the truth above the roar?' (76)

One actor plays all twelve members of the jury, while even Roxie's account of the pivotal moment with Fred Casely is illustrated in the form of a Charleston (79). Roxie's conflicted situation, caught between Fred and Amos, is stylized to a point where it appears as a theatricalized comic strip cartoon with a further musical underscore that climaxes with the company singing, 'Hallelujah! Hallelujah! Hallelujah!' (81). Roxie then narrates and acts out a melodramatic performance of Fred's shooting, which culminates in, 'And they'll make you a star!' (83). At this moment Roxie, Billy and the whole company bow.

Scene 7 opens with Mama Morton listening intently to Mary Sunshine on the radio, while Velma, also sitting at the table, plays with a deck of cards. The trope of performance is suggested when the reporter stands at a microphone on the bandstand above as she describes Roxie's 'gracious' behaviour at the trial, leaving Velma outraged:

VELMA. First she steals my publicity, my lawyer, my trial date, and now, my shoes.

MATRON. Well, whaddya expect? She's a low brow. The whole world's gone low brow. Things ain't what they used to be (*Music up.*)

VELMA. They sure ain't. It's all gone. (84)

The bathos of 'Class', the next number begun by Velma, is a particularly good example of gestic music, its clash between the music's mournful lamentation and the mock-politesse of the uninhibitedly coarse lyrics providing precisely the type of 'surprise' effect that Brecht and Weill aimed for in songs:

Whatever happened to fair dealing?
And pure ethics
And nice manners?
Why is it everyone now
      Is a pain in the ass?
Whatever happened to class?

MATRON.
Class. (84)

[..............]

VELMA and MATRON.
Nobody's got no class.

MATRON.
Everybody you watch

VELMA.
's got his brains In his crotch;

MATRON.
Holy crap,

VELMA.
Holy crap,

MATRON.
What a shame!

VELMA.
What a shame!

VELMA and MATRON.
What became of class? (85–6)

When Roxie is declared not guilty, the announcement is obscured by the hubbub offstage as another woman commits murder, thereby leaving Roxie lamenting, 'and I wind up with nothin' (88), as Billy commands, 'My exit music, please' (88), then leaves to the strains of 'All I Care about Is Love'. After Roxie admits to Amos that 'there ain't no baby' (88), he also insists, 'My exit music, please . . . ' (88), but the band remains silent so he is obliged to 'shuffle off like Bert Williams' (88).

Chicago had initially ended with two up-tempo vaudeville numbers, 'Looping the Loop' and 'It', which featured Verdon playing the saxophone and Rivera the drums; in Philadelphia, Fosse decided it seemed too much like an amateur musical concert, so he asked Kander and Ebb to spend the following day coming up with an alternative number for the finale. Feeling extremely pleased, they went to their hotel room and in three hours wrote 'Nowadays', a much more plaintive, mock-nostalgic song that slowly turns into a cynical celebration of equivocation, cupidity and greed.[29]

Verdon's delivery of the number was poignant, her ambivalent delivery adding to the gestic nature of its many-layered ironies:

It's good, isn't it?
Grand, isn't it?
Great, isn't it?
Swell, isn't it?
Fun, isn't it?
Nowadays. (88–9)

The alliteration of the three 'g's' in 'good', 'great' and 'grand', prime audiences to notice the regression from 'good' to 'fun' in the first chorus, while the brevity of each perfectly demotic line is teasingly set to a lugubrious melody, as though the hedonism of the life being celebrated has already become nostalgia for a lost time.

There's men, everywhere.
Jazz, everywhere,
Booze, everywhere,
Life, everywhere,
Joy, everywhere,
Nowadays. (89)

The second chorus once again creates a trope of nostalgia *before* the event, here generalized to invoke the myths of the Prohibition era – jazz, (illicit) booze, 'joy everywhere' – while deliberately avoiding the reality of smuggling, gangster culture and violent crime that the show has increasingly exposed. The universal allusiveness of 'Life, everywhere' presents a witty equivocation: certainly, the musical shows the audience life in all its multifarious forms, but the exaltation of the quotidian includes adultery, cheating, extortion and bribery as the currency of daily existence in the picaresque milieu that is both the 1920s and today.

Inevitably, Velma (also recently acquitted) and Roxie team up for an act. Their criminal notoriety has finally allowed them to achieve the success in vaudeville they have always dreamed of. The lyrics make it abundantly clear that what they are actually celebrating is a tawdry life of adulterous hedonism.

You can like the life you're living
You can live the life you like
You can even marry Harry
But mess around with Ike
And that's

Good, isn't it? (89)

The tautological 'you can like the life you're livin' with its inversion that begins the song, forms a repeated chorus attached to the verse to resemble a continuous loop, suggesting the vacuity of the pleasure they celebrate. Sung four times, the chorus is progressively emptied of meaning to become a truism implying only that illicit pleasure is its own reward. Ebb's compressed lyrics in tandem with the equivocal nostalgia of Kander's music transform what is on the surface a simple celebration of success into a tangle of ambiguities, whose effect is to indulge Roxie and Velma's vulgar aspirations while undermining them as pointless crimes.

In opposition to the conventional sexiness of show dancing, the scanty and tacky costumes in the number and its louche choreography quite cruelly exaggerate Verdon's and Rivera's ages as dancers – 50 and 42, respectively.

Ladies and gentlemen [. . .] Not only one little lady but two! You've read about them in the papers and now here they are – a double header! Chicago's own killer dillers – those two scintillating sinners – Roxie Hart and Velma Kelly. (89)

The vulgar image of the two stars clashes with their traditionally unctuous valediction to the audience at the end, emphasizing how tawdry the reality of America is by comparison with its mythical status as the ideal democracy:

VELMA. You know a lot of people have lost faith in America.

ROXIE. And what America stands for.

VELMA. But we are the living examples of what a wonderful country this is. (*They hug and pose.*) [91]

Figure 11. Chita Rivera and Gwen Verdon at the end of 'Looping the Loop' in *Chicago*. Photo: Martha Swope, NYPL, Billy Rose Division.

Some years after the production closed, Verdon stated that Fosse repeatedly claimed *Chicago* was his response to Watergate, although critics in 1975 did not seem to pick up on this. Nevertheless, since 1996 a global audience appears to have identified its ironic world view as one that they share. In that year, *Newsday* magazine called the show's revival 'so prescient about '90s justice, the press and celebrity that it's almost eerie'.[30] Contemporary audiences and critics have finally joined in this collaborative act of theatre-making to transform *Chicago* into the longest-running American musical.

The revival (1996)

In accordance with the Encores series of revivals, Ann Reinking (Fosse's long-standing mistress and a dancer in the original production) revised the choreography in a pared-down monochrome production on a bare stage that placed the orchestra on a tiered platform behind the actors. By changing the costume design in order to both glamourize and sexualize the bodies of the actors in contemporary clothes, as well as cutting some of the scenes and shortening a few songs, Walter Bobbie's production seemed to mirror the routine eroticization of media images for postmodern spectators. This remained the case when the revival transferred to Broadway. The 1996 production became sleeker, slicker and less ugly. Where the 1975 costumes and choreography appeared in context more eccentric and clown-like, with many of the male dancers appearing somewhat ridiculous in leotards, Reinking's choreography and the new high-fashion design concept highlighted Fosse's lifelong trope of sexy bodies as a manifestation of the life force. Bobbie and Reinking's slimmed-down production was less Brechtian in its hyper-sexualized pleasuring of audiences, thereby losing some of the original production's oddball satirical bite.[31]

Fosse's original production had been a Brechtian representation of the prostitution of justice by trashy journalism – of the selling power of sex as a scandalous brand of performance. Not only the gaudy underwear of the female stars but also the fumbling striptease of Billy Flynn behind the feathered fans of the female dancers in 'All I Care about Is Love' revealed the unlovely truth beneath their lies. In Fosse's production, Jerry Orbach played Billy as something of a middle-aged pimp, his cynicism indicated by his dirty moustache and hangdog look, whereas in the revival the character has most often been played as a traditional leading man by younger and often extremely handsome actors.

In 1975, *Chicago* was metaphorically rubbing the noses of its audience in the hypocritical and corrupt nature of their country's imperialism at the very moment that Americans were trying to repress or come to terms with its implications. Writing in the *New York Times* shortly after the destruction of the World Trade Center on 9/11/2001, Anne Taylor Fleming described the habitual difficulty Americans have in coming to terms with the destruction of their heroic self-image:

> Americans have been serial innocents. Not just with Pearl Harbor . . . but also with Vietnam, Watergate [. . .] Each time Americans have said, like abashed children: we've lost our innocence. Then that innocence is somehow re-donned like an alias or costume [. . .] If the country is going to go back, then let it be done in an uplifting, myth-reinforcing way [. . .] What is lost in this posturing is any grasp of the tragic.[32]

Psychologically, 1975 was not the moment for cynicism or satire; the general cultural response to the trauma of Vietnam and the shock of Watergate took the form in most movies of tough journalistic reportage (*All the President's Men*, 1976) or mythic tragedy (*The Deer Hunter,* 1976; *Apocalypse Now*, 1979). In this context, it is perfectly understandable that *A Chorus Line* assumed pride of place on Broadway in 1975 as a meta-musical whose gesture of self-critique is recuperated by the ritual triumph of show business at its conclusion. Its backstage exposé of the emotional traumas and physical suffering that typify the struggle to become a dancer on Broadway ends by celebrating the performers' overcoming of those hardships in 'One', the show's glittering, golden paean to the star system.

Chicago, by contrast, offers no recuperative valorization of show business, only mockery. After its satirical revelation of endemic corruption in the justice system, the show ironically celebrates the only value system that appears functional in America – celebrity. The two singing-dancing murderesses effectively thank the actual audience in the theatre for applauding their crimes:

> VELMA. (*To the audience.*) Thank you. Roxie and I would like to take this opportunity to thank you. Not only for the way you treated us tonight, but . . . for your faith and your belief in our innocence [. . .]
>
> VELMA and ROXIE . . . God be with you. God walk with you always. God bless you. God bless you. [91]

This ending is an indictment of a narcissistic culture of permanent immaturity. As Cornell Professor of American History, Michael G. Kammen writes:

> Most societies repress bad memories . . . But I do think there are reasons why short memory and collective amnesia are more pronounced and more problematic in our society. Tragedy is not part of the national self-image [. . .] Without a sense of the tragic, its citizens are naked, unprotected, eternally childlike.[33]

The televized trial of O. J. Simpson in 1995 was the catalyst for a profound cultural shift in the United States. Simpson's huge celebrity as a retired football legend who became a movie star and TV personality provoked the first international trial by modern media, a trial that reinforced the Black community's rooted mistrust of the LAPD by means of its unequivocal exposure of the racism of at least one of its officers[34] while at the same time totally undermining the white population's faith in a justice system that appeared to place celebrity murderers above the law. The estimated 95 million television viewers who watched as the television broadcast of a national football match was interrupted to show O. J. Simpson attempting to evade arrest by fleeing to Mexico, were witnessing news as a new form of entertainment. According to Kent Babb,

> In the years since, the lineage of so many cultural phenomena – the 24-hour news cycle, a never-ending stream of reality television shows and many Americans' unquenchable thirst for celebrity gossip – can be traced to this [moment].[35]

It seems fortuitous that Bobbie and Reinking's concert staging for the City Centre Encores series opened in May 1996, eight months after the trial verdict was announced. The revival's popular and critical success was undoubtedly fuelled by a new scepticism concerning the uneasy relationship between celebrity and the law in the wake of the Simpson case. The transfer to Broadway of the Encores production finally enabled the show to become not only the longest-running American musical on Broadway (still playing after almost thirty years) but also the longest-running Broadway musical in the West End (1997– 2012). The revival, with choreography 'in the style of Bob Fosse', made the premier production more user-friendly in 1996. The adaptation subtly changed Fosse's gleefully sleazy exposure of the shabbiness of a justice system indistinguishable from showbiz to a more chic and sexy visual spectacle of capitalism as catwalk show. The vogue-ish costuming of sleek flesh in tight and skimpy black plastic/leather fetishized the constantly undulating bodies of its dancers, creating a visual metaphor that covertly valorized the narcissism of post-O. J. Simpson culture. The sexiness of Ann Reinking's Fosse-styled choreography imbued the sculpted bodies of the performers with an erotic charge, making the omni-sexuality of the performers' images appealing as 'entertainment'.

When the show transferred to Broadway for an open-ended run, the creative team kept the black Encores set, with its gilt proscenium-style picture frame surrounding the raised onstage band. Not only did the band watch the performers and the audience throughout, but a few characters who were not immediately involved in a scene sat at the sides on black bentwood chairs, a Brechtian strategy that highlighted what Fosse had done to stress the role of the audience as expert witnesses of a series of vaudeville acts. The production – especially in London – sped up the musical tempi so that the music sounded more cheerful and the lyrics less explicit in their deadpan parody of twenties clichés.

Audiences were still able to laugh at the pungent satire on the perversion of justice by a celebrity-obsessed culture, but whereas in 1975 the garishness of Fosse's design concept had evoked striptease, Bobbie and Reinking displayed long-legged and comparatively

Figure 12. Bebe Neuwirth and dancers in 'All That Jazz' from *Chicago.* Photo: Carol Rosegg, NYPL, Billy Rose Division.

young women in sheer black stockings bumping cheeks and grinding groins with muscular bare-chested male dancers.[36] The intertextual play of imagery drawn from show business, fashion and soft-core pornography created the spectacle of an omni-sexual orgy of gyrating bodies whose indiscriminate pleasuring of gay and straight male and female spectators seduced them into complicity with the greed and lust of the characters. In comparison, the colourful vulgarity of Tony Walton's original twenties costume designs was reminiscent of the visual grotesquerie of Fosse's film, *Cabaret*, illustrating Billy Flynn's insouciant confession in the cleverly rhymed lyric,

> What if your hinges all are rusting?
> What if, in fact, you're just disgusting?
> Razzle dazzle 'em,
> And they'll never catch wise! (75–6)

The distancing of the audience from every character's tawdry cupidity in Fosse's production represented an authentically Brechtian *Verfremdungseffekt*; by contrast, the 1996 revival used an array of distancing devices but at the same time undermined their effect by turning the audience into sexual voyeurs, in thrall to the spectacle of the performers' self-gratification. In Fosse's production, the spectators were detached observers of the characters' glorification of crime:

> Who says that murder's not an art?
> And who in case she doesn't hang,
> Could say she started with a bang?
> Foxy, Roxie Hart. (45)

In the 1996 revival, the audience became hedonistic accessories, the sexualization of their investment in the performance collapsing the satirical attack on the cult of celebrity and the endemic corruption of the justice system into a tongue-in-cheek acknowledgement of their own selfish natures.

The 2001 film

Ironically, it had taken twenty-seven years, a hugely successful Broadway revival (1996) and a number of failed attempts by Bob Fosse, Nicholas Hytner and others to finally translate the 1975 stage show to the screen. The transposition from stage to screen posed many difficulties for director/choreographer Rob Marshall and screenplay writer Bill Condon. On the face of it, the quintessentially theatrical conception of Fosse, Kander and Ebb's Brechtian meta-musical appears wholly resistant to film adaptation because the stage musical frames the entire narrative as a vaudeville performance, the audience itself being cast as the 'suckers' in a vaudeville theatre.

After twenty-five years of failed attempts to film *Chicago*, it was Rob Marshall who kick-started the project again. While meeting to discuss filming *Rent*, he asked if he could describe his concept for a film of *Chicago* and pitched this to Harvey Weinstein, who held the film rights and agreed to do it after two hours. Marshall believed 'that it needed to take place in two worlds: a real one and an imaginary one' [11]. When he interviewed Bill Condon as the movie's potential screenplay writer, the two men discovered they had similar ideas about how to transpose the show to film. Condon succinctly identified the challenge:

> How is it possible to retain the vaudeville metaphor that informed every single moment of the play, when these characters had no reason to be on a stage? . . . On stage, all of *Chicago* is a vaudeville. Not only the numbers, but also the book scenes, which are highly stylized [. . .]. Roxie is someone who's obsessed with being on the stage – being noticed . . . and when things get too unpleasant, she projects herself out of reality and re-imagines the experience as a vaudeville number. But [this] . . . meant that there had to be a real world for her to escape from.[37]

The approach permitted them to combine the conventions of the gangster film (representing 'the real world') with those of the backstage film musical.

In reconstituting its vaudeville conceit as Roxie's escapist fantasy, Marshall and Condon reveal their debt to Fosse's *Cabaret*, which adhered closely to the conventions of classic film realism by avoiding the inclusion of any musical numbers that were not diegetically motivated by being performed on a stage-within-the-film, even though that stage was the vaudeville theatre of Roxie's imagination. According to Condon, 'Roxie became more central than she was in the play. After all, we're seeing everything through her eyes. And movies demand that a central character be someone you engage with on some level' (17). In fact the film opens with a close-up of Renée Zellweger's eyes accompanied by the 'slow, sexy wail of a jazz trumpet' (53), followed by the camera zooming and panning until her right eye fills the frame and dissolves to become the flickering middle 'C' of the electric CHICAGO sign of the screen title. Having established Roxie as a viewer of the vaudeville show cued by the bandleader's 'A five-six, seven-eight', the editing creates the impression of movement across a panorama of auditorium and backstage views as an anxious stage manager tries to find the Kelly sisters.

The opening seven minutes of the film reveal the key difference between the stage musical and the film. The overture from the stage production (the 'Looping the Loop' number repurposed) provides a soundtrack to the opening 'reality' montage in and around the vaudeville house, the camera cutting to an image of a woman's long legs as she walks from a taxi towards the theatre before ripping the name 'Veronica' off a bill advertising Velma and Veronica. This sequence cannot actually be part of what Roxie sees or imagines but establishes an independent perspective on the environment of crime and its detection that grounds the vaudeville acts in a historical reality. Velma's cryptic reply to the stage manager's question about where Veronica is ('She's not herself tonight') provides a motivation for her solo performance of the Kelly sisters' intended double act. With dancers in orgiastic heaps on the floor, flailing legs and arms in all directions silhouetted in glowing blue and lilac backlighting, 'All That Jazz' resembles an homage both to Fosse's *Cabaret* – although it is more glamorous and less grotesque – and a direct echo of the sleek black-and-white aesthetic of the 1996 stage revival of *Chicago*.

Roxie is then shown standing in the auditorium, apparently transfixed by Velma's performance, and for a moment her image and voice replace Velma's as she imagines herself a vaudeville star before reality intrudes in the person of Fred Casely, who summons her to leave. The environment outside the auditorium is filmed in the sepia tones of old-fashioned photographs, stressing the contrast between the 'documentary' recording of events in the material world and Roxie's theatricalized fantasy. From here, images of Roxie and Fred having sex in her apartment are continually intercut with Velma's stage act, suggesting the aphrodisiac nature of stardom that motivates Roxie's ambition to get into vaudeville and her violent reaction when Fred shatters her illusions.[38] Just before the number ends, a detective and police officer enter the auditorium, presumably to arrest Velma. The situation is later fully clarified by Velma's admission in the 'Cell Block Tango' that she had murdered Veronica after catching her in bed with her own lover Charley, thereby explaining the bandleader's mistake in announcing the opening solo as 'two jazz babes moving as one . . . the Kelly sisters' (58).

The parallel set-up of Velma's and Roxie's crimes exemplifies the way the film attempts to connect every event witnessed on screen with a 'backstory' in order to supplement the sketchy, revue-like plot of the stage show with the realistic detail expected of Hollywood film narrative. Condon recognized that such a translation into cinematic terms might risk sentimentalizing the characters:

> The challenge in the script was to create a world that was more real, and to create in the character of Roxie somebody with some psychological complexity, somebody you might feel more for [. . .] It's very easy to soften characters in movies, where suddenly you're told [. . .] they have a pet, they're nice to their mother [. . .] you think they're nice people, and [. . .] you like them. And we didn't want to do that with Roxie, because she's not. [. . .] But at the same time you [. . .] have to fill her out. ([44)

What Condon's sharp self-reflection masks is the way in which the reification of stage types as three-dimensional cinematic characters blunts the social satire. His claim that 'what makes her so compelling is that she's a shrewd, ambitious animal' (17) reduces a critique of the society that first romanticizes and then glamourizes Roxie in order to construct a criticism of her individual behaviour, betraying a modern tendency to comprehend fictional characters as virtual human beings by explaining their behaviour in the psychoanalytic clichés of contemporary journalism. Casting younger actors than even the revival had done,[39] the film made characters plausible in the way classic Hollywood realism always does: viewers are required to understand the social context of Roxie's crime because the shooting is visually presented, character and circumstance being concretely imbricated in the flow of narrative fiction as opposed to the stage version's Brechtian enactment of the shooting with the gunshots being comically mimicked by a snare drum, a *Verfremdungseffekt* that enables spectators to judge the ethical standards of the society rather than to be engrossed in stage violence.

Although many aspects of the film are brilliantly achieved, Marshall's approach subtly transforms the original in all sorts of significant ways. The viewer's connection with Roxie's point of view not only dissolves the distance established in the theatre through the objective presentation of the stereotypical musical comedy character by generating excitement concerning the outcome of her role in the gangster story, but the fantasy vaudeville motif also promotes empathy for Roxie's aspirational desire to be a star. In the theatre, murder is presented as a vaudeville act, whereas on screen, vaudeville becomes a means of escape from the harshness of the gangster milieu. As it is, Marshall's version preserves much of the wonderful score while the sexy dancing is effectively lit and filmed, but in the endeavour to achieve box-office success, the satirical attack of the original stage production has been blunted. The most obvious sign of the desire to mute the satire is the excision of the final lines of the stage version:

VELMA. You know a lot of people have lost faith in America.

ROXIE. And what America stands for.

VELMA. But we are the living examples of what a wonderful country this is. (*They hug and pose.*) (91)

A Hollywood movie desperate to win Academy Award approval and to make a hit with the US moviegoing public would never be so bold as to bite the hand that feeds it. The huge critical and commercial successes of both *Chicago* (2002) [$306,776,732, on a budget of $45,000,000] and *Moulin Rouge* (2001) [$179,213, 414 gross against a budget of $50,000,000] are widely regarded as responsible for the resurgence of the Hollywood screen musical in the twenty-first century. Marshall's homage to Fosse is visually exciting and comically entertaining, but it mutes the comic satire of the 1996 revival and avoids the harsh world view of Fosse's 1975 production. After the surprising success of his Fellini-esque *All That Jazz*, one cannot help wondering whether Fosse's intended film of *Chicago* with Liza Minnelli and Goldie Hawn might not have resulted in a screen masterpiece that managed to retain both the abrasive vulgarity and the dazzling wit of his stage production. Nevertheless, the enormous commercial success of Marshall's film has, together with the widespread fame of Fosse's *Cabaret*, kept Kander and Ebb's work in international circulation, fuelling hundreds of stage productions of the former and major revivals of the updated version of *Chicago* around the globe.

Notes

1. Lin-Manuel Miranda, Jonathan Larson as well as British authors Noel Coward and (occasionally) Lionel Bart are famous for having written book, music and lyrics.
2. The film, with a screenplay by Nunnally Johnson, sentimentalizes the play, removes the character of Velma and turns Roxie into a dancer: William A. Wellman, *Roxie Hart*, https://www.youtube.com/ watch? v=14 Vz Oy1wXul.
3. Sam Wasson, *Fosse*, Boston and New York: Houghton Mifflin Harcourt, 2013.
4. Even before Verdon and Fosse were married they had been intimately connected on every show he had choreographed in Hollywood and on Broadway since the early 1950s; Kander and Ebb had written new songs for his film of *Cabaret* and material for *Liza with a Z*, which Ebb had scripted; Tony Walton had recently designed the sets for Fosse's production of *Pippin*.
5. Fred Ebb called him The Prince of Darkness.
6. See Scott Miller, http://www.newlinetheatre.com/chicagochapter.htmlfile:/kanderebb/, accessed 12 April 2023; The Drama Teacher, https://thedramateacher.com/chicago-bertolt-brecht/, accessed 12 April, 2023; https://www.brainyquote.com/authors/ann-reinking-quotes.
7. https://scandalsandsweets.com/belva-gaertner-the-real-velma-kelly-2, accessed 13 April 2023.
8. https://scandalsandsweets.com/belva-gaertner-the-real-velma-kelly-2, accessed 13 April 2023..

9. Didier C. Deutsch, 'A Look Back', liner notes for *Chicago: A Musical Vaudeville*, CD reissue, Arista, 07822-18952-2, 1996.

10. Richard Philp, 'Bob Fosse's *Chicago*: Roxie's Razzle Dazzle and All That Jazz', *Dance Magazine*, November 1975, 40, quoted in Kevin Winkler, *Big Deal*, New York: Oxford University Press, 2018, 194.

11. Fosse's view of the production process is represented in his film musical, *All That Jazz* (1978).

12. John Kander in *Colored Lights*, New York: Faber and Faber, 2003, 126.

13. *Colored Lights*, 12.

14. Fred Ebb in *Colored Lights*, 126, 127.

15. Fred Ebb in *Colored Lights*, 127.

16. See Scott Miller, http://www.newlinetheatre.com/chicagochapter.htmlfile:/kanderebb/, accessed 12 April 2023; Kevin Clarke, http://operetta-research-center.org/berliner-ensemble dreigroschenoper/, accessed 13 April 2023; Stephen Gallagher, 'Goodbye Berlin, Hello Broadway', https://www.guidetomusicaltheatre.com/shows_c/cabaret_berlin.htm, accessed 14 April 2023.

17. James Leve, *Kander and Ebb*, New Haven: Yale University Press, 2009, 89.

18. Quotations from the stage version of the musical refer to Ebb, Fosse, Kander, *Chicago*, New York: Samuel French, 1976.

19. 'Jass' or jazz was originally slang for copulation. See Etymology of Jazz at https://www.apassion4jazz.net/etymology.html, accessed 20 October 2023.

20. The song is modeled on 'You Gotta See Mama Ev'ry Night' by Con Conrad and Billy Rose, originally recorded in 1923 by Sophie Tucker.

21. Ted Lewis' actual catchphrase was 'Is everybody happy?'

22. This episode was cut from the 1996 revival.

23. Watkins probably based Mary Sunshine in her play on Ione Quinby, a rival journalist and well-known Chicago sob sister. In Watkins' play Mary Sunshine plays a much larger role in the action. There is also a reporter called Jake, who is in cahoots with Billy Flynn.

24. The song was made popular when Marilyn Miller sang it in *Sally* (1920).

25. The *V-effect* as Brecht called it is usually translated into English as alienation effect, but is perhaps more accurately a distancing or defamiliarization effect.

26. Between the 1890s and 1922, Bert Williams was the biggest African American star in vaudeville, with a signature tragicomic song (Nobody') in 'Jim Crow' blackface, his lugubrious performance evoking the sadness of a Black clown, who is totally ignored by white people; in the 20th Century he became a headliner of the Ziegfeld Follies, the highest-paid Black performer in the USA.

27. This scene between Hunyak and her lawyer was also cut for the 1996 revival.

28. 'Another Openin', Another Show', 'Comedy Tonight', 'That's Entertainment' and 'This is the Greatest Show' are the best known.

29. In order to convince Fosse and the producers that they had put a great deal of effort into producing the number, they pretended to work until late the following afternoon before handing it to the director. Fosse loved the song and claimed that it was an exemplification of the duo's 'genius'.

30. *Newsday* review of *Chicago*, 1996, https://www.newsday.com/entertainment/theater/chicago. Accessed 21 April, 2019.

31. In my opinion, the dramaturgy and lyrics of *Chicago* are sufficiently ironic to undercut the erotic appeal of the bodies in motion.

32. 'Aftermath: Innocence Lost; A Tragedy for an Optimistic Land', *New York Times*, 23 September 2001.

33. Michael Kammen, *Mystic Chords of Memory*, New York: Vintage, 1993.

34. The judge in the O J Simpson trial ruled that Mark Fuhrmann had committed perjury in order to frame Simpson and Fuhrmann's repeated use of the N-word in a series of interviews with a journalist led to Simpson's eventual acquittal.

35. Kent Babb, *The Washington Post*, 9 June, 2014, accessed 30 April 2016

36. At fifty, Reinking was only four years younger than Gwen Verdon, but her height, her incredibly long legs and very slim figure made her appear much younger than Verdon onstage; Bebe Neuwirth was 38 as compared to Rivera (42) but in London, Ruthie Henshall as Roxie was 31, while Ute Lemper was 41.

37. Peter Kobel and Timothy Shaner, *Chicago, the Movie and Lyrics*, New York: Newmarket Press, 2002, 16.

38. This is another crib from Fosse's *Cabaret*, directly imitating the intercutting of stage performance with offstage reality in 'Maybe This Time'.

39. Renée Zellweger and Katherine Zeta-Jones were both 33 when the film was released.

8   A star reborn

The Act (1977) as vehicle for Minnelli

The Act (1977) and *Woman of the Year* (1982) were star vehicles. Both manifest the high level of professional craftsmanship the team had attained by the time of their writing. Yet *The Act* offered them the chance to play the type of meta-theatrical games that had become a dramaturgical trademark, whereas the latter show was commissioned as a conventional book musical that would at one and the same time show off Lauren Bacall's charisma and mask her vocal and dance limitations, denying the songwriters much opportunity to experiment. In spite of the fact that *Woman of the Year* won Tony Awards for Best Actress in a Musical, Best Score and Best Musical, it was the work the pair was least proud of:

> EBB: I think *Woman of the Year* was a mistake. We did that show because it was Lauren Bacall and it was a good title. But I didn't have any real conviction or passion about it. We won Tonys but mostly because there was nothing else much up against us. [. . .]
> KANDER: [T]here are shows that we have done which I think were really good but received no attention at all – I mean major flops – and then suddenly we get a Tony Award for a show that is just professional.[1]

In the event, it is paradoxical that it was only the star power of Liza Minnelli in 1977 that made *The Act* commercially profitable; it earned her a Tony but was so dependent on her performance that it closed as soon as her contract ended (fifteen weeks on tour and 234 Broadway performances). By contrast, *The Woman of the Year* ran for two years on Broadway, with Ms Bacall being succeeded first by Raquel Welch and then by Debbie Reynolds, while in 1983, Bacall toured the show nationally in a slightly revised version.

Not originally intended as a vehicle for Minnelli, *The Act* was conceived for Shirley MacLaine, whose mid-career stage comeback in a song-and-dance concert (*The Gypsy in My Soul*, 1976) was written by Ebb; others mentioned for the leading role were Ann-Margret, Debbie Reynolds and Doris Day. According to Fred Ebb, it was Marvin Hamlisch who first approached him with the idea for a show about a movie star making a comeback by putting together a Las Vegas nightclub act, to be interspersed with a stream-of-memories prompted by her estranged husband's surprise attendance on her first night. Rather than a typical backstage musical that might conventionally illustrate the struggle of a movie star to re-establish a failing career, *In Person*, as it was first known, was to begin onstage at the opening of the act itself while its narrative would consist of backstories told as a series of flashbacks between onstage numbers, which culminate in the insecure Michelle (Mike)

Craig's assertion of her self-reliance as an independent woman and newly empowered stage star.

In order to emphasize the stylistic differences of the various songs Mike has selected for her act, Hamlisch thought it would be effective for him to compose half of the music while Kander contributed the rest, with Ebb supplying all the lyrics. Ebb was more taken with Hamlisch's concept than Kander, but 'turned him down [. . .] as an act of loyalty' to his long-standing writing partner[2] so Hamlisch bowed out. Stanley Donen had initially been asked to write the book, but George Furth[3] became the writer when Kander and Ebb took it forward, at which point Minnelli offered to play the lead. In order to accommodate her, Michelle's age was lowered to 32, while at her insistence, Martin Scorsese was brought in to direct. He was at the time completing post-production work on *New York, New York* (1977) as well as editing *The Last Waltz* (1978), but had no experience as a stage director, with the result that during the musical's pre-Broadway tryout, the touring production (Chicago, San Francisco, Los Angeles) proved a saga of disagreements, rewrites and replacements (actors and costume designer). Scorsese had the idea that the show should continue the narrative of *New York, New York* – itself a *homage* to Judy Garland's *A Star Is Born* (1954) – but his inability to effectively deploy theatrical conventions undermined his attempts to shape the book. With the exception of Minnelli's performance, *Shine It On* as it was then titled, received poor reviews. Nevertheless, the entire tour was sold out, so it was mutually agreed that Gower Champion should be invited to re-stage the show, set to open in New York on 30 October 1977.

Seven days before the opening, *New York Times* journalist Cliff Jahr reported on how Champion had revised the musical in less than eight weeks:

> Mr. Champion caught the Saturday matinee and evening shows Sept. 24, rehearsed the company on Sunday, and inserted several changes Monday night. Gone suddenly were 2 minutes worth of the overture, the abortion scene, a scene where Michelle Craig is slapped around by her lover until she subdues him with karate, and a pair of scenes in which she twice loses the Academy Award. At the same performance Mr. Champion put in a new opening, a tag on the second act show-stopper 'City Lights', and a number of minor adjustments to lighten and simplify. Though he has taken full charge and continues the process, his name will not appear in the credits.[4]

Gower Champion had done what he was famous for – musical staging. In streamlining the book so that nothing interfered with the seamless flow of performance from action to a musical number, he certainly clarified the narrative and tightened the pace of the entertainment, though he clearly had no time to do more than produce a concise but conventional show business narrative, expediting scene changes with the use of a gauze scrim that allowed flashbacks to occur simultaneously with the performance of Mike's act – and vice versa. Advice to potential directors on the setting located at the end of the published play script (63) is clearly derived from Champion's staging principles:

> A unit set with a 'city' drop was used in the original New York production. Scenes are created by the use of a scrim, lighting, setting boxes and props. Champion's staging offered a theatrical version of cinematic editing: 'Each scene should be a smooth, almost instant transition. There should be no breaks in the action.' (63)

In some respects, this deployment of filmic conventions serves to heighten the difference between the flashbacks to Hollywood (memory) and the staging conventions of a Las Vegas nightclub where the act is unfolding in the present. One element of the production retained by Champion exactly as devised was the choreography: 'I didn't change one single step of Ron Lewis' choreography. Lewis is brilliant.'[5]

Furth himself had initially delivered a script with far greater narrative detail and emotional depth. According to James Leve, he had 'originally included intricate backstories, but under Scorsese's direction they were cut in favor of more nightclub scenes.' The set designer Tony Walton believed 'Scorsese eliminated the most interesting parts of Furth's script [. . .] and by the time Champion took over it was too late to salvage the cut scenes.'[6] Perhaps inevitably, in the rush to iron out the problems in time for a Broadway premiere, the character of Mike (Michelle Craig) inevitably began to overlap with 'Liza with a Z', the image that Fred Ebb had worked so closely with Minnelli to perfect, even though Mike's character biography had little in common with the star's own career trajectory. When attempting a rewrite of *The Act* in 1987, George Furth wrote to Ebb that he regretted having 'left Liza naked'.[7]

In the event, the Broadway production was a public triumph for Minnelli and a (private) vindication of Champion's skill as a 'showbiz' stager. The *New York Times* critic Richard Eder wrote:

> "The Act" is precisely what its name implies: It is an act, and a splendid one. On the other hand, it is a little less than its pretensions imply. Theatrical though it is as a performance, it is indifferent musical theater. It displays the breathtaking presence of Liza Minnelli, and her command of a force that is the emotional equivalent of what a good coloratura achieves in top form – although in her case it is a mixture of singing and other things. It has a small but brilliant chorus line; and its costuming, lighting and all-over cutting edge are a kind of vaunting of the talent available to American show business.[8]

American show business talent is precisely what Kander, Ebb, Minnelli, Champion and Lewis represented to the reviewers and public at this moment:

> "The Act" is Liza Minnelli. Rarely has a vehicle been so tailor-made for a star. [. . .] "The Act" is a swell show which does exactly what it sets out to do, show off the striking, vital talents of Liza, unveil some grand songs from Kander and Ebb and reveal, through seven immensely individual dancers, some dazzling choreography by Ron Lewis.

While he was not actually responsible for the way the book had been cut and reshaped on tour, George Furth came in for most of the criticism:

> What is mainly lacking in "The Act" is a book. George Furth's story about the professional and personal troubles and triumphs of an insecure movie star who becomes a nightclub performer [. . .] has little development or characterization of its own; and except for a stray line or two, only the most trite and synthetic dialogue. [. . .] "The Act" is a first-rate cabaret show expanded for theater, rather than theater itself.[9]

The concept of a series of stand-alone numbers required Kander and Ebb to construct generic songs for a nightclub performer. These were of a kind they had seldom written for musicals, yet had regularly contributed to their favourite star's concerts. This type of song made no reference to any particular dramatic context in a musical, but each was a speciality number that allowed Liza to exploit her talent as a singing actress in order to depict a character or story in less than five minutes. Obviously, this scheme ran the risk of reducing the book to a sketchy stream of memories that was being replayed in Mike's mind while she performed her act. Gower Champion abandoned this conceit in order to tie the songs to the dramaturgical context of the memories through which the narrative unfolds, placing each number in juxtaposition with the appropriate dialogue and action and, in some instances, creating 'musical scenes' by interweaving dialogue and song. But the hasty dramaturgical repairs could not entirely resolve what remained a superficial book. 'Good Thing Going', deleted before the tryout run, was something of a dramatic tour-de-force, an ironic love song dramatizing the gradual break-up of Mike and Dan's marriage.[10] Retrospectively, this deletion seems a pity, as the song might have introduced a more nuanced texture to the relationship between Mike and Dan that became somewhat generic in the shortened dialogue scenes, while the addition of the overtly cynical Las Vegas-style 'Hot Enough for You' to illustrate the seamier aspects of the typical Vegas revue may have been a mistake.

During the pre-Broadway tryout tour, six new songs were written to replace six others. The new songs were the Shaker hymn, 'Turning'; 'Hollywood, California'; 'The Money Tree'; 'City Lights'; 'There When I Need Him'; and 'Hot Enough for You'. Those deleted were 'Good Thing Going'; 'The Princess'; 'Love Songs'; 'Please, Sir'; 'The Only Game in Town'; and 'Walking Papers'. The last song was later reinstated, while the satirical 'Hollywood, California' was cut after the opening night.[11] 'Please Sir' is another one-act drama in song that would have been perfect for Minnelli. A story number about a poor child who has been brought up to 'mind her manners' by her drunken mother so that she can 'be a lady' who doesn't need to be 'slavin' in a slum till you're dead', transforms into the memories of a girl whose polite, obliging personality stops her from protesting when she is groomed and sexually molested by her uncle ('Yes, sir, please sir') leading her eventually to marry and control a rich man while regularly indulging in submissive sex with strangers at the docks. In my view, this number is an improvement on 'Hot Enough' so one can only surmise that it was cut because it held up Mike's story by drawing too much attention to a traumatic experience that was not in fact her own. Another deleted number, 'The Only Game in Town', is a quiet ballad that would have helped delineate the arc of Mike's development in the second act:

> Seeing through your dancing days
> The hustle's not the waltz;
> Saying you were wrong
> Without a single shame,
> That's the only game in town,
>
> So let all the cynics
> Dash off to their clinics
> [.......]
> And hearing them rail at
> The love that they fail at,
> [........]
> Just leave them alone.
> Turn them to stone.
> Let them stick to their own.[12]

A gentle and melancholy ballad, its integration of music and lyrics is, as often with Kander and Ebb, unobtrusively perfect, allowing Mike to express the wisdom she is acquiring through experience. It may well be that Champion decided that the number was too introspective to be part of a nightclub act, but again, it might have added subtlety and depth to Mike's process of self-discovery. The song does reinforce the quasi-feminist trope by which Michelle Craig demonstrates her ability to move from emotional dependency on men to total independence in her life and her career. Interestingly, this is almost exactly the opposite of Minnelli's own career trajectory, as she brokered her success on her own from the age of sixteen, trying as far as possible to resist her mother's influence, even refusing a number of times Garland's invitation to share the bill with her at the Palladium in 1964 (she was eventually tricked into it) and only garnering regular advice from Kander and more particularly Ebb, who became a friend and mentor after *Flora, the Red Menace*. There is no evidence that they ever made career decisions for her; she came to rely on them only to shape the musical material of her concerts and musicals.

Another deleted number that would have added more dramatic contours to both narrative and character was Mike's 'I'm Not in Love Today':

> I'm not in love today
> I don't need any cheering up
> [.................]
> No, not in love,
> No no, that's wrong
> I am in love;
> I'm not in love, I –
> Well, either way, it's a helluva day.[13]

While he may not have had time to restore Furth's original scenes or add much subtlety or depth to characters and situations, Gower Champion did render the overall narrative coherent and the staging fluent. Placing the band on two moving platforms that met in the middle of the stage to back Mike in her solo songs, he ensured they could slide out smoothly into each wing to effect easy transitions from the nightclub stage to her dressing room and other locations.

Champion's contribution was judged by Martin Gottfried to be 'polish as sleek and cool as chromium';[14] the restructuring may have been a reason why Richard Coe could proffer a less negative evaluation of Furth's work than other critics:

> Michelle Craig goes into her specialty numbers while remembering career and marital incidents which led to her present uncertain status. Her older director-husband, a footless [*sic*] lover and a gay composer flow in and out of her past and present. By the end of her act, Mike Craig will have her audience and life in control. The story by Furth [. . .] is hardly new but the trappings are.[15]

Most critics believed the success of the show was solely dependent on Minnelli's performance. The *Variety* reviewer stated, 'Minnelli gives an almost unbelievably dynamic performance. A personal triumph. [. . .] It's hard to conceive of *The Act* without her.'[16] Clive Barnes urged readers, 'See her and stock up an experience to tell your grandchildren about.'[17]

Nevertheless, there were distinct possibilities in the subject for a biographical narrative that might address various feminist issues, such as a woman's attempt to assert her own agency by breaking out of her straitjacketed image as constructed by men. Or a story of Mike's inability to have children, reinforced by bad romantic choices, which culminates in a decision to choose her career over marriage and a family, thereby signalling that she was forced to behave like a man in a male-dominated world. Or a *Gypsy*-like tale of a daughter whose debut in her domineering mother's show ultimately eclipses her mother's success, permitting her to stand on her own as an independent woman and performer. In *The Act*, Mike's biography most closely resembles the first possibility, yet hints of the alternative versions are detectable in the narrative that finally emerged.

What renders the book unremarkable, however, is its refusal to take an unequivocally feminist stance on the questions about gender it inevitably poses. Even though the second possibility quite closely follows the trajectory of Minnelli's own life and the third hints at her struggle to step out of the shadow of her own mother's legend, Champion and the authors appeared loath to create a persona that did not permit Mike/Liza, after some struggles, to have it all – career, children and a loving marriage. Emerging most clearly from the structure engineered by Champion are the epistemological games that typify Kander and Ebb's musicals. These were given free rein, transitions from present to past and vice versa allowed to occur almost as slickly as cinematic dissolves from one image to another, emphasizing the processes of learning and growing that produce the immediate present of Michelle's act.

The opening of the musical deliberately wrong-foots the audience by introducing Lenny Kanter after the overture as a rather conventional stand-up comic, who does two minutes of rather lame *schtik* before Mike is revealed backstage. The audience watch Lenny mime the remainder of his routine while she anxiously attempts to steady herself. 'Shine It On' introduces Michelle Craig in her nightclub debut at the Hotel Miramar in Las Vegas. She is so nervous she has mislaid one of her shoes. Finding it as the curtain rises, she enters carrying the shoe as though it were a microphone, to which she sings the first few bars until a dancer comes on stage with her microphone and helps her put on the shoe as she continues the song backed by the chorus. 'Shine It On' is a somewhat generic nightclub opener, a more facile version of other songs Kander and Ebb have written about putting on a happy face, for instance, 'Sing Happy' and 'Yes'.

The up-tempo number has some funny lyrics, but there is no fresh approach to the topic, nor, presumably, was there intended to be. The trite opening verse is replete with the kind of jargon a 1970s nightclub number might exhibit:

'Shine It On' means when depression comes upon you,
Does a downer number on you;
Take no notice,
Shine it on![18] (11)

Although concise and rhythmically insistent in its repetition of the 'Shine It On' hook, many of the chorus sections are arch and formulaic. The excessive use of rhyme, while slick, appears contrived:

Morning news
Brings the blues;
Shine it on.

Just dismiss it,
Boo and hiss it,
Bracket and parenthesis it;

Figure 13. Liza Minnelli and chorus performing 'City Lights' in *The Act*. Photo: Martha Swope, NYPL, Billy Rose Division.

That's the way you
Shine it on. (12)

Nevertheless, the number enables Minnelli to present Mike overcoming her paralyzing nerves in order to perform effectively, as well as allowing an easy segue to the confession that her ex-husband has surprised her by turning up to the opening night, '[T]his, tonight, may not be as much an act as it may be an anxiety attack' (13). Admitting her feelings to the audience in a supposedly improvised conversation is a typical ploy that Ebb and Minnelli had previously exploited to get concert audiences on her side and perhaps steady her own nerves. It works well at this moment under Mike's exceptional circumstances. However, most of the remaining numbers are of a very different kind. Unlike most singers of her mother's generation, who sang swing or jazz standards, Minnelli in her concerts chiefly performed songs that told stories. Under the influence of her friend, the French *chansonnier* Charles Aznavour, she later took the art of the 'storytelling' song to a very high level. Yet as early as 1973, such stories in song were already being devised for Minnelli by her in-house writing team.

The most obvious example is, of course, 'Liza with a Z', in which the Liza persona is constructed as someone warm and open, who buttonholes her audiences to tell them 'confidentially' about her annoyance at the continual mispronunciation of her name. The other best-known number of this type is 'Ring Them Bells', in which an unmarried New Yorker named 'Shirley Devore [. . .] travelled round the world to meet the guy next door'.[19] Once the pair knew that *The Act* required nightclub songs for Liza with a Z, they could simply write for the vocal range and style of the personality they had I helped to invent. The first number in the show that told a story is 'Bobo's'. The song is in fact, motivated by

Mike's life, but is written by her friend Nat with little genuine knowledge of it. In Scene 3, she tells Nat in passing:

> Look, back in Omaha I grew up in my mother's saloon, 'Bobo's' where the losers ruled. And the drunks drank until they had enough to die. The first time I sang there I was laughed off the stage. [. . .] 'Bobo's.' My mother's name. And don't you use it in a song. Don't you dare. Every time I tell you something personal about me, you turn it into some song. (21)

Needless to say, 'Bobo's' turns up in Mike's stage act in Act 1, Scene 4. The genesis of the song was complex. Originally intended as a 'happy little song' about a bar, Fred Ebb later told a television audience of an occasion when the pair were working on the number and received a phone call informing them that a friend had recently committed suicide.[20] After reflecting and reminiscing for a few hours, they continued, but the news changed the mood of 'Bobo's' as they invested their real memories and feelings in it, so it transmuted into an elliptical piece concerning failure and desperation – more a vivid sketch of a locale and situation than a complete story.

The scene that precedes the number is the set for Mike's third movie; she feels so insecure that Dan, as the producer, is obliged to reassure her not only that she is good but also to propose marriage to her before she is ready to do a take. The song has nothing to do with the scene Mike has been recalling, but the lyric depicts the location as follows:

> Outside uptown Omaha
> There's a small piano bar
> Where a neon sign keeps flashing Bobo's
> [..........................]
> Bobo's not around today
> But still it's Bobo's anyway;
> He left that stipulation in his will.
> And when you look around, it's clear
> All us steadies love it here
> At Bobo's bar and grill. (23)

Mike includes herself as one of the regulars before going on to give snapshots of the 'steadies' around the bar – Mr Miller, 'shooting pool with Bobby', Peg and Mabel 'Waiting for a sucker to buy a round', Mr Johnson 'from the filling station/Pouring out his troubles/To Ruth McGore' and Deputy McQuire who 'talks about the fire/[. . .] At the package store' (24).

These thumbnail sketches merely indicate the conversations taking place around the unfashionable venue, but the country and Western style with its syncopated rhythms evoking a carefree mood makes an ironic contrast as the lyrics change to express the pain beneath the friendly chat around the bar. The neon sign that keeps flashing now assumes a grotesque effect, its celebratory mode in stark contrast to the experience of the venue's regulars:

> Bobo's
> So noisy that a heart could break and,
> Bet a buck, you'd never hear it
> [.....................]

Bobo's
'I lost my job,' 'The kid is sick', and Jesus, God, how can I take it?'
Bobo's
The laughter's much too loud to let you
Think of how you'll never make it
You'll never make it
You'll never make it. (25)

The music suggests despair as the short notes are replaced by sustained ones, and the tempo slows until the song grinds to a halt when Mike/Minnelli screams the repeated line for a third time. After this terrible moment of truth ruptures the sociable veneer, the song returns to its jolly, jingling rhythm as Bessie continues to play her Yamaha, and the 'losers' become a memory while the singer moves ahead in her own career. In some respects, the number suggests a backstory for Mike at her mother's bar. Even though the details of the scenario have been invented by Nat, the song offers a strong contrast to Mike's insecurity in the previous scene. By revealing the pain of failure in a show dedicated to celebrating success, 'Bobo's' offered an opportunity for Minnelli to demonstrate her virtuosity as a singing actress.

Two such 'story' numbers in *The Act* that do not reflect Mike's life in any way are 'Arthur in the Afternoon' in Act 1 and 'City Lights' which opens Act 2 – both show-stoppers, which Minnelli subsequently performed in numerous concert tours between 1978 and 2002. The former is shoehorned into Mike's act (Scene 6) as *faux*-autobiography with an almost entirely arbitrary dramaturgical motivation:

There was a lovely period in my life when I was ceaselessly pregnant. I had four children. One at a time. Oh, once in a while, I'd do a little film but – musicals became rare and frankly other parts got rare too. So most of that time I was plain old Mama . . . carpooling, perpetual children's birthday parties, or sitting with other housewives drinking coffee and talking recipes. That's where I watched one woman change – well not since Jekyll and Hyde. She had found a secret recipe indeed which she shared with me. And it wasn't guacamole. Now she made me swear I would never tell. So I have to ask you the same. But here's exactly how she dropped it on me. (27)

Although the personal details about Mike's children and the scarcity of film roles do not in any way reflect Minnelli's life at this time, they do articulate certain anxieties she may have felt about her Hollywood career after the two major movies she had made since *Cabaret* had been box-office flops, and the fate of *New York New York* hung in the balance. In fact, these anxieties anticipate the end of her career as a major Hollywood star after the commercial success of *Arthur* (1981). Not only might Mike's pseudo-confidential address to the audience have been taken directly by Furth and Ebb from one of Minnelli's stage concerts, but the pretence of spontaneously sharing a secret with her audience was to become a standard ploy in Minnelli's introduction of story numbers: '*MIKE [. . .] comes back D.C [Downstage Centre] "in character" and begins [. . .]*'. This stage direction mirrors the way the actress would start a 'story' number by assuming a role in view of the audience, in this case, a rather 'ditzy' lady:

Everyone's noticed the change in me
The startling, heartening change in me

No longer depressed
I'm feeling my best
And I'm totally in control. (27)

While Kander supplies music that enacts the narrative arc of travelling/progression from a depressed state to a joyous one in a dance rhythm that helps the choreographer Ron Lewis express the character's physical and mental well-being by kinetic means, Ebb invents lyrics to portray the wacky woman as attracted by the fashionable health fads of the 1970s, including dieting, drugs, 'primal scream' therapy, transcendental meditation, psychotherapy ('this kid's id's in tune'), Est and scientology:

> And my secret isn't diets, drugs or pills
> I've simply found a new routine
> To banish all my ills.
> I have my coffee in the morning,
> My brandy in the evening
> And . . .
> (MIKE flips the top of the set box to find a MALE DANCER 'ARTHUR'.
> They dance and MIKE sings.)
> . . . Arthur in the afternoon. (27–8)

Arthur was played by the short Hawaiian-born dancer Roger Minami, who popped out of the box to do a sexy and energetic dance with Mike, which pantomimed her descriptions of their afternoons together:

> [...........................]
> Hello Arthur
> Got a little headache
> All my nerves are worn a little thin
> I was wondering
> If you had an opening
> And if you do well, could you squeeze me in? (29)

The orchestration mimics the sound of a person dialling as she books an appointment for an afternoon of 'sex' therapy. A woman paying for sex may have been a *risqué* topic for a Broadway audience in 1977, but it worked perfectly to provide an unexpected *frisson* in an era in which feminism and gay liberation had challenged a number of sexual taboos in the process of liberating people from repression. The number is a naughty and entertaining celebration of sex as a cure for psychological dysfunction:

> Go activate Arthur
> That animal Arthur
> Get bitten by Arthur in the afternoon. (31)

The lyrics include some clever rhymes ('psyche's steaming' with 'primal screaming'; 'grey days' with 'matinee days'; 'est dear' with 'unimpressed dear'), puns such as 'get bitten by Arthur' and the memorable hook ('Arthur in the afternoon') for every alternate chorus. Inserted by Gower Champion before the last two choruses of 'Arthur in the Afternoon' is a brief scene in which Mike argues with her husband Dan (played by Barry Nelson), who does not wish her and their children to accompany him to Colorado where he is directing a TV series. She feels excluded from his career: 'I want to do pictures with my husband like I did for a hell of a lot of years for a hell of a lot of money' (30). When Dan exits, Mike ends the scene by saying to herself, 'Dan, I've met someone' before finishing her musical celebration of the pleasures of extramarital sex. The combination of the character's manic delight, Liza's natural gusto and the pair's comic dance made this number a highlight of the show.[21] When Arthur exits and Mike calls him back on again to share more applause, another man, Seth, enters in his place and shares her bow, so that when she turns to bow to Arthur, she sees Seth, who moves in to kiss her before they exit.

In complete contrast is the self-reflexive chorus number that follows – the only musical routine in the piece that does not feature Mike/Minnelli. Two years after *A Chorus Line* had celebrated the life of the Broadway 'gypsy' (chorus dancer) with its spectacular finale 'One', in which the entire cast of gypsies vocalizes their adulation of an absent star ('S/He's the one'), obliterating individual personalities to become one perfectly synchronized line of dancers, Ebb offers an alternative view of what it feels like to be a gypsy – typically more wry and cynical than that of the somewhat sentimental *A Chorus Line* – and openly admits that the number exists merely to cover the leading lady's costume change. Lying on their backs, members of the chorus sing the verse:

> So the star leaves the stage to change her clothes
> And the natives are restless
> Their anxiety shows
> And their hostile posture seems to say
> 'When will she be back?'
> 'Who the hell are they?' (31)

Whereas *A Chorus Line* purports to celebrate show dancers, while in fact reinforcing the inequality of the star system, Kander and Ebb are more honest in portraying the gypsies' disapproval of the unfairness that their rigorous training prepares them merely to provide anonymous support for a star who receives all the kudos: 'But the knowledgeable gypsy knows/It's ridiculous to throw a fit'. With Ebb's trademark irony the dancers, who actually play numerous characters in the relatively small cast of *The Act*, sing,

> That's the way things are
> When they've paid to see a star
> But
>
> Little do they know
> And little do they see
> Without our paying court
> Without us in support
> How lousy she might be (31)

The joke about the star being lousy without her backup chorus is an obvious irony because the audience had paid as much as $25 – at that time the highest ticket price ever for a Broadway show – to see Liza Minnelli in a musical written as a vehicle for her talents. Yet in fact, Broadway critics praised the dancers,

The chorus line – four men, three women – is one of the evening's graces. It does not dim Miss Minnelli; it embellishes her, as a good listener embellishes a storyteller. She is not first among equals; she is first of her kind, but the dancers are also of her kind. [. . .][22]

Ron Lewis' numbers demonstrated the typical components of a Las Vegas show routine with great panache:

When we go

(*Dance break*)

They don't even stir
When we go

(*Dance break*)

They only look at her
Such inequality! (31–2)

Notwithstanding their low status, the small group of dancers in *The Act* 'are strong and precise, but they are also capable in "Little Do They Know" of a comical, slack-jointed rebelliousness.'[23] Instead of celebrating the long-suffering chorus line, the routine ends by more convincingly stressing the ambition of its individual members:

Yet I have a dream
That isn't mine alone;
Each gypsy that you see
Is just the same as me
The fact is widely known
Someday I'll go so far
That I'll become a star
With gypsies of my own! (32)

So Kander, Ebb and Lewis create a comic anti-*Chorus Line* number, which to a certain extent mocks that work's earnest pretensions of valorizing the careers of Broadway chorus dancers while covertly celebrating the star system. Richard L. Coe claimed, 'I could see "The Act" again just for this small but dashing chorus line'.[24] As a venerated Las Vegas choreographer, Lewis was adept at staging dance numbers with specific themes as components of a full-length revue, or storytelling numbers like 'Arthur in the Afternoon', in which the choreography mimed sections of the narrative to reinforce the song. Such self-standing numbers had exotically themed costumes, which showed off the dancers' bodies and spiced each revue with a variety of spectacular displays. While Lewis may never have developed a signature movement style like Bob Fosse, he was an inventive musical stager, a perfectionist who used the existing vocabularies of jazz and theatrical dancing from Jack Cole to Gower Champion in order to provide a style appropriate for each number. Dancers loved working with him.[25]

The speciality number sung by Michelle after the group's 'Little Do They Know' is 'Hollywood, California', its virtuoso series of lyrical gags making it different from any other in the show. It appeared as the conclusion of a scene in Nat's apartment when he tries to persuade her not to leave Dan. It was performed on the Broadway opening night but was cut before the cast recording was made – possibly because Gower Champion, who had attempted to introduce dramaturgical contexts for all Michelle's songs, thought the connection to Michelle's situation that had been introduced ('The gossips in this town lay in wait to get couples like you and 'Dan'), (36)' although providing a nice change of pace and tone, was too contrived or tenuous. While it did provoke a number of huge laughs at the expense of Hollywood gossip-mongers, it may have proved one 'situation' number too many:

> (*spoken*) Ruth's face lift?
> (*sung*) Oh now that was done by Doctor Pearl
> Now when she smiles, poor girl
> Not only do her earlobes curl
> But she looks like Milton Berle. (37)

The number included an in-joke for Minnelli with its repeated 'Don't you just hate New York?' tagline that teasingly contradicted the title song from the June 1977 release[26] of her film, *New York, New York*, yet was undoubtedly superfluous to the plot line:

> CHORUS:
> (Hollywood, California)
> MIKE:
> Well you know him, he'd screw a goat
>
> CHORUS:
> (Hollywood, California)
> MIKE:
> He was the stuntman for 'Deep Throat'. [38]

In 1987, Furth tried to persuade Ebb to restore the number with slightly rewritten lyrics (Ebb had thought not all were good enough), as he believed it provided some necessary comedy.

Although there had been a number of different endings to Act 1, the Broadway version ends with the scorching show-stopper, 'The Money Tree', a song motivated by Mike's rage at Dan for the way he has deceived and manipulated her:

> The day will come
> He'll come running to me
> The day the sun turns black
> And there's a money tree. (41)

The song performs a savage reversal of all the traditional 'love ballad' tropes, its bleakly ironic images destroying the possibility that love might ever triumph:

> Yes the time will come
> When he'll never stray
> On the never dawn
> Of the never day
> When we all pick coins
> On the silver money tree. (42)

In total contrast, 'City Lights' opens Act 2 with Mike sitting cross-legged on the floor dressed in a red-sequined Halston pantsuit, with an old straw hat perched incongruously on her head. She is assuming the guise of 'The little old lady [who] sat on the porch of the farmhouse' (43). Mike introduces a new character to the audience of her act, by recalling that when she gushed to her about the charms of rural life, the old lady's response had 'floored' her:

> She said, 'It's nice to meet someone who appreciates
> The beauty that nature initiates;
> It's sweet to hear
> But me, my dear,
> I'm truly bored' (43)

As she sings the last lines of the verse, Mike/Minnelli throws off the straw hat and replaces it with a red-sequined jacket and fedora to suggest the ultimate in show business urbanity, being joined by the five dancers to sing:

> I miss those city lights,
> Those spark-a-ling
> City lights,
> Those twink-a-ling
> City lights,
> Blurring my eyes (42)

What follows is a hymn to city life, pastoral pleasures being rejected in favour of 'urban crises', 'grime and grit and pretty city lights'. The number starts as a soft shoe 'strut' with Mike initially positioning herself sideways to the audience to put her hat on at a rakish angle as the five dancers enter in a bobbing walk that allows them to place themselves behind her to perform this vaudeville-style soft shoe routine. They are dressed in pastel-coloured men's suits – green, yellow, blue, lilac and peach, to provide a pale rainbow of contrasting colours that set off the star's glittering red. At this moment, Mike performs a dance break that uses a soft shoe shuffle to mimic tap dancing, with the dancers sitting around her to supply tap sounds by slapping their palms on the stage.

Mike's lover Seth had invited her to join him in New York in Act 1 Scene 10 (39) before Mike and Dan decided to divorce, so the number makes sense as an indication that by the second act Mike is living in New York. On Broadway in 1977–8, the song inevitably became a tongue-in-cheek celebration of Manhattan:

> Sties and stables sure are smelly
> Lemme sniff some kosher deli
> Brightly lit by pretty city lights. (44)

By the late 1970s, New York had acquired a bad reputation for dirt and street crime, with porn cinemas and prostitutes in the streets of the theatre district, so the praise of its dubious urban attractions by contrast with the tedium of country life is somewhat ironic. Nevertheless, critic Richard L. Coe opined,

Ebb's lyrics shine: 'Country air means zilch to me. I won't breath [. . . nothin'] I can't see' going over especially well with New Yorkers who proudly applauded references to the city's squalor. 'City Lights' seems to begin as a paean to country joys but becomes a hymn to the Manhattan skyline.[27]

While the gypsies perform a dance on the theme of 'A Day in New York,' illustrating the differences between 'high' and 'low' life, Seth enters and a new scene begins while the dancers move in slow motion in the background. Throughout the dance routine, three segments of dialogue are intercalated, during which Mike's relationship with Seth deteriorates from,

> SETH. May I have this dance?
> MIKE. (*beaming*) For the rest of your life. (*They dance.*)

to:

> SETH. And most of all I'd like to leave you with six words. 'I'm sorry I ever met you.'
> MIKE. And Seth, I'd like to leave you with two words. (45–6)

As Seth exits for the last time, Mike switches back to a short reprise of 'City Lights' while being lifted above the heads of the five dancers in a fully horizontal position to be carried triumphantly offstage. The implication is that Mike is obliged to perform this rousing comic song-and-dance number, while her mind is preoccupied with the bitter ending of her initially idyllic extramarital affair. As performed live at the 1978 Tony Awards, the audience burst into spontaneous applause four times during the number, followed by a rapturous ovation at the end.[28] Typical of the slightly retro, show-stopping production numbers that Ebb, Kander and Minnelli had popularized, the interruption of 'City Lights' with scenes detailing the disintegration of a relationship is a characteristic exercise in irony that concisely reveals Mike as a role-player in life as much as onstage.

In addition to the 'story' numbers, the most notable songs in *The Act* are three ballads and 'The Money Tree', the torch song that ends Act 1, with Mike directly expressing her rage at Dan's decision to divorce her. Two of the ballads are introduced conventionally in Mike's performance, but the first ('It's the Strangest Thing') is fragmented by flashback scenes of her screen test and first meeting with her husband, the director Dan Connors, while she is taught the song by its composer, Nat. The conceit is, therefore, that she learns to perform a love song in her first film while actually falling in love with Dan:

> MIKE. (*sung*)
> What do you suppose it is
> That's mine and his
> NAT. (*pushing her rising hands down*) What's the question?
> MIKE. (*sung*)
> What would you call that?
> NAT. You tell me.
> MIKE. (*sung*)
> I would call it something

NAT. What?
MIKE. (*sung*)
Magical.
NAT. (*backing away, S.L. watching her.*) Me too.
MIKE. (*sung*)
If I believed
In all that
Just the same

When I hear the telephone ring
As I hurry to answer the ring
If I know it's him, it's him
It's the strangest thing
It's the strangest thing.

[……………….]

DAN. That's the way to do it! Congratulations! (19)

The fairly standard ballad is 'doubled' in significance to give the audience a 'backstage' view of someone 'rehearsing' her love as she actually experiences it.

'There When I Need Him' in Act 2 Scene 2 is a *cri de coeur*, which the audience is not sure is non-diegetic or part of the act, because Mike sings it when she fails to reach Dan on a telephone in the wings after being rejected by Seth near the end of the 'City Lights' sequence. The placement of the song moves the drama closer to the present time of the performance because it motivates Mike's flight from Vegas to Los Angeles to ask Dan for help, prompting his suggestion that she perform a nightclub act. The number is an intense expression of her wish for support from a lover, in its repetition of the title line akin to 'Maybe This Time', representing a somewhat desperate longing for a man who will not desert her:

MIKE. (*sung*)
Someone to lean on, really rely on
A shoulder to cry on
No muscled Adonis with vine leaves in his hair
But there when I need him
There when I need him
There when I need him there. (48)

When Mike's friend Nat, who has arranged and directed her act, dies during a break in rehearsals, Mike is finally left entirely on her own to prove herself onstage. The final number of the act is 'Walking Papers', which she begins entirely alone, giving herself a note on the piano for the pitch before members of the orchestra enter in small groups to build incrementally into a 26-piece band backing. The number segues into 'Shine It On' to take the act back to its opening. As Mike publicly declares she agrees to marry Dan for the second time, she sings the final ballad, 'My Own Space' accompanied only by the conductor on the piano, which asserts her newfound independence as a precondition for marriage:

I love you more
Than I can ever say
I love you more and more and more
With every passing day

Allow me light
A breath of air
Leave me the only thing I own we cannot share
[.................]
Just my own space
And we'll be fine. (62)

On opening night in New York, life imitated art as John Kander entered in the role of conductor to accompany Liza/Mike on the piano. Although *The Act* closed the moment Minnelli's six-month contract was up, Furth, who had received most of the critical opprobrium, continued to produce new versions in which songs were restored, cut, repositioned and dialogue inserted, cut and rewritten. In his letter to Ebb in 1987, Furth stated that Minnelli was really old enough for it at forty-one and that he would value her opinion of the revised show. He went on tirelessly revising it, most significantly in 1995 and then in 2001 with the title *Comeback*, and a great deal of the narrative context was restored. At least twelve drafts of the script exist (from 1976 to 2001) but no one has yet dared to mount a revisal. While it would be interesting to explore the musical in an alternative version, it seems that most regard it as the exclusive property of Liza with a Z.

Notes

1. John Kander, Fred Ebb and Greg Lawrence, *Colored Lights*, New York: Faber, 2003, 155.
2. *Colored Lights*, 145.
3. Furth's most celebrated book was for *Company* (1970).
4. *New York Times*, Section D1, 'The Drama Backstage Is Not An Act', 23 October 1977.
5. Gower Champion, in John Corry, 'If You're Just Wild about Eubie, This Is for You', *New York Times*, 12 May 1978.
6. James Leve, *Kander and Ebb*, New Haven: Yale University Press, 2009, 235.
7. Fred Ebb papers, Box 50 f 6.
8. *New York Times*, 31 October 1977 in Fred Ebb papers, Box 50 f 6.
9. *New York Times*, 31 October, 1977 in Fred Ebb papers, Box 50 f 6.
10. This song was akin to 'It Was a Good Time', a number about divorce that Minnelli had done in *Liza with a Z* and 'Happy Anniversary', sung as part of a medley on marriage during her 1979 concert tour.
11. Information from Scott Schechter, *The Liza Minnelli Scrapbook*, Kensington: Citadel Press, 2004, 58.
12. Fred Ebb papers, Box 50 f 7.
13. Fred Ebb papers, Box 50 f 7.
14. Martin Gottfried, 'Liza Gets Her Act Together', *New York Post*, 31 October 1977, 32, quoted in John Anthony Gilvey, *Before the Parade Passes By*, New York: St Martin's Press, 2005, 267.

15. *Washington Post*, 31 October, 1977.

16. Hobe in *Variety*, quoted in *The Liza Minnelli Scrapbook*, above, 59.

17. Clive Barnes in WQXR, *New York Times Radio*, quoted in *The Liza Minnelli Scrapbook*, above, 59.

18. Quotations from *The Act* are taken from George Furth, John Kander and Fred Ebb, *The Act: A Musical Play*, London: Samuel French, 1987.

19. Kander and Ebb, 'Ring Them Bells', https://www.musixmatch.com, accessed 14 June 2022.

20. *The Songwriters: An Evening with Kander and Ebb*, https://www.youtube.com/ watch?v= UtW9IBH3GtY, accessed 14 June 2022.

21. Unsurprisingly, Minami was later chosen as one of two dancers who toured between 1979 and 1981 in Minnelli's international concert tour, during which the number was featured.

22. *New York Times*, 31 October 1977 in Fred Ebb papers, Box 50 f 6.

23. *New York Times*, 31 October 1977 in Fred Ebb papers, Box 50 f 6.

24. Richard L. Coe, 'A Tough Act to Follow', *The Washington Post*, 31 October 1977, https:// www .washingtonpost.com/archive/lifestyle/1977/10/31/a-tough-act-to-follow/48d53450-5692 -4536-9bbf-6e2b4d1fba30, accessed 14 June 2022.

25. See Facebook page, Alumni of Ron Lewis: https://www.facebook.com/groups/316012516 809774/, accessed 15 June 2022.

26. The opening night of *The Act* on Broadway was 29 October 1977, just four months after Scorsese's film.

27. Richard L. Coe, 'A Tough Act to Follow'.

28. See Liza Minnelli in 'City Lights', https://www.youtube.com/watch?v=TvAURkgx-D0, accessed 12 June 2022.

9 A film classic reborn

Woman of the Year (1981) as vehicle for Bacall

Arguably, *Woman of the Year* (1981) has the most formulaic book of any musical to which the pair contributed. Together with book-writer Peter Stone, they were constricted in many ways by needing to tailor the musical to exploit Lauren Bacall's movie star image and showcase her distinctive talents while disguising her vocal limitations. In the *New York Times*, Frank Rich attributed the success of the show almost entirely to the performance of its star:

> As hard and well as Miss Bacall works in "Woman of the Year", she never lets us see any sweat. That's why this actress is a natural musical-comedy star. By making life and art look as easy and elegant as a perfect song, Miss Bacall embodies the very spirit of the carefree American musical. She also, as a result, makes extraordinary demands on her theatrical collaborators.[1]

The challenge for the writing team was to create a vehicle for Bacall that might equal the success of *Applause* (1970), for which she had won a Tony. *Applause* had been based on the Bette Davis classic, *All About Eve* (1950), so it was probably an easier sell, yet in the event Bacall garnered her second Tony, the book and the score both won Tonys, as did Marilyn Cooper for Best Supporting Actress in a Musical.

> When we see Miss Bacall on stage, we want the entertainment that contains her to come together as simply and delightfully as her performance. If it doesn't, we're going to notice the esthetic gap between the star and her vehicle very fast. "Woman of the Year" [. . .] is an amiable show that suffers from such a gap. It boasts other assets besides Miss Bacall – most crucially a tuneful score by John Kander – but it often huffs and puffs to achieve effects that its leading lady can pull off with a flick of her regal head.[2]

Rich's comments on the book are entirely technical; he makes no mention of the problematic nature of the source material, nor does he acknowledge that some of the 'effects' that its leading lady apparently achieves so effortlessly are, in fact, created by dint of the authors' ingenuity. His response to Bacall mirrors the kind of reactions John Clum describes as typical of gay fans' love of a 'diva'. James Leve borrows Clum's appellation 'diva musical' in order to categorize *The Act*; conversely, he regards *Woman of the* Year as an 'anti-diva' musical.[3] Yet in most respects, it is only the public's regard for Lauren Bacall as a diva that renders the musical palatable in 1981: whatever surrender to patriarchal values Tess Harding professes at the end of the show, audiences are mindful that Bacall was by 1981 a middle-aged star who had moved beyond her Hollywood image, which required the heteronormative marriage to Humphrey Bogart, to achieve the legendary status of a diva whose power is greater than that of any men friends or lovers she might acquire.

After *Applause*, based on the great Bette Davies movie, *All About Eve* (1950) the film of *Woman of the Year* (1942) suggested as a source by Bacall herself, might have seemed an obvious choice. It would invoke her inevitable association with the Hollywood of the 1940s, recalling the era that she had helped to define while at the same time exploiting the parallels between herself and Katharine Hepburn, both of whom had later become iconic as models of strong women devoted to ailing partners. *The Woman of the Year* was the first of ten films starring Hepburn and Spencer Tracy, who had fallen in love during its making. Bacall married Humphrey Bogart shortly after their first film together, *To Have and Have Not* (1944); he died in 1957. Bacall and Hepburn were known as fiercely independent women, who over the course of almost fifty years developed a close friendship. Yet there were ideological problems inherent in the film that the musical, produced almost forty years later, could not resolve.

Hepburn's reputation as a feminist influenced the construction of her film characters. Her own ideas were often directly opposed to those of the screen industry, so although many of the films she appeared in seem promisingly feminist at the outset, they are almost always contradictory; the ubiquitous dramatic trope in which love transforms the headstrong woman into a devoted wife is typically employed in order to support a heteronormative 'happy ending'. According to the critic Stephanie Zacharek,

> The story's bones are simple and perfect: Tracy's Sam Craig and Hepburn's Tess Harding are two hardheaded newspeople who rush into marriage, only to learn they're seemingly incapable of adjusting to one another.[4]

In 1941, the original idea of allowing the female character to assume an equal right to pursue an independent career as her male counterpart may have been progressive. The fact that the film highlighted the difficulties facing a career woman married to a competitive husband was in itself surprising, but it was also prescient at the moment of the USA's entry into the Second World War, when women were required to work in factories and on farms, while their menfolk were away fighting. It was therefore a great disappointment to Hepburn that the intended scheme of the film was seriously compromised by the studio's decision to pander to the social conservatism of the preview audience by tacking on a new comic ending in which Tess fails completely in her attempt to make breakfast for her husband. The traditional values of patriarchy are reinforced: a 'real woman' must be at home in the kitchen. Notwithstanding this 'sellout', the expert performances of Tracy and Hepburn, who fell in love while making the film, charged the narrative with a remarkable, if suppressed erotic energy, resulting in the pairing of the two stars in nine subsequent films.

Some of the problems with Peter Stone's efficient yet generic musical comedy book might be attributed to the challenges presented by his source material. By 1981, after sixteen years of second-wave feminism, the film would surely have appeared dated in its special pleading for the equality of an exceptional woman. Peter Stone's revision of the screenplay for the stage sets the musical in the period contemporary with its production. Even a musical nostalgically celebrating the vibrancy of a Hollywood legend might surely be expected to embrace the social and cultural changes that have occurred in the intervening forty years. In attempting to do this, *Woman of the Year* (1981) is as fraught with contradictions as its screen progenitor. It also lacks the crackling intensity of the movie, which, for all its eventual recuperation of patriarchy, for the most part proffers a sincere argument in favour of Tess Harding's independence as a political journalist. With a tuneful 'golden age' score by Kander and Ebb, the musical is structured to celebrate Bacall. What it lacks is a male opponent of equal status.

By framing Act 1 with the awards show, the authors apparently intended to introduce the major argument of the musical directly. The chairperson of the ceremony establishes the terms of the debate:

> This year's winner [. . .] has not only achieved a phenomenal success as a broadcast journalist, a field heretofore dominated by men (*fanfare*) but she has also, through her blissfully happy marriage to the well-known cartoonist, Sam Craig, (*fanfare*) proved beyond all doubt that today's woman can be successful both in her career *and* her marriage –[5] (11)

Tess herself immediately undermines the claim by introducing the song with the following verse:

> Sam Craig
> Wherever you are
> You arrogant, ill-tempered, brutish, insensitive
> Chauvinist son of a bitch
> Listen to that! (14)

Given the shift in the time period to 1981, Bacall's Tess is shown at the outset to possess a sophisticated awareness of the persistent difficulties of married women to maintain a successful career. As the women chorus their celebration of the woman of the year while Bacall tops them with her baritone belt, her performance of the lyrics becomes a defiant rejection of Sam ('You don't need any husband/ I did not need a husband') while the music ironically appears to trumpet her triumph as she aggressively sings the final lines: 'Cuz Godammit, I am/The Woman of the Year!' (15)

Obviously, this makes an effective opening for a Broadway show, but by allowing audiences to be in the know at the start of the musical, it prepares them at the same time to anticipate the potentially doomed relationship while viewing the subsequent 'flashback' action of Act 1, privileging Tess' viewpoint as an experienced and famous older woman who has fallen in love with a slightly younger man. It may not make Bacall's Tess as likeable as Hepburn's, but it makes her the subject of the stage show, disempowering the character of Sam by reducing him in status to Tess' love interest, whereas in the film Tess and Sam were equals in a genuine battle of lovers. Bacall's acceptance speech includes the pseudo-feminist claim, 'You know, it's only been a few years since this award was given for a bright smile and a clean kitchen. Well, we've come a long way, baby –' (16).

Intended to update the 1942 film, the line might ironically reinforce the opinion that second-wave feminism still hadn't achieved its economic aims. As a sports columnist, Spencer Tracy's emblematically masculine preoccupations were more obviously lowbrow (and all-American) than the sophisticated interests of Hepburn's internationally known political journalist. In the musical, there is less at stake: the gender battle is reduced to a more humdrum series of squabbles between a grouchy male cartoonist and a famous media star, reminiscent of Barbara Walters, to whom everyone onstage defers.

The flashback to the start of their relationship is motivated by Tess's soliloquy:

> What did I need him for? I was doing just great on my own, why'd I have to screw it up? If I hadn't shot my mouth off that morning on the show we never would have met. When was that, eight months ago? (16)

This allows for an easy segue to her 'Early Bird' television show, in which the backstage preparations for the live broadcast by Tess and fellow anchorperson Chip Salisbury are revealed. The meta-theatrical presentation of activity behind the scenes in a TV studio parallels the backstage-onstage duality of the Woman of the Year ceremony, once again representing Tess both offstage and on. The meta-theatrical trope persists as the set for Sam's studio is also moved onto the stage to present four of Sam's fellow cartoonists and a giant-sized version of Sam's cartoon cat character Katz, at the tail end of an all-night poker game.

When Sam places a television set down stage centre to watch the live broadcast of Tess Harding's show because 'Those commentaries she does are the brightest thing on the air' (20), he is unprepared for what she is about to say:

> TESS: At the risk of sounding un-American, I'm getting sick and tired of the funnies. Oh they're all right in their place I suppose, on the back pages of our daily newspapers, but when [. . . they] start invading our art museums, then it's time to [. . .] send them back where they belong, back to the funny papers –' [. . .] In short I'm beginning to see nothing funny about the funnies. (20)

While Sam initially feigns indifference to her denigration of the cartoonist's art, he soon joins in attacking Tess for her unpalatable opinions: '*Who the hell does she think she is?!!* That lame-brained, over-educated, under-developed moron!!' (21)

When his friends leave, Sam utilizes Katz, his cartoon cat, as a device to enliven his monologues by turning them into conversations. Amplifying the media trope to include newspapers, the authors now depict Sam in the process of drawing the new 'Tessie Cat' while singing 'See You in the Funny Papers'. While the scene changes to Tess's office, her secretary Gerald reads aloud from a tabloid newspaper:

> Katz is eating his morning cereal in front of his television set. He is watching – Tessie Cat? – [. . .] who says: 'Dear viewers – how will you ever amount to anything if you don't stop wasting time with low-brow pursuits like television and start doing something worthwhile with your lives.' (24)

The media trope functions as an effective means of amplifying many of the cinematic techniques so that they register clearly on stage. Although it might put one in mind of Kander and Ebb's sophisticated deployment of meta-theatrical frames in *Cabaret*, *Zorba* and *Chicago*, its use here appears less ambitious. Rather than prompting epistemological reflection on its subject, the self-reflectiveness of the device exploits Bacall's star image to impart an aura to the character, whose celebrity is a media construction. In comparison with the movie's comic realism, the trope reduces both Sam and Tess to figures of popular media culture. In the film, the genuine contest of equals is an argument between two serious newspaper journalists on the *New York Chronicle*, caused by Tess's assertion on the radio that baseball should be abolished during the war. The sports columnist naturally defends the 'low-brow' value of baseball as virtually iconic of American nationhood (masculinity?), while Tess represents the highbrow national and international interests of a political journalist.

As a romantic comedy, the film attempts a genuine portrayal of the contested status of relationships between men and women at the start of America's involvement in the Second World War. Hepburn's Tess is a serious and well-educated political journalist. By comparison, Bacall's Tess is a media celebrity but less of an intellectual – a TV anchorwoman who happens to be clever and well-connected. Hepburn's Tess is at an age when she might well expect to have a child, while that is certainly not an option for the character as represented by the 57-year-old Bacall. In the movie, Tess' attempt to adopt an orphan is important in determining the outcome but is not featured at all in the musical. Neither Tess's father nor her feminist aunt, who later marries him, appear in the musical, so the class difference between Sam and Tess is eliminated, as is the loving example supplied by the older couple who take their wedding very seriously.

In the film, the sexual attraction is visually signalled at the moment when Sam sees Tess straightening her stocking as he meets her for the first time in their editor's office. While this is typical of the way Hollywood movies conventionally privilege the male gaze to sexualize the woman as an object, the instant spark of attraction is progressively transformed into a romance, including a key episode in which Tess accompanies Sam to a game at Yankee Stadium. On stage, the moment is effective but exaggerated to suit the theatrical medium: at the climax of Tess's witty patter song, 'When You're Right, You're Right' during which she vents her anger against Sam, she meets him for the first time and her rage is instantly transformed into attraction:

> There's only one way to treat vermin like that
> I'll show him what cats are, that beady-eyed rat –
> (*She stops, turns and sees him.*) Mr Craig?
> SAM. Look Miss Harding, I know you saw the newspaper. I came here to tell you – You know, you're really better looking than you are on television – a lot better.
> TESS. Mr Craig, before you say something more, let me tell you straight out – (*She sings.*)
> I was wrong
> That's right
> I was totally wrong –
> [.........]
> And not to confess would be small
> That's right
>
> When you're wrong, you're wrong, right?
> I know when I'm wrong
> And you're not what I pictured at all. (29–30)

The musical permits both Sam and Tess to register their reactions, employing the number to generate a laugh: in its construction of a farcical plot reversal, this effect is less subtle, if slightly less sexist, than the cinematic version.

Figure 14. Lauren Bacall and male chorus in 'One of the Boys' from *Woman of the Year*. Photo: Martha Swope, NYPL, Billy Rose Division.

Near the end of Scene 4 in Sam's studio, the number 'So What Else Is New?' dramatizes Sam's anxiety about the sudden change in his affection for Tess through a conversation with Katz as his alter ego. An animated onscreen Katz sings the hook, 'so what else is new?' in response to Sam's accusations that Katz is falling for Tessie Cat in the way he is for Tess. The screen projection of Katz further extends the exploitation of media devices on stage, reinforcing the self-deprecating irony of Sam's succinct lyrics and the music's catchy dance rhythm with its visual personification of the rueful cartoon cat. When Tess returns to the studio on the pretext of retrieving her gloves, the two exit to the words, 'POW! BLAM! GULP!' followed onscreen by a firework explosion. Once again, the fun of the cartoon effects, with their suggestive climax, provides a comic comment on the sexual relationship, rendering it as merely naughty rather than charged with the unspoken intensity of the film. For all the stage show's clever farcical effects, as a musical comedy it eschews any attempt to create a convincing representation of a social environment.

When Sam, accompanied by Tess, enters a Third Avenue Saloon where his fellow cartoonists have sung a reprise of an earlier number in which they repeat their attack on Tess's derogatory comments on 'the funny papers', they are soon surprised by her detailed knowledge of their cartoon strips, even though she then admits that she has merely read up on cartoons in Sam's encyclopaedia. After charming them with her ability to keep up with their drinking, as well as with her straightforward apology for the ignorance of her comments on the breakfast show, one of them (Phil) in short order proposes a toast to her as 'One of the Boys'. Possibly the best song written to suit Bacall's range, the number is engineered as a show-stopper, in which other men in the bar join Sam's friends to back Bacall in a few moments of Broadway razzmatazz. There is a joking acknowledgement by the men of their own sexist attitudes ('Come ye men misogynistic') as they sing the praises of an exceptional woman, 'Now and then some broad is /One of the boys!' (45)

In constructing a kind of antidote to the angry 'Woman of the Year', Kander and Ebb capitalize on Bacall's androgynous charisma as a mature woman with a deep masculine growl that signals strength and the ability to do combat in a masculine environment:

I'm one of the girls
Who's one of the boys
Enjoying the jokes and the smokes and the noise
You wanna go fishing?
Well hand me a reel
I majored in poker
So shut up and deal
[...............]
In spite of the dress, the finesse and the poise
I'm one of the girls
Whose really one of the boys (46–7)

The lyrics suggest the gender ambiguity of a glamorous woman ('Despite all the Gucci, the Pucci and pearls') who is willing to do battle with men on their own terms.

The number is carefully choreographed to showcase Bacall's graceful movement in a bright red pantsuit, while not exposing her lack of genuine dance training, so she is turned, lifted and carried a great deal by the line of chorus dancers. Echoing her star turn from *Applause*, in which she had sung 'I'm Alive' while dancing with a group of chorus boys in a gay club, 'One of the Boys' conveys a much more complex and nuanced approach to gender, collapsing distinctions between being 'one of the girls' and 'one of the boys' in order to provoke a subliminally feminist interrogation of the significance of gender and the possibility of moving between traditionally masculine and conventionally feminine activities. Kander and Ebb transform a song-and-dance kickline number typical of Broadway musical comedy into a teasing challenge to sexist norms.

At the end of Scene 5, immediately after the song 'Table Talk', in which Sam unequivocally declares his love for Tess, the two dance onstage, followed by the onscreen Katz proposing on his knees to Tessie Cat before they drive off in a car with a 'Just Married' sign on the back. Other numbers skilfully adapt incidents from the film to suit the conventions of a stage musical. The farce of the wedding night in the film, when a crowd of Tess's friends and professional associates gather in her Fifth Avenue apartment, thereby preventing the married couple from having any time on their own, becomes in Scene 6 a musical scene interspersed with episodes. 'The Two of Us' changes as first Gerald joins to sing 'The Three of Us', then Chip Salisbury and Tony the doorman enter and form a kind of glee club that vocalizes about 'The Five of Us', until the entrances of further characters, the lyric successively increases the number to eight and, finally, thirteen. Eventually, the couple is left alone:

TESS.
Here we are
With one of us
Who hates to sleep alone
SAM.
That squalling, sprawling crew of us
Our huge supporting cast
BOTH.
Has left the brand new two of us . . . (60)

Just as they are finally able to go to bed, the 'handsome young Slavic ballet dancer' Alexi Petrikov bursts through the open terrace door to inform Tess he has defected and needs to stay in her apartment. As Tess goes off to make coffee, the scene concludes with Sam sitting beside Alexi on the sofa, drinking champagne while singing,

> Here we are
> The two of us
> I can't believe my eyes – (62)

Another example of the superior craft skills of Kander and Ebb, this musical scene exhibits not only the perfect matching of music and lyrics typical of their songwriting but also their close collaboration with Peter Stone in shaping a highly effective piece of musical dramaturgy in which action, dialogue and song are wittily woven together to advance the comic narrative.

A further example of the artful transformation of narrative material into musical comedy format is the next ensemble number, in which the various groups of characters polyphonically assert their negative view that 'It Isn't Working', in contradiction to the repeated observation that neither Sam nor Tess has ever seemed happier. The elaborate three-part chorus utilizes both round and counterpoint structures to reveal the cartoonists being joined by Chip, then men from his TV studio, succeeded by Tess's German housekeeper Helga, who is accompanied by two other housekeepers, then some neighbours and eventually Gerald, until virtually the entire cast apart from Tess and Sam have joined in. This is a virtuoso musical scene, built up from the incessant repetition of a simple vamp and uncomplicated lyrics: the effect of the gradual accumulation of vocalists is extremely funny in the narrative context while it enhances suspense at this moment in the action of the show.

Cracks in the couple's relationship are initially visible in Scene 8 when Sam learns that he and Tess had both been in Milwaukee the previous day, yet because she hadn't listened when he had told her this, they missed the chance to have dinner together. When Tess responds in a slightly dismissive way, an argument begins, reaching a climax at the moment Sam offers a very muted 'congratulations' after being told by Tess that she has been voted Woman of the Year:

> TESS. Would you have voted for me, Sam? (*They continue to stare at one another, then exit. TESS, offstage, says:*) Men, who needs them – ?!! (*There is a CRASH!*)
> HELGA. Did you hear that, Gerald? It's the beginning of the end, ja? (73)

Gerald and Helga then gleefully sing 'I Told You So' to emphasize their view that everyone would be better off if the two were to separate.

Backstage at the award ceremony (Scene 9), as in the opening, but now a few minutes earlier, Sam, who has been scribbling some ideas for a comic strip on the programme, insists on reading them to Tess:

> Katz says 'There's an award for everything these days – movies, plays, books, *women,* dogs, floor lamps, aluminum siding – there's even a new award awarded for the best award of the year. So what else is new?' (76)

Naturally, this sparks a row, culminating just as the chairperson is delivering a eulogy to Tess, in Sam's decision not to stay for the ceremony, he exits with the sexist insult, 'Wouldn't all those people out there be surprised to learn that the Woman of the Year isn't much of a woman at all?' (77) At this moment, Tess reprises part of the opening number while waiting in the wings to be presented with her award:

> It's my night, Sammy
> All mine, Sammy
> And you can't give it
> Your well-known whammy (77)

She closes the act by singing her defiant declaration again, 'Cause Goddam it, I am/The woman – [. . .] of the year!' (77)

The second act of the musical diverges from the film narrative in several respects, giving each one of the pair the chance to offer more complicated explanations for their contradictory behaviour in song, soliloquy and dialogue. In the first scene, Sam tells his saloonkeeper friend,

> The funny part is now that I'm living alone again it's not so different to being married to Tess. But I had to move out – I couldn't take it any more. [. . .] It's been six months since I heard of anyone I haven't heard of. She hasn't got time for us, Maury. (79)

When Tess, who has been waiting in another room, enters, she is extremely conciliatory, encouraging him to resume their former living arrangement, but after a mild disagreement, he kisses her a passionate goodbye before leaving her with Maury, to whom she admits that 'It looks like it's "Miss Harding" again' before singing the ironic 'I Wrote the Book', reinforced later by the four cartoonists who have been waiting for Sam in the kitchen:

> [I wrote] the book
> On how to have style
> I wrote the book
> On wisdom and wit
> I wrote the book on every great
>   English statesman
> From Churchill to Pitt
>
> So when it comes to losing a man
> You'll find it unsurprisingly true
> That last week
> I wrote that book too. (83)

Dramaturgically, this is Tess's first proper admission of defeat, the number permitting her the opportunity for some witty but rueful self-reflection, during which she is able to admit that for all her worldly sophistication and intellectual accomplishment, she is incapable of maintaining an intimate relationship with a man. Musically, it is one of the highlights of the show, a 'charm' song[6] with a bouncy rhythm, a clever hook and effective use of idiomatic phrases. The next number, 'Happy in the Morning', at the ballet rehearsal (Act 2 Scene 2) dramatizes the dancer Petrikov's thoughts as he responds to Tess in a taped interview and functions as a lesson in the relative value of a loving relationship and a career.

There is an attempt at this point to revise the sexist assumption in the film that it is a woman's responsibility to forego her career in order to be a proper wife by disclosing a man who is prepared to give up a brilliant ballet career in the West to return to his wife in Soviet Russia: 'Dancing is nice. Is beautiful. But is only dancing. Is not to be confused with *life!* I think perhaps you do not understand this. Is why you are not so happy' (85). As he sings a rhythm song, which evokes the dance rehearsal, he attempts to convince Tess that she has confused her priorities:

> Happy in the morning
> Laughing, joking
> Happy in the morning,
> Kissing, stroking
> Ready to endure whatever lies ahead
> Jumping out of bed (85).

This explicit example of the joy of a satisfying marriage represents the beginning of Tess's gradual rethinking of her attitude towards Sam, followed in Scene 3 by Sam reading his latest comic strip to Katz before confessing to his injured manhood in a specious attempt to justify divorcing Tess:

> How would *you* like to be married to someone who's *more successful*, more *important*, makes more *money* than you – someone who's never around when you need her [. . .] and who spends more time with Yuri Andropov than she does with you?! (87)

In a more contemplative vein, Sam sings the ballad, 'Sometimes a Day Goes By', one of the beautifully romantic songs which Kander claims to be his favourite mode: 'I think I'd like to be remembered as an emotional stirrer, whether the emotions are happy or tender or sad. But emotions that have impact, feelings that don't just wash over you and do nothing.' Although Ebb's lyrics appear to be simple, the irony produced in the context of the previous soliloquy conjures up powerful feelings of yearning and pain:

> Sometimes a day goes by
> One whole entire day
> When I don't think of her (88)

The conceit of the lyric is to allow Sam to betray himself by boasting that there are times when he doesn't think of Tess for a whole day, an assertion that betrays the fact that he thinks of her most of the time. Even though the song is brief, the repetition of the third, fourth and fifth choruses together adds poignant intensity, an example of the consummate yet understated craftsmanship of the songwriting team:

> It's hardly every day
> It's most unusual
> In fact I can't remember when
>
> But, sometimes a day goes by
> When I don't think of her
>
> 'Til morning comes and then —
> There she is again. (88)

Thematically echoing the scene with Alexi Petrikov, Scene 4 offers a comic example of a happily married couple – Tess's ex-husband Larry and his wife Jan in their rustic home in Colorado. Jan is frumpishly dressed in a shapeless robe with her hair up in curlers. When Larry suggests she get ready for Tess to come down for breakfast and enquires why the house is not ready, she retorts that she is ready – and the house is ready, too.

> LARRY. Just because she happens to be my ex-wife –
> JAN. [. . .] I can deal with an ex-wife. But that happens to be Tess Harding up there [. . .] She's made the best-dressed list nine years straight – she's been on more magazine covers than Miss Piggy [. . .] At my best, Larry, *at my very best* – to her I'd look like this any way, so what's the use? (89)

When Tess appears a few minutes later, 'looking wonderful', she does her best to be polite, 'The entire house is so – warm and – and *lived* in' but when Larry asks about Sam, 'she looks him straight in the eye' and says, 'He left me' (91), prompting Jan to hint heavily that Larry should leave the two women alone to talk. Tess tries to explain what went wrong:

> One minute we were deliriously happy, and the next we were fighting about everything. At first I thought he was the one who was wrong. But last week someone I know gave up everything I thought was important just to save his marriage. Jan! *I* must be the one who's wrong! [. . .] And then it occurred to me that the most happily married man I know was my ex-husband. Show me what to do, Jan – you know how to make a man happy [. . .] (91–2)

Jan's response is to remind Tess of how 'wonderful' her life is in the form of a show-stopping comic number, 'The Grass Is Always Greener'. In the rhythm sections, there are two hooks, 'That's wonderful!' and 'What's so wonderful?' emphasizing how the women compete in their praise for each other:

> JAN.
> You're always in the magazines
> That's wonderful!
>   TESS.
> What's so wonderful?
> You can hold a husband
> That's wonderful!
>   JAN.
> What's so wonderful?
> There's more to life than husbands
>   TESS.
> I could use a husband
>   JAN.
> You can have my husband
>   TESS.
> (*mumbling*)
> I've already had your husband —

These wry exchanges alternate with the chorus they belt out together:

> Ah, the grass is always greener
> On somebody else's estate!
> Ah, the meat is always leaner
> On somebody else's dinner plate! (93)

Clearly anticipated to 'bring down the house'[7] in performance, Kander and Ebb wrote an encore that was nearly as long as the number itself. Marilyn Cooper's dry, deadpan delivery in the dialogue and song was so funny that she earned a Tony for appearing in one scene only. A highlight of the show, the scene and song are obviously intended to generate laughs, but the number functions as well to depict Tess thinking aloud about what is important in life, thereby motivating her cryptic decision, 'Larry! You don't know how lucky you are! Oh Jan, you've given me a wonderful idea! And both of you, make sure you watch my show tomorrow morning' (96).

Scene 5 is an attempt to rewrite the (in)famous scene in the movie where Tess fails with disastrously comic results to cook breakfast for Sam in his apartment. By trying to bake a cake live on the 'Early Bird' programme, the musical transforms the amusing but sexist episode into a slapstick sequence with broad gags that reduce Tess to a caricature – naïve, cunning and exhibitionistic – while Sam is humiliated in front of millions of TV viewers:

> TESS. This is the final appearance of 'Tess's' Corner, because it's the final appearance of Tess. From now on you'll be able to find me right here, in the kitchen. My own kitchen. And sitting across from me [. . .] will be my husband, Sam Craig. The problem is, you see, I've been having breakfast every morning with eighteen million people. And while that's earned me a 36% share in the ratings, I wound up with a zero share at home. (98)

Potentially, this version of the kitchen scene is not only as sexist as the revised ending of the film, but it is also extremely far-fetched as a representation of the gender conflict. Peter Stone underlines the significance of every activity by inserting direct comments on the situation by each character, so what is implicit in the film is spelt out didactically in the musical:

> SAM. Tess – I don't want you to quit your job, you're too damn good at it. You don't want to quit, either. You're a big phony. [. . .] Why didn't you just tell it to me – why'd you have to say it on television? (*grabs the mike boom, starts imitating her*) Hi there! This is Tess Harding [. . .] – telling all you wonderful folks out there in televisionland – my most private personal business [. . .] (102)

This moment is not just overtly didactic but incontrovertibly true so that it represents Sam, somewhat unconvincingly, as the mature and fair-minded man who points out how silly and self-deceiving the woman has been. In contradiction to his own expressions of resentment in Scene 3, Sam suddenly appears magnanimous – tendentiously implying that the male protagonist is more equable and fair-minded than the female:

> Don't you see, Tess? Just because I couldn't take being married to Tess Harding that doesn't mean I wanted you to be Mrs Sam Craig.
> TESS. What *do* you want?
> SAM. You could try being Tess Harding Craig. I don't want you to stop being you. All I ever wanted was for you to leave some room in your life for me.

TESS. I love you –
SAM. So what do you say, Tess Harding Craig – do we give it a shot? (102)

As a conclusion to the conflict, which ends in a reprise of their love ballad 'Table Talk', with the jointly sung, 'We'll be the couple of the year!' (103), this rationalization of their behaviour is too glib. Typically, the man doesn't need to change at all, which merely reinforces the patriarchal moral of the film's rewritten ending. Sam and Tess now start dancing to be followed by Katz and Tessie dancing onscreen before walking into a technicolour sunset. Again, a gag is utilized to mask the unsatisfactory conclusion of the argument as '*A legend appears: "AND THEY LIVED SCRAPPILY EVER AFTER." And then: "SO WHAT ELSE IS NEW?"*' (103)

Although the stage version fails to resolve the contradictions posed by the cinematic narrative, it nevertheless succeeds in transforming its source into a broadly funny and romantic musical comedy, demonstrating the impeccable craftsmanship of the authorial trio in constructing an extremely successful vehicle for Lauren Bacall.

Notes

1. Frank Rich, *New York Times*, 30 March 1981, https://www.nytimes.com/ 1981/03/30/theater/stage-lauren-bacall-in-woman-of-year.html, accessed 19 September 2022.
2. Rich, *New York Times*.
3. James Leve, *Kander and Ebb*, New Haven: Yale University Press, 2009, 229–38.
4. Stephanie Zachrek, Criterion Collection, *Woman of the Year*: Essays, Criterion Collection, 2017, https://www.criterion.com/current/posts/4514-woman-of-the-year-a-womans-place.
5. Page references are to Stone, Kander and Ebb, *Woman of the Year*, New York: Samuel French, 1984.
6. A charm song is one in which a character charms the audience or other characters in the show. It was one of the categories of musical theatre songs invented by the famous musical director, orchestrator and teacher Lehman Engel to indicate the different types and functions of numbers in a 'golden age' musical. His taxonomy influenced lyricists and composers between the 1950s and 1960s.
7. Frank Rich, *New York Times*.

10 The drama of memory

The Rink (1984)

The Rink is a show whose poor critical reception at its première in 1984 is, in some respects, inexplicable. In my view, it has one of the strongest scores and most coherent books of any musical since *Sweeney Todd* (1979). Both Chita Rivera and Liza Minnelli acted superbly and were vocally on top form.[1] Kander described A. J. Antoon's staging as 'the most complete realization of our intentions on any production we have ever done'[2] and asserted, 'I loved doing *The Rink* [. . .] it was a piece I was especially proud of [. . .] I thought it was directed and cast wonderfully. But we really got slammed.' According to Ebb, 'It also looked fabulous on the stage'[3], but they both later came to feel that although Liza Minnelli as Rivera's prodigal thirty-year-old daughter (Angel) 'played the role beautifully', the audience were wrong-footed by her casting because they were expecting to see her in a 'show biz' context: 'they didn't want to see her without the sequins'.[4] A viewing of a series of brief extracts from the production, recorded and maintained by Theatre on Film and Tape Archive, New York Public Library, reinforces their point. Minnelli eschews any of the 'Liza with a Z' mannerisms of voice and gesture to give a naturalistic performance, almost Stanislavskian in its careful delineation of the 32-year-old daughter Angel, emphasizing the genetic disposition towards stubborn independence inherited from her mother combined with her father's romantic imagination.

What surprises is Minnelli's ability to submerge her well-known concert persona beneath the details of a naturalistic characterization – quite the opposite of her approach in her previous Broadway musical, *The Act*, in which she exploits her performer persona to represent a character who appears, on the surface, to share her vulnerability, insecurities and ambition. The danger with *The Act* on Broadway had been that the role of Mike had been constructed as a vehicle for Minnelli to showcase every facet of her singing, dancing and acting talent. The character herself was something of a blank page, a neutral agent necessitated by the narrative, into which the actor was required to project her own identity in order to construct a believable persona.

It's certainly not a coincidence that the musical was originally titled *In Person*, implying that the action was motivated by the live performer, whoever they were, rather than a fully fleshed-out character. The change of title to *The Act* even more directly alludes to the star's role-play: perhaps under the layers of role-playing all that exists is the persona – an 'act'. Mike's life problems with both her husband and her daughter are resolved only when she successfully launches her nightclub act by herself, rather than as dictated by a man. This self-reflexive drama of the self as role was very typical of the 1970s conceptions of the 'dramatistical' quality of life that was popularized by Kenneth Burke, R. D. Laing and E. R. Goffman. Yet *The Rink* tackles a drama of memory from a completely alternative dramaturgical perspective. Conceived much more naturalistically as historical narrative, each character has a role in the extended family that is motivated by a complex web of what Stanislavsky referred to as 'given circumstances'.

The recovery of the 'true' past by both Anna and her daughter Angel involves continual flashbacks so that the past is almost constantly present, side by side with the unfolding action. To achieve coherence, Anna and Angel must individually relive key moments of the family history in order to comprehend the clash they experience between their opposed perspectives.

Perhaps it was an inauspicious moment to present this kind of musical. While never mentioned at the time, the spike in street crime in New York City in the early 1980s, linked to a rising incidence of crack cocaine usage, as well as the reputation of the theatre district for porn movie houses and street prostitution, may have made audiences and critics wary of a musical that, towards the end of Act 1, presents two incidents of violent street crime as signs of the disintegration of communities that has led to the dilapidation of the neighbourhood around the boardwalk. Yet its sequences of dancing on roller skates anticipated *Starlight Express*, making the production in some respects groundbreaking. The difference was that *The Rink* had a book for adults.

In the wake of *A Chorus Line* (1975), *Sweeney Todd* (1979), *Evita* (Broadway, 1979), *Dreamgirls* (1981) and *Cats* (Broadway, 1982), *The Rink* may on the surface have seemed like a rather old-fashioned book musical. Although it focused on the relationship between the past and the present, it was not a retro musical comedy in the style of *My One and Only* (1983). Yet, as is typical of Kander and Ebb, *The Rink* combined psychologically and socially challenging subject matter with musical comedy tropes and styles. In a cultural climate dominated between 1980 and 1984 by the effects of the worst economic recession since Second World War, and a theatre dominated by 'concept' musicals of various kinds, the show deployed older forms of Broadway entertainment for ironic purposes.

The starting point for *The Rink* was John Kander's desire to base a musical on Ibsen's existential drama *Peer Gynt*, in which the eponymous hero travels the world in search of a less constricted life. Peer discovers that each of his adventures is merely an act of role-playing to escape the truth of his own identity by seeking it abroad instead of forging authentic relationships with his mother, Aase, and his beloved, Solveig. Throughout his eventful life, the two women have waited faithfully for him to return home. Peer Gynt's conflict between his sense of self at home and his personae abroad is clearly parallel to those of photographer Jacques Bonnard in *The Happy Time*, yet the remnants of the initial *Peer Gynt* motif can be observed in Angel's journey of self-discovery before she returns home to reclaim her family identity: her desire to revive the roller-skating rink is an attempt to retrieve the past.

Two playwrights were, in fact, commissioned to write the book. The first was Albert Innaurato, whose play *Gemini* (Broadway, 1977) had been the longest-running non-musical show on Broadway since the Second World War. The precise location of the musical kept changing until it became the generic 'somewhere on the Eastern seaboard' in 1979, but the battle between mother and daughter over whether to sell the family-owned rink remained the constant factor in the different versions. In the first version, the mother, Anna Antonelli, wishes to sell the rink to a disco promoter for $200,000 in order to retire to her birthplace, Abruzzi in Italy, but her daughter, Pia, is trying to prevent the sale. In a final reversal, Anna decides to keep the rink and throws her daughter a surprise party to celebrate.[5]

In the second of Innaurato's two versions, Pia is being encouraged by her friend Bob to rent the rink out to aspiring performance artists as a rehearsal space. The playwright also created love interests for both Anna (Hans Rolf, a retired school principal) and Pia (Bob's neurotic brother, Frankie), even proposing a double wedding for mother and daughter before it is announced that the rink has been officially condemned, reducing the price of the building to $10,000 and obliging Pia to abandon her initial idea of reopening it. Kander and Ebb wrote a complete score for Innaurato's draft book, the second version of which was particularly over-complicated and contrived. Eventually, Terrence McNally was asked to replace Innaurato as the book writer. Four of the songs were retained to become key moments in the new version: 'Colored Lights', 'Chief Cook and Bottlewasher', 'Don't Ah Ma Me' and 'All the Children in a Row'. The team wrote twelve new songs for McNally's first draft, thereafter deleting seven while adding six more for a final version.[6]

It has been claimed that McNally never read Innaurato's versions. His major innovation was to eliminate distracting subplots and instead focus wholly on the mother-daughter interactions, which in turn generated the confrontation of each character with her past. McNally also introduced a male chorus of wreckers, who have come to empty and tear down the building. Unlike the chorus of ancient Greek drama, every member of this group also played at least one of the characters in the flashbacks to each woman's past, enabling the narrative to alternate cinematically between present and past. This element of the show transformed what had at first been envisaged as a conventional book musical into a more modern 'concept' musical in line with a large number of Kander and Ebb's works.

When A J Antoon replaced Arthur Laurents as director, he determined to emphasize the tougher elements of the script – the blue-collar characters in a derelict environment – and to minimize any potential sentimentality. He identified a classic dramaturgical structure in the confrontation between mother and daughter, whose conflicting memories are gradually pieced together to form a coherent picture of their past lives. Although British critic Benedict Nightingale later called the show 'an inverted "Electra" on wheels',[7] tragedy is averted by the reconciliation at the end. *The Rink* begins with the atmospheric sounds of an old fairground organ, which cues the appearance of Angel sitting on a suitcase in what might be a bus station. The sound of the organ seems to trigger Angel's stream of memories in 'Colored Lights'.

The song mimics the way in which a person might recall past acts of remembering an even more distant past, so while Angel doesn't sing directly of the rink, the 'oom pah pah' of the organ underlies all the layers of memory.[8] The contrast between the memories of the more recent and more distant past provides some explanation of her journey back to confront her mother and reclaim the rink. In contrast with the organ chords is the 1970s orchestration of the song with its acoustic guitar accompaniment.

> I was sitting on a sand dune in Santa Cruze,
> Or Monterrey –
> Well anyway.
> I could feel the trickle on my cheek
> Of ocean spray.
> A perfect day –
> Well anyway.[9] (10)

The casual conversational style of the lyrics with its repeated parenthetical phrases not only characterises Angel's casual, off-beat idiom – she is regarded by her mother as a drug-taking hippie – the images also conjure impressions of the West Coast of the USA in the early 1970s when California was regarded as a kind of Utopia for the alternative lifestyles of the counterculture.

Angel's recognition that 'something's missing' from her life in California is always provoked by her attempt at a precise memory of when and where the realisation occurred, evoking a sense of alienation in contrast to the natural beauty of her surroundings:

> I was sailing out of Long Beach on a catamaran
> Or fishing scow –
> Well anyhow –
> I was leaning, chewing cashews off the starboard bow.
> That sunset, 'Wow' –
> Well anyhow –
> I remember telling Joey,
> 'God you're sweet,'
> Or was it Pete? –
> Well anyhow.
>
> I wonder why I feel so incomplete;
> Something's missing Joe,
> Something's missing Pete,
> Something's missing here. (10–11)

As the number progresses, the moments of remembering lead repeatedly to Angel's underlying nostalgia for the rink where she grew up. The sound of the organ becomes a musical motif associated with feelings of security and love from her childhood:

> Where are my colored lights,
> Beads and bleachers and colored lights?
> Passing smiles round and round,
> Thumping oom pah pah organ sound.
> Noisy boys long and lean,
> Giggles of girls in the mezzanine,
> Filtered through colored lights,
> Gold and amber and green. (10)

By the end of the number, Angel is beginning to question why she left home in the first place, so as the motif is repeated, the organ sounds triumphantly as a kind of 'welcome home'. As Angel admits to having forgotten why she left home in the first place, the kind of fairground sounds evoked by the theatre organ creates nostalgia for a past that may never really have existed, except in the mind of a child. Nevertheless, the atmosphere of the rink is established by its 'oom pah pah' as the location in and around which the action of the show will occur, the sound of its accompaniment to the skating seemingly justifying the singing and dancing that occurs throughout.

When Angel exits, a demolition gang of six enters, ready to carry out their orders to pull down the building. During their conversation, Anna enters and sings a song that explains why she has sold the rink. 'Chief Cook and Bottlewasher' introduces Anna's perspective on her own past life, setting up an alternative to her daughter's nostalgic memories of childhood. The different styles of the first two songs distinguish the younger generation and its music from that of the older generation. In contrast to 'Colored Lights', this number is a traditional Broadway show-stopper: like many of the songs in *70, Girls, 70* and *Chicago*, this 'I Want' song has its roots in musical comedy and vaudeville, which enables Anna to 'perform' her personal reasons for selling the rink:

> To Antonelli's Roller Rink and Recreation Center, I have only one thing to say. Va Fangul!

> When I sit and remember the past,
> Though I'd rather not sit and remember the past.
> If I happen to sit and remember the past,
> I hear so many voices – (16)

At this point, the six wreckers transform themselves into male characters from the past calling for her, to which she responds with the verse:

> I was running the rink
> Running the household
> And being a wife.
> 'Working her ass off'
> Should be the title of the story of my life. (16)

The verse brilliantly creates an idiolect for Anna, which combines her own sharp sarcasm – a stock-in-trade of Ebb's lyric-writing – with the typical street slang of a first-generation Italian American. The earthy language suggests Anna's tough attitude and ability to defend herself, building up a rhythm of speaking that illustrates her thinking aloud in the song. Before the first chorus, one of Kander's trademark vamps establishes the humorously aggressive tone in which Anna complains about her life as a mother and wife:

> Chief cook and bottle washer
> That's what I always was
> Doing what some cook and bottlewasher does. (16)

Fred Ebb's concise lyrics brilliantly condense Anna's impressions of domestic life so that the routine labour of a humdrum existence is rattled out furiously as a list of the chores from which she wishes to escape:

> Go stand and take the tickets
> Go make the corn go pop
> Bread to bake and beds to make
> And rugs to shake and floors to mop. (16)

The multiple internal rhymes, the alliteration and the repeated use of words of one syllable contrive to heighten the staccato effect and emphasize Anna's anger. The lyrics compress the experience of bringing up the baby (Angel) into a series of verbs that repeat some of the chores mentioned earlier:

So now it's warm the bottle
See what she's crying for
Bathe and wipe and rock and diap
And bake and take and mop and pop
Exactly like I did before. (17)

As much focused on summoning the past as 'Colored Lights', Anna's number is derived from traditional musical comedy tropes and styles. Its combination of sassy up-tempo music and salty vernacular lyrics provides the opportunity for Chita Rivera to give a virtuoso demonstration of classic Broadway belting. After the number, the sound of the roller coaster gives a momentary intimation of a time when the rink was at the height of its glory until Angel's intrusion from the outside world jolts the action into the present moment once more.

A vituperative argument between mother and daughter comes to sound like an old routine until it, in fact, segues into song. One of the four numbers retained from the very first draft of the musical, 'Don't Ah Ma Me' is a highly effective transposition of dialogue into song, whose opposition of Anna's detailed accusations with Angel's often overlapping protests ('Ah Ma') ritualizes the recurrent conflict of mother and daughter at the core of the drama. This is the first of the numbers in *The Rink* written in a manner that might be described as operatic – a duet, which mimics vernacular speech on a heightened emotional level. After a few repeats of Anna's chorus, the song climaxes:

> Ah Ma, I thought there'd be some tears
> And after all these years,
> You might have mellowed some
> But Jesus, was I dumb.

ANNA.   [.....................................]
Should the sound of your hello
Be like music to my ears,
When I haven't seen your face
In what is it, seven years?
Now you walk back in my life
Should I really bless my luck
That's an outfit you could wear
On a sanitation truck
Have a daughter I was told
They're a blessing when you're old
Ah Stroongatz
[..]

I quit

ANGEL   Ah Ma

ANNA.   Now I got a good thing going
And I don't need you to hex it
Did you notice where you enter
You can also make an exit?
So go out and find a husband
Join a convent

> Be a whore
> But I'm sick and tired of your
> Ah Ma

ANGEL.   Ah Ma. (25)

After 'I quit', Angel holds the note until the end of Anna's two choruses, both performers giving virtuoso displays of skill (Anna has to maintain clear articulation while singing her lines very quickly).

By this stage in the action, the writers have clearly established the resentments that undermine the abrasive relationship between mother and daughter in the present, so the remainder of Act I consists of excavations of different layers of the past in order to identify the cause of the current impasse. The first flashback is to 1950 when Anna's boyfriend Dino returns from a trip that he does not satisfactorily account for. When she tells him she is pregnant, he claims this to be the reason he went 'to the moon and back' to purchase her blue crystal goblets. The song 'Blue Crystal' reveals Dino as a romantic, even something of a fantasist, whose charm has become a strategy for avoiding family responsibilities. Angel, who watches the re-enactment of the past from her position in 1979, morphs into her childhood self, complimenting her father, whom she adores. After the song, the action shifts forward to the present (1979), as four of the wreckers return with the box of blue crystal glasses, which Lino offers to buy. Angel is horrified and struggles to prevent her mother from selling them. There follows a flashback to 1952, in which Anna accuses Dino of having an affair while he threatens to volunteer for the Korean War; the quarrel wakes the child Angel before the scene jumps forward to 1979.

Angel's next song, 'Familiar Things', concerns her newly acquired appreciation of the value of home and the security of the environment in which one grows up. An 'operatic' aria, Angel's paradoxical reflections on why she wishes to preserve the rink and all its contents, from which she had previously run away, are once more expressed in an emotionally elevated style. The verse at the beginning of the number is a kind of jingle evoking the mechanical sounds of the various holiday attractions on the boardwalk in a rhythm that creates musical onomatopoeia:

> Under the rollercoaster
> Next to the jungle ride
> Right of the caterpillar
> Left of the water slide
> [.................................]

These recollections of the surrounding environment prompt the more intimate flow of Angel's thoughts:

> Familiar things
> The thing about familiar things
> Is how you keep imagining
> They'll never go away.
> They're nothing special
> They've always been there
> And so you really don't appreciate familiar things. (31)

The chorus, with its tautological repetitions of 'familiar things', enacts the quality of permanence implied by familiarity, subtly put in question by 'how you keep imagining'. This rhetorical strategy is repeated by the two further reiterations of the chorus, with their slight modifications, the last one stating Angel's discovery of the importance of familiar things she has at first 'underestimated'. The 'aria' is completed by a repetition of the opening verse, reproducing the familiar noises of the boardwalk again.

When Angel realizes both the organ and the glitter ball are broken, she feels elements of her past have been taken from her, but Anna simply retorts, 'You're not a child anymore, Angel', which triggers a flashback to Dino's return from the Korean War in 1953. When the drunken Dino brings his army buddies home, his father attempts to protect the sleeping Angel, but Dino wakes her up to ask her to make a wish on her birthday. She whispers to him, prompting him to reply with, 'There's Not Enough Magic', after which he asks her to close her eyes and he produces the glitter ball, which enchants the child:

DINO.   'Round it goes, 'round it goes, just like the world

ANGEL. Only much more beautiful

DINO.   Turn, turn, glitter and twirl
       Light up the eyes of my little girl
       Shine like stars in the snow

ANGEL &
DINO.   Only much more beautiful (37)

Dino has changed the atmosphere completely to reflect the fantasy he has created for Angel, but the mood soon reverts to one of danger and aggression when the number becomes a dance for Anna and Tom after Dino drops out.

Anna then presents Angel with a birthday cake and asks her to make a wish as she blows out the single candle, at which moment the little girl is asked to make a speech: 'I have the best Daddy in the whole world and this is the best rink in the whole world and we're all gonna be here like this forever and forever and forever.' Dino breaks the festive atmosphere when he inappropriately communicates with the child as though she were an adult ('Nothing's forever, Angel', 38), causing his father to try and cheer things up by proposing a toast ('Here's to the rink/And all of us together', 38) but Dino shatters the mood completely by smashing one of the crystal glasses 'in frustration and anger'. Dino asks everyone to leave before confiding in Anna:

I don't know what's wrong, Anna. It all used to be so . . . Everything fit [. . .]
ANNA.
It's not easy coming back.
DINO.
All of a sudden nothing's the same. I'm scared.
ANNA.
[. . .] It's okay. I'm right here for you. (39)

Anna sings another 'operatic' aria, to my mind the most moving song in the musical, in order to try to comfort her husband:

Long as I know you're trying
Long as I know you care
Long as we stick together
We'll take on anyone
Anytime, anywhere (40)

The music builds to a soaringly romantic crescendo in the last two lines of the 'bridge'. The intensity continues until the last line of the chorus when the declaration turns soft and gentle,

I have you
You have me
Right to the end of always
Down to the finish line
We can make it fine. (41)

When working lights come on, the scene has returned to 1979. Now Angel discovers that the wreckers have a demolition order because Anna has sold the rink without consulting her. Their intense argument continues in a dumb show as the chorus sings the breezy old-time 'After All These Years', ironically celebrating the 'loving' mother-daughter reunion:

Gee, it's good to see you
After all these years
Gee, you've really lifted my morale
Kept it all together after all these years,
What's your secret old pal? (43)

The heavy irony here is much like that used in *Chicago*, in which songs are deployed equivocally to express feelings inappropriate to the dramatic moment – here a cheerful, up-tempo number in contrast to Angel and Anna's engagement in an extremely intense exchange of anger. During the song, Angel sees that her mother has forged her signature in order to go ahead with the sale. As before, the dialogue segues easily into Angel's sung declaration,

I got plans, Ma
Lots of plans
Stick around Ma
Watch them happen (44)

An amplification of the operatic mode of expression employed earlier, Angel sings defiantly of her determination to reopen the rink. The thumping staccato of the orchestration evokes Angel's determination as well as the heyday of the rink:

Angel's rink and social center
The chic-est place you'll ever enter
[............................]
So that's the future, that's the story
I'll have the rink in all its glory
And I can make it happen, that much I know,
'Cause now I'm gone, and now I'm stronger
I ain't your Angel any longer

I got this dream and I ain't letting it
Go! (47)

Angel's determination seems overstated, as if she needs to convince herself by acting out in song her ability to achieve her goal. After Angel phones a lawyer from a payphone, the battle builds up to a point when she says 'fuck you' to her mother, who slaps her and is slapped back. Anna finally explains to her that all the attractions on the boardwalk have closed down, cueing a flashback to the recent past in which two old women (played by men from the wreckers' chorus) join Anna to lament the disintegration of the neighbourhood, as two punks disturb the peace with loud music from a ghetto-blaster.

While Angel observes from the present, her mother and the old women sing the nostalgic, 'What Happened to the Old Days?' The clichés they accumulate in recalling a less threatening past produce a rich vein of comedy while at the same time eliciting sympathy.

What happened to the old days
What happened to the unlocked door
What happened to the 'Come on in, it's open' kind
of phrase?
What happened to the nice times?
Who put the 'hood' in neighborhood? (53)

Some lyrics suggest the genuine fear that older people experience as the streets are taken over by young hoodlums. Idiomatic exclamations ('It's murder'; 'those scumbags') punctuate the song, which twice reiterates Angel's earlier motif,

Under the rollercoaster
Next to the jungle ride
Right of the caterpillar
Left of the waterslide. (32)

At the end of the song, Anna approaches the three punks who have returned with their radio on full blast in order to demand that they turn the volume down. The electric guitars form an accompaniment to a stylized movement sequence in which Anna is mugged, the action returning to 1979 after the punks leave and the 'old women' exit. Anna and Angel each remain firmly resolved: as Anna goes upstairs to her apartment to finish packing, Angel telephones a friend to say, 'This is gonna take a little longer than I thought' before ending the act with a reprise of the last few bars of 'Colored Lights':

Leaving home years ago, what was I looking for?
I don't know

I can't recall
Well, anyway soon I'll have my days and nights
Of wonderful, glimmering, beautiful, shimmering
Colored lights! (55)

Act 2 begins with Anna and Angel getting stoned. From their friendly banter and the wisecracking nature of the comic 'list song', 'The Apple Doesn't Fall', there appears now to be a reconciliation between mother and daughter, but this proves to be temporary. Kander and Ebb exploit the style of 'The Grass Is Always Greener', a huge crowd-pleaser from *Woman of the Year*, to create a typically self-referential comic lament. When Angel learns that Anna is returning to Florida with Lenny Pegedis, there is a flashback to the 1940s when Anna knew Lenny as a teenager who was besotted with her. At first. he introduces himself in song:

> They never call me Lenny
> Or Leonard or Len
> It's always good old Lenny
> Good old, good old Lenny
> Since I can't remember when. (61)

Then, he proposes to Anna in an insistent refrain that suggests he has asked her a number of times:

> So marry me
> Give in and marry me
> Though you don't love me now you will in time
>
> You may not know it yet
> But I'm the best you'll get
> Wake up and marry me
> Marry me
> Marry me [62–3]

The scene switches from the 1940s to the present as Anna remembers how many boys wanted to date her, although she only had eyes for the arrogant Dino Antonelli, whose family owned the skating rink: 'The day your father handed me a broom was the day I should've guessed what being married to him was going to be like' (65). At this point, a flashback to her wedding (posing for a photograph) not only reminds Anna of her honeymoon in Atlantic City but also that, while her sexual relationship with Dino was pleasurable, 'after a while it wasn't enough' (66). There is a series of short shifts in time forward from 1956, during one of which Dino leaves home. Later, Anna explains his absence by telling Angel he has died. A sequence of brief scenes advances the years to the point where Angel is fifteen. The musical number 'Mrs A' is intercalated with dialogue to evoke Anna's guilt in succumbing to the pressure to have sexual relations with a number of men in the neighbourhood. On her knees at the end of the first iteration of the number, Anna addresses God in song:

> What kind of God are you really anyway
> I guess you're not really there
> You're not really there
>
> I don't believe
> I don't believe in you (71)

From this point, the unravelling of what happened in the past is expedited as mother and daughter prompt each other to remember. Anna's rendition of 'Mrs A' is followed by a three-part version, in which Angel and Anna are joined by three men in recreating the memory. Angel reveals that she could hear her mother having sex with various men:

Hearing sounds
Mysterious familiar sounds
And I would lie there picturing
The scene behind the door (72)

This further iteration of the number is a dramaturgically and musically complex interweaving of Angel's accusations against her mother, Anna's defence of her behaviour and the men's desire to exploit Anna's loneliness for their own gratification. It mixes motifs from Angel's earlier song ('Familiar Things') with the repeated choruses from 'Mrs A' ('Someday I'm gonna/Tell you about/The nights', 73) and the three men's repeated staccato demands ('Hey, Mrs A,' 72–3).

After Angel exits, Ben (one of the wreckers) expresses some sympathy with her desire to save the rink:

It's a shame to see a place like this come down. [. . .] This place survived the hurricane of '37, that big boardwalk fire of '58. It survived two world wars, rock 'n' roll and disco. The only thing it's not gonna survive is us. [. . .] They're never gonna build something like this again.[10]

When the other wreckers enter on roller skates, a past era is recreated as they all sing and skate in tribute to the rink's bygone glory:

I wanna go see the spot go pink
I wanna go hear the skate-key clink
If you wanna good go round with me
We're gonna go round the rink. [75–6]

After Lenny has phoned to check that Anna is ready to leave for Florida, there is a flashback to Angel's spring prom in 1965, with Anna encouraging her in a song-and-dance duet to

Figure 15. Liza Minnelli and Chita Rivera rehearsing for *The Rink*. Photo: Martha Swope, NYPL, Billy Rose Division.

be bold in inviting any boy she wants to dance with her at the prom ('Wallflower'). In one version Angel's Uncle Fasto tells her that her father has not died but simply walked out on her and her mother. In a later revision, it is the rather uncouth Bobby Perillo who, when Angel refuses to dance with him, spitefully refers to her mother as being almost a whore as well as revealing the truth about her father. In a scene in 1972, Angel, shattered by this startling discovery, searches for Dino Antonelli.

In the original 1984 version, Angel's virtuoso 'All the Children in a Row', ostensibly a lament for American soldiers who died in Vietnam, functions both as a reminiscence of the end of the protest movements of the late 1960s and early 1970s and as a personal story of her progressive disillusionment with her father.

> All the children in a row
> Running for their lives
> Seems to me I wrote the book
> How a kid survives. (81)
> [..................]
>
> California's warm as love
> I belong I know
> To the secret army of
> All the children in a row (82)

Within the song is interpolated a chorus that reveals her boyfriend Danny's death as the result of driving a car while stoned.

> Do you need to take that stuff
> Come on Danny, that's enough.
> We can make it, we'll survive.
> Danny, you're too stoned to drive.
> *(In the distance a car crash. A siren wails. Danny is gone.)* (83)

After the car crash, the audience observes Anna watching Angel finally make contact with her older father: the daughter is devastated because he refuses to allow her to share his new life and family. When she tells him she is pregnant, Dino's reaction is, 'Do me a favour and don't come back. It ain't fair to either one of us' (85). Angel reverts to a reprise of the opening 'Colored Lights',

> I was sitting on a sand dune in Santa Cruz
> Or Monterey, well anyway . . . (85)

At this point, Angel's little girl, also called Anna, enters from across the road to ask Angel for five dollars to pay for the hamburger she has eaten. Looking at Anna, she asks:

> Who are you?
>
> ANNA:
> I think I'm your grandmother.
>
> LITTLE GIRL:
> You think?

(*To* ANGEL)
You're right, she's far out for an old lady.
[...............]

(*to* ANNA)

I'd kiss you but I don't know you well enough and she's raising me not to be a hypocrite.

ANNA:
In the meantime what do I call you?

LITTLE GIRL:
Anna. (86–8)

After this there is a tearful scene of reconciliation and Angel agrees that the demolition of the rink can go ahead. She has made peace with her mother and with her past. The show ends with a reprise of the triumphant toast to the rink. ('Here's to the rink') as an underscore of 'Colored Lights' heralds the end of the show.

Notes

1. There is a private recording of a performance of the Broadway production at https://www.youtube.com/watch?v=QxJstIozp60.
2. *Colored Lights*, 161.
3. *Colored Lights*, 161-2.
4. Ibid., 162.
5. See James Leve, *Kander and Ebb*, New Haven: Yale University Press, 2009, 212–3.
6. See Leve, *Kander and Ebb*, 213–4.
7. *New York Times*, 10 February 1984, Section C 3.
8. This dual process is what Jacques sings of in *The Happy Time* as 'Remember you/ Remembering the happy time' (See Chapter 4).
9. Page references are to McNally, Kander and Ebb, *The Rink*, New York: Samuel French, 1985.
10. This quotation is from the revised version of the show presented at the Southwark Playhouse in June 2018, with the script provided by director Adam Lenson.

11 The political is personal

Kiss of the Spider Woman (1993)

The theme that may instantly have sparked Kander and Ebb's interest in Manuel Puig's novel is articulated in a central argument between the two cellmates. Molina, the homosexual window-dresser, uses memories of his favourite movies as a mental escape from the cruel and monotonous regimen of life in prison, while the Marxist revolutionary Valentin rejects such escapist strategies as harmful delusions, preferring unflinchingly to confront the reality of the fascist regime that has caused their incarceration by studying social conditions as a preparation for changing them:

> I'm locked up in this cell and I'm better off thinking about nice things so I don't go nuts. [. . .]
>
> [T]hat business of only thinking about nice things [. . .] can be dangerous [. . .] It can become a vice, always trying to escape from reality like that, it's like taking drugs or something. Because [. . .] reality, I mean *your reality*, isn't restricted by this cell we live in. If you read something, if you study something, you transcend any cell you're inside of [. . .] That's why I read and why I study every day.'[1]

The philosophical debate between coping with the pain of a harsh existence by imagining a fantasy world of pleasure and romance or directly confronting that existence by pursuing a path of political action parallels the dialectical relationship between the escapist illusions of the cabaret and the disturbing reality of the rise of Nazism in *Cabaret*.

In the novel, Molina's vivid retelling of a series of five films is intercalated with the unravelling of a skeletal narrative in which the prison warden bribes him to obtain information concerning the political activities of Valentin's revolutionary organization in exchange for his own early release from jail. One of the novel's extraordinary literary features is its construction as a series of dialogues and long monologues in which Molina relates his films in the manner of a stream-of-consciousness, and Valentin recounts his past romantic attachments. This permits the evocation of a Freudian transaction between the effeminate Molina and the macho Valentin, in which the clash between their points of view can be played out in terms of a rational argument as well as through an unconscious process in which their opposed personalities are subtly transformed by their surprising friendship.

According to Puig's biographer and his usual English translator, Suzanne Jill Levine, 'Manuel [. . .] would even satirise the analyst's couch by turning it into a prison cot and by taking the talking cure to its ultimate mutual transference: Valentin and Molina become, through verbal as well as sexual intercourse, each other' (Levine, 258). Levine regards his work as by its nature political:

Manuel was genuinely, intuitively political in his writing – and most explicitly in *Kiss of the Spiderwoman*, though he was not a public spokesperson like other writers. His novels can also be regarded as feminist in that his constant subject was the political nature of our sexual lives, or the sexual dynamic of the body politic. [. . .] Manuel consistently spoke for difference, not so much for groups as for the individual [. . .] Despite his ever-present, mischievous irony, Manuel did have a political mission: to educate both the victims and the perpetrators of homophobia in Latin America.[2]

In one of the elaborate footnotes he appended to the novel, Puig expressed his own view of the psychological genesis of homosexual identity in the guise of the fictional Danish psychoanalyst, Anneli Taube. The 'theory' propounded mirrored his experience of growing up within the typically patriarchal Argentinian family structure:

[T]he rejection which a highly sensitive boy experiences toward an oppressive father – as symbol of the violently authoritarian, masculine attitude – is a conscious one. The boy, at the moment when he decides not to adhere to the world proposed by such a father – one of weapons, violently competitive sports, disdain for sensitivity as a feminine attribute, etc. – is actually exercising a free and even revolutionary choice inasmuch as he is rejecting the role of the stronger, the exploitative one. Of course [. . .] Western civilization [. . .] will not present him with any alternative model for conduct, in those first dangerously decisive years – above all from three to five – other than his mother. And the world of the mother – tenderness, tolerance, and even the arts – will turn out to be much more attractive to him, especially because of the absence of aggressivity: but the world of the mother, and here is where his intuition would fail him, is also the world of submission, since the mother is coupled with an authoritarian male, who only conceives of conjugal union as a subordination of the woman to the man [. . .][3]

The footnote offers a psychoanalytic explication of the novel's radical subversion of the patriarchal ideology of gender that determined not only conservative discourse but also oppositional Marxist ideology. Puig identifies a boy's early rejection of traditional gender roles as 'a free and even revolutionary choice', subverting the stereotypical masculinism of the revolutionary left to reveal it as a mirror image of the primitive machismo of fascist oppression. The novel proposes a deconstruction of the categories of 'masculine' and 'feminine' as they traditionally operate to determine gender and sexuality – an early articulation of the idea that 'the personal is political', which became the mantra of feminist and queer activists in the 1980s. The lengthy footnote also outlines a developmental scenario that matches Puig's own family circumstances: '[I]f [. . .] the father is extremely primitive and the mother quite refined but nonetheless submissive, the extremely sensitive and precociously intelligent boy almost inevitably will reject the paternal model'.[4] Puig appears to project many aspects of his homosexual identity through the character of Molina, but he does not reject Valentin's intellectual sophistication and political idealism. As Levine suggests, 'Molina and Valentin [. . .] represent two sides of Manuel'.[5]

As with most of his novels, *Kiss* expresses Puig's lifelong love of the melodramatic and unselfconscious camp of certain popular Hollywood and South American film genres and reflects his belief in the efficacy of cinema as a necessary means of escape:

There are many people who live in the sticks and have nothing. They are soaking in machismo, in a hostile environment. What do they do? They have no choice. The movies provide an alternative. They help you to not go crazy. You witness another way of life. It doesn't matter that the way of life shown by Hollywood was phony. It helped you hope.[6]

Although Puig invented two of the five movies narrated by Molina, the novel explores the ways in which the content of popular films becomes a crucial factor in the construction of a cultural imaginary. In doing so, it cuts across conventional aesthetic distinctions between high art and mass entertainment,[7] interrogating the relationship between high culture and kitsch to provoke a dialogue between Marxist politics and camp. According to Kimberley Chabot Davis,

> The novel could be described as a tragic love story that tugs at the heart strings, not unlike the B-movies that Molina cherishes and retells to Valentin. [. . .] Despite these attributes of a popular sensibility, *Kiss* has most often been received as a high-cultural postmodern text. [. . .] *Kiss* upsets narrative expectations, criticizes the banality of popular culture, and deconstructs such accepted cultural dichotomies as male/female, rational/ emotional, and homosexual/heterosexual. Many critics regard *Kiss of the Spider Woman* as a high cultural, critical meditation on popular culture, rather than as a participant in popular culture. I contend that the text establishes a symbiotic relationship between the popular and the postmodern that is crucial to its political impact upon audiences.[8]

The novel's pervasive dialectic of high art against mass culture made it an obvious candidate for translation into the medium of film. Puig was himself an avid collector of old films; his knowledge of popular movies was compendious and his taste eclectic, although he had a particular predilection for the melodrama intrinsic to genres such as 1940s film noir, horror movies, Latin American musicals of the 1930s and 1940s, and even German, Italian and Spanish fascist cinema of this period, which were the only foreign films he could see during his adolescence when all Hollywood films were banned under Peron's dictatorship. In Puig's preparation for *Kiss*, he researched Nazi films to find material for the invented fascist film *Destino,* which would provoke Valentin into giving the ignorant Molina a political education.

The novel begins in the middle of Molina's retelling of *Cat People*, a classic Hollywood horror film made by RKO in 1946:

> – Something a little strange, that's what you notice, that she's not a woman like all the others. She looks fairly young, twenty-five, maybe a little more, petite face, a little cat-like, small turned-up nose. The shape of her face, it's . . . more roundish than oval, broad forehead, pronounced cheeks too but then they come down to a point, like with cats.[9]

Molina ostensibly narrates the various films in order to help both men fall asleep; however, they gradually become their most powerful means of communicating. The dissection of the film narratives by Valentin, who often interrupts to ask questions or subject the values of a film to an ideological critique, initiates a genuine exchange of ideas between the two prisoners who would otherwise find no common ground for conversation. While Valentin regards the highly charged romantic content of most of the film narratives as politically oppressive, Molina is preoccupied largely with their aesthetic style and interprets the mise-en-scène – fashions, faces, bodies, gestures and décor – in minute detail. Each man projects himself psychologically onto the different narratives, empathizing particularly strongly with certain characters and viewing others as objects of desire. On the page, the distinction between Valentin and Molina is not always immediately clear as the author does not attach names to the speakers. This device allows a reader to experience each man's flow of feelings and ideas as an interior stream of thought, with a distinctive rhythm that allows unrestricted movement between conscious and unconscious registers of psychic life, rather than prompting her to construe each man's identity as a conventional, self-contained 'character'.

Puig's promiscuous mingling of highbrow literary tropes with kitsch cinematic references represents a postmodern challenge to Adorno's aesthetic distinction between high art and mass culture that chimes with the often surprising attempts of Kander and Ebb to bridge the gulf separating popular entertainment from 'serious' drama by exploiting the artistic vocabulary of the Broadway musical in extremely ambitious and sophisticated ways. As soon as Fred Ebb saw the film of *Kiss of the Spider Woman* in Los Angeles in 1985, he read Manuel Puig's novel and decided it would provide an excellent basis for a musical. John Kander and Harold Prince were equally enthusiastic and agreed that the novel was a better starting point than the film, so Prince engaged Puig as the book writer. According to Kander, the novel's evocation of its central characters' interior lives was the key to imagining it as a musical:

> It's easier to work from a book when you can really go inside the mind of the character [. . .] It was perfectly obvious to the three of us that not only do you have the exotic locale of a South American prison, but you're spending half the evening inside of somebody else's fantasy, and if that isn't a clear invitation to do something musical, I don't know what would be. What seems unlikely musical material to many people often seems like very likely material to us [. . .] I think these pieces that are kind of bold [. . .] are much easier to write than a little story about boy meets girl in New York.[10]

Nonetheless, it was clear that a series of alterations in the structure of the narrative would be required in order to adapt the novel as an effective stage musical. After being invited by Prince to write the book of the musical, Puig drafted an outline, which was completed by May 1986. According to James Leve, he exploited the device he had employed in his 1981 stage adaptation, replacing the novel's multiple movie narratives with a single film. The newly conceived 1940s Hollywood film musical portrayed the love affair between a 'playboy film director'[11] and a beautiful young woman, whose demise was ominously foretold at birth. When she saves the director from death by stepping in front of him to block the bullets of gunmen hired by a jealous producer, the woman's heroic gesture of romantic love seals her predicted fate. Although Fred Ebb expressed reservations about the outline for this film-within-the-show, the ambiguous foreshadowing of death as the inevitable consequence of pure romantic love remained key to the meaning of the Spider Woman's kiss throughout the long developmental process.

When Ebb suggested *Follies* and *Cabaret* as theatrical models that might help transfigure the novel into a musical whose structure would be very different from that of the novel, Puig's response was extremely perceptive, asserting that Ebb's two examples were 'atmosphere pieces, . . . not dominated by two strong characters, like *Spider Woman*'. The full-length draft that Puig later sent to Prince reflected his belief that the film narrative should heighten and develop the drama of the two prisoners: its new movie fantasy, *It Was Written in the Stars*, was the story of Perla, a young woman raised by prostitutes, who 'falls in love with a wanted man and in the end dies tragically' – an obvious parallel to the relationship between Molina and Valentin. Although the interweaving of the movie musical fantasy with the brutal facts of prison life was to become even more problematic in the version of the show performed in Purchase, the importance of revealing parallels between the two was never in question. A few years after the team's initial attempt to collaborate with Puig in New York, it became apparent that his residence in Rio de Janeiro and Cuernavaca in Mexico precluded a lengthy commitment to the project. His lack of experience in the technical aspects of musical theatre and the fact that English was his second language created additional difficulties, so in the late 1980s, Prince invited Terrence McNally to author the book of the musical. Nevertheless, the experience of getting to know Puig greatly helped Kander and Ebb in writing the show.[12]

Puig's treatment (1987) begins with the faces of the two protagonists in 'pin' spots while Molina narrates the film *Cat People*; only after six minutes do the lights widen to reveal the whole cell. The treatment is very much a condensation of the novel, similar to the stage play that Puig had adapted from it in the 1980s; the spotlit faces served to foreground the interplay of consciousness between the two men in dialogue and internal monologue as a key to the oneiric quality that is so brilliantly exploited in the novel. At the end, Valentin is heard in voice-over speaking the hallucinatory narrative of escape with which the novel ends.[13] Clearly, this approach did not permit obvious opportunities for musical numbers so one can see why Prince felt it necessary to hire a new book writer.

Terrence McNally's first draft (dated September 1988)[14] began with a prologue 'Her Name Is Aurora' intended to be performed by Molina, Aurora, the star of his favourite movies, and chorus boys. It is motivated by the words 'I will dance alone' and would have opened the show with a flourish very different from the hauntingly quiet sung phrases that actually began the show when it finally opened in Toronto in 1992.

Some of the songs listed in this draft remain in the final version of the show: 'Over the Wall (three fragments to be sung at different moments)', 'Dear One', 'I Do Miracles', 'You Could Never Shame Me', 'The Day after That' 'She's a Woman', 'Let's Make Love'. Others, such as 'Man Overboard', 'No Law against It', If I Were in Your Shoes', and a duet for Valentin and Molina, 'Something in Common'. Valentin seems to have a larger role in this version, with 'Valentin's Thoughts' listed several times, while 'Molina's Thoughts' is listed only once. They do not sleep together in this version, and the Spider Woman is not yet totally symbolic.

Kiss of the Spider Woman had the longest development period of any Kander and Ebb musical. It was the first show to receive a tryout production at SUNY, Purchase[15] as part of a 'New Musicals' initiative that offered Broadway-bound musicals the chance to test what had been written in a full staging. The intention was to permit authors and other creatives to see precisely which aspects of the dramaturgy, score, design and choreographic approach worked and which needed changing so that the show could be revised or even re-conceived in preparation for its Broadway opening. Given the aim of the 'New Musicals' project to provide a platform for the gestation of musicals free from the commercial pressures of Broadway, newspapers were explicitly requested not to review the show. When the *New York Times* announced it was going to send its chief theatre critic, Frank Rich, to see the show, seventeen representatives from all of the musicals that were scheduled to participate in the first year visited the newspaper's offices in an unsuccessful attempt to persuade them not to review it. When other newspapers heard that the *Times* intended to publish a review, some of them decided to send reviewers. Frank Rich and a number of other critics were fairly negative about the musical, which was not only a severe setback for *Kiss* but effectively put an end to the 'New Musicals' enterprise.

In the version of the show at Purchase in 1991, Terrence McNally had attempted to interweave two narratives – a direct representation of one movie recounted by Molina and the story of the two men in a prison cell. This approximated the device used in Hector Babenco's film version, in which Molina and Valentin's conversations are intercut with sequences from *Her Real Glory*, a sepia-toned film-within-the-film, which serves as a vehicle for Nazi propaganda. By contrast, McNally's newly conceived movie musical *Man Over Board,* was a pastiche of the style that typified Rita Hayworth's film musicals, including an elaborate pattern of deliberate echoes of the actual situation in the prison. Molina is figured as Aurora, a South American actress who is the mistress of 'the Monster', while the obvious surrogate for Valentin is Armando, a young sailor with whom Aurora falls in love and who is later discovered to be the leader of a resistance movement fighting organized crime.

The scenography for the Purchase version of *Kiss of the Spiderwoman* was much more literal than that later used for the Toronto production, with the spectacle represented through bulky painted set pieces.[16] There was an attempt to render the Latin American flavour of the story, which was signalled before the show began by the enormous surreal painting on the front scrim of a fan, fruit, flowers, leaves and butterflies, which remained in place throughout a conventional Broadway overture. The show began with prisoners marching followed as in the final version, by the announcement of Valentin's arrival at the prison. Here, however, the Spider Woman is not represented in a stylized manner as a symbol but appears as the young actress Aurora, who simply walks into the cell to talk to Molina. He is not as self-consciously camp as in the final version, and both he and Valentin sing extremely operatically.

The film-within-the-musical creates a parallel between Valentin and the heterosexual hero, Armando and also between the prison warden, who in reality is bribing Molina to try and solicit political secrets from Valentin, and the Monster, who as crime boss represents the corrupt system Armando is fighting to destroy. After Aurora is forced by the Monster to reveal her lover's hideout in the mountains, she rushes to the guerrilla camp to warn Armando, who hatches a counterplot that results in the Monster's death. The climax of the action occurs in the 'Embassy Ball' scene during which Armando poses as a waiter, Aurora sits on the Monster's lap while a chanteuse sings 'Kiss of the Spider Woman' and surreptitiously stabs him as the song ends. As Armando sweeps Aurora off her feet, Molina explicates the conclusion of the film as the victory of virtue and love over evil and hate.[17]

The creative team agreed that the constant switching between the prison cell and the locations of *Man Over Board*, together with the detailed scheme of correspondences between reality and fiction, was too complicated: it split the focus of the plot and confused the audience. Viewing the piece in performance also permitted Hal Prince an opportunity to observe that the overall style of the production was too realistic. The design approach was conventional: large pieces of scenery necessitated mechanized set changes that lacked the fluidity needed to alternate cinematically between prison reality and escapist fantasy. According to Prince, the form of the musical had from the outset been influenced by Dennis Potter's BBC television drama series, *The Singing Detective* (1986).[18] Its continual shifting between the figure of the writer in his hospital bed and scenes from a Raymond Chandler-style novel he is imagining about a detective who sings with a dance hall band offered the team a model for the kind of relationship between the reality of the men's confinement in a prison cell and Molina's escapist film fantasies.

The problems of this version are clearly apparent from a viewing of the TOFT audiovisual recording. The storytelling is too literal, and the alternation between *Man Overboard* and the prisoners is clumsy, inadvertently ignoring the dual stream-of-consciousness writing that gives the novel its peculiar power. The pastiche musical film-within-the-musical turns any sense of its melodramatic potential into broad parody – an 'Anything Goes'-type number with dancing sailors on the deck of a boat is a camp version of a bad Broadway show, rather than a pastiche of the South American melodrama that Puig may have had in mind: ('Sailor boy, hear my SOS/Sailor boy, won't you answer yes').[19] Armando's girlfriend is La Suena, to whom he somewhat arbitrarily sings 'An everyday man', a pastiche number, which includes a wholly inappropriate tap dance that finally becomes wilder and more Latin. In a mountain setting, Armando and a group of insurrectionists sing and dance 'A Good Clean Fight', an irrelevant number about guerrilla warfare that appears to be a pastiche of 'Nothing like a Dame' from *South Pacific*. In this sequence, the 'Monster' is the Chief of Police.

In describing his moment of political conversion by the revolutionary leader Golizar, Valentin explicitly compares his dream of revolution to Molina's escapist films ('You have your movies, I have mine – it's one scene'). 'The Day After That' is introduced by Valentin's admission that 'I came hot on the trail of a pretty girl' and he sings 'You Are a Man' to Molina as both a reminder that his companion is indeed masculine and an exhortation to be so. Molina directly declares his love for Valentin ('I've fallen in love with you – it only makes it worse') who takes his shirt off to indicate his willingness to sleep with Molina and a curtain is drawn to hide the sex scene. In this version, Valentin hears that Molina has been killed taking his message and there is a final scene in which Molina's mother visits Valentin and thanks him for helping her son achieve love and pride as a man ('A Life Without Dignity'). At the ending of the show, Molina rises from death but now he refuses to dance with Aurora as before: 'I can't live in my movies any more.' A new cellmate joins Valentin, who promises to tell him the stories of movies to pass the time and begins to narrate Molina's story.

Although it gave *Kiss* unwanted negative publicity at a crucial moment in its development, Frank Rich's review did highlight a few of the problems which Prince and his creative team themselves had recognized they would need to rectify:

> [T]he fantasy film – here fittingly changed to an old movie musical – overwhelms the reality so completely that the compelling story of Molina and Valentin seems a mild, often incoherent intrusion [. . .]. By evening's end, when Molina and Valentin are supposed to be achieving a redemptive symbiosis, the male stars hardly seem to have met each other. Instead of concentrating on the performances crucial to this psychodrama, Mr. Prince seems fixated on the big production numbers and scenic effects, as if he felt obligated to warp his show to placate Broadway audiences' presumed insistence on spectacle [. . .] [S]omewhere in "Kiss of the Spider Woman" is the compelling story its creators want to tell, which is nothing less than an investigation of what it means to be a man, in the highest moral sense, whatever one's sexual orientation.[20]

The resolution of the problem demanded the cutting of the film-within-the-show, which entailed the scrapping of the entire set design. Sensing the show's potential, the Canadian producer, Garth Drabinsky, joined the team as producer of a new version. Extensively rewritten for a première in Toronto in 1992, which was followed by a critically successful run in London, *Kiss of the Spider Woman* finally opened on Broadway in May 1993, where it played for 900 performances.

In order to illustrate Molina's escapist use of movies in the cell without wholly submerging the portrayal of the men's developing relationship, Prince, McNally, Kander and Ebb decided to cut *Man Over Board* and replace it with songs or fragments of scenes from a number of films supposedly starring Molina's favourite screen idol Aurora, who stars as the glamorous heroine of every movie he recalls. As a director, Prince substituted song and dance and exotic spectacle for most of the verbal relation of film narratives, while Kander and Ebb seized the opportunity to write pastiche songs for a variety of fictional film musicals. As a consequence of these changes, the figure of the Spider Woman underwent a series of radical transformations in the process of moving from novel to musical. In the novel, the symbolic implications of the figure are merely hinted at in a conversation between Valentin and Molina that occurs shortly before Molina leaves the prison:

> _ I'm curious . . . would you feel much revulsion about giving me a kiss?
> _ Mmm . . . It must be a fear that you'll turn into a panther like with the first
> movie you told me.
> _ I'm not the panther woman.
> _ It's true, you're not the panther woman.
> _ It's very sad being a panther woman; no one can kiss you. Or anything.
> _ You, you're the spider woman, that traps men in her web.
> _ How lovely! Oh, I like that.
>
> _ . . .
> _ Valentin, you and my mom are the two people that I've loved most in the world.[21]

In Hector Babenco's film, Sonia Braga played Leni Lamaison, who is the heroine of the romantic melodrama set in occupied France, the Spider Woman spoken of by Molina, and, in a flashback sequence, Valentin's lover, Marta. In the musical, the Spider Woman is more or less detached from her screen context to become a figment of Molina's imagination, appearing above the prison cell as a mysterious choric commentator who prophesies a fatal destiny for a romantic lover the audience comes to recognize as Molina.

In order to avoid the dramaturgical problems of the film-within-the-show, McNally, Kander and Ebb needed to devise a traditional theatrical framework that would support the disclosure of the various shifts in the relationship between the two men, mapping the changes in their points of view while permitting smooth segues from dialogue scenes to musical fantasy sequences and back. By physically representing the Warden, the prison guards and other prisoners from the outset, the musical creates a naturalistic context for the conversations in the cell, which are greatly abbreviated to permit the elaboration of action, songs and dances.

Having reduced the complexity of the inset film narratives, the authors reveal slightly earlier in the musical that Molina is being bribed to extract information about Valentin's guerrilla organization, enhancing the ambiguity and complexity of Molina's motives and creating greater tension regarding the outcome. Inevitably, Puig's novel focuses more intensively on the conflict of sensibilities than on the details of the prison drama. While the novelistic medium is perfectly suited for the subtle interplay of interior reflections and reported conversations, the materiality of theatre demands that the events occurring in prison be witnessed as much as heard. At the same time, the dramaturgical structure of *Kiss of the Spider Woman* must enable repeated interpolation of visual and aural representations of the oneiric dimension (dream, fantasy, hallucination) that reinforce rather than undermine the logic of the action.

The Broadway version (1993) opened on the image of Molina behind bars with prison inmates at the back of him. Valentin is dragged across the stage in front of the bars while the Warden is in place above the cell, surveying the action. A convention for the interweaving of material action and oneiric experience is established a moment later with Molina sitting on his prison bed surrounded by darkness to the accompaniment of a singing voice (later to be identified as that of the Spider Woman):

> Come and find me
> Hear my song
> Let me hold you here where you belong
> Lips are waiting
> Pain will cease
> Calm your anguish I can bring you peace.[22] (9)

In the first scene of the musical, the Warden directly informs the audience of the reason for Valentin's arrest – 'Apprehended in act of passing travel documents to political fugitives. Suspect is key link to terrorist groups.' At the end of this announcement, an offstage scream reveals that Valentin is being tortured, after which the cryptic chorus of the Spider Woman's song sounds again as a voice in Molina's head:

> Sooner or later
> You're certain to meet
> In the bedroom, the parlor
> Or even the street (11)

When Valentin is thrown onto the floor of Molina's cell, the Warden reappears to introduce Molina: 'Prisoner 57884. Name – Luis Alberto Molina. Age 37. Sexual offender. Arrested for corrupting a minor. Male.' In order to try and avoid contemplating Valentin's bloody body,

Figure 16. Chita Rivera as the Spider Woman. Photo: Martha Swope, NYPL, Billy Rose Division.

Molina conjures the first movie sequence in the show, an extract featuring Aurora rising from a bathtub, attended by a group of male servants:

MOLINA.
Aurora, help me! What movie? There were so many. What scene? Aurora, I need you. Come to me, like you always have.
[.........................]

> Her name is Aurora
> And she is so beautiful
> No man who has met her can ever forget her
> They're madly in love
> Forever in love (12)

The one film memory that Molina summons without sharing, this first glimpse of her represents Aurora as the gay prisoner's idealized image of himself: she is a desirable woman whose extraordinary beauty gives her the power over men that Molina lacks in reality but might possess in fantasy.

As in all the extracts from Molina's film musicals, Aurora embodies the power of romantic love, a state of being that transmutes mundane existence into a transcendent realm. Ironically, such love usually proves fatal in these films. At first, it seems as if Valentin's scream is the 'sharp, piercing' cry that signals the arrival of the love of Aurora's life, but the quick cinematic cut to the cell reveals Molina in what might have been Aurora's position, kneeling over Valentin's body: 'Oh my God, I didn't know how they'd hurt you. I didn't look. [. . .] I'll tell you about my Aurora. I'll tell you her movies, her wonderful movies! We'll be friends' (14).

The contrast between the seductive images from Aurora's film and the harshness of reality in the prison is amplified by 'Over the Wall', a song in which prisoners in other cells recall the pleasures they once experienced beyond the prison walls. The abject tableau they form behind prison bars contrasts starkly with the sensuous images conveyed by the lyrics:

FIRST PRISONER.
There are big busted women
Over the wall
[.........................]
SECOND PRISONER.
There is rum from the cane field
Over the wall.
[.........................]
THIRD PRISONER.
There is sun on my taxi
FOURTH PRISONER.
And cakes in my oven
FIFTH PRISONER.
And fish in my netting
[.........................]
ALL.
And big busted women
Over the wall

Over the wall
Over the wall
Second Prisoner.
And I wonder if I'll ever see them again. (14–15)

The prisoners' idealized memories of the good life beyond the prison walls are equivalent to Molina's recalling of film sequences as a means of escape from confinement in the prison, establishing the idea that a prisoner needs some images of a better life, whether drawn from reality or fiction, in order to survive the intolerable existence in a fascist jail. This opposition between the necessity for a degree of escapist fantasy and the demands of an unbearable reality is the major trope elaborated in the musical numbers, threaded as a recurrent motif throughout the show.

Once again, the Spider Woman appears on the catwalk above the prisoners, in the same position as the Warden at the opening, singing another chorus of her mysterious song,

And the moon grows dimmer
At the tide's low ebb
And your breath comes faster
And you're aching to move
But you're caught in the web . . . (15)

Her significance is still not clear, nor is it certain whether this is an appearance by Aurora in another movie or an isolated hallucination experienced by Molina. Motivated by his memory of being taken to the cinema as a small boy by his mother, who worked as an usherette, Molina describes to Valentin the momentous occasion when he first saw Aurora on screen. The only one of her films he did not like was one in which she portrayed the Spider Woman, a figure he believed to be real – a belief he still holds. The film terrified him because it showed that anyone she kissed would die. Valentin's contemptuous reaction is interrupted by a prisoner's scream, which prompts Molina to blot out the fearful sight of another tortured inmate by summoning Aurora for the second time:

MOLINA.
I'll look but I won't see. Deaf, dumb and blind. Take my advice, Mr Revolutionary,

When you feel you've gone to hell in a handbasket
And the world in which you dwell's no paradise (28)

At this point, Aurora appears in a spotlight at the side of the stage, posing insouciantly *a la* Dietrich in an elegant, pearl-grey gentleman's silk suit to perform the song Molina has begun to sing:

You've got to learn how not to be
Where you are
The more you face reality the more you scar
So close your eyes and you can be a movie star
Why must you stay where you are.

A homage to the kind of jazzy production number for which Kander and Ebb are themselves famous, 'Where You Are' represents a paean to Molina's escapist ethic, proffering images of 'showbiz' spectacle as an antidote to grim reality:

> You've got to learn how not to see
> What you've seen
> The slice of hell you call your life is harsh and mean . . . (28)

Where the novel and the film had simply evoked the narratives of Molina's movies as escapist fantasies, Kander and Ebb's songs exploit the trope of escapism in a self-reflexive way to amplify and justify his deliberate use of film as a means of avoiding the extreme brutality of the environment in which he is trapped:

> And if you find that you land in jail
> A little fantasy will not fail . . . (28)

At this moment, two guards escort prisoners in chains across the back of the stage, indicating that the film musical sequence is taking place in a prison. The number develops to a point when Aurora is accompanied in whispered song by prisoners, now blurring the distinction between Molina's film memory and reality so that Aurora seems to have transmuted the actual prison into the set of her movie musical. This is subtly reinforced by the way in which the rhythm of the number combines the driving energy of a Broadway song-and-dance sequence with a Latin beat, while the percussive effects of a steel drum evoke the metallic sounds of prison bars and inmates in chains. During the dance break that follows, nine prisoners in matching fedoras form a chorus line, lifting the high-kicking star in the air before grabbing canes to bring the number to a climax that celebrates the victory of imagination over probability.[23]

The quieter final chorus of the song, however, seems directly addressed to Molina: in fantasy, *he* is Aurora's 'leading man' who, by following her advice, can magically convert horrible surroundings into an imagined world of escapist pleasure.

> Turn off the lights and turn on your mind
> And I can promise you you will find
> You will like my plan, my sweetest fan,
> My leading man,
> Anywhere you are (29)

As the performers freeze in a final tableau, the applause for this celebration of film as fantasy is interrupted as two guards drag on stage a prisoner whom they suspect is known to Valentin. When they remove the sack over his head to expose his bloody face, Valentin claims never to have seen the prisoner, but as soon as they exit, he starts to tremble, confirming to the audience that he did know the man. Such an alternation between fantasy and reality will continue throughout the show, dialectically embodying the argument between Valentin and Molina.

Despite Valentin's macho rejection of Molina's escapist strategy, his vulnerability is being tested:

VALENTIN.
> I'm not one of your goddamn movies. I will probably die here and I will have accomplished nothing but my death. Nothing. [. . .] Look at me. I'm shaking. I'm as pathetic as you. (30)

After a scene in which the Warden receives a visit from an Amnesty International observer, Valentin attempts to obliterate the unpleasantness of being caged with other inmates in a small cell by daydreaming about his girlfriend, Marta. His song has a function equivalent to

Molina's movie sequences as a means of momentarily substituting pleasurable images in place of the horror of his actual circumstances.

Although the sceptical Valentin ironically resembles Molina in exploiting his memories as a form of escape, he cannot avoid the realization that the image of Marta is merely a dream he creates from fragments of memory in order to alleviate his misery:

VALENTIN.
So I close my eyes
And I hear her step
And I know she's come to hold me
So my senses stir
PRISONERS.
Over the wall
VALENTIN.
But its never ever her
It's just a dream of her
PRISONERS.
And I wonder
If I'll ever see them again (32–3)

The final chorus reprises the coda from the earlier 'Over the Wall'. As sung here by the crowded prisoners, it heightens Valentin's mournful realization that the dream may never materialize.

The next appearance of Aurora occurs when Valentin is brought back to the cell after interrogation and torture. As Molina gets a cloth to clean Valentin's bloody wounds, Aurora sings 'I Do Miracles'. This is not a film sequence but an imaginary conversation, which illustrates Molina's psychological identification with Aurora as a lover and carer.

MOLINA.
Aurora, I don't know how much more he can endure. What makes a man like that so brave?
AURORA.
Love, you fool, love!

> I do miracles
> [....................]
> Blood
> On your firm young thighs
> Let me kiss it away
> So that I can hear you say
> That
> I do miracles (38–9)

While it is Aurora who appears to Molina, it is Marta whose singing Valentin hears:

MARTA.
As I cradle you close and caress each bruise
What I come here to give you must not refuse

BOTH.
There is love in my touch that is yours to use
[……………………………………………]
There are miracles in me. (39)

In the following scene, Molina is required by the Warden to give Valentin a plate of food that has been poisoned (the large portion), while he himself is to take the small portion. Ignorant of the Warden's plan, Valentin switches the plates, generously insisting that Molina eat the large portion, which later makes him violently ill. During the meal, the men tell each other about the people they love, Valentin for the first time acknowledging Molina's desire and affection for a man as equivalent to his own for Marta, even though Gabriel, the waiter with whom Molina is in love, is married with a child and cannot reciprocate his feelings. Later, the audience will learn that Gabriel did not reply to Molina's letters, so the song projects what he wished the waiter to have written, casting Gabriel in the role of a sympathetic friend in contrast to Valentin, who sings in counterpoint about the prostitute who was 'my first woman' (42) in the clichéd idiom of male heterosexual initiation, without noticing Molina's symptoms of food poisoning.

After being taken to the infirmary, Molina is given morphine to ease his pain, a drug whose effect is equated in song with the palliative escapist pleasure he obtains from his nostalgic film memories. It is drugs that precipitate Molina's bizarre visions in 'Morphine Tango'. Now he dreams or hallucinates images not of Marta or Aurora but of his mother and the Spider Woman, while the orderlies sing an uncanny hymn to the pleasures of morphine as they wheel his gurney around the room in dance-like patterns of movement. The lights change to reveal Molina's mother standing beside the hospital bed in an episode that represents an imaginary or dream conversation between mother and son. The conversation represents Molina's fantasized version of coming out to his mother as a gay man:

MOLINA.
There are no girls, mama. I've brought you such shame.
MOTHER.
No, Luis. Only if you did something cruel, uncaring.
[……………………]
MOTHER.
You like this Valentin, don't you?
MOLINA.
To him I'm a silly window dresser. That's all I am to everyone but you.
MOTHER.
Hoo! What nonsense.
[………………………………]

And you could never shame me
Let me say out loud
I've a son
A loving son
Who makes me proud. (44–5)

The song is simple but deeply moving, providing one of the few positive images in the show of Molina being loved and admired. The scene dissolves to reveal the Spider Woman sitting on Molina's bed in the cell, with her giant web appearing above a dimly lit stage. Her appearance contradicts the comforting warmth of Molina's mother. In a kind of *Sprechgesang* or recitative, the Spider Woman asks Molina why he has always been afraid of her as the music swells to support her singing.

SPIDER WOMAN.
Someday you'll give in
Of course you will. All men do.
Yes, all men kiss me and you will too
[.......................................]
Your cries of pleasure
Will heat the cool, night air
When you kiss me
And you will kiss me!
But not now! Not yet! Not now! (46–7)

The terrifying spectre of the Spider Woman is the dark secret concealed beneath the hedonism and glamour of Aurora's movie sequences, the figure from a horror film whose images became the stuff of Molina's nightmares as a child. The vision of the Spider Woman dissolves while the orderlies lift him from the floor and place him on the gurney as the morphine overcomes him.

Every fantasy sequence is followed by a prison scene, during which one of the protagonists is forced to endure some kind of suffering. When Molina returns to the cell from the infirmary, the guards give Valentin his first meal in three days. Valentin admits to Molina that his girlfriend Marta is not a political activist, revealing for the first time a mature understanding of the irrational and contradictory nature of human instincts: 'I have a confession to make. She's upper class, drives a little red Mercedes 180 SL, and plays golf. [. . .] She's everything Golizar says we're supposed to hate and I'm crazy about her' (48–9). The food given to Valentin by the guards has been poisoned, causing him to be so violently ill that he defecates in his trousers. He is cleaned up by Molina, after which he faints. Then Molina sings to the unconscious Valentin as Aurora and Marta have before. While he assumes the position of a female lover who gives succour to her man, Molina imagines Marta as an impossibly glamorous movie heroine, the woman he fantasizes he could be: 'And I wish that she were me/That/Woman!' (51)

By visualizing himself as Valentin's female lover in 'How Lucky Can You Be', Molina's growing romantic attachment to his cellmate becomes more apparent; his vulnerability makes him anxious when Valentin inadvertently mentions details about his political activity. Ironically, it is the Warden who first explicitly articulates Molina's nascent feelings: 'Are you falling in love with him, Molina?' (52)

A turning point in the relationship between the two prisoners occurs as the men collaborate in recalling the nightclub sequence from the film, *Bird of Paradise:*

MOLINA.
Her lover has escaped. She alone knows where he is.

VALENTIN.
Will she betray him?
MOLINA.
She tries to pretend [. . .] that it is not her concern what happens in the world for
good or evil.
VALENTIN.
But she can't do it. She does care.
MOLINA.
Yes, Valentin, she is only a woman who loves! Let them kill her even. She will not
betray the man she loves. (53)

Although Valentin now appreciates the consolations offered by Molina's films, there is a subtle difference in the way each man comprehends their significance. In this exchange, Valentin expresses his belief that Aurora cannot pretend she is unconcerned about morality, whereas Molina interprets her courage not as a reflection of moral or political values, but from a deeply traditional perspective as 'a woman who loves'. The number opens with a group of men softly singing a rhythmic mantra of 'Gimme love, gimme love, gimme kisses, gimme love', which they repeat six times with very small variations before Aurora sings from inside a giant birdcage:

> If there's a war on don't bring me the news
> Ask me to bull fights and I must refuse
> But if you want to get my attention
> Let's make love (54)

Exaggerating the escapist philosophy formulated in 'Where You Are', the performer trivializes human catastrophes (war, earthquakes, plague, poverty, fire) by adopting a more sinister attitude of callous indifference to other people's misfortune.

> **AURORA.**
> It's like giving to the needy
> And I don't mind being greedy
> Come on, Chico, please be speedy
> And bring me what I long for (54)

In the role of a jaded sophisticate, Aurora demeans the poverty of 'the needy' by equating their genuine hunger with her selfish desire for sexual gratification. After a few minutes, the cynical song in celebration of the hedonistic pleasures of a lost Eden segues into an extended dance sequence set in a spectacularly lit jungle, but the narrative context of *Bird of Paradise*, as explicated by Molina and Valentin, ironically reveals the lyrics of 'Gimme Love' to be an elaborate lie. Surrounded by a group of bare-chested male admirers who turn and move her cage around the stage before carrying her onto the floor to the accompaniment of salsa music, Aurora's routine exposes show business at its most decadent. Nevertheless, the chic conventions of the erotically charged nightclub floorshow, with the star fetishistically costumed in orange and green ostrich feathers to evoke the image of a gigantic caged bird, mask the hidden intensity of the dancer's authentic passion, which the film has previously revealed.

The baroque intermingling of melodramatic narrative and spectacular musical revue in the *Bird of Paradise* sequence prefigures Molina's courage in trying to protect Valentin – now symbolically cast in the role of his lover – by helping him disguise the fact that he is ill. As the movie scene freezes, Molina tries to convince the two guards who arrive to escort Valentin to the infirmary that he is beginning to extract information from the vulnerable prisoner. Although the guards are suspicious, they reluctantly leave Molina to care for Valentin, who faints as soon as they are gone. In a complicated overlapping of movie and stage narratives, the dance number continues again as Molina opens the little curtain in the cell to discover that the Spider Woman, who had appeared there before the start of the musical number, has vanished. As he carries Valentin 'into his movie' (56), Act 1 ends with the sound of bird calls. Molina's rescuing of Valentin and their retreat into the film indicate that he has totally identified himself with Aurora's heroic role as a woman who sacrifices everything to save her lover, the boundaries between film narrative and stage 'reality' dissolving to foreshadow Molina's tragic sacrifice in Act 2.

As the second act begins, the musicalized cries of the prisoners give way to the Spider Woman's sung voice-over:

> Sooner or later
> Your love will arrive
> And she touches your heart
> You're alert, you're alive
> And there's only one pin that can puncture such bliss
> Her kiss. (57)

Like a Greek oracle, her warning is both ominous and puzzling. The mood in the cell provides a complete contrast, the relaxed jollity of the two men partly due to the pleasure of having just eaten a fine meal, which Valentin believes has been delivered to the prison by Molina's mother. However, the warmth of their conversation also reveals the camaraderie that has developed between them since Molina tended to him when he was ill. In a reversal of the usual pattern, it is Valentin who desires to prolong the pleasant atmosphere by asking Molina to recount *Flame of St. Petersburg.* For obvious reasons, this is Valentin's favourite movie:

VALENTIN.
To save her lover, Aurora agrees to marry a man she doesn't love on the eve of the Russian Revolution.
MOLINA.
[. . .] HE'S HOOKED!
VALENTIN.
Of course I'm hooked. You don't get this sort of thing in dialectical materialism. Please Molina. (57)

Once again, the film reflects the situation of the two prisoners, with a surrogate for Molina in the figure of Tatyana Alexandrovna, 'vedette du cabaret' (58), and a fictional version of Valentin in the character of her lover Anatol, the student revolutionary whom she dies defending. As in *Bird of Paradise,* the circumstances of the narrative render the song lyrics equivocal:

As addressed to the aristocratic St. Petersburg audience, the song pretends to celebrate the Tsarist order, but beneath the surface, Aurora/Tatyana is actually heralding the revolution that will destroy this decadent feudal society and replace it with the liberty and equality promised by Communism.

Kander and Ebb deploy the oppositional pairing of optimism and despair that has recurred in their shows since *Flora, the Red Menace*, but in this instance, the good times-bad times trope motivates a broad parody of traditional Russian folk songs: the melodrama of the film's action is mocked by means of both the clichéd sentimentality of the writing and the camp style of its performance. Molina stands in for Aurora's maid in a dressing room scene accompanied by a typical melodrama underscore:

MOLINA.
"Madame."
AURORA.
"Yes, Lisette?"
MOLINA.
"A note arrived for you."

(*MOLINA "hands" a note to AURORA who "reads" it.*)

AURORA.
"Count Ostrovsky has deceived you. Your lover, the student revolutionary Bolshevik anarchist, Anatol, will be shot as he waits for you in vain on the Pushkin bridge this evening at the stroke of midnight. Signed, A friend." I must save him. Summon my troika.
[...]
To be in love is the sweetest thing, Lisette. But to risk everything for love is even sweeter! (59)

While the 'Good Times' song itself is the shortest of all the movie musical sequences in the show, the putative excerpt from *Flame of St Petersburg* is the only sustained segment of the film narrative dramatized by McNally. Dialogue, action, underscoring and diegetic song illustrate Molina's narration to produce a parody of a complex musical scene, even Aurora's tragic end being played comically as she appears to die at the conclusion of one chorus, only to rise again and sing triumphantly before actually expiring:

And –

There's going to be good times
Nothing but good times
Viva la Guerra, viva la Revolucion, viva – ! (61)

Valentin's completion of the song signifies his strong identification with this melodrama of revolution:

VALENTIN (*Speak-singing.*)
Good times are coming our way . . .

(The vision of Aurora fades. The two men are silent a moment, touched by what has happened.)

VALENTIN.
You know there's one thing that's profoundly wrong about your movies, don't you?
MOLINA.
What is that, doctor?
VALENTIN.
They're not real. (61)

The men's continuing debate about the pleasures of escapist movies as opposed to the value of confronting harsh truths has advanced to a point at which Valentin no longer rejects the emotional relief they offer but instead laments the fact that the tragic or utopian narratives are fictions. Molina's counter-argument that such narratives provide ideal images of a better world includes a Freudian slip which unconsciously exposes the intensity of his love for Valentin:

> **MOLINA.** Of course [. . . the movies are] not real. They're better than real. I need my movies to remind me that there can be beauty and grace and bravery and loyalty and kindness and love [. . .] and happy endings even and love. I already said that.
> **VALENTIN.** Why don't you try to find them in your own life? (61)

Valentin recognizes the parallel between his own political struggle for freedom from fascist oppression and Molina's desire for a utopia of love and beauty but cannot understand the gay man's sense of helplessness in the face of a homophobic society. In this scene, there is no hostility between the two men; rather, the way that each relates his own life experience to his ethical and political ideals constitutes the most complex and unguarded of all their exchanges.

Perhaps in order to generate a more overt conflict between the two characters that allows them to exhibit their mental attitudes in behavioural terms on stage, the musical, in comparison with the novel, represents Valentin's homophobia as a more obvious source of antagonism, provoking Molina in turn to act out his effeminacy in a defiantly camp display of difference. Molina's greater prominence in the novel as the narrator of the films is paralleled in the musical by the fact that most of Aurora's songs are the product of his memory or imagination and that he is given more musical numbers than Valentin.

Another significant change made for the musical is the transformation of Valentin from an educated middle-class man whose Marxist ideas are derived from knowledge of political theory, which he teaches to the working-class Molina to a poverty-stricken orphan. In setting the scene for 'The Day after That', Valentin likens the process of his own political enlightenment to a movie but warns Molina that there is, 'No singing, no dancing, no pretty costumes. Just the truth' (61). The song takes the form of a rousing anthem in praise of the promised freedom that revolution will bring. The surprising change of style and tone invokes grand opera, with the unfolding of Valentin's memories of key moments from his youth constituting a kind of recitative that forms the prologue to an intensely emotional aria followed in turn by a stirring choral reprise.[24] Valentin emotively recalls the tin shanty where he and his sister went to sleep on the floor until their mother died at thirty:

And my sister and I
Swore the day that we left
There'd be no more children like us
In the filth there, in the heat there, in the smell there (63)

After travelling to the city in order to beg for food, they heard a revolutionary leader[25] addressing an enormous crowd. By contrast with the 'Good Times' number, Valentin's song is anthemic, repeating words that had been sung by thousands of people in response to the leader's inspiring call for revolution:

Some day we'll be free
I promise you we'll be free
If not tomorrow
Then the day after that

[...................................]

And the war we've fought to win
I promise you we will win
If not tomorrow
Then the day after that
Or the day after that (63)

An unseen chorus joins Valentin to reprise the song in an evocation of the overwhelming response of the crowd at the political rally. In equating the fervour of his belief in the revolution against fascist dictatorship with the utopian values inherent in Molina's cinematic fantasies of the power of romantic love, Valentin demonstrates a more mature understanding and acceptance of the gay man's battle to defend his humanity in the face of the repressively macho regime of fascism.

The repetition of key lyrics in the final chorus section is dramatically complex and subtle, implying the possibility of an endlessly deferred Utopia:

Then the day after that
Or the day after that (64)

The last line is sung five times, the reiterations suggesting that Valentin's Marxist belief in the ultimate achievement of a classless society represents an aspiration rather than a realistically conceived possibility. Valentin's willingness to give his life for the sake of the revolution is equivalent to Molina's identification with the heroic woman who dies to save the man she loves.

A key moment in Molina's own personal self-actualization is signalled in his words, 'Will you stop trying to make a man out of me?' when Valentin jokes that Molina is a 'bad influence' after he unwisely offends the guards (65). As a homosexual man in a homophobic macho culture, Molina has, up to this point, assumed the female gender identity ascribed to men who cannot or will not subscribe to the hyper-masculinity determined by the gender hierarchy of fascist society. Such a 'feminine' man is indicated in Spanish by the word *maricon*. By somewhat hopelessly identifying himself with a glamorous woman, Molina has confused his desire to love and be loved by a man with the need to be a woman, thereby failing to challenge the fascist denial of the freedom to express homosexual desire. From now on in the show, Molina's growth as a human being is demonstrated not merely by his consciousness of legitimate identity as a gay man but by his growing awareness that – like Aurora in *Flame of St Petersburg* – he could be heroic in risking his life for someone he loves.

The Warden's ploy to extract information from Valentin by bribing Molina to act as an informant in exchange for his freedom creates a conflict for Molina between his devotion to his mother and his passionate love for Valentin. 'Mama, It's Me', a telephone conversation in song, reveals the strong temptation for Molina to betray his friend. Frank Rich's claim that '*Spider Woman*, [. . .] is the first large-scale American musical told from an unapologetic and unsentimental gay point of view',[26] reflects another shift away from the novel's dialectically balanced structure to a more conventional portrayal of Valentin's character and ideology. Although Valentin's initial homophobia is gradually dispelled by the men's burgeoning friendship, the musical, unlike the novel, does not suggest that in sleeping with his friend, Valentin accepts the fluidity of sexual identity implicit in acknowledging the feminine aspect of his personality. Whereas in the novel it is apparent that the men develop an ongoing sexual relationship, in the musical they have only one sexual encounter the night before Molina's release, motivated by Valentin's need to manipulate Molina into telephoning his girlfriend Marta with a coded message for the guerrilla organization:

> He'd do anything for me
> I can tell.
> [……………….]
> if we touch before he goes
> He'll make that call (70)

Also less ambiguous in the musical is Molina's motive for agreeing to communicate the message. He is prepared to risk his life to support Valentin's political ideals simply because he has fallen in love with him:

> I'd do anything for him,
> I want him so.
> I've no interest in his cause;
> Let that be. (70)

The intercalation and counterpointing of the men's choruses are framed by the Spider Woman's three interpolated choruses:

> Soon, I feel it,
> Soon, somehow
> I will have him,
> Any minute now. (70)

Like Aurora in *Flame of St Petersburg,* Molina dies heroically in the service of his lover's cause, but like all tragic divas, he dies, not for a political principle, but for love. As Valentin initiates the sexual encounter with Molina in the darkened cell, the scene cuts cinematically to the image of the Spider Woman in her web. The title song is the emotional climax of the show, an eleven o'clock number that draws together all the fragmentary choric intimations of doom she has sung into an uncanny paean to sexual pleasure that startlingly evokes the inevitable fate of the true romantic lover:

> And you're aching to move
> But you're caught in the web
> Of the spider woman
> In her velvet cape,
> You can scream
> But you cannot escape.
>
> Sooner or later
> Your love will arrive
> And he touches your heart,
> You're alert, you're alive
> But there's only one pin that can puncture
> Such bliss
> Her kiss. (73)

Although each man has become more sympathetic to the other's world view, it is only Molina who has changed in any significant way. What matters in the musical is that the gay window-dresser finds that he has the courage to risk dying for his own belief in the value of romantic love, so that both men are shown as willing to sacrifice their lives in the struggle to make the world better. Instead of the open ending of the novel in which Valentin is alone in his cell, fitfully dreaming about escaping with Marta on a yacht in a fragmented narrative that borrows images from one of Molina's films, the musical appears to provide closure by depicting the gay man's tragedy as an existential triumph, imbuing his life with meaning as a romantic hero.

The events of Molina's life subsequent to his release from prison are framed by the prisoners' envious reprise of 'Over the Wall', counterpointed with the Warden's variation of 'Anything for Him'. Ironically, while Molina has a happy reunion with his mother, his other experiences of life outside prison are a disappointment. After returning to his former job as a window-dresser, he realizes he cannot go back to his repressed life of self-deprecating camp banter, but his unkind rejection by Gabriel, the waiter with whom he was previously infatuated, offers no alternative opportunity for new kinds of friendships. It is understandable that after these disillusionments, he would be prepared to risk his life in the service of Valentin, the one man whose friendship has brought meaning to his life. Sadly, the phone call he makes on Valentin's behalf to Marta reveals this wealthy, upper-class woman has no wish to get involved with her ex-lover's political cause; by contrast with her self-serving response, Molina remains loyal to his friend, as is revealed when the abject Valentin is brought face to face with the horribly bloodied Molina, who has been captured and brought back to the prison.

Molina has been tortured because he has refused to reveal Marta's telephone number, but defiantly he acts like a soldier in a movie melodrama, waiting for his captain's orders while the Warden puts a pistol against his head. When Valentin, horrified by his realization of the consequences of Molina's actions on his behalf ('I betrayed you'), tries to save his friend by himself revealing the information to the Warden, Molina says, 'Then you *will* have betrayed me' and dies telling Valentin, 'I love you'.

In attempting to locate the reasons for the musical's change in emphasis most notable in the second act, two factors stand out, both of which reflect the traumatic impact of the AIDS crisis on the New York theatre community. The first is its representation of heterosexual and homosexual orientations as completely distinct identities. At a time when proponents of queer theory were elaborating conceptions of gender and sexual identity as cultural performances rather than biological norms, prejudice and fear of AIDS had in many quarters stigmatized gay men for bringing the 'plague' on themselves through indulging in promiscuous sexual activity. Maintaining a more sympathetic image of homosexual men as 'innocent' victims required adherence to the view of homosexual identity as genetically determined rather than a 'choice' influenced to a great extent by cultural factors.

Allied to this conservative view of sexual identity is the Spider Woman's equation of sexual passion with death. Amplifying the tradition of representing orgasm as a *petit mort* (little death), she implies that in the consummation of a powerful desire, gay men may literally risk death. In the musical, the inexplicably linked images of desire, disease, blood and death function powerfully in the unconscious to promote images of the gay man as a martyr to his impossible desire and as a nurse or carer to a sick friend.[27] In cities with large gay communities like New York and San Francisco, people were, in the 1980s and 1990s, confronted with a generation of comparatively young men dying of a series of frightening AIDS-related diseases, while at the same time, large numbers of gay men were faced with the challenge of trying to alleviate the suffering of their infected lovers and friends. The musical opened a few years after the urban AIDS crisis had reached its height[28] and before the danger of HIV infection had been somewhat mitigated by the success of new combinations of drugs.

In honouring Molina's courageous choice of dying to save Valentin and defend his cause, the authors exploit one more unexpected Pirandellian strategy to produce a final *coup de theatre*. The scene dissolves from the Warden's office into a ghostly cinema auditorium in which Molina's mother once again assumes her job of usherette, leading the Spider Woman to her seat after Valentin has entered to sit among the entire company. When Molina appears dressed in white tie and tails, he has become the star of his own movie biography, singing to the onstage cinema audience:

> Optimistic endings,
> Passionate romances,
> Beautifully beefy heroes
> Taking death defying chances.
> Only in the movies. (83)

By amplifying the meta-dramatic nature of the *Kiss of the Spider Woman,* 'Only in the Movies' offers an appropriately provisional form of closure. The musical number paradoxically celebrates Molina's courage in a stylized retelling of his death that elevates the status of the humble window-dresser to that of a romantic (male) diva in a musical melodrama. The song cleverly weaves together the escapist desire for the happy endings of kitsch entertainment with the unremitting harshness of the real world,

> And though I knew the difference,
> I kept on pretending
> I was in the movies. (84)

The full surprise occurs when Valentin joins Molina on the 'stage' and Molina ironically creates a more complex form of authentic experience from the interweaving of reality with film fantasy:

> Everything changed when I met you,
> I find I walk in tecnhicolor now. (84)

The number re-enacts Molina's death when the Warden's earlier threat to Molina ('Talk you fucking faggot or I'll blow your fucking head off') is replayed over a speaker. Now the image from *Flame of St Petersburg* with Aurora as the dying Tatiana being cradled by her lover Anatol is recalled and transfigured as Valentin cradles Molina's head in his arms. Like Aurora/Tatiana, Molina seems momentarily to revive in order to musically 'narrate' his own death,

> Looking into those steely blue eyes of his, she cried,
> 'Viva la Guerra'
> 'Viva la Revolucion'
> 'Viva whatever it is!' (84)

By contrast to the novel's open-ended conclusion with Valentin's surreal dream of being on a yacht with an idealized Marta, and yet parallel to it, the musical recuperates Molina's death in a fantasy film sequence that questions the epistemological status of the entire performance. Although the final moments of the narrative may have encouraged Broadway spectators to construe Molina's assassination as part of a naturalistic portrayal of a fragment of the historical 'reality' of the Argentinian dictatorship in the 1970s, the shock of witnessing Molina 'come to life' in 'Optimistic Endings' distances them from conventional expectations of narrative closure to experience the powerful emotional affect of movie musicals in the final one of a series of numbers that interrogate the meaning of spectatorship. The novel's sophisticated bricolage of high art techniques with the sentimental strategies of mass entertainment is translated into the form of a musical that embodies Puig's postmodern recognition that contemporary existence is entirely mediated by the agencies of mass culture.

Notes

1. Manuel Puig, *Kiss of the Spider Woman,* New York: Vintage Books, 1991, 78.
2. Suzanne Levine, *Manuel Puig and the Spider Woman: His Life and Fictions,* New York: Faber, 2000, 257–8.
3. Puig, *Kiss of the Spider Woman*, 207–8.
4. Puig, *Kiss of the Spider Woman,* 210.
5. Levine, 259.
6. S. Freedman, interview, 'Manuel Puig and His Hollywood Lure', *International Herald Tribune,* 14 August 1985.
7. See the Introduction for a discussion of Adorno and the Frankfurt School.
8. Kimberley Chabot Davis, *Postmodern Texts and Emotional Audiences,* West Lafayette: Purdue University Press, 2007.
9. Puig, *Kiss of the Spider Woman* 3
10. John Kander and Fred Ebb, *Colored Lights*, New York: Faber, 2003, 178.
11. James Leve, *Kander and Ebb*, New Haven: Yale University Press, 2009, 152.

12. 'Just absorbing him – his personality and insights – gave us a lot of clues into how to write "The Window Dresser's Song" and others like that. Manuel Puig himself was so flamboyant [. . .] When he talked about doing a tango, all of a sudden – he would get up and do a tango. [. . .] Or he would do a samba. As writers, we tried to absorb his energy and joy and love in our work. We inherited that or you could say we inhaled that. We never used Manuel's libretto, but he came to Purchase with us, and he was our conscience. [. . .] If you put Puig in that cell and call him Molina, that's what the story would be' (*Colored Lights*, 179-80).

13. Fred Ebb papers, Box 69, f 1.

14. Fred Ebb papers, Box 70, f 7.

15. State University of New York at Purchase.

16. Audiovisual recording of the production in TOFT Archive, NYPL. Accessed on 5 June 2018.

17. From Leve, *Kander and Ebb*, 153.

18. Harold Prince on *The Kiss of the Spider Woman*, YouTube A&E, https://www.youtube.com/watch?v=mqyV_WTKt20. Accessed 18 December, 2017.

19. Lyrics taken from audiovisual recording of Purchase performance in the TOFT Archive, accessed 5 June 2018.

20. *New York Times,* 1 June, 1990, https://www.nytimes.com/1990/06/01/theater/review-theater-in-a-prison-cell-2-men-and-a-movie-musical.html. Accessed 10 June, 2018.

21. Puig, *Kiss of the Spider Woman*, 260–1.

22. Page numbers for the musical refer to McNally, Kander and Ebb, *Kiss of the Spider Woman the Musical*, New York: Samuel French, 1993.

23. Ironically, the fact that audiences at the original production enthusiastically applauded Chita Rivera and the chorus appeared to signal their preference for escapist entertainment over authentic depictions of human abjection.

24. The operatic quality of the song derives from the version of the show presented in Purchase, in which the songs for the two men are in a fairly operatic style, while the *Man Overboard* sequences are conceived in a musical comedy style. The operatic mode of composition is likely to reflect Kander's love of nineteenth-century opera and his wide-ranging knowledge of the repertoire.

25. He is named in a previous scene as Alberto Golizar.

26. *New York Times,* 4 May 1993, https://www.nytimes.com/1993/05/04/theater/review-theater-for-the-musical-a-love.' Accessed 10 June, 2018.

27. In their excellent essay, 'Caught in the Web: Latinidad, AIDS and Allegory in *Kiss of the Spider-woman the Musical'*, *American Literature*, Vol. 67, No. 3 (1995): 553–85, David Roman and Alberto Sandoval argue that the images of blood, illness, poisoning and defecation displayed on stage vividly evoke gay men's experience of AIDS, suggesting an allegorical dimension of the musical.

28. Manuel Puig is believed to have died of an AIDS-related illness on 22 July 1990, although this was strenuously denied at the time.

12 The American Dream as dance marathon

Reality and illusion in *Steel Pier* (1997)

Why would a Kander and Ebb musical with a highly-rated score, a great deal of 1930s dance by the talented choreographer Susan Stroman, as well as challenging themes concerning the desperation of many Americans during the Great Depression, have been a huge commercial failure on Broadway in 1997? In *Colored Lights*, Kander recalls, '[T]here was a certain amount of panicking and a certain distance from the show in the theatre, whereas in the studio, we had been right on top of these people. It was very emotional and funny'.[1]

Reviewers, bloggers and the writing team themselves have sought to pinpoint the musical's weaknesses, yet as none of their new work produced after *Kiss of the Spider Woman* (1993) turned a profit, it might simply be the case that these shows did not match changing audience expectations on Broadway from the mid-1990s. Even *The Scottsboro Boys*, which has a claim to being artistically their finest work, was a resounding commercial flop when it transferred to Broadway in 2010. As with some of Sondheim's musicals, their most controversial or complex shows have had difficulty in finding large audiences in a commercially driven environment. Yet, because of the unequalled success of *Cabaret* and *Chicago* in revival on Broadway and globally since the mid-1990s, each of their later shows has been measured against these 'classics' of the genre – only to be found wanting.

In his quotation from the Sunday edition of the *New York Times*, Greg Lawrence unintentionally demonstrates how startlingly inaccurate many critics' comprehension of the duo's aesthetic approach was during this period: '[*Steel Pier*] reminds us that these two men represent the survival of a form of musical that no one else is writing today filled with that youthful joy that doesn't believe in despair or death.'[2] In truth, the majority of their musicals are permeated by despair as well as the apprehension of death. Although the team's approach to thematic motifs has proved remarkably consistent through the years, the balance between confronting life's cruelty and embracing hedonistic entertainment has varied from one musical to another to the point that critics and audiences have not consistently appreciated the tone or style of every show. At different moments, one of their shows has absolutely chimed with the times: in the aftermath of the AIDS crisis, *Kiss of the Spider Woman* seemed to offer a critique of homophobia and – less overtly – a lament for queer victims of AIDS. In 1996, the revival of *Chicago*, coinciding with the heightened scrutiny of media and celebrity consequent on the high profile of the O J Simpson trial, struck completely the right note.

In the event, *Steel Pier* did not manage to fully satisfy either those who were looking for pure entertainment or those expecting something more hard-edged from the writers of *Kiss of the Spider Woman*. Several intrinsic factors may have contributed to its lack of commercial appeal. For one, the tension between Kander and Ebb's opposed attitudes did not create the kind of dialectic in which Kander's romantic emotional attitude was ironically in play against Ebb's tough yet equivocal cynicism. All the elements appeared to be there. At times harsh and brutal in its depiction of the milieu that Ebb had wished to represent, *Steel Pier* may nevertheless have over-emphasized the desire of Kander and book-writer David Thompson to create a romantic dance musical as a vehicle for Karen Ziemba.

The commercial and technical demands of the Broadway industry combined with the illness of the director Scott Ellis may, in the event, have undermined the aim of counterpointing harsh satire against the mythically inspired love story. The lack of balance in the staging of 'book' scenes and musical numbers appears to have resulted in the downplaying of Ebb's desire to create a grim spectacle of the cruelty of American capitalism, an idea inspired by Sidney Pollock's film *They Shoot Horses Don't They?* (1969). When the authors failed to obtain the rights to adapt this film, they were obliged to invent their own narrative of events occurring at an Atlantic City dance marathon. Typically, Kander and Ebb did not agree on the viability of the film as a source. Kander maintained, 'I felt differently than you [. . .] it's a story which has always seemed to me a bit unrealistically dark and bleak' whereas Ebb 'thought it was terrific'.[3]

The possibility for a harsh exposé of the dishonest and degrading treatment of contestants at the marathon dance competitions of the Depression may have been compromised by an anxiety to entertain. Whereas Harold Prince had, in directing *The Kiss of the Spider Woman* four years earlier, made the juxtaposition of the genuine suffering of the inhabitants of the South American prison with the escapist film fantasies of the gay prisoner (Molina) the key trope of the musical, it seems that in *Steel Pier* the 'kinetic poetry'[4] of the dances outweighed their evocation of desperation. By subliminally pleasuring audiences, the 'Come Dancing'-type exhibition of sexiness and talent may oddly have reinforced the aspirational American values that Fred Ebb had wished to interrogate. Paradoxically, Ebb 'thought Susan's dances were wonderful. My God, she staged a jitterbug that was fabulous but the audiences seemed to overlook the miraculous pieces like that'.[5]

Ebb's appreciation of Stroman's appealing choreography as pure dance does unintentionally imply that their charm may occasionally have masked the subversive quality of the drama, while their inevitable repetition in portraying the unending continuity of the marathon certainly threatened to overwhelm the intensity of the more intimate dialogue scenes. Clearly, the production lacked the sophisticated ingenuity of an *auteur*-director like Fosse or Prince, either of whom might have transformed the dancing into a more pervasive metaphor for the brutal competitiveness of the typically American value system in which material rewards are the promised prizes for a select few.

Not all of the collaborators were entirely happy with the fable-like framing device.[6] Fred Ebb found the love story between Ziemba's character Rita Racine and the deceased exhibition pilot Bill Kelly far too sentimental: 'I wasn't moved. You [Kander] are way more romantic than

I am. I appreciated it [. . .] but I don't think the show ever worked.' The pilot Bill, after having crashed in the attempt to perform an aerial stunt, has been given three more weeks to live in order to woo Rita Racine, the singer who captivated him at the air show. The reviewer Greg Evans noted: '"Steel Pier" borrows a conceit from "Carousel" by having its hero [. . .] return from the dead.'[7] An off-Broadway audience might simply engage with the inverted Orpheus myth as a plausible dramaturgical trope, but its transposition from fable to concrete plot device might, if not convincingly elaborated by a theatre director, seem like a meretricious gimmick. While its inclusion in an accurate historical representation of the 1930s may have struck some as anomalous, *Hadestown* made extensive use of the Orpheus myth, winning a number of Tony Awards for what was in 2019 hailed as groundbreaking!

As it stands, the show's dark undertow might seem at odds with its romantic music, lushly orchestrated as big-band Kansas City swing. In conversation, Fred Ebb confirmed the stylistic duality as essential to the team's artistic aim:

> We were looking for a project that was a challenge and the idea of the dance marathon craze appealed to us. It incorporated all the glitz and glamour of show business but also showed the American dream gone awry. I like our shows to have a dark side.[8]

With the hugely successful Broadway revival of *Chicago* in 1996, critics and audiences were no doubt anticipating another complex yet cynical satire of ambition and greed, so the nostalgic charm of *Steel Pier*'s 'relentless' montage of 1930s dance styles may have proved a disappointment – indeed, two major reviews confirm this. In *Variety*, Greg Evans makes a disparaging comparison: 'Another first-act song also recalls a "Chicago" number, but with lesser results: "A Powerful Thing," in which the emcee sings the praises of manipulation, lacks the punch of "Chicago's" "Razzle Dazzle."'[9]

Most of Ben Brantley's review in the *New York Times* addresses the same theme:

> 'Steel Pier' is in a sense the anti-'Cabaret,' or the anti-'Chicago,' the 1975 Kander-Ebb hit now playing to packed houses in a revival just two blocks away. Both earlier works are pumped with the ambition-fed energy of performers who want to be top fish in a tank of piranhas, no matter what the cost [. . .] Now meet Rita Racine, the more passive, ingenuous cousin of these ravenous song-and-dance gals [. . .] Rita, a weary marathon dancer [. . .] just wants to settle down in a little cottage by the sea [. . .] what sets the tone of the show is not the urge to make it but the urge to escape. [. . .] Disadvantageous comparisons to 'Chicago' and, especially, 'Cabaret' are inevitable [. . .] One wants to fall in love with 'Steel Pier' for so many reasons. It is, after all, one of the few book musicals in a season of pop operas, and its kind, open heart is a welcome relief from the push-button irony of most current shows. [. . .] Yet [. . .] 'Steel Pier' is insulated by a fuzzy cover of blandness.[10]

What Brantley fails to remark is that both earlier shows present their heroines in an entirely critical light as women in corrupt societies, deluded by the tawdry chimera of show business success. Like Rita, however, Sally, Roxie and Velma desire to escape, yet for them, escape involves the triumphant vindication of earlier privations by the attainment of celebrity. Rita, on the other hand, has seen through the misguided dream that success brings happiness: indeed, she is in the process of discovering the cruel duplicity of her ruthless husband Mick, who has made her complicit in cheating hundreds of hungry competitors out of the chance of winning a prize at the dance marathon. For Rita, escape means contented domesticity rather than the dishonest cut-and-thrust of show business.

The decidedly mixed reception of *Steel Pier* was therefore a reflection of the very same ethos that made the revival of *Chicago* so much more of a hit in 1996 than it had been in 1975. According to Fred Ebb, 'The critics attacked [. . . the] piece like we were getting arty at the end. We didn't seem to be able to do anything right with *Steel Pier*. They just weren't having it'.[11] American popular culture in the mid-1990s was clearly more cynical and sceptical of romance than it had been when *Chicago* titillated and startled Broadway audiences with its sleazy glitter.[12] To some extent, the general public had by 1996 caught up with *Chicago* – so much so that the idealistic romance of *Steel Pier* may have been perceived as dated and sentimental. According to Ebb, 'It was the wrong show at the wrong time'.[13] Nevertheless, Greg Evans asserts that 'some of Kander and Ebb's strongest writing in years overshadow whatever missteps this musical makes'.[14]

'First You Dream': utopian dream versus economic reality

The ironic nature of *Steel Pier's* dramaturgical structure in itself produces a pervasive motif of illusion versus reality that relies on the dialectical tension between opposed performance elements to emerge as integral to the work's meaning. The *Variety* reviewer Greg Evans succinctly identified Scott Ellis' failure to maintain such a counterpoint:

> The performance [of the character Mick] and the production would be better served by an edgier, more menacing quality early on. Both his character and 'Steel Pier' only gradually move beyond stretches of blandness. [Scott] Ellis, whose best work arguably was the frothy revival of 'She Loves Me,' is particularly good at this musical's romantic elements, but seems less comfortable with the darker strains of Thompson's book.[15]

In Ben Brantley's opinion, 'Mr. Harrison gives a smooth performance [as Mick], but he lacks the compelling, darkly erotic aura the character requires'.[16]

According to Kander, 'there was an emotional distance in the theater that was not there in the studio', where 'small audiences [. . .expressed. . .] great enthusiasm and everybody would be in tears at the end'.[17] When *Steel Pier* played in the tiny Union Theatre on the London fringe, a feature of the production that several theatre critics appreciated was the intimacy of the performance, which created an effect of immediacy in the confrontation between performers and audience. Alice Audley's comments are typical in this respect:

> With the combination of the energy of the dancers, the volume of the music and the closeness to the actors, the fourth wall was continually broken. On the one hand you were the audience of [Taylor-]Mills' *Steel Pier*, but on the other you really were the audience to the Atlantic City 1933 dance marathon.[18]

Audience members were given coins to throw at the dancers, so that by contrast with the large-scale Broadway production they began to participate as though they were sponsors of the marathon instead of merely spectators of a terpsichorean spectacle. Simultaneously, an empathic auditor and a more detached spectator at the dance marathon, an audience member's split identity initiated a disturbing dialectic of affective responses. Both humanely engaged with the vulnerability of individual subjects/characters and more distanced from their abjection by the desire to be entertained, members of the audience were torn between the moral judgement of the exploitative event and voyeuristic pleasure at their own power over begging contestants.

Although the libretto establishes a pattern of repeated dissonance between the sensuous flow of dance disrupted by moments of shock, pain and human degradation, the Broadway production did not allow these darker instances of action and dialogue to subvert the 'relentless'[19] pleasures of the dancing. Ambivalence characterizes the score and libretto from the opening of *Steel Pier* to the final moment when Rita escapes from Mick's infernal illusion of happiness as power and material success to embrace her more realistic aspiration for peaceful domesticity – on her own, if necessary.

In New York, preview audiences were confused by the second act revelation that Bill is actually dead. To help clarify the narrative, the creative team therefore inserted, at the start of the piece, a group of ghostly dancers.

> At the top of the show, the dancers line up across the back of the stage and come towards the audience in slow motion. Moving through fractured blue and white light, they glide and slink through various styles of dance, undulating like an ocean wave as the sound of seawater plays underneath.[20]

After this, the supine pilot stood up and stated that he had three weeks more to live in order to claim his prize of a dance with 'Lindy's Lovebird'.[21] Neither Kander nor Ebb wholly approved of the expository device, which, in the context of a literal interpretation, had the effect of reducing suspense. 'Kander: "You shouldn't find out" that he's dead until the second act when the girl, his partner in the marathon, finds out. Ebb: "It worked much better without that business at the beginning."'

With the benefit of hindsight, neither version seemed to be entirely satisfactory in performance. Had the collaborators all trusted their audience to engage with experimental dramaturgical forms, the overall narrative might have been construed as a Brechtian fable[22] with spectators in the know from the start, thereby being primed to judge characters' decisions more critically, which, as Rita starts to fall in love with Bill, offers her the hypothetical alternative of an escape from her Machiavellian husband. If a director were to able enhance the exotic aura of the mythic framing device before Rita's entrance in Act 1, all of the action that revolves around Bill might assume an oneiric dimension as a dream, memory or fantasy, thereby enabling an audience to accept the device of the 'ethereal' dancers as part of a ghost trope disclosing the more otherworldly narrative.

In the Broadway production, the evocative moment when the ghost dancers move on sand, which they take from their pockets and let slip through their hands, alludes to the sands of time in a moment perhaps too subtle to be instantly comprehended. A more emphatic iteration of such a motif would motivate the action by means of the Brechtian conventions with which the 'concept' musical has been conversant since Sondheim and Furth's *Company* (1970). Yet, unlike *Company*, the primary action of *Steel Pier* is structured as a traditional linear narrative rather than as a concept musical, so that the symbolic and non-linear images would need to be given prominence in a way that might transform the show into a concept musical.

Cinematic mise-en-scène and thematic ambivalence

Although the book and score of a musical provide clues to its intended performance, it is almost impossible to imagine its overall effect without seeing it staged because the shape of a show's original mise-en-scène usually establishes its unique qualities as a performance text. The libretto and cast album of *Steel Pier* offer tantalizing glimpses of the show that might have been, hinting at a number of interesting possibilities for a different staging that might deliver an innovative and exciting dramatic experience. Unfortunately, the financial risks of mounting a musical commercially are so great that so-called flops are seldom revived professionally if they do not initially succeed at the box office. In my view, *Steel Pier* requires only small adjustments to work well. It is not so much 'anti-*Cabaret*' as 'anti-Sally Bowles' – but then so was *Cabaret*.[23] Both musicals challenge the moral sensibility of audiences eager to evade reality by means of entertainment: they probe the spectators' collusion in the decadent pleasures intended to give them a good time when times are hard. The bottom line of *Steel Pier* is that the suffering and humiliation of the marathon dancers actually becomes a voyeuristic spectacle: the extent to which it shocks audiences is a measure of their capacity for empathy.

Kander's beautiful swing music is less raucous than that of *Cabaret* or *Chicago*. The strains of a female trio crooning, 'Life's a party, / Why don't you come / To the Steel Pier' (16–17),[24] mimic the kind of radio jingle that might permeate the seaside atmosphere of Atlantic City in 1933. The siren call of the song lures those with a little money to forget the suffering and deprivation around them in the pursuit of pleasure. The famous Steel Pier has replaced the Berlin cabaret as an emblem of the escapist seduction of popular entertainment. As one might expect from Kander and Ebb, the interweaving of action, dialogue and dance is skilfully done, but it does make difficult demands on the director and performers to segue seamlessly from large ensemble song-and-dance numbers into more intimate scenes revealing the intricate motivations of a considerable range of characters.

From the entrance of Rita in the opening scene until the end of Act 1, the show moves in a cinematic fashion from one centre of attention to another. Bill's idealization of Rita as 'Lindy's Lovebird' is set against her resolve to make this her 'LAST marathon' (13). Yet the music and lyrics for Rita's opening number 'Willing to Ride' are equivocal. The waltz rhythm of the song recalls the exhilarating sonic landscape of a funfair, with the never-ending cyclical revolve of its 'merry-go-round' and 'ferris wheel', in paradoxical contradiction to Rita's determination to put the marathon dances behind her:

> This time
> Although I'll do it
> I swear it's the last time
> I'll ever put myself through it (14)

Nevertheless, she repeats the song's triumphant 'hook' ('Willing to Ride') four times, bringing it to a rousing climax with her defiant belting of the line, which actually contradicts the decision *never* to 'ride' again, on what for Rita is a punishing treadmill. The ambiguous nature of the song gives way to the tawdry glamour of the exterior of the steel pier, all sparkling light bulbs, that offer her a joyful entrance to what will later be represented as an inferno.

At the start of Act 1 Scene 2 on the dance floor, Tony Walton's stylish set revealed all the paraphernalia of the contest at the periphery of the stage, with a bandstand at the centre. The overall tableau was followed by a narrow focus on the bandstand from where the female trio sang 'Steel Pier' intercalated with Mick's speech of welcome, after which his rendition of 'Everybody Dance' exhorted the contestants in an unctuous manner to dance until 'worries waltz away' (17). The insistent subsequent repetitions of the order to 'Dance!' transform the cheerful paean to escapism into a more sinister demand for conformity as the marathon continues. The equivocal attitude motivating Mick's rhetoric once again contradicts the joyous fluency of the dancing, echoing the inherent doubleness of the central trope. Four lines initially seem out of place in Mick's clichéd lyrics, yet they imply a key to the ambivalence of many who commit themselves to parading their abjection by participating in this contest:

When you feel an
Anger deep inside
That smoulders,
Dance! (17–18)

As Stroman's virtuoso ensemble dance continued in the background, Rita was picked out by a spotlight so that Mick could introduce her by announcing she had no partner, thereby indicating that a man should invite her to dance. This foregrounding of Rita permitted Bill to be seen inviting her in mime to be his partner as 'Everybody Dance' continued to be sung by Mick and the trio while the competitors danced. A number of experienced contestants then introduce themselves to the audience, whom they address as a group of potential sponsors. These include Olympic wrestling champion Johnny Adel and the brother-and-sister vaudeville team Buddy and Bette Becker. The theatre audience is thus identified as a group of spectators to whom the dancers will pitch their ploys for attention.

As in several other scenes, the fairly lengthy sequence (Act 1 Scene 2) is a musical scene: action, dialogue, song and dance are interwoven to introduce expository information, indicate the locale, as well as to establish the conventions of staging that will apply. After the competition has been officially started by Mick's firing of a gun, the focus narrows to Bill and Rita conversing as they dance, later leading to Bill's singing of the hopeful 'Second Chance', in contrast with Mick's more cynical rendition of 'Everybody Dance'. The central theme of *Steel Pier* might be regarded as the conflict between the merciless competitiveness manifest in Mick's attitude and the naively optimistic ethos of the American Dream – Bill's belief that success can be born from failure.

Dream and fantasy: Brechtian fable on Broadway

In 'Second Chance', Bill tries to convince Rita to accept him as her dance partner because hers still hasn't arrived, and she teaches him some steps. In the rewritten version as printed in the published text, the audience knows his second chance is to have been allowed to live for an additional three weeks after his crash, but Rita's is the opportunity to return home and remake her life as a housewife. In a disturbingly ironic twist of the plot, she will eventually discover not only that her husband, Mick, is an adulterous liar who had already mortgaged the house they owned on the chance of earning much more money from rigged dance marathons, but also that Bill, who appears to offer a romantic alternative to her cheating husband, is a phantom. The somewhat fanciful situation constitutes a perfect metaphor for the vanity of choosing a dream of romance in preference to the competitive hustling of capitalist enterprise, its reference to the Orpheus myth exposing even the relationship with Bill as an illusion. Yet Bill cheerfully 'sells' this dream to Rita while she teaches him to dance:

> And you can start all over
> With a second chance
> Whenever life has gone from bad to worse
>
> You've got to run your movie in reverse
> Re-rehearse
> Soon that curse
> Will disperse (26)

In truth, the show reveals there is no utopian second chance that can magically reverse the flow of time – only the sober realization that one can make a mistake and rectify it in the real world by sacrificing naïve fantasies in favour of building a satisfying life through honest work and personal commitment.

It may be that a failure of nerve among the creatives prevented a more direct enactment of the mythical aspects of the story. Instead of emphasizing Bill's status as a mythical character (through lighting or other scenographic means), his exchange with Rita in 'Second Chance' exploited the conventions of linear narrative derived from 'integrated' book musicals of the golden age. Yet, in many respects, the symbolic implication of Bill as Rita's wish-fulfilment fantasy figure might plausibly be represented in more abstract terms by means of theatrical stylization – pushing the show further in the direction of a 'concept' musical by invoking the dream motif of 'Leave the World Behind' and 'First You Dream', which illustrate Rita's escapist fantasy of Bill as her daredevil rescuer.

The audience is permitted a triple perspective – that of the contestants and marathon spectators; that of Mick, Rita and Walker, who share the secret that Rita and Mick are in fact married; as well as the pilot Bill Kelly's knowledge that he has died and only has three weeks more on earth. As the first act unfolds, it becomes apparent that the entire competition is rigged – a way for Mick to award the prize money to Rita, while he gains additional money from sponsors for putting on the show. For most of Act 1, the technique of cutting from group scenes to 'close-ups' provides a highly effective format, but there were moments in the première production when the montage of images lost focus, partly because the performance delivered an embarrassment of riches. The sheer size of the subsidiary cast made it easy to miss details of character motivation and plotting as one struggled to identify the important characters in each scene. Interpolated between the spectacular dance sequences are scenes introducing the audience alternately to the men in their dressing room and the women in theirs. The rapid succession of locations includes a number of brief scenes in Mick's office, revealed as the space behind the carousel-type bandstand at centre stage when it revolves.

In some respects, the structure of the show stretches the limits of traditional linear dramaturgy. Until Act 1 Scene 5, the songs are presented either as internal monologues (Rita's 'Ready to Ride') or are woven into the staged marathon 'show' ('Everybody Dance' and 'Second Chance'), but the duet 'A Powerful Thing' (Act 1 Scene 6) is presented as a sung conversation *a la* Rodgers and Hammerstein.[25] At this moment, the artifice of the song appears to disrupt the book's musical conventions by failing to effect a seamless transition from the preceding dialogue scene:

> MR WALKER. Boss, you never stop. Do you?
> MICK. No, Walker, I don't.
> When I was a toddler
> Daddy took the strap
> [. . .]
> Don't ever be an employee
> Always be the boss. (36–7)

As it stands, the lyrics appear didactic or overly self-conscious, with Mick giving his assistant a lesson on how he behaves as an all-powerful dictator, controlling the outcome of dance contests by tempting desperate people with the false promise of financial reward. Interpreted at face value, the song demonstrates overtly how Mick wields power, commanding Walker to lie and cheat. However, by highlighting the images of theatre in the lyrics, this motif at the same time exposes the elaborate role-playing involved in Mick's machinations. He pictures himself first as a stage director, ordering people to sing or dance, then he explains that he planned the celebrated moment of Lindbergh and Rita's apparently random meeting:

> 'Cause when Lindy landed home from France
> She kissed him first but not by chance
> I staged that happy circumstance
> The first of many brilliant routines (37)

Mick's jubilant performance produces a kind of psychological subtext, implicating both him and Walker in a sadomasochistic game of master and servant that motivates their mutual exultation of the power play: 'So here's the deal / Good old sport / I'm the star you support' (38). The awkward transition from dialogue to song at its start could be recuperated by staging the number in a manner akin to 'Razzle Dazzle' in *Chicago* so that the actors deliberately 'perform' as though it were a type of vaudeville act – one of Mick's 'brilliant routines' – in tandem with Walker's perverse acceptance of his abjection: 'I'll kneel down and kiss your ring' (39). In such a staging, the lyrics would convincingly depict two actors rehearsing a well-worn number. Such stylization would nicely suggest the characters' heightened self-awareness, but a break in the realistic flow of the action such as (a snap lighting change) would be required to avoid straining credulity.

Pleasure as escape

The comic highlight of Act 1 is undoubtedly Shelby's 'Everybody's Girl':

> You won't be disappointed,
> I'm also double-jointed.
> I'm everybody's girl.
> [.............................]
> And so to reaffirm my status,

It's absolutely gratis
To use my apparatus,
I'm everybody's girl.

Men and me are like pianos. When they get upright, I feel grand. (50–1)

Shelby's number gives the audience on and off the dance floor a fantasy of sexual pleasure to escape the exhaustion and monotony of the marathon.[26] Precious tries to steal Shelby's thunder by faking a cramp thereby bringing 'Everybody's Girl' to a premature conclusion and allowing Precious to scoop up coins thrown for Shelby.

The romance that has bloomed between Rita and Bill is given concrete shape by the charming duet on the rooftop by the Diving Horse, in which the two strip to their underwear to get 'Wet':

Think of all the pleasure
You'll get when you're
All wet
Not a trouble you can't forget
When you're
All wet. (57)

Here the theme of sensual pleasure as an escape from the harshness of reality – in this case, the sweaty punishment of the dance floor – is reinforced by the physical presence of water when Bill jumps in. After Bill is tricked into proposing to Rita in Scene 11, Mick invites Rita to sing 'the song that made her famous'. As Bill gazes at Rita, the scene dissolves to the Trenton air show, where he first encountered her before crashing his plane, hearing the lines 'Love Bird, / Let's make a pair' (65) as her expression of desire for a lover like him.

The strangest part of Act 1 is 'the sprints', feared by all the contestants apart from Buddy:

[. . .] you're ALWAYS running. You wake up running. Running after something. Never stops. [. . .] You're it. You're not. You're up. You're down. You're always somewhere between hell and glory. Unless you stop running. And then you're out for good. (71)

The race, like the marathon, is an endurance test, in Buddy's words, a metaphor for the competitive nature of their lives in the Depression: 'Show business. Eats you up. Spits you out' (71). In the sprint competition, couples must run for ten minutes, with some falling by the way before the end. When Rita falls, Bill reverses time so that the contestants move backwards in slow motion to the moment before this, magically allowing her a 'second chance'. This fable-like element in the sprints sequence must have struck many as an artificial contrivance, which had no place in a historically based evocation of the Depression era, yet it certainly provides a *coup de théâtre*. At the climax of Act 1, the curtain falls while the race continues.

Dream and desperation

Steel Pier is no different from the majority of Kander and Ebb's works, which problematize their representation of events in order to provoke a process of critical reflection on the nature of authentic representation and spectatorship. Meta-theatrical devices or the expressionistic method of focussing the narrative through a prism of subjective consciousness in the form of dream, memory and fantasy are methods of initiating such epistemological discourse. 'Leave the World Behind', the spectacular dance number that opens the second act, is a dream sequence, utilizing a clever pastiche of a number in *Flying Down to Rio* (1932) that includes a Busby Berkeley-esque aerial ballet, but here it has a more complex dramaturgical function. Extending the trope of escaping from the unendurable grind of reality into dreams of Hollywood romance, the elaborate song-and-tap-dance routine on the wings of a biplane represents Bill as Rita's heroic rescuer, a pilot who risks his life to save hers.

In Act 2 Scene 2 the dreamlike romance of 'Leave the World Behind' begins crumbling to expose the harsher psychology of the quotidian life of competition that motivates the characters. In a corridor away from the dance floor, the quarrel between Precious and Happy is the first sign that their romantic bliss is an illusion. Precious realizes that her childhood sweetheart is determined to leave the marathon to return home: 'Happy, how could you do that? We were doing so well', to which he replies, 'Grovelling around like that?' (80). Happy reluctantly agrees to allow her to stay and dance with another partner until the pre-arranged 'wedding' of Rita and Bill so that she can sing on the radio. Back on the dance floor in Scene 3, the good-natured enthusiasm of the competitors has disintegrated. The professional dancer, Buddy Becker, has started to shake with nerves in his state of hallucination, addressing the front rows of the audience as though they were the audition panel for a new Broadway show that he is trying to convince to employ him. In desperation, he jests, 'Hey fellas – you ain't seen nothing yet. Take a look at this', before he '*begins to do trenches. Then pullbacks. He stumbles a bit and then recovers*'. (86)

The moment when Buddy literally begs for a job is possibly the most agonizing in the show, deploying every performer's nightmare image of rejection as an emblem of the endless standing in line for soup, shelter or a menial job that was commonplace in the Depression:

> BUDDY: What's the matter with me? There's nothing the matter with me! 'I WANT A JOB! I WANT A JOB! I WANT A JOB! [. . .] LET GO OF ME! (*The music stops. Stunned. Face to face with MICK, BUDDY turns, looking at everyone on the dance floor.* [. . .] *And then quietly, he says. . .*) I can walk out of here myself, thank you. (86)

When Mick orders the audience to throw coins, Johnny Adel's partner Dora first reacts by grovelling for them, but then rises and walks away from the humiliating incident '*with as much dignity as she muster*' (87).

In her loneliness, Shelby responds to the innocent Happy's realization that he has been dumped by Precious in 'Somebody Older': 'Somebody older can help you get through / What you're going through now' (88). It is a well-placed song, poignant in its simple depiction of both Shelby's desperation and Happy's sense of failure.

The wedding as illusion

Mick's construction of Bill and Rita's wedding as a spectacular encomium to the 'two little words' – husband and wife – with Precious as a warbling soprano in a mock-operetta, and the wedding party dressed in transparent cellophane outfits, idealizes marriage in an inflated manner that appears to parody itself in Precious's hilarious coloratura performance:

Figure 17. 'First You Dream' from *Steel Pier*. Photo: Joan Marcus.

> And two other words
> To tell you what bliss is
> One word is Mister
> The other is Missus.[27] (94)

The conflict of escapist dream versus harsh reality is at its most intensely emotional when Mick tricks Bill and Rita near the end of the sham wedding, followed by a degrading honeymoon night in an onstage tent.

Spontaneously invoking the imagery of flying as they use a bench to mime a biplane, the song 'First You Dream' enables Bill to offer Rita hope of genuine happiness in a mutually loving relationship. The lyrics allude to Orpheus and Eurydice:

> Take my hand
> I promise that I won't let you fall
> Don't look back
> The looking back could end it all
> [...................................]
> But first things first
> First you dream. (99)

Dreams and mythic elements are woven together as an ongoing oneiric trope that signifies the desire for a better world in stark contrast to the harsh realities experienced by the desperate marathon contestants. Somehow, Rita must find a way of penetrating the fog of illusions and lies surrounding her involvement at the Steel Pier in order to construct a domestic life not built on fantasy.[28]

The final section of *Steel Pier*, after Rita discovers she has been tricked into another marathon in St Louis reveals Mick's attempts to persuade and eventually to bully her into agreeing to participate in the St Louis marathon. Rita refuses to move; she will not accept Johnny Adel as a partner when Bill effectively abandons her in Atlantic City. This is dramatized in a series of dialogue scenes and a stylized movement/dance sequence in which the rest of the cast circles around her, singing 'Life's a party / Why don't you come / To the Steel Pier' as a series of taunts. Although not clearly indicated in the libretto, it seems to me that the most powerful way to present the last ten minutes of the show (Limbo) is as a stylized movement/dance sequence that forces Rita to confront her own involvement in the corruption of the marathon, building to a grotesque climax when she decides she must end the duplicitous life created by Mick. The other dancers mock her for her sanity in leaving. This was one part of the beautifully staged production that seemed to lack the requisite savage quality of the final section of the show, with its dark atmosphere undermining any possibility of a 'second chance'.

Social perspectives on the Depression setting

Another 'missing' element that might have produced a more powerful recognition of the despair of the marathon dancers was an explicit reference to the context of the Depression. Other than the hopeless condition of the participants, Scott Ellis's production provided no genuine representation of the economic situation beyond the false optimism of the steel pier.[29] The lack of a social perspective undermines the irony of the 'Life's a Party' lyric because an audience has nothing to measure the claim against. Some projected images, such as newspaper headlines as well as historical photographs of people on breadlines and in shantytowns, might anchor the musical historically for audiences who might in the 1990s and after have scant awareness of the severity of the Depression.[30] It may be that the entertainment culture on Broadway in the late 1990s was simply inimical to the hermeneutic complexity of *Steel Pier*, valuing operatic exhibitions of pure emotion over detailed nuances of feeling, while at the opposite end of the spectrum, prizing farce and burlesque over the wit of Kander and Ebb's subtle pastiche.[31] In spite of its stunning choreography and universally admired score, the musical's first production clearly did not help.[32]

In a fashion reminiscent of the 1966 production of *Cabaret, Steel Pier* mixes the conventions of the backstage musical and its attendant show-within-the-show with a Brechtian framing device. Clearly, many audience members in 1997 were unwilling to accept a combination of conventions that had never seemed problematic when utilized forty years earlier by the Berliner Ensemble or even in international approaches to Shakespeare production. Yet more recently, shows such as *Xanadu* (2007), *The Book of Mormon* (2011), comically exploiting mythical or fable structures, as well as *Hadestown* (2016), based on mythical narrative, have become widely popular with young audiences in particular, who do not appear to regard the mixing of contemporary and mythical settings as problematic.[33]

Notes

1. *Colored Lights*, 196.
2. Greg Lawrence in *Colored Lights*, New York: Faber, 2003, 196.
3. *Colored Lights*, 201.
4. Ben Brantley, *New York Times*, 25 August 1997. Accessed 15 July 2021.
5. *Colored Lights*, 200.
6. In an early draft the show was subtitled 'An American Fable' (NYPL, Ebb papers, accessed 12 August 2023).
7. Greg Evans, *Variety* Review, 5 May 1997, https://variety.com/1997/legit/reviews/steel-pier -1200449981, accessed 15 July 2021.
8. In the programme note, 19.
9. Greg Evans, in *Variety*, as above.

10. Ben Brantley, *New York Times*, as above.

11. *Colored Lights*, 199.

12. *A Chorus Line* won all the Tony Awards that in another year would certainly have been awarded to Bob Fosse's production because *A Chorus Line*, for all its gestures towards an honest representation of the life of Broadway dancers, maintains a sentimental attitude towards show business success.

13. *Colored Lights*, 199.

14. Greg Evans, in *Variety*, as above.

15. Greg Evans, in *Variety*, as above.

16. Ben Brantley, *New York Times*, as above.

17. Kander, in *Colored Lights*, 200.

18. Alice Audley in *The Upcoming*, https://www.theupcoming.co.uk/2012/11/09/theatre-review-steel-pier-at-the-union, accessed 21 July 2021.

19. Greg Evans in *Variety*, as above.

20. Susan Stroman, https://www.susanstroman.com/productions/steel-pier, accessed 20 July 2021.

21. 'Lucky Lindy' was the nickname of aviator Charles Lindbergh, the first person to fly solo across the Atlantic in 1927. In *Steel Pier*, Rita has been designated Lindy's Lovebird in a publicity stunt arranged by Mick.

22. There are many precedents in Greek drama, Shakespeare, Brecht, Edward Bond, Hollywood films et al but none in naturalistic theatre.

23. I have seen Paul Taylor-Mills' London amateur production of *Steel Pier* at the Bridewell Theatre (February 2011) and his professional off-West End production at the Union Theatre (October-November 2012).

24. All page references are to David Thompson, John Kander and Fred Ebb, *Steel Pier*, New York: Samuel French, 1998.

25. This replaced 'Everybody's for Sale' originally sung by Mick to Walker (Fred Ebb Papers, Mss 2005–001).

26. An earlier song for Shelby was 'Salt and Pepper' (Fred Ebb, Papers Mss 2005-001).

27. Another song was written to reveal Precious as ambitious and calculating; 'I Can See Right through You' was eventually deleted as was 'The Little Woman' (Fred Ebb Papers, Mss 2005-002).

28. Rita had a song, 'Blue Flame', that was deleted just before the show's première (Fred Ebb Papers, Mss 2005-004).

29. By contrast, *Cabaret* has numerous allusions to what is occurring in the world outside the cabaret: the appearance of a swastika on Ernst, Cliff being beaten up by Nazis and the attack on Herr Schultz's fruit shop are prime examples, as are 'Tomorrow Belongs to Me', Fraulein Schneider's 'What Would You Do' and Cliff's explicit criticism of Sally's wilful blindness to the political situation in Germany.

30. Erwin Piscator's epic theatre techniques were the first to use documentary images and text to provide supplementary historical contexts that explained aspects of the drama.

31. Opening the night before *Steel Pier* in April 1997, *Titanic: The Musical* was a commercial hit, as was *Ragtime*, which had already premiered in Toronto in 1996 but appeared on Broadway in 1998 soon after.

32. For some indication of choreography and production values of the Broadway production, see: https://www.susanstroman.com/productions/steel-pier or https://www.youtube.com/watch?v=xtkOj9EUAbI, accessed 20 July 2021.

33. In fact, *Hadestown* is entirely based on the myth of Orpheus and Eurydice alluded to in *Steel Pier*.

13 Ghosting *The Skin of Our Teeth*

All about Us (1999) over and over

Their last two musicals, *All about Us* (2001) and *The Visit* (2014), are theatrical meditations on the burden of living in the shadow of death. As in the majority of the team's musicals, the vocabulary of *All about Us* is pure showbiz. Yet its theme is an existentialist reflection on the resilience of the human spirit in defiance of the dangers of universal annihilation. It is as if Ebb's troubling lyric, 'Life is what you do while you're waiting to die' from *Zorba!* were transmuted into a narrative demonstrating the cyclical shape of human history from prehistoric times to the present. Like *Zorba!* much of the duo's work (*Cabaret*, *The Rink*, *Kiss of the Spiderwoman*, *Steel Pier*, *The Scottsboro Boys* and *The Visit*) depicts the encroaching danger to each character's way of life as the comforting illusions of hope or escapist fantasies are successfully destroyed.

The dark comedy of Thornton Wilder's seemingly intractable *The Skin of Our Teeth* is presumably one reason why the songwriters were drawn to musicalize the play. The other reason may have been its non-stop self-reflexive discourse on the imperfect nature of theatre as a mode of representing human existence, exploiting the meta-theatrical form of which they are masters. Indeed, in 2004 Michael Billington succinctly opined that a Young Vic production 'suggests [. . . *The Skin of Our Teeth*] is the missing link between Pirandello and Ionesco'.[1]

Reviewing *Over and Over* (1999), the musical's first iteration at the Signature Theatre in Arlington, Virginia, Lloyd Rose commented perspicuously:

> "The Skin of Our Teeth" is a masterwork but a very peculiar one. Absurdist, whimsical, optimistic, mystical, realistic, a little mean, Thornton Wilder's play just barely hangs together – succeeds, so to speak, by the skin of its teeth. By contrast [. . .] the musical based on it [. . .] comes apart, scattering into seemingly unrelated components. [T]he show has very little energy. [. . .] Though the fantastical elements seem perfect for musical comedy, the all-over-the-place, incident-packed story has to be scrupulously focused. [. . .] Arguably the greatest engineer of dramatic structure in the American theater, Wilder made his wobbly material [. . .] stand up and skate lightly across the stage.[2]

Whereas Wilder was able to create an intricate weave of absurd humour in the anachronistic clash between the milieu of Excelsior, New Jersey, during the Second World War (1942, the year the play was originally produced), the prehistoric period and the Biblical era of Genesis in Acts 1 and 3, and of Atlantic City in the 1920s with the period of Noah's Flood, *Over and Over* inevitably reduces this surrealist philosophical conceit to tongue-in-cheek archness:

In contrast, Kander, Ebb and Stein seem to have approached the problem of telling this odd, awkward story by figuring out how many songs could be gotten out of it. [. . .] The problem is, the numbers aren't set up by the book so that the audience not only wants them but has to have them. They're just thrown at us one by one.[3]

Joseph Stein inadvertently reveals the problem of reworking his book for its new incarnation as *All about Us*:

The Virginia version was [. . .] badly mishandled. Characters were added which I felt were unnecessary, [. . .] but we saw what was wrong. [. . .] I made a lot of changes, and the third act of the play practically doesn't exist in the musical. Basically, the line of the play, we have kept. And the three major characters. [. . .] We made the changes that will improve it for a contemporary audience.[4]

Paradoxically, by maintaining 'the line of the play' while paring its dialogue down to the bone to allow for the intercalation of songs that repeatedly freeze the action, the team heightened the show's revue-like collection of songs and sketches to advance the rather static action. By all accounts, in revising the show Stein made the correct decision to cut most of the multiple characters (Lulu Shriner, Lola Fitt and the Blessed Virgin Mary) overplayed for laughs by the irrepressible Dorothy Loudon. In Wilder's play, the scene changes form a circular pattern from Excelsior in 1942 to Atlantic City in the 1920s with a return to the first act setting in the final act, yet the characters remain fixed in spite of the 'flashback' to twenty years earlier, growing neither more nor less mature. By telescoping the entire panorama of human history into a three-act parable, his characters are not mere comic stereotypes, but neither are they presented through subtly motivated naturalistic action or feeling. They come to life by speaking in a modern idiom of quotidian domesticity, which animates the universal human types by encouraging audience members to empathize with commonplace experiences they too have been through.

Sensitive to the peculiar nature of their source play, Kander and Ebb eschew the usual method of trying to deepen the characters' inner lives in the fashion of the integrated book musical: instead of utilizing the songs in either version to externalize a sub-textual thread of progressively developing emotions, the authors strive to match the static quality of Wilder's archetypal characters by presenting every song in a slightly abstract style, which communicates a single idea or emotional attitude that does not advance the plot or amplify character but explicates action rather than maintaining its flow. While the juxtaposition of the opposing periods and styles in the play is a surrealist technique, the radical pruning necessitated by the musical format of *Over and Over* reduces conversations into fragmentary and isolated signposts whose overt didacticism threatens to render them arch or camp.

On *All about Us*, the creative team made some intelligent casting choices, while director Gabriel Barre managed to avoid the knowing mockery or deadpan delivery by means of which the actors had burlesqued the intellectual whimsy of the first version. In this sense, the later production manifested a deeper insight into the function of Wilder's dialogue and characterization, echoing the songwriters in fashioning the songs to function either as Brechtian commentaries or as illustrations of thought patterns rather than evoking the characters' emotional engagement. Yet this makes greater demands on an audience. The one misstep was possibly in replacing David Garrison as Mr Antrobus with the operatically trained Shuler Hensley: although a highly talented performer, Hensley's sombre and booming vocal approach did not possess the witty lightness of touch that might evoke the fanciful flight of ideas in the songs.

In dramatizing a theory of time indebted to Vico via Joyce's *Finnegan's Wake*,[5] Jung, Pound and T. S. Eliot, Wilder created a palimpsest of superimposed time frames. In addition to twentieth century New Jersey, the prehistoric Ice Age and the Biblical epochs of Genesis and the Flood, there are even in Act II allusions to Sodom and Gomorrah. Such a complex pattern of correspondences is intended to cue each member of the audience's private association with the parallel moments within multiple time frames, so that each individual character or happening becomes a universal archetype of human experience. According to Wilder,

> Every action which has ever taken place – every thought, every emotion – has taken place only once, at one moment in time and place. 'I love you,' 'I rejoice,' 'I suffer,' have been said and felt many billions of times, and never twice the same. Every person who has ever lived has lived the same unbroken succession of unique occasions. Yet the more one is aware of this individuality in experience [. . .] the more one becomes attentive to what these disparate moments have in common, to repetitive patterns.[6]

Mary Williams' summary of Wilder's conception of time illuminates the artistic method he elaborated to abolish the notion of linear and progressive time 'through the use of circular structures, fragmented narratives and situations, deliberate anachronisms, the use of myth, the emphasis of mystical resolutions'.[7] To parody the representation of archetypal experiences by reducing it to a set of comic clichés is to disengage the complex philosophy from its unique form in the dramaturgy. Hence the more Joseph Stein tried to clarify the putative narrative line of *The Skin of Our Teeth*, the more he might have betrayed its author's intentions. Adopting a non-linear approach to the structure of the show – Sondheim and Furth's *Company* here provides the paradigmatic example – would be wholly in keeping with Wilder's philosophy, allowing the team to 'spatialise'[8] the temporality of the play in a collage-like scheme, rather than attempting to introduce narrative drive or suspense.

It is fairly common when a musical is revised to lose some significant features of the original in order to capitalize on the opportunities offered by a different approach. In my view, this is precisely what occurred when the Prologue of *Over and Over* was replaced by the entrance of a Stage Manager who stuns the audience with her warning that a cataclysmic wave of ice is blowing across the land. The intention was no doubt to establish at the outset a convention of asides by the actors who comment on the script or editorialize about an item of world news, thereby breaking the flow of action. Once members of the audience understood that such interruptions would recur repeatedly, it was assumed they would be less bewildered and more receptive to the continual self-reflexiveness of the show.

The Prologue combines the sounds of a raging storm with an operatic chorus of frightened male voices followed by female ones:

> Ah ah ah ah ah ah ah ah!
> Oh me, oh my, oh me, oh me oh my!
> The icicles are falling from the sky
> [.......................]
> Oh God oh dear!
> Oh God it's clear

The end is near
Let loose God
The deluge God
The deluge God
Oh God oh God!
Oh God oh God oh God.
Oh oh oh oh oh[9]

Cutting this prologue risks losing the introduction of the Armageddon motif that is threaded throughout the play in opposition to the softly voiced belief that humankind will survive by 'the skin of our teeth'. The almost childlike terror evoked in the quasi-Biblical choral song is produced acoustically by the integration of wind and vocal sound, illustrating the trope musically. The staccato repetition of the exclamations in a quick tempo produces the wry, comic impression of crowds of people rushing around helplessly in panic and confusion. By rendering the mood through music, the affect of the trope is far more moving than the effect of the rather cynical ploy in the revised version. The swift realization that the 'surprise' interruption is a joke instantaneously identifies the direct address as a stage convention, thereby dispelling any genuine tension:

> Stop this! Hi everyone, I am the Stage Manager. One special announcement – we just received word that there is a giant wall of ice accompanied by winds of hurricane proportions approaching this area, so should it be necessary to evacuate the premises please do so calmly. Thank you for your cooperation and – enjoy the show!

The final exclamations in the sung Prologue make a nice segue into Sabina's initial dialogue scene, an abbreviated version of Wilder's. Yet a comparison between Stein and Wilder's dialogue suggests that even though Stein directly quotes the play on occasions, his deletion of certain sections (indicated below in square brackets and italicized script) has subtly but completely altered both tone and meaning. The cutting of the reference to the Hudson River leaves the musical's setting less specific, so that the archetypal significance of an 'everyman's' family hailing from New Jersey loses its ironic resonance.

> Oh oh oh oh! Six o'clock and the master not home yet! Pray God nothing serious has happened to him crossing the [*Hudson*] river. [*. . . The fact is I don't know what'll become of us*]. Here it is the middle of August and the coldest day anyone can remember [*of the year*]. It's simply freezing; the dogs are sticking to the sidewalk, Can anyone explain that? [*No. But I'm not surprised. The whole world's at sixes and sevens, and why the house hasn't fallen down about our ears long ago is a miracle to me . . . Every night this same anxiety as to whether the master will get home safely: whether he'll bring home anything to eat. In the midst of life we are in death, a truer word was never said.*] Oh I pray the master returns home safely. This is the Antrobus home where I work. As you can see, normal American home – husband, wife, son, daughter . . . the maid. A typical New Jersey family.[10]

The precarious survival of humanity, in spite of the apparent entropy of a randomly ordered universe, is no longer registered when the reference to the world being 'at sixes and sevens' is removed, as is the significance of a house about to fall down as an emblem of the precarious nature of human life. Stein has inserted an overt comment by Sabina on the Antrobus family as 'normal' to compensate, but this is more didactic and knowing than

Wilder's original portrayal of the maid through the platitudes of homespun philosophy, which in some respects makes her more like 'all of us'. When she proudly registers agreement with the portentous cliché 'In the midst of life we are in death, a truer word was never said', while recognizing it as a commonplace, her anxiety allies her with the play's scheme of archetypal references rather than the camp commentaries of Sabina in Stein's script.

Sabina's first song is an unusually muted version of the typical Kander and Ebb exhortation to enjoy the hedonistic pleasures of life. Whereas the best known of these consistently celebrate the cheerful escape offered by maintaining a positive attitude amid difficult circumstances ('Sing Happy', 'Cabaret', 'The Happy Time', 'Life Is', 'Yes', 'Nowadays', 'Where You Are', 'Steel Pier' and 'Show People'), Sabina's scope for pleasurable relief is much more restricted. Perfectly in character, 'Eat the Ice Cream' conjures a world of little treats – children's parties and surreptitious visits to the cinema or funfair – in which it is necessary to snatch comfort through self-gratification in the brief intervals between disasters.

The homespun quality of the advice is reinforced by the fact that it is a quotation from Sabina's mother – a further use of Wilder's allusive strategy showing how comparable truths of experience are echoed by individuals in every time and place. In the verse Sabina sings,

> And it says in her autobiography
> In an often-quoted text,
> 'Gather those rosebuds while ye may,
> God knows what you're in for next.'
>
> 'There's always some calamity
> To knock your road askew
> Today you're in the pink
> But by tomorrow black and blue
> And I think you should consider
> This very good advice
> Coming from a mother
> Who was violated twice.'

The alternation between optimism and disillusionment is incessant, leading to the cautionary banality of the chorus:

> You gotta eat the ice cream
> While it's on your plate.
> Wait till tomorrow
> And it's sure to be too late.

Yet her mother's warning, 'You've only got yourself to blame', reinforces the trite moralism of Sabina's song, in which it is the responsibility of the individual to grab whatever fragment of pleasure offers itself. As in other songs, Ebb supplies lyrics that amplify Wilder's concept of the insecurity of human history, necessitating the snatching of happiness from the jaws of disaster. Sabina's version of this commonplace exemplifies a hand-me-down version of the prevailing trope of humanity being thrown upon its own resources to survive 'by the skin of our teeth'. The prehistoric anachronisms incorporated into the 1942 setting include the necessity of keeping the fire burning, implied by Mrs Antrobus' short pseudo-operatic song 'Sabina' in which her repeated melismatic delivery of 'You've let the f-i-i-i-ire go out' parodies the high-flown style of an aria. On one hand, she reiterates the obvious in a portentous melodramatic vocal gesture, but on the other, there is no doubt that losing fire during the Ice Age constitutes a risk of extermination, so ironically her apparent over-dramatization of a quotidian accident in 1942 is entirely appropriate in the prehistoric era.

The paradigmatic family is successively introduced as first daughter and son, Gladys and Henry ('We're Home'), then their father, enter. While the children unintentionally betray signs of the quarrelsome nature that previously caused Henry (a surrogate Cain) to kill his brother (a surrogate Abel) with a stone, they pretend to have been well-behaved. The next example of a deliberately anachronistic song is George Antrobus' hymn to his own invention, 'The Wheel'.

> I'm thrilled with what I do
> As nearly everybody knows,
> They know
> I invent.

Phrased in brief statements in the style of a haiku, the song describes George as an enthusiastic inventor whose creations have been of more use to the human race than he takes credit for.

> I invent lots of things,
> Like the toothpick, the tweezer,
> The orange-juice squeezer . . .

Antrobus sees himself as a kind of artist, inventing implements for the personal satisfaction their intrinsic beauty brings him:

> But the wheel the wheel
> I'm proudest of the wheel
> For it clearly is a work of art I've found
> And I couldn't love it more
> If I knew what it was for
> But I'm satisfied to watch it
> Go round and round and round.

His list of 'all kinds of useful, wonderful practical things [. . .] / Like the scissors, the towel, the gardener's trowel [. . .] / The bonnet, the sweater / Each alphabet letter' bears testimony to the way individual human beings have historically mastered a hostile environment by designing a wide range of tools to help cultivate and control it. The number creates a series of Brechtian defamiliarization effects, which present each domestic item in a fresh light as a historically significant phenomenon: the clash between the naming of ordinary objects and the exultant affect of the music produces the 'gestic music' beloved of Weill and Brecht.

The musical sound of the repeated hook line, 'Go round and round and round' enacts, in the manner of programme music, the sense of endless repetition emblematic of Wilder's cyclical conception of time, as indeed does the trope of the wheel. Meanwhile, the exhortation to the audience to 'Invent!' at the conclusion of the song suggests their shared investment in George's celebration of the instinctive creativity of human nature. Sabina's pragmatic advice to 'Eat the ice cream while it's on your plate' is a degraded version of this exhortation. While

George's instincts are creative on a high mental plane, Sabina's merely involve grabbing opportunities for escape from reality whenever offered. When George welcomes a number of homeless people and animals out of the blizzard, there is a vague echo of the Biblical Noah, but Maggie's resistance to his generosity (like that of Noah's wife) obliges the group to try and manipulate the family's sympathies in the lugubrious yet wryly comic 'Warm', which reinforces the severity of weather conditions in the Ice Age and the desperate struggle of mammals to subsist.

Among the homeless are Socrates, Plato, Homer and Moses. As George makes them welcome, Sabina comes in to complain that Henry had a violent altercation with the boy next door and almost killed him; Henry contradicts her tale with an obvious lie, starting to become violent as the quartet of wise men interrupt by joining to become a 1940s close harmony group (such as the Ink Spots).[11] They plaster over the cracks in the dysfunctional family situation by singing a typical jive song, 'A Whole Lot of Lovin', which is a parodic celebration of 'the family'. Again, the song teasingly pastiches a popular musical form of the period in order to exemplify the philosophy motivating the survival of the family unit, employing the anachronistic contrast of historical figures with the 1940s song for comic effect:

> You need a whole lot of raindrops
> To make a pouring rain;
> You need a whole lot of windstorms
> To make a hurricane.
>
> You need a whole lot of water
> To make the deep blue sea;
> And you need a whole lot of love
> To make a family.

Wilder's Jungian notion of archetypes of experience is animated in the folk wisdom of 'You need a whole lot of suffering to make your average life', yet another reminder of the conflict between the positive (loving) impulses of individuals and their hostile conditions. One of the changes made in the transformation of *Over and Over* to *All about Us* was the substitution of the song 'When Poppa Comes Home' in place of Gladys' poem – the rather obscure 'Abou ben Adhem' – based on Wilder's text and 'Remember Them' in place of 'The Library'. Henry and Maggie now sing a medley of 'Numbers' and 'Remember Them', so the three numbers together constitute a musical scene highlighting the rote learning of the children in the context of George's reflection on how to keep past civilizations alive in the collective memory. Although Gladys delivers the poem she wrote faultlessly, Henry angers George by making a mistake in the recitation of his arithmetical tables; George himself must decide whether it is necessary to burn furniture and material artefacts (presumably including books) to maintain the fire that keeps people alive, or to risk the destruction of the human race by ice and snow.

The later section of 'When Poppa Comes Home' is counterpointed with 'Numbers' to include the moralistic platitudes: 'Home is where the heart is', 'There's no place like home', 'Make a house a home'. The price of survival might mean the destruction of past culture, as Maggie demonstrates in 'Remember Them', a list of famous authors whose work Maggie exhorts George to treasure in memory: Proust, Balzac, Dickens, Galileo,

Keats, Milton, Charlotte Bronte, Oscar Wilde, Thornton Wilder, Edith Wharton, et al. In *All about Us*, the musical scene brings Act 1 to a powerful climax with the choral singing of 'Save the Human Race'. If the opening number from *Over and Over* were retained, this would be an ironic musical echo with the 'end of the world' motif inverted to end the act on a hopeful note.

In Act 2, the authors conflate the last two acts of *The Skin of Our Teeth* in order to conform to the two-act convention of musical comedy. This may not have been the perfect solution to the problem that a faithful musical version of Wilder's play would be far too long, as it has some implications for the structure of Act 2 in *All about Us*, which consequently bungles Wilder's image of a war that threatens universal holocaust, leaving only the savage ironies of the number 'Military Man' to evoke its full horror.

The act begins with the self-reflexive 'A Discussion', an extremely funny number that enables the four wise men to freeze the action in order to debate the merits of the musical:

> They say to make the musical successful
> The audience should know just why they're here;
> The authors should make sure in every moment
> That the narrative is absolutely clear.

The constant self-interrogation in Wilder's play is mimicked by the wise men's comic bafflement in failing to grasp the musical's avant-garde approach to form and meaning.

> I don't get it, I don't get it,
> If you think I do, forget it!
> And what's more I never got it all along

They speak for the average audience member in their inability to interpret the show's abstract philosophical issues, thereby actually helping the audience by giving a quick recap:

> It started with this family in New Jersey
> Who seemed to find the going very rough,
> About the big calamities that befell them –
> As if New Jersey wasn't bad enough.

These lyrics also produce a Pirandellian commentary, which mocks the naïve expectations of musical theatre audiences:

> Sabi says it's called an allegory,
> Her uncle's a producer of the show.

The meta-theatrical trope continues as one of the men reads the stage directions that describe the location of Act 2. The threatened catastrophe of destruction by snow and ice at the conclusion of Act 1 is followed by circling back in time from Excelsior, New Jersey, in 1942 to the conspicuous consumption and orgiastic pleasures of Atlantic City in the 1920s, with its train of overt references to the Biblical prediction that the world would be destroyed by a flood, while Noah's family and representative animals would be saved in the ark he'd been instructed to build. As in Wilder's play, this loopback of roughly twenty years deliberately disrupts the linear progression of the musical's plot. George is introduced as president of the 600,000th convention of friendly mammals, before the breathless promise of the 'delightful entertainment' by the fortuneteller Esmerelda. The 'star' build-up to her grand entrance together with the mysterious mood of magical hocus pocus conjured by her appearance is redolent of the tacky milieu of boardwalk entertainment in Atlantic City, rather than Biblical prophesy.

Eartha Kitt's idiosyncratic and oddly oracular performance of 'Rain', attired in the Newport, Connecticut production in a shiny red gown, stole the show, solemnly invoking the disturbing promise of the flood, while at the same time highlighting the deliberately cheesy atmosphere of gambling and escapist fun typical of seaside holidays. Wilder's specific inclusion of bingo in Act 2 involves an implicit comparison between chance (gambling) and fate as two kinds of human destiny, with Esmerelda exposed as an ambiguous figure who might just as well offer Biblical prophecy as cut-price readings of tea leaves. On entering, Kitt looked directly out at the audience before seeming to extemporize, 'Nice crowd!' which inevitably elicited gales of laughter.

She then addressed the audience as delegates of the fictional convention, 'Well, I guess some of you have come to this convention to have fun, some to gamble, some to make your fortune [. . .] I can't help you make your fortune, I just tell it like it is', establishing the audience as complicit with the Atlantic City revellers. On one hand, gambling symbolizes pure chance while prophecy, on the other, represents predestination by God, Noah/Antrobus choosing to obey the word of God whereas the superstitious pleasure-seekers refuse to heed the Fortuneteller's equivocal fortune-telling:

I can see the future
[.....................]
Yes I can see the future
Clear as sunshine morning
But I cannot see the past –
No-one can see the past.
[...................]
All I see is filled with pain.
As for further matters
I can tell the weather
And believe me brother
It's gonna be
Rain rain rain rain rain
Rain.

At Newport, Kitt then picked out particular individuals in the audience and told their fortunes, ending always with her screaming the fearful warning, 'And you'll die, brother'. In one case she promised someone she jokingly identified as a sex addict, 'No matter how many times you lower your pants, / Death by romance' and at the end, cautioned the whole audience to anticipate 'death by pouring rain'. Ironically Esmerelda's prediction in this instance proved to be true, blurring the line between 1920s Atlantic City and the Biblical world.

In Kitt's performance, 'Rain' became a climactic moment in the show, the sinister yet tantalizing mood of the song providing a ritualistic evocation of the dangers of universal annihilation as well as a world-weary acknowledgement that people ignore at their peril the signs of entropy and destruction in the pursuit of immediate gratification. (In the context of current arguments about climate change, both the play and musical prove prescient.) From the beginning of Act 2, Kander, Ebb and Stein have prompted the audience to experience the central tropes of *The Skin of Our Teeth* in an extraordinary language of musical theatre, initially by musicalizing a self-referential critical discourse on how to explicate the meaning of the show itself. In 'Rain', Esmeralda's linking of the recent past (the 1920s) with the return of the Biblical calamity of the flood then amplifies the pervasive trope of history as cyclical in a vividly theatrical demonstration of prophecy.

The authors next illustrate the typical difference in outlook between men and women in the following few moments. In his address, George asserts that, 'the watchword of the past was "work, work, work" but this is a new day, and I say we have earned the right to a new slogan, "Let's enjoy ourselves, have fun, fun, fun"' whereas Maggie, in a comic and self-defeating re-purposing of feminist rhetoric, espouses 'Save the Family' as the guiding principle of 'the female of the species':

> My husband and I have been married 5,000 years today. [. . .] We women had to crusade for marriage; we marched; we fought, we chained ourselves to lampposts until we finally won the wedding ring.

The age-old plea for faithful marriages gives way to the 'Beauty Pageant' in which Cleopatra, Helen of Troy and Joan of Arc state their aims, each of which involves either free love or war – or both. As the fourth contestant, Sabina's reassuring crooning of 'World Peace' hyperbolically describes her ambition to save the world by means of several initiatives:

> I wanna make world peace
> I've gotta make world peace
> And when I make world peace
> I'll take a little rest.

In each of the two subsequent choruses, Sabina promises with naïve sincerity to solve a different global problem – by ending hunger and discovering a cure for cancer. 'World Peace' is a typical example of Ebb's ability to elicit laughter out of a series of ironic lyrics delivered in this instance with deadpan comic effect by Cady Huffman:

> Giving with my body
> And giving with my soul,
> Giving both together
> I'm giving as a whole.

The song amplifies Sabina's archetypal significance as 'the other woman', at the same time characterizing her as a literal-minded do-gooder who fails to recognize the inherent self-interest in her professed generosity. In her sung rejoinder ('He Always Comes Home to Me'), Maggie confirms the traditional archetype of the long-suffering but faithful wife, 'For no matter what he may do / With women as easy as you, / He always comes home to me.' The stereotypical antithesis of mother/wife versus mistress is given voice immediately in 'You Owe It to Yourself', Sabina's comfortingly seductive reassurance to George that extramarital pleasures are normal for men.

> Take a long hard look at me
> You owe it to yourself;

I'm not the lamb I seem to be
You owe it to yourself.
[.......................................]
I've got a brain and just below it,
I've got talent, let me show it.

After a few minutes of dialogue, Cady Huffman stops the performance with her announcement that she is not going to play Sabina's next scene:

It's just a short scene and we're gonna skip it but I'll tell you what happens and then we'll just continue from there. Now in this scene we talk and he decides to leave his wife and divorce and marry me – that's it [. . .]

At first, this appears to be simply another hilarious meta-theatrical interruption that reiterates the trope whereby actors comment on their roles or interfere to criticize or suggest rewrites of the script, but it soon emerges that the episode explores the connection between audience reception and self-censorship, as Sabina explains in what today might be considered a trigger warning:

I happen to have a friend in the audience who'll be hurt by some of the lines in the scene [. . .] Has it ever occurred to you just how hurtful it is when a man walks out on a woman . . . A man tells a woman who he's been married to for 15 years, perfectly happily, that he's gonna up and leave her for her kid sister [. . .] I feel for you, Harriet.

The actress' extra-dramatic identification with her friend Harriet through her personal response to Maggie's role in the play is an extraordinary instance of Brecht's conception of performance as a mode of rehearsal for life; it tests every individual in the audience as to the kind and degree of their empathy with the archetypal situations and characters – a further elaboration of Wilder's notion of the distinctive relationship between particular and universal experience. When Harriet storms out of the auditorium, the Stage Manager's unsympathetic response generates huge laughter, 'Well she's gone now so you can play the scene,' reducing a philosophical argument to a crudely pragmatic level.

Before George makes his radio broadcast to the conventions of the world, he tells Maggie:

I'm moving out . . . for good. I'm gonna marry Miss Fairweather. I shall provide generously for you and the children . . . In a few years you'll see that it is all for the best. That's all I have to say.

Maggie replies ironically to George's mouthing of a husband's clichéd declaration of his intention to seek a divorce, thereby shattering the 'happy family' myth of Act 1: 'Well, after living with you for 5,000 years I guess I have a right to say a word or two, haven't I?' The wife/mother here exposes the first act's 'faithful' marriage idyll as a charade obscuring the historical pattern of the husband's compulsive philandering.

The start of the next number, Henry's sneering 'Nice People', confronts members of the audience directly with their own hypocrisy:

What are you looking at?
Go on tell me!

[................]
You don't like me, do ya?

I know what's wrong with the world.
[..............]
It's people like you.

Henry provokes laughter by amplifying this trope in order to mock the desire of any audience to be recognized as 'nice people,' employing the colloquial speech that they themselves may habitually use:

You're all such
Namby-pamby, wishy-washy,
Fuddy-duddy, irritating
Nice people

Giving love and
Never thinking twice
That's nice and sugary and
Spice people

You know the kind

Ebb's rhetorical strategy is ultimately to goad an audience into becoming complicit in the rejection of Henry's specious truth-telling as malevolent sarcasm, while the mocking tone of the music matches it perfectly, invoking 'Kandernebb' at their best.

Reviewing *Over and Over*, Lloyd Rose opined, '[T]he evening's one show-stopper [is] the funny, scary, worthy-of-"Cabaret" "Nice People," choreographed to furious perfection by Bob Avian.' The number extends the deconstruction of Act 1's mythical image of the 'perfect' family by presenting the pathological pattern of Henry's behaviour as a retrogression from naughty boy taunting do-gooders ('The kind that follow all the rules / The kind that tells you/Where to go and what to do') to an unwitting admission of the murderous instincts that reveal Cain as his Biblical archetype:

Henry go comb your hair;
Henry go wash your face;
[.........]
Henry, that knife is sharp;
[.........]
Henry, don't kick that dog;
Henry, put down that rock;
Henry, you're much too rough;
Henry, I've said enough
Enough! Enough! Enough!

When Gladys reports to her parents that Henry/Cain has almost killed a man by hitting him with a stone 'just because he didn't like his looks', thunder starts to rumble, causing someone to shout, 'The end of the world!' Then George announces flatly on the radio, 'Folks, good evening. Nothing much to say . . . because it's the end of the world. Good luck! Thanks for listening'. After Maggie exhorts George to round up two creatures of every species while she searches desperately for Henry, who she calls Cain for the first time, Esmerelda sings a short reprise of 'Rain' and speaks a few sentences, ending thus, 'Well, Mr and Mrs Antrobus, it looks like you're safe – for the time being. But there are other dangers. [. . .] A moment of peace. [. . .] Nothing else left but trouble. Nothing else left. Nothing . . . left.'

The Skin of Our Teeth ends the second act here, but at this moment *All about Us* segues directly into 'Military Man', a grimly cheerful march sung and danced by Henry with a corps of soldiers:

> Left left left right left
> Left left left right left.
> Don't you just love a parade?
> [......................]
> Were that not quite enough for now
> You know in thirty years somehow,
> There'll be another war
> In Russia or Japan.

Following a double-quick patter section[12] a chorus of cheering women waves the young men off with:

> Three cheers for conflict, my boys,
> Three cheers for war (war, war, war).
> [..................]
> Let's heat up the cannons my boys
> Hot as we can,
> Because by keeping our ability
> To manifest hostility,
> There'll always be a military man.

Henry and the soldiers repeat the patter section as part of a round before the jingoistic final chorus. Another ironic show-stopper, its apparently unthinking celebration of the horrors of war as a musical comedy 'parade' song reminds the audience of the unending cycle of war and peace. It might, however, have been more effective dramaturgically to have found a way to mimic Wilder's own reiteration of the circular nature of historical time in a third act. As it is, the representation of war immediately succeeds Esmerelda's little speech, so the audience has no time to observe the return to life after Noah's Flood.

In their reference to 'another war in Russia or Japan', Kander and Ebb invent an equivalent to Wilder's coded references in 1942 to the dangers of total annihilation during the Second World War, yet now their mention of Japan exploits the benefit of hindsight by prompting images of the atomic bombs dropped on Hiroshima and Nagasaki, as well as suggesting the dangers of nuclear holocaust throughout the Cold War that succeeded. (This implication has only been strengthened by the threat of a nuclear war in response to Russia's invasion of Ukraine.) The song is later interrupted a few times by the sounds of exploding bombs until only Henry is alive to sing it, preceding a final section where only the sound of explosions is heard. Then there is silence. A baby cries and is hushed by two women singing a sweet lullaby, signalling that even after the disastrous destruction of war, life goes on.

Possibly something more is needed to match the effect of Wilder's deployment of the second interval to imply the passage of time from the destruction of humanity by flood to the imagined end of the Second World War. In fact, Sabina begins the third act of *The Skin of Our Teeth* in the living room of Act 1 (the set is somewhat the worse for wear, with stage flats missing or askew) by announcing:

> Mrs Antrobus! Gladys! Where are you? [. . .] The war's over. The war's over. You can come out. The peace treaty's been signed. Where are they? – Hmpf! Are they dead too? Mrs Annnntrobus! Glaaaadus! Mr Antrobus'll be here this afternoon. Huuurry and put things in order. He says that now that the war's over we'll all have to settle down and be perfect.[13]

At this point, Fitzpatrick, the Stage Manager, breaks the stage illusion yet again, disrupting the flow of action by ordering the house lights to be switched on so Mr Antrobus can apologize for the fact that 'an unfortunate accident has taken place backstage'. Seven actors have ptomaine poisoning and are in hospital 'having their stomachs pumped out'.[14]

The act continues in meta-theatrical mode as Fitzpatrick is obliged to explain the author's intentions in the scene that cannot be properly enacted without the right performers:

> [A]t the end of this [second] act the men have come back from the war and the family's settled down in the house. And the author wants to show the hours of the night passing by and the planets crossing the sky – uh – over their heads.[15]

There follows a ten-minute discursive detour in which actors, stage crew and friends who have sat in at rehearsals argue about how to represent the planets and abstract concepts of time. The friends attempt to rehearse a Socratic debate by famous philosophers until the stage manager announces the start of Act 3, whereupon the actress playing Sabina begins the action all over again.

Such a radical dramatization of the artistic problems involved in trying to compress an existentialist history of human life into a play would clearly be unwieldy in a musical, which should be approximately seventy-five minutes shorter than the original drama to allow time for musical numbers. Yet, by cutting the deconstruction of the play's metaphysical meaning as well as Wilder's evocation of a historical gap between the second and third acts, there is a danger of the putative realism of the narrative appearing even more facile and sketchy. Stein, Kander and Ebb compensate by intelligent song placement that creates an emotional arc to imitate the progress of the play's argument in affective rather than discursive terms.

When Henry first and then George return, the ceaseless intra-familial conflict is restated, the motivation for wars being identified as men's competitive instinct for battle. In a line taken directly from the source play, Sabina wisely observes, 'The enemy is Henry. Henry *is* the enemy'. After another violent altercation in which the actor playing Henry accuses George of infidelity, the Stage Manager intervenes again to remind everyone that they are all just actors. When they resume, Henry/the actor has left the stage, and George believes that his books are gone, threatening the end of human knowledge and, therefore, civilization. ('How can I go on without them?') The Stage Manager discovers the books, and they start to read various quotations from great authors, ending with 'Do unto others as you would have others do unto you. All the rest is commentary' from the Bible.

In answer to Gladys' question, 'Why is God mad at us?' George replies, 'God is not mad at us. God is mad. To bring all these calamities on us. If he exists, he must be mad.' This conversation leads to the eleven o'clock number, 'The Skin of Our Teeth', one of the most deeply emotive songs the pair ever wrote. Perfectly placed in dramaturgical terms, it transforms the characters' mood of despair to the guarded optimism that typifies human tenacity in the face of disaster, while both music and lyrics unobtrusively assert the unquenchable desire to survive. The show might well end on George's triumphant final note, but with the assurance of genuine craftsmen, the authors extend the action to show George and Maggie petting Gladys' baby girl while Sabina asks if she can go to the reopening of the old Rialto cinema, a wry and touching assertion of the need of ordinary people for escapist distraction from the harshness of the greater realities:

> You only get so much to work with
> Before the seltzer's lost its fizz
> And so it's wise to realize
> This is all there is
> […………………..]
> And the Rialto changes movies
> Every Friday
> What a wonderful thing to know

In the middle of the number, Sabina returns to the script from the opening of Act 1, bringing the action full circle for the second time: 'Oh oh oh! Six o'clock and the master's not home yet. [. . .] The whole world's at sixes and sevens', before completing the song:

> Go to the movies
> And reserve me a centre seat
> At the Rialto
> At the Rialto
> Friday.

Having finished the number on a mutedly elegiac note, Sabina breaks the musical spell by turning to the audience to bid them farewell: 'Now this is where you all came in. We have to go on for ages and ages, yet you get to go home. Oh Mr and Mrs Antrobus [. . .] They told me to tell you – good night!'

Although Kander and Ebb's penultimate completed show appears in retrospect to be a potential masterpiece, almost managing to match their hallmark dialectic of escapist illusion versus harsh reality to Thornton Wilder's impossibly complicated meta-theatrical meditation on human history, it may remain a pleasure for the true aficionado only, because the Wilder estate appears to have withdrawn permission to perform it.

Notes

1. Review of *The Skin of Our Teeth* in *The Guardian*, 6 March, 2004, https://www.theguardian.com/stage/2004/mar/06/theatre. Accessed 28 April 2023.

2. Lloyd Rose, 'Over and Over: Bits and Pieces', *The Washington Post*, 5 February 1999. https://www.washingtonpost.com/archive/lifestyle/1999/02/05/over-over-bits-and-pieces/596882b4-ed51-4333-86b2-dd1eb33ea818/. Accessed 29 April, 2023.

3. Rose, 'Over and Over: Bits and Pieces'.

4. *Playbill*, Interview with John Kander, May 2015. https://www.npr.org/2015/11/25/457289950/broadway-composer-john-kander-reflects-on-a-career-of-hidden-treasures. Accessed 3 May 2023.

5. Joyce's conception of the cyclical nature of time is ultimately derived from the Italian philosopher Vico.

6. Thornton Wilder, Preface to *Three Plays*, https://www.thorntonwilder.com/blog/2021/1/28/preface-to-three-plays-by-thornton-wilder, xxvii. Accessed 3 May 2023.

7. Mary Williams, quoted in Tesi di Laurea, 'Translation and Analysis of *The Long Christmas Dinner*', PhD thesis, http://dspace.unive.it/ bitstream/handle/ 10579/ 5752/ 827458-1183288.pdf ?sequence=2. Accessed 5 May 2023.

8. There is a strong connection here between Wilder's view and the influential ideas of the Symbolist poets and playwrights of the late nineteenth century, who believed in the *correspondances* between discrete moments of sensory experience and the ineffable powers of the universe.

9. All quotations transcribed from private audio recording of *Over and Over*, Signature Theatre, Arlington, Virginia 1999.

10. All quotations transcribed from private audio recording of *All about Us*, Westport Playhouse, Connecticut 2007.

11. The Ink Spots' recording of 'Java Jive' is a good example.

12. This part of the song echoes a major section of 'Sitting Pretty' from the original stage score of *Cabaret*.

13. *The Skin of Our Teeth*, 41, at https://www.academia.edu/31391046/THE_SKIN_OF_ OUR_TEETH_A_Play_by_Thornton_Wilder. Accessed 6 March, 2023.

14. *The Skin of Our Teeth*, 41–42.

15. *The Skin of Our Teeth*, 42.

14 American racism as minstrel show

The Scottsboro Boys (2010)

In dramaturgical terms, Kander and Ebb's collaboration with David Thompson must rank as their most complex and sophisticated exploration of twentieth-century history and the popular culture that reflected and reconstituted it as cultural imaginary. Surprisingly, perhaps, it is the only one of their musicals to treat actual historical personages and events in detail, although another three of their works (*Chicago, Cabaret* and *Steel Pier*) are set in the twenties or thirties, with the songs inspired by popular musical styles of the period being among their very best. Certainly, their ability to produce pastiche versions of characteristic song types of this epoch is unparalleled, suggesting a special affinity with its predominant stylistic qualities. Nevertheless, the enjoyment produced by their clever mimicking of period music and lyrics is never straightforward, for the placement and individual style of each song always indicate some degree of incongruity with its dramatic context that functions self-reflexively as a critique of the system of representation itself.

In its approach to history, *The Scottsboro Boys* derives from a tradition of musical theatre that might be said to have originated with Joan Littlewood's innovative and influential *Oh What a Lovely War!* on the surface, a re-animation of the Edwardian end-of-the-pier pierrot shows[1] that in fact confronted the nostalgia for Empire lurking in memories of popular First World War songs in order to expose their ideological function as a feature of the imperialist rhetoric of war.[2]

In its ceremonial re-enactment of race hatred, *The Scottsboro Boys* borrows and inverts the deliberately unsettling meta-dramatic strategy of Jean Genet's play *The Blacks: A Clown Show* (1959). Genet explicitly foregrounds the political conflicts incited by having Black actors perform a play about racial conflict for a white audience:

> This play, written, I repeat, by a white man, is intended for a white audience, but if, which is unlikely, it is ever performed before a black audience, then a white person, male or female, should be invited every evening. The organizer of the show should welcome him formally, dress him in ceremonial costume and lead him to his seat, preferably in the first row of the orchestra. The actors will play for him. A spotlight should be focused upon this symbolic white throughout the performance.[3]

The action of *The Blacks* takes the form of a play-within-a-play presented for the Queen and her court (played by five Black actors who 'white-up' for the performance) about the trial of a white woman who is murdered by order of a kangaroo court. The explosive scenario of race hatred and revenge is both articulated and defused by the staging of the trial as a kind of voodoo ceremony, while the politics of actor-audience engagement become as important, if not more so, than the narrative content of the drama.

While there is no evidence to suggest that Kander, Ebb and Thompson consciously imitated Genet in the construction of *The Scottsboro Boys*,[4] its musical dramaturgy does invite white and Black members of an audience to witness American history reduced to a disturbing ritual of racism against African Americans (and by implication, Jews). At various moments, the interplay of a multiplicity of different ethnicities and political prejudices risks offending one or another member of the audience. The choice of the historically racist frame of the minstrel show in some respects mocks the 'feel-good' factor of the Broadway entertainment industry, which may be the chief reason why, although nominated for twelve Tony Awards in 2011, it did not win one.

David Thompson initially aimed to present the historical material of what was then entitled *Minstrel Show* in a three-act format that would have reflected the various phases in the complicated series of trials, appeals and delays that occurred in Alabama during the thirties. The writers may also have wished to follow the three-act structure established as a minstrel show convention by the Christy Minstrels after its formation in 1843. This included an opening section followed by the 'olio' and concluding with a one-act plantation skit.[5] Although many elements of the minstrel show are imaginatively exploited throughout *The Scottsboro Boys*, the three-act format must have proved too constricting as the collaborators ultimately rejected it in favour of a continuous two-hour performance without intermission.

The earlier version begins with Haywood Patterson alone on stage in a Prologue, speaking directly to the audience:

The truth? Nobody's much interested in the truth. Inside the courthouse, truth was no defense anyhow. Not for the nine boys standing trial. They just wanted a show. The same goddamn show they'd been lining up to see for the past hundred years. What choice did we have? But to sing and strut . . . sing and strut. [*Patterson is hit with a hard-edged spot. The minstrel show begins.*] Hang 'em from up high! Spin 'em 'round and 'round! Stretch 'em by the neck! Dey make you gasp. Make you sigh! Make you cry sweet tears of joy! Dey's de dancin', prancin', entrancin' Scottsboro boys.[6]

The hectoring tone of the initial announcement that people's prejudices prevent them from recognizing the bare truth of facts insists on a ready-made explication of the musical's most significant trope, plainly disclosing the inherent racism of the 'show' desired by the white population of Alabama. The version that premiered at the Vineyard Theatre off-Broadway in 2010 does away with the didacticism of this prologue. The opening of the latter version is much more disorienting, precisely because it does not separate historical fact from minstrel mayhem. Simply by performing history in the form of a minstrel show, *The Scottsboro Boys* challenges its audiences to question how that history has been written, deconstructing a 200-year discourse on racial difference to reveal the brutality and injustice of the power structure it masks. According to James Leve, it was intended for the first three-act version to be performed by the entire cast in blackface, with the actors removing the makeup towards the end of the show. In retrospect, the decision not to do this seems wise, as it allowed the audience to engage with the performers spontaneously and to empathize directly with their humanity in ways that would have been blocked by blackface performance.

Instead of Patterson's prologue, the action of *The Scottsboro Boys* begins silently as a Black woman sits on a chair, opens her white cardboard cake box to smell the aroma and waits. The silence is broken by the hint of an archaic ritual as a regular drum beat is accompanied first by a tambourine rattle to create a hollow and slightly sinister sound, then by the solo plucking of a banjo, which is soon augmented by other instruments to transform the slow, marching rhythm into a recognizable dance tune. Reminiscent of the entrance parade of the typical minstrel show, each of the nine Black actors in turn enters dancing, bows to the woman on stage and positions a chair to create part of a semicircle, adding to the sense of ritualistic performance until the music climaxes at the entrance of the Interlocutor – the only white actor on stage[7] – who speaks the ceremonial words that announce the formal opening of every minstrel show: 'Gentlemen, be seated'.

Although spectators might wonder why at this stage the Interlocutor ignores the woman (does he regard her merely as a servant?), as yet they have no idea that she will, at the conclusion of the show, be recognized as the iconic figure of Rosa Parks who defied the segregationist rule preventing Black people in Alabama from sitting in the designated 'whites-only' front section of a public bus. Unlike the opening sequence of *The Blacks*, the ceremonial nature of the theatrical event is not fully recognizable until the final moments of the show because both narrative and ritual elements are disrupted in the manner of a minstrel show by seemingly inconsequential fragments of song, dance and low humour whose purpose appears to be merely to entertain. The Interlocutor launches without hesitation into the verse of the jolly opening number, 'Hey. Hey. Hey. Hey', without any ostensible reason other than to please the audience:

> Tonight's a night of merriment
> Of laughter, songs and jokes.
> I'm host and interlocutor,
> The master of these folks![8]

If the idea of the sole white man on stage as the 'master' of the Black performers comes as a slightly unpleasant surprise, then his next few lines will seem truly shocking:

> I introduce two jolly pranksters
> Each one as black as Sambo,[9]
> But they're men of many faces,
> Mr Bones and Mr Tambo!

The vigorous and up-tempo song-and-dance develops from the minstrel march, but in Susan Stroman's premiere production, only the Interlocutor and the end-men, Mr Bones and Mr Tambo, are in minstrel costume while the nine middle-men, who represent the Scottsboro boys are dressed in the assorted street clothes they might have worn when they jumped onto the freight train in Chattanooga in 1931.

Tambo (in a bright check jacket) and Bones (in a shiny red one) recreate the kind of direct interplay with the spectators in the front rows that would have guaranteed a minstrel show audience the kind of low humour expected of such entertainment. The jokes are simple and sexually suggestive, the convention of blackface – that is, the notion that the performers are representing African Americans – licences and defuses its potential offensiveness for a heterogeneous audience. The number climaxes in the time-honoured cakewalk, one of the core dance elements of minstrelsy. While invoking the classic form of the minstrel show in many ways, Stroman's production of the final version does not adhere to all its conventions but, for example, rejects one of the writing team's initial ideas that the nine boys would appear in blackface. By subtly varying and jumbling the traditional elements, *The Scottsboro Boys* demands that the spectator remain alert to nuances of meaning signified in slight subversions of the form, which might at first seem merely confused or contradictory.

The Interlocutor's declaration, 'That's right we're telling your story boys, just like we always do' signals that whites have historically assumed authority over the representation of Black people's history, so when Haywood Patterson asks the Interlocutor, 'This time, can we tell the truth?' it is both clear that the Black actor is obliged to ask permission from his white 'master' and that minstrel shows normally distorted the truth of the African American experience. The implication that truth is a relative value, constructed in context-specific situations in order to validate the dominant ideology, is amplified when the Interlocutor continues by asking, 'Have you ever told the truth before, Mr Tambo?' the end-man's puzzled reply, 'Is that what we're doing? No, I've never done that before.' Not only does the exchange again indicate scepticism towards the possibility of absolute truth, but it also demeans the Black actor by implying he is an inveterate liar.

Rather than reproducing in any way the pernicious myths perpetrated by minstrel shows of the past, the fracturing of the traditional three-act structure frustrates the easy accumulation of meaning and provokes a spectator to recognize and interrogate gaps and inconsistencies in a deconstructive process that relishes the dissonance of the unexpected in its radical confrontation with the racist assumptions of a paternalistic white culture. Occasionally, a gesture or speech may be incomprehensible without detailed knowledge of the form's history. Few spectators today will understand the precise reference to the ghostly figure of Jim Crow haunting the end of the song, 'Wheel about and turn about and do just so, / Every time I wheel about I jump Jim Crow.' In context, the lines may be construed as a curious and possibly sinister mumbo-jumbo, a suggestion of the ritualistic quality of a performance not fully comprehended by its audience. In fact, the lyric invokes the provenance of the naïve and foolish slave archetype invented in the early 1830s by T. D. (Daddy) Rice in what is regarded as the first 'blackface minstrel' performance,[10] the demeaning stage type that gave its name in 1877 to the 'Jim Crow' laws. These infamous laws, which instituted segregation by local and state legislatures in the South more than a decade after the federal government had abolished slavery, continued to be enforced by southern states until 1966, memorializing the name of Jim Crow for over a century.

Although the mode of storytelling through song and direct address does not correspond to any particular aspect of a traditional minstrel show, the Interlocutor's demand reduces the re-enactment of the historical narrative to the status of an item on the variety bill. The Interlocutor emphasises the function of storytelling as entertainment by introducing the song with the time-honoured 'puff' of a professional narrator:

Our story begins one fine spring morning! March the twenty-fifth. Nineteen-hundred and thirty-one: on a boxcar heading for Memphis. And nine young boys, nine complete strangers, are about to begin the ride of their life! Go on, boys! Favor us with your story. Tell us where it all started.

By singing 'Commencing in Chattanooga' as a means of narrating the events leading up to their arrest, the young Black performers are innocently cooperating with what the audience will gradually come to perceive as a degrading performance of their African American identity, scripted by the whites who originated the minstrel show tradition. Like those Black performers in the mid-nineteenth century who themselves adopted blackface minstrelsy professionally as one of the few opportunities to make a living as free men, the actors appear at this stage of the show eager to please the white 'master' by performing the stereotypical roles he has invented to valorize the inequality of the status quo.

The name 'Chattanooga' provides an immediate reference to the most popular train song of the swing band era, 'Chattanooga Choo-Choo?' whose patronizing reference to a shoeshine 'boy' is unselfconsciously racist.[11]

ALL
Whoo whoo whoo-oo
Whoo whoo whoo-oo
[.......................]

HEYWOOD
Then I thanked the lord above
That I was still alive
And I waited for the 'six-o-five'

ALL
Commencing in Chattanooga

This is a country and Western-style train song, its rhythm designed to echo the sound and depict the locomotion of a steam train, while the actors sit and sway on grey tabletops depicting the way bodies are swung about by the jostling of the freight cars:

HEYWOOD
And it chugga-chugga'd in
And I said
There you are
As I scrambled in the old box car
Then I settled back believin'
That the world was fine
I was travellin' on the Southern Line.

Ironically, the number may also call to mind 'Freight Train', a remarkable song by an eleven-year-old Black girl in the folk tradition whose metaphor of the train's progress as the journey of life qualifies the carefree mood of 'hopping a freight' with the reminder that the end of the journey is death. At this moment in the performance, however, the cheerful singing conveys a sense of the early morning promise of the journey as the young men begin their ride full of hope for new prospects. Oblivious to the ironic perception of the audience, Haywood evokes the joyous sense of liberty induced by travelling on a train in his cry: 'Far away places! They are in my bones! [. . .] I am free! I am free! I am FREE!'

The first hint of trouble occurs at the end of the song when the brothers Roy and Andy realize the train is unexpectedly stopping at Paint Rock, Alabama, although it is not scheduled to do so until Memphis, Tennessee. The incident at Paint Rock involves the first fully dramatized enactment of historical events. Nine appropriately costumed Black actors

Figure 18. Ensemble from *The Scottsboro Boys*. Photo: Johann Persson.

represent the Scottsboro boys as they are forced off the train to be questioned by the Sheriff and his deputy. Historical facts are now simplified as Bones enters in the comically exaggerated guise of the Sherriff. Here the performance switches to a mode of grotesque caricature that can be understood as a form of whiteface minstrelsy – a fitting rejoinder by Black performers to the norm whereby white performers created distorted stereotypes of Black people. There is a viciously satirical edge to Bones' portrayal of the Sherriff as a Southern redneck, strutting legs wide apart in a comic display of butch masculinity and unthinking prejudice. An audience becomes aware at this point of how the meta-theatrical role-play typical of the minstrel show is complicated in *The Scottsboro Boys* by the various kinds and degrees of role-play essayed by end men Bones and Tambo.

While up to this moment, Bones has only been represented as the compliant minstrel who plays the foolish slave at his white master's bidding, the audience now encounters his stinging mockery of the historical figure of a white oppressor, revealing an acute intelligence that had not hitherto been apparent. This is a highly sophisticated dramaturgical effect, akin to Brecht's experimental *Lehrstück, The Measures Taken* (*Massnahme*), in which four actors undertake multiple switches in role as well as play roles-within-roles to oppose the bourgeois idea of a fixed self by modelling events in which members of a revolutionary group submerge themselves into a collective identity, while not surrendering their critical judgement as individuals. The fluidity and changeable nature of identity staged in Brecht's short 'learning play' provides a striking parallel with the meta-theatrical role-play that in *The Scottsboro Boys* subverts the notion of the self to reveal the complex webs of identity constructed by hegemony and the modes of resistance possible to individuals oppressed by it.

The irony implicit in Bones' performance of the Sherriff is that a Black actor is required to play a scenario of white prejudice that has, in effect, been scripted by white police and judicial systems for two centuries. Yet, in impersonating the Sherriff, Bones is in addition able to represent a white oppressor from the viewpoint of a Black victim, inventing and adding specific character traits that communicate this oppositional perspective. As he remarks in the scurrilous style of the minstrel joker, 'When it comes to justice, there's just us'. The satirical strategy demands that an audience remain alert to sudden shifts and unexpected changes in perspective so that it notices inconsistencies and contradictions between actor and role in order to grasp the fluidity of identity and the complex layers of irony implied by the comic replay of historical incidents.

This type of role-play is amplified when the actors portraying Charley Weems and Ozie Powell assume, in addition, the roles of Victoria Price and Ruby Bates, the two young women who accuse the boys of rape. The scene borrows the convention of burlesque directly from the nineteenth-century minstrel show. Performing in an exaggerated drag convention, wearing capes, scarves and cloche hats over their male street clothes, with Victoria carrying a small handbag, the actors expose the women's elaborate attempt to deflect attention from a possible charge of prostitution by acting as innocent victims of rape:

VICTORIA
We're only two

RUBY
Two

VICTORIA
True

RUBY
True

BOTH
Alabama Ladies
Loyal Daughters
Of the solid South

By adopting the minstrel tradition of female impersonation, the performers are able to travesty the fake propriety of these two disreputable and highly suspect figures. The women's collusion in lying is explicitly stated by Victoria's instruction to Ruby, 'Follow me. Do exactly as I do. And don't fuck up', their deceit grotesquely figured in the crude attempt at theatrical deception practised by two young actors only partially disguised as women.

Victoria's hypocritical effort to devise a scandalous news story by peppering her account with salacious details is undercut by the fact of its performance by a Black male actor:

Another Negro
Opened up his trousers
And I struggled
Like an alley cat
And then he raped me

RUBY

An Alabama lady
Doesn't tolerate
A thing like that
[.....................]

RUBY

The other

BOTH

Negroes

RUBY

Took their turns upon me
And my privates
Which were private
Weren't private
Any more

The implication that they were gang-raped is an obvious attempt to fuel white prejudice against African Americans by invoking the persistent myth that Black men are insatiable in their sexual desires – especially for white women. As embodied on stage in an elaborate ragtime song-and-dance, the outrageousness of the lie becomes immediately apparent, the women's travesty of the truth being signified by the transvestite parody of a vaudeville act. Once more, any assumption that the truth is pure and simple[12] is undermined by a show-within-the-show that pretends to be an accurate depiction of historical reality.

When questioned by the Interlocutor ('Boss') as to whether the women's account is true, Patterson twice answers, 'No Sir', prompting the Interlocutor's casual decision, 'I suppose instead of hanging these boys, we better give them a proper trial', even though the Sherriff insists that Victoria and Ruby couldn't be lying because, in spite of being 'miserable white trash', they are 'our white trash'. The scene in the county jail is a straightforward dramatization, revealing that all but four of the young men were strangers to one another. Such moments of documentary-style realism are contrasted with the extreme stylization introduced in the previous scenes, inviting the audience to question the status of the drama either as history or racist ritual. Dialogue and action portray their fears and the divisions among the men, causing one to accuse two others of the alleged rape in a misguided attempt to prove he is himself innocent. When required to list their names, it becomes apparent that only Roy Wright knows how to write. Most of the young men naively assume that the forthcoming trial will prove their innocence, but Patterson understands the force of white prejudice:

They ain't gonna give us no trial. They gonna hang us just like they hanged my cousin for looking a shopgirl in the eye. He was strung up from a telephone pole. The whole town turned out [. . .] They cut off his fingers, privates, sold them for souvenirs.

When the Interlocutor enters to calm the quarrelling boys, he confirms Haywood's view that the townspeople are 'in a lynching mood'.

The semicircle of minstrel show tradition represents the courtroom, with the accused boys ranged between the inebriated defence attorney (Lawyer Tambo) and the prosecuting counsel (Lawyer Bones), with the Black woman – a silent witness – positioned on the Interlocutor's right-hand side. In court, Haywood answers the prosecutor's unfounded accusation that he 'ravished' the girls in a song that expresses his rage:

> I haven't done
> Nothin'
> And I never did
> Nothin'
> Since I never did
> Nothin'
> This is a fine
> How do you do

By switching alternately between a dignified, if desperate assertion of innocence and the sarcastic and self-lacerating convention of minstrel performance, Haywood depicts the helpless dependency of the African American on the authority of white institutions. Rolling his eyes and wiggling his bent body, Haywood's imitation of the humiliating obsequiousness adopted by blackface performers is bound to embarrass a present-day audience as he continues:

> So I won't say
> Nothin'
> It wouldn't help
> Nothin'
> When you can't help
> Nothin'
> I believe it's true
> It's a real fine
> How do you do

The song's repetition of 'Nothin' echoes the repetition of 'Nobody'[13] in Bert Williams' legendary tragicomic act, ironically exploiting the self-mockery of the Black performer in blackface to lay bare the complicity of all white people who turn their backs on the suffering of African Americans. Blithely confirming the travesty of justice that has taken place in court, the Interlocutor, in the role of judge, reads the verdict: 'It is the opinion of this court that these here innocent boys are guilty as charged; I set the date for your execution by electric chair. July 10th, 1931 at Gilbey Prison.'

Silhouetted against a red screen at the back of the stage, the actors strip off their clothes to be 'deloused'. The horrid glee that motivates racist lynch mobs is visually represented in the form of a luridly lit tap dance number, 'Electric Chair' – Eugene's nightmare of what is about to happen. Possibly the most grotesque moment in the show, it is sung and danced in two white follow spots by the prison guards Tambo and Bones, with the *sang-froid* of experienced vaudevillians.

> If on that chair
> You put your rear

Your hair frizzles out
And your eyes disappear

As the dance break builds up momentum to the accompaniment of a Benny Goodman-style swing band arrangement led by a clarinet, flashes of strobe lights and buzzing electronic sound effects mimic the terrifying ordeal of an actual execution:

Just to hear that sizzlin' sound
People come from miles around

Mom and Dad get crammed inside
While their sonny boy's electrified

After Guard Bones orders the twelve-year-old Eugene Williams to dance, he is joined by two other electrocuted boys 'who rise from the dead' illustrating the perverse cruelty of a form of show business that laughs at the suffering of Black victims of injustice:

GUARD BONES AND GUARD TAMBO
So little boy
[…………..]
Don't sit there and cry
It's not ev'ry guy
Gets to light up the sky
What a fabulous way
A fab-yu-abulous way

SCOTTSBORO BOYS
To die

What is most disturbing about the number is the jarring contradiction between the wish to laugh and applaud Susan Stroman's witty and brilliantly performed choreography and the callous celebration of a death by electric chair implied by the lyrics. At this point in the musical, even the knowledge that this is an ironic strategy cannot undo an audience's uneasy sense of complicity with white racism.

The first phase of the narrative concludes in the prison cell with Haywood's singing of 'Go Back Home', a poignant song of lamentation for the loss of home. Irony is suspended as the song invokes empathy for the loneliness and fear of nine innocent young men facing an unjust death. For the first time, the Scottsboro boys are dressed not in street clothes, but in spotless white shirts and trousers. Standing stock still, they are no longer 'performing' but simply expressing their emotions in the most intense and personal way. As the youths are being prepared for the electric chair, the Interlocutor halts the proceedings with the startling news that he has received a telegram from the Supreme Court informing him that the trial has been declared invalid because the boys didn't have a proper lawyer. Despair turns to hope as they learn they have been given a 'second chance' in the form of another trial. The Interlocutor instructs them to sing 'Shout' – a joyously infectious gospel number like 'Sit Down You're Rockin the Boat'.[14] Again the young men are manipulated into exploiting their momentary joy as minstrel show entertainment:

Shout! Let it be celebrated
Stand and slap your tambourines
Blues have been annihilated
Blown to smithereens

When I thought to meet my maker
When they said, 'You're gonna fry!'
God supplied a circuit breaker
Giving me another try

After Haywood makes an attempt to escape from prison, he is caught and placed in solitary confinement as punishment. Here, Roy begins to teach him to read and write by spreading sand out on the floor of his cell and tracing letters in it. The 'story about the truth' that Haywood claims to have written in his cell is enacted as a minstrel number, the narrative illustrated by a shadow dance behind a screen, using the silhouette of a dancing Jim Crow. The discourse on truth and dishonesty, which has been a central trope of *The Scottsboro Boys*, is explicitly if ironically, articulated in 'You Better Make Friends with the Truth', which takes the form of a mock cautionary tale about the danger of telling lies. From stealing cookies as a little boy to accidentally killing his teacher by shooting him with a pistol he has stolen, Billy's punishments for lying about his guilt become progressively more severe until he is lynched. In an ironic reversal 'outside the pearly gates', Billy is finally rewarded for telling the truth to Saint Peter,

HAYWOOD
(*as Saint Peter*)
'Did you steal those cookies?'
(*as Billy*)
'Yes I did'
(*as Saint Peter*)
'Did you break that windshield?'
(*as Billy*)
'Deed I did'
(*as Saint Peter*)
'Did you shoot that teacher?'
(*as Billy*)
'Fraid I did'
(*as Saint Peter*)
'Look at that! He didn't lie!'
He finally made friends with the truth
Welcome to heaven!

Yet the full irony is only apparent at the conclusion of the next chorus when Billy knocks on heaven's door: 'Now son, you know you gotta use the back door. And that's the real truth!' The complex web of ironies finally implies that it makes no difference whether Black people are guilty or innocent, they will still suffer discrimination at the hands of whites. The Southern judicial system is exposed as an elaborate pretence, in which any Black person accused by a white is arbitrarily assumed to be guilty. The Interlocutor alluded to the format of a minstrel show when he asked Haywood if his song was a 'plantation skit';[15] now he again invokes the minstrel show in the arch manner in which he enquires, 'Mr Tambo are you ready for the second trial?' The series of trials has become a spectacle. White boys sell souvenirs to the crowd outside the law court in which Blacks play the traditional comic role of willing stooges in a losing battle against complacent white racism: 'Put on those smiles that make folks so happy.'

The arrival of Samuel Leibowitz, the highly successful lawyer from New York, heralds the third phase in the retelling of historical events. Although 'That's Not the Way We Do Things' is a comic number, the impersonation of Leibowitz by Tambo is very different from any of the grotesque characterizations he has undertaken thus far. Instead of merely adapting his minstrel garb as before, Tambo is now fully costumed in a fashionable houndstooth suit to provide a more complex and detailed representation of a clever and confident New York lawyer. Perhaps calculated to flatter a Broadway audience, the song encourages the boys to believe that Americans outside the southern states support them:

> Although the law may be disgusting
> Here in Alabama
> [....................]
> That's not the way we do things
> In New York

In Leibowitz's words, 'The world is on your side. Black and white. Unite and fight. Save the Scottsboro boys'. Yet the endorsement of a less prejudiced Yankee attitude to their plight is at the same time accompanied by a wry comic observation of white liberal complacency:

> Back in Manhattan, ask anyone
> There's no bigger voice
> For equal rights than me
> I fight for it
> I live for it
> Just ask my maid Magnolia
> And I'm sure she'd agree

The courtroom is again set up in the semicircular format of a minstrel show. Leibowitz has persuaded Ruby Bates to recant the dishonest accusation she was pressured by Victoria Price to make at the first trial, and she transforms her new testimony into a public act of atonement that she believes will transform her into a celebrity witness: 'I want to make a statement about those Negroes jazzing me. It is not true. It is the opposite of true. It is a lie.' Somewhat akin to Roxie Hart's public 'confession' in *Chicago*, Ruby's attempt at honesty during the second trial is staged as a vaudeville number ('Never Too Late'), with Ruby accompanied by the boys, who sing in close harmony that it is 'Never too late to atone.' Although she blithely announces, 'So help me God, this is one time I am going to tell the truth', she is still concerned to create a favourable impression: 'Help me up on the witness stand, boys. Make me look good.'

Dancing on a small bench, Ozie Powell postures and pouts in the guise of the newly reformed Ruby, somewhat disarmingly admitting that as a skilled prostitute, she would never have taken on nine men at once and that she wishes to change her testimony:

And so despite my rave and rantin'
I'll tell the jury I'm recantin'
I lost my head and lied when I was a youth

As the attorney general of Alabama, Bones retains his minstrel costume and exaggerated persona as end man while acting for the prosecution. Bones' song 'Financial Advice' represents the cross-examination of Ruby, who he claims has been bribed to retract her original testimony by the 'Jew money' of Leibowitz:

When there ain't no cash
For the days ahead
And you got no job
And you wish you was dead
There's one solution, honey,
Go get you some Jew money.

By speaking to the anti-Semitic prejudices of southern rednecks in his smoothly insinuating rendition of the blues song, Bones shows that the trial is not actually concerned with establishing the truth of the boys' guilt or innocence but involves a brazen manipulation of the jury's racist prejudices. Ironically, Ruby's honesty is of no value in this situation: 'I lied because Victoria told me to. I was scared. Why did everybody believe me when I was telling a lie, but nobody believes me when I'm telling the truth.'

While the boys await the verdict in their cell, Haywood, who has now learnt to read, quotes from the Bible, 'The truth will set you free'. When the Interlocutor presents them with a cake given to them by the silent Black woman, they indulge in various fantasies about what they will do once they are free, and Haywood imagines himself walking proudly past the courthouse, looking people straight in the eye and being smiled at for having told the truth. The Interlocutor interrupts to ask them to 'sing that song 'bout home we love so much', claiming that the South is where they belong ('We take care of you down here'). As expected, 'Southern Days' begins as a nostalgic plantation song, the boys' close harmony appearing to memorialize the myth of slavery as a paternalistic system of white protection for Blacks. They sing the first two choruses softly in an earnest and melancholy style, assuming the pose of school choirboys:

Don't you miss
The sight of willows drippin'
On a balmy southern day?

Although the Interlocutor relishes the nostalgic mood, his admonition that 'It wouldn't hurt if you smiled a bit' provokes an immediate flash of the boys' toothy smiles, which comically exposes their beautiful harmonising as a performance of enforced complicity demanded by a white audience in order to justify white supremacy in the South.

Tell the truth now
Don't you miss
Those honeysuckle days in Alabam?
How the sights and sounds
Come back to me!
Like my daddy hangin' from a tree

[...]
Or the fire that made
Those crosses burn

The unexpected jolt of the lyrics that reveal the reality of lynching and burning of African Americans is even more shocking because it is sung by smiling and seemingly compliant Black performers. The effect of beautiful music accompanying horrifying lyrics challenges the theatre audience to interrogate the underlying attitude of the Black singers. How much have they suppressed genuine rage against the injustice of a racist society in the obsequious attempt to reassure white audiences that the recreation of minstrelsy is just satirical fun? Are they attacking us, laughing at us or just teasing us? The instability of the performers' identities problematizes the performance event by challenging every member of the audience to ask if this is ritual or entertainment.

The boys' illusions about receiving justice at the hands of a white southern jury are shattered by the Interlocutor's announcement of a second guilty verdict. For the first time, they defy his instruction to perform a cakewalk 'just like we always do'. The final phase of the musical begins at the point when the boys refuse to continue the minstrel show representation and more realistically recreate their work as a prison chain gang, breaking rocks while singing 'On the Southern Railroad line' as a sinister and fragmented reprise of their hopeful number, 'Commencing in Chattanooga'. They no longer perform to entertain the audience but to demonstrate the grim experience of their imprisonment. Again, Haywood escapes, this time to see his dying mother, and again he is caught and incarcerated.

After vaudeville-style placards carried by Tambo and Bones announce the passing of five years, the Interlocutor informs the audience directly that the Scottsboro boys are in 1937 still on Death Row, repeating his ceremonial 'Gentlemen, be seated' in order to command the boys to sit in rows of chairs arranged as in a bus. The boys reshuffle themselves six times to indicate the number of times they were tried and found guilty after 1932, until Ozie Powell tries to kill the guard driving the bus and is injured so badly he is permanently brain-damaged. This is played out as a kind of nightmare in garish pink light with the actors moving in slow motion while the Interlocutor's voice drawls, 'Gentlemen, be seated'. The last phase of the narrative is recounted much more concisely with Victoria Price declaring in a fragmented and mocking reprise of her 'Alabama Ladies' number that she is tired of repeating her testimony: 'Six years I'm stuck in this hellhole of a town delivering the same testimony trial after trial after trial after trial . . . ' Her lie has taken on the hackneyed quality of a meaningless routine as she can no longer convince anyone of its authenticity, singing sarcastically, 'But then a negro threw himself upon me / I can still smell his hot black breath . . . ' The actor sustains an incredibly long note on the last line of the chorus, before exiting in disgust with a line that is virtually an echo of Velma Kelly's reference to Texas Guinan in *Chicago*, 'So long, suckers'. The singer is applauded at this moment for so wittily exposing an act of duplicity that has failed.

The silent Black woman watches as Haywood, the bravest and most defiant of the group, refuses not to tell the truth while Leibowitz, in an attempt to persuade him to compromise, insists, 'You're guilty because of the way you look', informing him that the Governor of Alabama will only pardon him if he pleads guilty: 'The truth will not set you free but a lie can.' In recalling a day when he harmed his mother by lying, Haywood addresses the audience simply, blaming himself for the damage done: 'You can never lie or bad things will happen to you.' In the following number, 'Zat So?' the Interlocutor as Governor offers Haywood a pardon in exchange for his admission of guilt; it is written and staged as a parody of grand opera with the Governor as a kind of Mephistophelean figure in a long black cloak standing on a chair to tower over Haywood, while Leibowitz argues with Haywood from the sideline. In a manoeuvre typical of white patriarchy, the Governor blames the colonized victim for the injustice he himself commits: 'You people sometimes don't know what you've been asked. That's because you don't listen.' Although he is informed by the Governor that he will be in prison for a very long time, Haywood refuses to assume the identity of a criminal: 'In my mind I'm free.'

Dressed in his angelic white costume, he quietly sings 'You Can't Do Me' as a final act of defiance. Haywood performs a ghostly soft shoe shuffle almost in slow motion, as if to deconstruct and appropriate the gestures of minstrelsy as an assertion of his integrity. The lyric suggests two possible meanings for 'do me': on a literal level, 'being done over' is a colloquialism signifying the guileful exploitation of a naïve person, but in the context of show business, it suggests someone impersonating someone else. So Haywood is here insisting on the authenticity of his own performance and metaphorically rejecting the whole system of white representation, which, like the early minstrel shows, purports to speak for mute Black people:

> You can't do me
> Like you done me
> Like you did me before

For the first time, the Black woman does not merely witness the number, but by copying Haywood's fragmentary dance steps, she provokes questions about her relationship to the central narrative. The other boys join the chorus from offstage in lyrics that imply the rebellion of African American people against domination and discrimination:

> We won't stand still
> Our hands in our pockets
> What was a whisper
> Is now a roar

At the moment when it appears that the minstrel show format has disintegrated to make way for a straightforward retelling of historical facts, the Interlocutor announces 'the grand finale of our Minstrel Show' as eight actors, dressed in top hats and tails, enter the stage doing the traditional 'choo choo' train steps of vaudeville hoofers. The moment when one notices that they are all actually blacked up exactly as they would have been over a hundred years ago is horrifying:

> Every member of society
> Celebrates our notoriety
> Step right up and meet
> The Scottsboro boys

An audience is torn between admiration for the jazzy perfection of the number and the grim realization that to applaud it is to sanction the minstrel show's celebration of a long history of racism.

The boys have become freak celebrities whose news value is fleeting. Andy steps forward to tell the audience that Leibowitz put the four boys who had been released into vaudeville so that 'people wouldn't forget about the rest of us in jail. But guess what. They already had.' As the men turn in succession to the audience to present details of their failed lives, the contrast between the factual account of the injustice and the aura of show business that threatens to reduce history to gossip is startling. The gravest injustice is suffered by Haywood who died in jail, still protesting his innocence, 'I wrote it all down. I told the truth. There's nothing more I can do'. As the actor exits, he gives his book to the woman who watches from the sideline, a gesture of resistance against the trivialization of suffering and the falsification of history as a minstrel show. The rousing final chorus of the song is a travesty of their memory, its triumphant musical climax manipulating the audience to participate in the ritual of a show business finale by applauding:

> Read the morning papers every day
> Read what all the gossip columns say
>
> Hey hey hey hey
> Join in the merriment
> Come on make some noise
> Hey hey say
> Goodbye to the Scottsboro boys

As the Interlocutor tries to transform tragedy into entertainment, the actors sullenly defy his attempts at making them dance the cakewalk that typically provides a carnivalesque ending to a minstrel show. His repeated attempts to bring them to order ('Gentlemen, be seated!') are ignored as each actor begins wiping the blackface makeup off his face and silently exits the stage. Audience expectations are ambushed yet again when the woman sits on a chair facing the front, confronted by the Interlocutor, now dressed in a blue jacket as a bus driver:

> Lady, you can't sit there. Move to the back of the bus. Colored to the back of the bus. Move to the back.

THE LADY
> No. Not no more.
> I'm gonna sit here and rest my feet.

After the movement and noise of the Scottsboro boys' minstrel number, the stillness and hushed intensity of this moment of defiance is extremely powerful, as the audience finally understands that 'the lady' is Rosa Parks. The scene is a ritual re-enactment of Black protest against racism, which completes Haywood's transformation of the degrading conventions of minstrelsy initiated in 'You Can't Do Me' and continued by the boys' refusal to dance the cakewalk. What the audience realizes it has unwittingly been witnessing is a different kind of memorial celebration for the creation of a revisionist Black history aimed at replacing the white supremacist viewpoint embedded in the minstrel show.

Given the disturbing effect of witnessing a zestful and funny animation of demeaning racist stereotypes of African Americans and Jews, it should come as no surprise that *The Scottsboro Boys* caused offence and sparked a protest when it transferred from the Vineyard Theatre to Broadway for a short run. Quite properly, Susan Stroman argued that the show was not uncritically exploiting minstrel show conventions but that it was deconstructing them in order to expose the racist ideology inscribed in this distinctively American popular cultural form. Yet it is impossible to dismiss the protest as an overreaction because sensitivity to such prejudice is ultimately a historical response to the aftermath of American slavery. John Kander himself claimed that there was something in *The Scottsboro Boys* to offend everyone, revealing that the show was designed to disturb the complacency of what would on Broadway be a largely white, middle-class audience, but might also offend the sensitivities of Blacks and Jews. By seeming to collude in the humiliating depiction of African Americans, the twelve Black members of the cast might appear to be endorsing the stereotypes. Yet this is to ignore the savage irony of the musical, which insists that both Black and white members of the audience confront a shameful history of oppression in order to liberate themselves from it.

Implicit in Charles Isherwood's review of the musical in the *New York Times* is the expectation that a musical should primarily aspire to delight its audience as pure entertainment:

> Mr Kander and Mr. Ebb have written a zesty if not top-tier score, but the pleasures of a jaunty ragtime melody and a clever lyric are hard to savor when they are presented in such an unavoidably grim context. [. . .] [T]he intermissionless 'Scottsboro Boys,' which runs a bit under two hours, suffers from a problem of monotony, as the scabrous comic tone spreads like shellac across almost every sequence. [. . .] And outside the minstrel-show framing device is yet another framing device, which rather heavy-handedly stresses the inspirational aspects of the story in the history of the civil rights movement. [. . .] But the musical never really resolves the tension between its impulse to entertain us with hoary jokes and quivering tambourines and the desire to render the harsh morals of its story with earnest insistence.[16]

The critique of the musical as overly didactic is common to the majority of New York reviewers, who appear to berate the authors for not having created another *Chicago*. Without the attraction of a contemporary rock-style score or the feel-good factor of a musical comedy or a jukebox show, *The Scottsboro Boys* not only lacks the commercial appeal of other Broadway shows but also insists that an audience confront unpleasant historical truths that remind them of the history of injustice that is their own inheritance.

Unsurprisingly, perhaps, the show had a very short run on Broadway, where between 2000 and 2010, the majority of musicals had succeeded on the basis of their 'feelgood' qualities. Even in London, where critical reactions were much more enthusiastic than in New York and the show won the Evening Standard Award for Best Musical in 2014, the painful historical reality in which it is grounded did not make the production an easy sell when it transferred to the West End. Dominic Cavendish summed up the uneasy reactions of a British spectator when the show transferred from the Young Vic Theatre to the West End:

> [A]n easy response – particularly in a white audience-member – is something problematic. Julian Glover's aged 'Interlocutor' [. . .] is not the only one implicated as a slave-driver – we are too. For every high experienced, there's an equal and opposite prickle of shame. So, yes, do rush to see this ingenious, pain-filled, feel-good show but be prepared to be ambushed by ambivalence. You may be torn between wanting to clap and beat yourself up.[17]

Cavendish recognizes the characteristic paradox of Kander and Ebb's approach to musical theatre in his description of *The Scottsboro Boys* as a 'pain-filled, feel-good show'. In their desire to satisfy the strictest criteria of art to express truths, no matter how unpleasant, while at the same time pleasing a public wishing to be entertained, the authors engineer a critique of the values of the minstrel show that exploits the guilty pleasure of savouring the old clichés of the form while shining a spotlight on its unthinking endorsement of racism. In London, Michael Billington was unequivocal in recognizing the show's artistic excellence: 'But what staggers me is that, although nominated for twelve Tony Awards, this dazzlingly daring show was defeated in virtually every category by *The Book of Mormon*. It just goes to prove that in the world of showbiz, as in the American South of the 1930s, there ain't no justice'.[18]

Susan Stroman's production was a model of style and tact, in which dance and scenography were brilliantly expressive of the values of the writing without ever being excessive. Unlike directors of recent Broadway shows with large casts of African Americans, like *Fela* (2008) or *Shuffle Along* (2016), she has demonstrated a sophisticated grasp of the politics of stage spectacle – particularly problematic as a consequence of two centuries in which the power of white slave-owners and their descendants over slaves – and later servants – motivated the habitual projection of sexual fantasies onto the bodies of Black men and women, mythicizing Black people as over-sexed and Black men as a danger to white women. Whereas Billy T. Jones' choreography for *Fela* repeatedly fetishizes the Black female body by presenting the cliché of nubile women in scanty mix-and-match versions of African dress, gyrating erotically for the pleasure of the audience, the only moment in the production of *The Scottsboro Boys* when the body is in any way on display is at the point when the young men are supposedly being deloused at the back of the stage, but this near-nudity is shown in silhouette as they change from street clothes into prison garments. While they are doing this, Haywood says, 'Strip me naked', as he stands centre stage with his shirt open, but his posture and the dramatic context entirely justify this moment and his body is certainly not being fetishized. In fact, when the rest of the boys do appear in the cell, they are dressed in pristine white trousers and shirts rather than actual prison uniforms, the abstract costume apparently designed to dignify the characters and avoid any banal recourse to historical realism or minstrelsy.

By contrast to the first productions of *Cabaret* and *Chicago*, in which the dances are intentionally erotic, playing in both grotesque and appealing fashion on the inherent voyeurism of spectating, any representation of sexuality in *The Scottsboro Boys* is comic, as in the exaggerated drag performance of the men who play Victoria and Ruby. Yet as in the two earlier musicals, the show problematises the relationship between performers and audience, daring spectators to take responsibility for the pleasure they derive as witnesses of the ironic representation of a travesty of justice. To the extent that the Black performers are made to sing for their supper, the musical potentially exploits pre-existing stereotypes. Yet by showing a white actor commanding Black performers to enact a white racist version of their own history, the musical obliges spectators to participate in a theatrical ceremony that gradually unravels to reveal as false the very language in which it is articulated.

In concert with Kevin Adams' evocative lighting, Beowulf Borritt's minimalist set of silver-grey chairs and a table framed by two oddly angled proscenium arches becomes an element of the dramaturgy as the performers shift and upend the furniture to conjure up all the necessary locations of a minstrel stage, freight train, prison cell, courtroom, bus and prison yard and convey the changing moods of the unfolding story. The Interlocutor highlights the self-reflexive nature of the dramaturgy by his command to present the historical events as an act of storytelling – 'Our story if you please'. In this way, the actors' seemingly improvised arrangement of each scene serves to remind the audience that history, just like drama, is always constructed from specific viewpoints. So too, the switch from one mode of dramatization to another – blackface performance, realist dramatic style and direct narration – and the disjunction between dialogue and song are Brechtian distancing devices that enable the audience to maintain a critical attitude towards the representation rather than simply empathizing directly with the central characters.

Stroman's virtuosity in integrating the various components of scenography and dramaturgy possibly derives from her expertise as a choreographer. The production is beautifully paced with changes in tempo and shifts in mood and tone from one scene or musical number to another, provoking a variety of conflicting feelings. As always with Stroman's work, the choreography is thoroughly grounded in the drama as well as being informed by meticulous historical research. At times, she revivifies indigenous African American dance styles deployed in minstrel shows and vaudeville from the mid-nineteenth century to the 1930s, such as the buck dance, wing dance, tap dancing and cakewalk while at others (e.g. 'Electric Chair'), she inventively utilizes traditional steps in an expressionistic manner, mixing old and modern styles eclectically to evoke specific atmospheres and emotions.

Notes

1. These shows involved white performers 'whiting up' as pierrots.
2. In Britain, a continuing history of revivals of *Oh What a Lovely War!* has persisted to the present day, popularizing its anti-Establishment view of the First World War. The controversial Conservative Party politician Michael Gove made an infamous attack on this attitude to the war in the right-wing *Daily Mail:* 'The conflict has, for many, been seen through the fictional prism of dramas such as *Oh! What a Lovely War*, *The Monocled Mutineer* and *Blackadder*, as a misbegotten shambles—a series of catastrophic mistakes perpetrated by an out of touch elite.'
3. Jean Genet, trans. Bernard Frechtman, *The Blacks, New York: Grove Press*, 1958, 4.
4. It is likely that Ebb saw an off-Broadway production of *The Blacks* that opened in 1962 and ran for a large number of performances.
5. The three-act structure of a typical minstrel show included the introduction, with its variety of songs and dances; the olio, with some clowning and a pun-filled 'stump sketch', concluded by a plantation skit, a short play, often a burlesque of a popular play, with topical references.
6. Leve, 2009.
7. In the original white minstrel troupes, the Interlocutor was the only performer who did not perform in blackface.
8. Quotations of lyrics from *The Scottsboro Boys* are taken from the CD liner, CD Jay1421, 2010.
9. *Little Black Sambo* was the South Indian hero of a children's story written by Helen Bannerman in 1899. The name became ubiquitous and is now regarded as racist.
10. Rice claims to have based his blackface performance of the character he popularized as Jim Crow on his observation of the song and dance of a disabled slave, but there is evidence to suggest that the name may have been in use for many years before he adopted it.

11. 'First recorded by the Glen Miller band in 1941, the reference to a shoeshine 'boy' in the opening lyric 'Pardon Me Boy, Is That the Chattanooga Choo Choo?' is somewhat offensive today. The fact that the boys are travelling to Alabama may prompt echoes of Irving Berlin's popular ragtime number, 'When the Midnight Choo-Choo Leaves for Alabam' (1912).

12. 'The truth is rarely pure and never simple.' (Oscar Wilde, *The Importance of Being Earnest*.)

13. Bert Williams was the most highly-paid Black performer in the early twentieth century who eventually headlined for Florenz Ziegfeld's *Follies*. His signature song 'Nobody' tragicomically depicted the plight of a poor Black itinerant who has done nothing to harm 'nobody', yet has nevertheless received no relief from poverty and hardship from 'nobody'. See 'Mr Cellophane' in *Chicago*, Chapter 7.

14. This is one of the most popular numbers in Frank Loesser's *Guys and Dolls* (1950).

15. A plantation skit was a short, one-act play performed as the third act of a minstrel show.

16. Charles Isherwood, *New York Times*, 31 October, 2010. https://www.nytimes.com/2010/11/01/theater/reviews/01scottsboro.html. Accessed 10 May 2021.

17. *The Daily Telegraph*, 21 October 2014, https://www.telegraph.co.uk/culture/theatre/theatre-reviews/ 11177121/Scottsboro-Boys-Garrick-review.html, accessed 10 May 2021.

18. *The Guardian*, 21 October 2014.

15 Subverting the happy ending

The Visit (2015) as anti-operetta

Originally intended as a vehicle for Angela Lansbury, the show was scheduled to open on Broadway in March 2001 after a Boston tryout in December 2000; the production was shelved when Lansbury withdrew as a result of the illness and subsequent death of her husband in mid-2000. Frank Galati (director) and Ann Reinking (choreographer) were then scheduled to stage the show at the Goodman Theatre in Chicago on 1 October 2001, with Chita Rivera as Lansbury's replacement. The original treatment for *The Visit* included far more dialogue and character detail taken directly from Durrenmatt. There was an 'I Want' song ('Never in a Million Years') as well as a number called 'Memory'.

The representation of anti-Semitism was more overt, with lines like 'The real surprise is how the Nazis missed her' indicating the post-war context more unambiguously than in any later version. In a draft from 1999, 'You, You, You' is introduced, while Anton's 'You Know Me' is taken up by the townspeople. The two eunuchs, then called Lenny and Benny, act out the roles of young Claire and Anton in a grotesque role-play. In this draft, 'Love and Love Alone' is introduced. Galati's notes from 2000 indicate that 'Winter' was added and that two young actors playing Claire and Anton's younger selves were introduced. The rehearsal script used in Chicago in 2001 still included Durrenmatt's stylized conceit of trees played by actors; Claire's butler and the two eunuchs have more singing than in later versions, while she sings 'Golden Apostle' about her philanthropy.

The 2001 production was intended to transfer to Broadway, but the traumatic events of 9/11 intervened, preventing *The Visit* from getting to New York. According to Galati, 'It was generally a success but we couldn't get anyone from New York or California to see it'.[1] Writing in the *Washington Post* In 2008, Nelson Pressley noted, 'After the 9/11 attacks the mood was wrong for a transfer to Broadway'.[2] Ann Reinking later recalled, 'By the time you could travel and people felt safe again, our run was up.'[3] The musical was then developed further before being produced at the Signature Theatre in Arlington, Virginia, in 2008. By now Fred Ebb had died, so Kander and Frank Galati changed certain details to make the show more 'ferocious',[4] adding two songs for Anton Schell, which was one of the reasons why George Hearn was now cast in place of John McMartin. 'I think we wrote it wrong', opined Kander in 2008. 'In the first version he was very much a nonentity in the town. Here he's a rougher, tougher guy.'[5] A further revised (streamlined) version directed by John Doyle was performed at the Williamstown Festival in 2014, transferring to Broadway in 2015.

Although *The Visit* makes no overt use of meta-theatrical devices, its score is an ironic pastiche of a Viennese operetta. John Kander viewed the show as a grim version of Lehar's ubiquitous operetta, *The Merry Widow* – an anti-operetta, perhaps:

The first thing that I wrote for *The Visit* is a song that appears early on and goes through the entire show – it's a waltz and it's called 'You, You, You'. It's a very simple waltz. [. . .] The play, *The Visit,* by Friedrich Durrenmatt, I first saw many, many years ago with the Lunts, and I realized since that the story of an impoverished country or place about to meet the richest woman in the world and hoping to nab her to marry one of its citizens so they would have the money is the story of *The Merry Widow*.

Durrenmatt was a Swiss playwright who wrote two plays that became modern classics – *Der Besuch der alten Dame* (*The Visit of the Old Lady*) in 1956 and *Die Physiker* (*The Physicists*) in 1961.[6] Both are black satires on post-war European society, presenting a world of existential absurdity without being directly affiliated with the movement Martin Esslin named Theatre of the Absurd. Kander believed that Durrenmatt was aware of his play's references to Lehar:

I am convinced that Durrenmatt knew that, too [. . .] What he did was take the story of *The Merry Widow* and stand it on its head and turn it into something really quite vicious. [. . . T]he very first song that Fred and I wrote for the show is 'You, You, You' – it is a very seductive waltz and it was a kind of style-setter for the piece musically as a kind of operetta [. . .] filled with waltzes and sort of beguiling love songs, if you will. Once I hit on that idea, then that song almost wrote itself. It was the idea of us doing our own *The Merry Widow* waltz. So, the 'You, You, You' theme was the first thing that we wrote and then we went back to the beginning and wrote 'Out of the Darkness'.[7]

The score is lush in the manner of Viennese operetta, but it also contains some more dissonant moments of emotional music in a manner that owes nothing to the tradition of Lehar and the Austrian Strausses who dominated the world of the waltz ('Out of the Darkness' is a case in point).

According to Kander,

The whole thing that attracted us to the piece was to take Durrenmatt's story – which is quite political and quite nasty in its comments on Swiss society – and to open up the relationship between the two main people, which, when you think of it, is about as intense a love/hate experience as you can possibly find. That was what drew us to the material itself and is also what led us to write the song Claire sings toward the end called 'Love And Love Alone' – all these disastrous things that happen and this rage and need for vengeance is about love . . .[8]

Ben Brantley, in his review of the Broadway opening, misses the ironic tension between operetta and black comedy, asserting that 'the show [n]ever quite make[s] peace between its uneasily twinned strands of merciless cynicism and a softer sentimentality.'[9] What Brantley fails to notice is that the affect of the musical is never either sentimental or cynical because its overall scheme superimposes the grotesque comedy of revenge upon its *Merry Widow* love story. Nostalgia is never endorsed by the score; it is savagely undermined by the clash between present and past. As Mark Kennedy has written:

Trust a John Kander-Fred Ebb musical to make the sunny color of vitality and youth positively menacing . . . [Kander's] music is wonderfully complicated; some are fully fleshed out numbers and others seductive sketches that pull you in [. . .] 'The Visit' is sophisticated and beautiful and yet has that typical glorious chilling view of man that you expect from a Kander and Ebb show.[10]

Few changes were made by Terrence McNally to the outline created in Durrenmatt's play, but there are two significant alterations: Claire Zacchanasian is now half-Jewish and half-Gypsy, which gives another level of significance to Durrenmatt's parable of post-war reparation. In 'Problems of the Theatre', the Swiss dramatist had written,

> Tragedy presupposes guilt [. . . and] a sense of responsibility. Comedy alone is suitable for us [. . .] The tragic is still possible, even if tragedy is not. We can achieve the tragic out of comedy. We can bring it forth as a frightening moment, as an abyss that opens suddenly.[11]

Durrenmatt's 1956 play revisits past events that are vaguely indicated as forty-five years before; yet, as a parable, it invokes the guilt concerning Switzerland's neutrality in the Second World War and her culpability for making a profit by storing art looted by the Nazis and money illegally squirrelled away in Swiss banks to protect wealthy people's ill-gotten gains. In rejecting Claire's shocking condition for giving the town money, the mayor inadvertently invokes a post-war perception of the Third Reich's precipitation of an era of European barbarism:

> Madame Zacchanassian: you forget, this is Europe. You forget, we are not savages.
> In the name of all citizens of Guellen, I reject your offer; and I reject it in the name of
> humanity. We would rather have poverty than blood on our hands.
> (*Huge applause.*)
>
> CLAIRE [. . .]: I'll wait.[12]

In New York in 2015, the resonance of a person of Jewish and Romani descent insisting on repayment or revenge for past wrongs is just as powerful in its provocative implication of Nazi victimization of Jews, in particular. Also, in the musical, Claire does not get married again, focussing exclusively on her desire to wreak terrible vengeance on the man who wronged her. McNally changes the name of the town from Guellen to Bracken. He also shortens the first half to cut some details of the townspeople's memories of Claire Wascher as she was, as well as of the current poverty, which motivated the invitation for the return of the now-wealthy woman to rescue Bracken from total collapse. Terry Teachout rightly, in my view, praises the score for the way it expresses the dark irony that suffuses the fable: 'Mr Kander and his late, lamented partner never wrote a finer score, and . . . you'll thrill to their cruel tale of what men who dare to call themselves decent will do to one another if the price is right.'[13]

Durenmatt's play is fairly static, resembling the inevitability of a ritual, with a great build-up to the entrance of the billionaire Claire with her bizarre entourage, in which dramatic tension is created by the gradual unfolding of the town's financial, and it is finally revealed, moral bankruptcy. The plans to honour and then seek the charity of the wealthy heiress occupy the first half of the play. In her 2023 memoir, Chita Rivera indicated the grotesque qualities of *The Visit* by joking, '[I]f [. . .] you said, "A woman, a butler, two eunuchs and a coffin enter the stage," you would have not only one helluvan entrance, but one helluva musical'[14].

The first shock after Claire's astonishing entrance from a train is her announcement that she will give a huge amount of money to help the town recover on the condition that they kill Anton Schell, the ex-lover who has wronged her. Naturally, this introduces a moral dilemma, which becomes the major source of tension in the play, prompting members of the audience to guess whether the townspeople will actually go along with her or persuade her to change her mind. In her review, Jesse Green astutely pinpointed the musical's ironic duality in its,

> tension [. . .] on one hand, [between] the unimpeachably cold – almost terrifying – production design . . . [and] on the other hand [. . .] Rivera, whom everyone adores and hopes to see succeed in a challenging role at age 82. This is a tension that's useful, at least insofar as it puts the audience in sympathy with the devil . . . The songs, too, pull in two directions . . .The better the songs are, the weirder the show gets . . . Alienation and gregariousness make strange co-stars, but then so did Kander and Ebb.[15]

'Out of the Darkness' establishes the awful reality of a town that is in economic distress, its inhabitants desperate to try any means possible to improve their appalling circumstances:

> Out of the darkness
> Come two piercing lights
> Slicing the cold night air
> An angel descends
> From the steps of a train[16] (5)

Even this early in the narrative, an audience might have difficulty taking the description of Claire as an angel at face value.

> At last, at last
> The old lady pays a visit
> Let's stop and think
> Just how many lifetimes is it? (5)

In response to the townspeople staring at her jewels and furs, Claire sings, 'I married very often / And I widowed very well' (6). She lists all of her husbands in a number that resembles a patter song:

> Number three was born in Warsaw
> He was high class Slavic folk
> Though at first he was amusing
> He became my Polish joke.
>
> When he died of liver failure
> Someone read me Freddy's will
> And it said, 'To my dear Clara
> I bequeath three hundred mil.' (7)

Claire's philosophy when 'love is dead' is to 'walk away'. At the end of the song, she observes, 'Anton Schell. I don't see Anton Schell. [. . .] Is he dead?' (8) At which point he enters, 'No, not dead, Clara. Still here' (8).

When Claire tells Anton, 'I've waited a lifetime for this moment' (9), he misses the depth of her vengeful intentions. Claire embarrasses Anton, forcing him to repeat his pet name for her, 'my little wildcat', in front of his wife. In reply, she remembers, 'I called you my panther. How young we were, how beautiful together', initiating a process of memory, which is enhanced by the appearance of two (mostly silent) dancers who represent their young selves. Claire demands to revisit some 'familiar scenes' with Anton on the way to the hotel, 'I want to visit our old trysting places: Peterson's Barn and then on to Konrad's Village Wood' (10). As she exits with her entourage, Anton assures the mayor in the song that Claire will be kind ('I Know Claire'), but the schoolteacher is more sceptical.

The greatest irony in the musical is encapsulated in the singing of 'There's going to be a happy ending' (11) by the mayor and assorted townspeople in the forlorn hope that Claire will rescue the town from dereliction. When Claire asks Anton what happened to Brachen, he replies,

> It's as if we were struck down in our prime to teach us a lesson but no one knows what that lesson is or why we were punished [. . .] Oh, Clara, if only we could be the way we were again, when we were young and unafraid, if only for an instant. (14)

The drama of memory set in train by his reminiscence is both comparable and extremely different to the way Anna and Angel in *The Rink* remember things from opposed perspectives. Unlike *The Rink*, and in spite of the townspeople's determined fantasy of wish-fulfilment, it is not possible for the audience to believe there will be a happy ending:

> YOUNG ANTON
> You, you, you,
> Everywhere
> You, you, you
> In every dream I dream,
> There's a specter of
> You, you, you. (15)

As Kander has said, this lush waltz was the first song the team wrote; its poignancy is intense and complex in the light of the audience's knowledge of Anton's abandonment of Claire when she became pregnant. The atmosphere becomes more sinister as Claire anticipates what will be a macabrely vengeful ending:

> How could I behave
> As if we'd never met
> Oh no, my dear,
> Please rest assured
> I never did forget. (16)

The song continues with melodic lines for Anton and Claire, as well as their young selves, interwoven to create a juxtaposition of past and present in nostalgia, delusion and horror. John Doyle's Williamstown version simplified what had been an elaborate musical scene to emphasize the shocking contrast between present and past, with Claire and Anton's idealistic younger selves being incarnated by two dancers who perform in counterpoint to the older actors.

When Anton claims he only married Matilde for Claire's sake, she replies, 'She had money. I had nothing' (17). But Anton assures her that he is now bankrupt, 'My life is a disaster, Clara'. To which Claire replies icily, 'Don't flatter yourself, Anton. The world is a disaster' (17). Claire comments on her artificial leg and hand, the result of a plane crash but grotesquely insists, 'I'm unkillable' before assuring him that the only real thing about her is her heart. Galati's 2008 version of the number in Arlington offered a more complex musical scene, with more singing for Anton as 'I Know Clare' was interwoven with 'You, You You' and the up-tempo song of memory in which he remembers how he could manipulate Claire who adored him: 'She truly adored me . . . Oh / I must have been something . . . Yes. [. . .] I'm certain we'll have something again' (19).

Once again the audience is teased by the possibility of a happy ending. In Doyle's later version, 'I Must Have Been Something' merely follows Claire's exit, whereas in the 2008 production, the Konrad's Wood scene segues into Anton's shop to form a complicated interweaving of all three songs, now including Matilde, the two younger selves, who sing more than they dance, as well as Claire who sings from her visually juxtaposed hotel bed, while replacing her artificial leg. In my opinion, the earlier version is dramaturgically more powerful because it provides a more genuine hope of a happy ending, creating more plot tension and fleshing out Anton's vanity and self-delusion in comic detail. That same afternoon Anton's children wish to take some items (a party dress; a jacket) from the shop he owns but he cannot afford to let them have these. His son Karl retorts, 'At least let me have some of those yellow shoes. You ordered a gross' (21) before 'You, You, You' continues.

In the following scene, the mayor introduces a *tableau vivant* with music, to tell you our unhappy story':

Many years ago in Brachen
Joy would overflow in Brachen
[...............................]
Goethe spent the night here
In Brachen (27)

What seems like an innocuous folk song is amplified with the clichéd 'oom-pah-pahs' from the men and yodelling from the women.

We all got rich during World War Two
And we couldn't sell our cuckoo clocks faster
[. . .]
Then all of a sudden from out of the blue
We were faced with a terrible disaster:
Our factories closed
Our economy died. (28–9)

The musical explicitly compares the current bankruptcy of the town to what amounted to Swiss war-profiteering during the dominance of the Third Reich, thereby changing the setting of Durrenmatt's 1956 drama with its vague reminiscences of a 1911 past to forty-five years after the 1939–45 war. At this point, the townspeople beg Claire in song to be the 'angel' that saves the town. The references to cuckoo clocks taken from Durrenmatt's play at this point clearly invoke the bourgeois milieu of a Switzerland made wealthy by manufacturing watches and by banking during the Second World War. Claire replies:

My parents could not marry because Papa was a Jew. It's true he built your public lavatory but my mother wasn't allowed to use it. [. . .] You drove my mother from the village. She found her way to Germany where gypsies were no more welcome than here.

MAYOR.
Terrible! We all made terrible mistakes. (30)

Now Claire recounts how she and the handsome Anton fell in love and how she became pregnant:

> You said, 'You must not have the baby. Kill it. I am going to marry Matilde Blumhard. Her father has promised me his shop.' [. . .] Anton said he had friends who would testify that they had slept with me time and time again. And they did, Anton, under oath in a court of law. (32–3)

After her slow and melancholy song, 'Winter', in which Claire sings that the ending of her relationship did not and will not 'give me justice', she declares: 'I wish to buy justice' (37), offering the town ten billion marks before demanding, 'I want the life of Anton Schell' (38). In lines that omit Durrenmatt's reference to Europe's people not being savages, the mayor rejects her bargain with an expression of outrage ('In the name of all the citizens of Brachen, I reject your offer. And I reject it in the name of humanity. We shall never accept.') Rivera claims that reading this for the first time produced a revelation concerning Claire, who 'says the most devastating line in the play: "I can wait."'[17] Her determination to wait for 'truth and justice' is not merely vengeful, but a sign of the love that Anton almost destroyed.

When the townspeople start buying on credit from Anton's store, they start to sing a song in celebration of material pleasures: yellow shoes come to symbolize the cupidity of those in Brachen who believe they can buy happiness in place of current misery:

> Yellow shoes
> Look at me wearing my yellow shoes
> Got me a pair of those yellow shoes
> Finally feeling secure (40)

In the midst of all this hope for the resuscitation of the economy, Anton grasps the grim reality: 'You're going to kill me, aren't you?' (41). In Kander's words,

> I'm trying to remember how yellow became our synonym for money – I guess it's just gold. Yellow shoes itself is kind of a stand-in or symbol for money and greed, and, pretty soon, everybody in the company has got them on.[18]

The song illustrates the way greed spreads incrementally through a community as individuals begin to compete for consumer goods. Kander remembered:

> ['Yellow Shoes'] was a lot of fun to write – that was really fun. And, also, that's a lyric of Fred's that just totally takes my breath away. There's a couplet in there that still makes me smile every time I hear it, which is: 'People who call themselves the elite / Are people who take good care of their feet'. That's really Fred – through and through.[19]

The number has the upbeat and syncopated rhythm of a tap routine (in the Chicago and Arlington productions, it actually was a clog dance) to accompany the whole community as they begin to dance gleefully in their new shoes. Anton tries to escape his murder by leaving the town on a train but is prevented by the townspeople as they sing in sinister fashion while showing off their yellow shoes.

When told by the schoolmaster that 'there are untold riches under the land here, land rich in oil and minerals' (46), Claire replies that she already owns all the land. When the schoolmaster asserts, 'Then it was you who destroyed Brachen', Claire assures him, 'As surely as you destroyed me'. The question of whether she has no 'feelings for humanity,' (47) prompts Claire to sing defiantly:

> Feelings for humanity, can't you see?
> Are for ordinary millionaires, not me!
> [...............................]
> The world has made me into a whore,
> [...............................]
> I make the world my brothel now. (48–9)

Although Claire tells her entourage they are free to leave her after her business in Brachen is over, they all sing, 'I Could Never Leave You', which, in the earlier versions, became a grotesquely funny vaudeville-style strut with canes, Claire occasionally kicking her real leg high in the air to punctuate the tango rhythm.

Both Anton's family and the wider community now begin to resent Anton for making them seem guilty of wanting to sacrifice him:

> Back and forth,
> Like a cat
> Why is he driving us mad like that?
> Back and forth,
> Pacing his room
> [.....................]
> Now he's home
> Spread the gloom. (55)

The schoolmaster then sings 'I Was the Only One' to Anton in explanation of the townspeople's wish to kill him and save Bracken:

Figure 19. Chita Rivera and Michelle Veintimilla in 'Love and Love Alone' from _The Visit_. Photo: Ben Hider, Getty Images.

And wouldn't it serve us well,
If Anton were dead, they said.
[......................]
Forgive me, Anton,
I wanted to help you
But I was the only one in all of our town . . . (58)

After refusing to commit suicide but instead insisting on having a formal trial, Anton asks his son, Karl, to take the family for a drive in Karl's new automobile. In a jaunty musical number representing Anton and his family's tour of the town, he feels he is 'Seeing it all for the very first time' (65) before they drop him off at the edge of the forest, singing 'See you soon' (65)

According to Chita Rivera, '*The Visit* is more than anything a love story. Maybe a little perverse, but a love story nonetheless'.[20] At the edge of the forest, Anton meets Claire, who sings one of the most disturbing songs in the haunting score, 'Love and Love Alone':

There's a truth young love
Simple as this
Every fond hello ends in goodbye
What seems certain to live will die
[.................]

When tomorrows come
And your heart is stone
What has made it numb?
Love and love alone. (66)

John Kander considers the song

[O]ne of Fred's best lyrics, I think. In the song, it's about the fact that almost everything that you can think of – all the things you are so sure of – are really caused by love in one form or another. Only towards the end of Claire's life does she realize that. Love and revenge – I guess the point is that they are really very connected.[21]

When Anton asks her what became of the child they conceived, she recoils, in lyrics that suggest the girl has died. Anton then informs Claire that

It's the last time we shall sit in our old wood and hear the cuckoo calling and the sound of the wind. They are meeting this evening. They will sentence me to death. And one of them will kill me. So ends the story of Anton Schell. (71)

Yet Claire insists, 'The story's not over' (71), explaining that she will bury him on a hill on the Amalfi coast, where she herself intends to be laid to rest, as they sing:

The waltz we waltzed is ending soon
We'll be together high on a hill
Our love surviving
Though our hearts are still (71)

After the trial, the townspeople surround Anton in a circle and he disappears. The doctor declares he died of a heart attack; Claire hands the mayor a cheque as she exits. With macabre irony, the townspeople sing as they did at the beginning: 'There's going to be a happy ending', followed by the entrance of a grey-haired Claire in 'a simple black cloth dress. She is without a wig, jewelry or adornment'; the members of her entourage bear Anton's coffin. The musical ends as her train is heard pulling out of the station.

Ann Reinking's grotesquely funny, if overlong, 'One-Legged Tango' interwoven with 'I Could Never Leave You' was cut in Williamstown; instead, new choreographer Graciela Daniele created additional dance material for Claire and Anton's younger selves in parallel with the older actors in order to reveal the poignant sadness accompanying the bitter spectacle of ageing.[22] In the words of Chicago-based reviewer Chris Jones,

> Watching Rees and Rivera, staring plaintively at each other even as their beautiful younger selves (played by John Riddle and Michelle Veintimilla) sing and dance around them, I was suddenly struck how much the meaning of this show had changed. In Chicago, and then later [. . .] at the Signature Theatre [. . .], 'The Visit' had felt very much like a sharp-edged exposure of self-serving expediency, or the twisted nonsatisfactions of revenge.[23]

In stressing the melancholy confrontation of present and past, the creative team highlights the inevitability that Claire will destroy Anton to exact her revenge. As sad as the death-of-love motif becomes in the second half of the piece, David Rooney reminds his readers of the harshly ironic scheme of *The Visit*, attesting to the heart of darkness at the core of Durrenmatt's fable, which is highlighted by Kander and Ebb's score: 'It's unsurprising that American musical theater's most Brechtian double-act was drawn down this dour road of revenge to explore the ravaged soul of humanity . . . [in a] dance of death.'[24] Nevertheless, he praises 'the thrilling choral singing and exquisitely textured harmonies', another instance of the Brecht-Weill concept of gestic music, which sets the music in tension with lyrics/ dramaturgy. It is significant that John Doyle's one-act production made no concession to a Broadway audience's demands for the reassurances of commercial entertainment; in fact, the ending of the show may have become even more desolate than it was in Chicago and Arlington, although its grotesque ironies may not have been so sharp. Jones interpreted Doyle's production as a comment on outsiders, which is as much a response to then-current controversies about Iraqi refugees in Europe as to the profits made by robbing doomed Jews:

> On Broadway, it feels far sadder and more plaintive, and perhaps a commentary on Europe's less than stellar record with outsiders. Most of all, though, 'The Visit' now feels to be about the pain of growing older and [. . .] our inability to assuage our past mistakes.[25]

Contrary to the creative team's positive endorsement of Doyle's slimmed-down version, the 2008 production in Arlington, Virginia, was, in my view, superior, maintaining suspense by allowing more musical weight to George Hearn's very powerfully sung Anton. His initial attempt to stop the population of Bracken from colluding with Claire created more doubt about the outcome than that of Roger Rees, who appeared, from the moment Claire stated her terms, to accept that he was doomed. Graciela Daniele's new dance trio for the young Anton and Claire, and for Rivera, who later partnered her younger self, was effective. However, a less defiant Anton and the even more melancholy dance lament for the loss of past innocence deprived *The Visit* of the intense desperation of Anton's hope against hope, an approach that provided more intense dramatic tension. *The Visit* was the last of the team's musicals for which Fred Ebb wrote all the lyrics.[26] It is probably their bleakest musical, in which they take the work of 'highbrow' theatre and attempt to make it accessible through the use of an outmoded operetta style.

Notes

1. Quoted in Robert Simonson, 'Many Visits Along the Way: the Long History of Broadway's Latest Kander and Ebb Musical', 23 March 2015, in Playbill/ ManyVisitsAlongtheWay:TheLongH istoryofBroadway'sLatestKander&EbbMusical/ Playbill.webarchive, accessed 20 June 2023.

2. Nelson Pressley, *Washington Post*, 29 May 2008, https://www.washingtonpost.com/ wp-dyn/ content/article/2008/05/29/AR2008052903277.html, accessed 1 June 2023.

3. Quoted in Pressley, *Washington Post*.

4. Quoted in Pressley, *Washington Post*.

5. Quoted in Pressley, *Washington Post*.

6. It is worthy of note that there have been two other musical versions of Durrenmatt's play, one in Rust, Germany in 2013 and a subsequent Persian version staged in Iran. Clearly, the dark parable still appears to resonate with authors and audiences alike.

7. John Kander in https://www.broadwayworld.com/article/BWW-EXCLUSIVE-5-SONGS-BY -John-Kander-On-THE-VISIT-20150526, accessed 4 June 2023.

8. John Kander, as above.

9. Chris Jones, *Chicago Tribune*, 23 April 2015, in https://www.broadwayworld.com/reviews/The -Visit. Accessed 15 June 2023.

10. Mark Kennedy, *Associated Press*, 23 April 2015, https://www.broadwayworld.com/ reviews/ The-Visit, accessed 21 July 2023.

11. Friedrich Durrenmatt, 'Problems of the Theatre', in *The Marriage of Mr Mississippi: a Play; Problems of the Theatre: an Essay*, Translated Gerard Nelhaus and Michael Bullock, New York: Grove Press 1971.

12. Friedrich Durrenmatt, trans. Joel Agee, *The Visit*, London: Jonathan Cape, 1973, 47.

13. Terry Teachout, *Wall Street Journal*, 23 April 2015, https://www.broadwayworld.com/reviews/ The-Visit, accessed 21 July 2023.

14. Chita Rivera, with Patrick Pachecho, *Memoir*, New York: Harper Collins, 2023, 274.

15. In *Vulture*, 2015, https://www.broadwayworld.com/reviews/The-Visit, accessed 21 July 2023.

16. All page numbers refer to Williamstown Theater Festival Performance script, 2 August 2014, unpublished.

17. *Memoir*, 275.

18. John Kander, in *BroadwayWorld*, above.

19. John Kander, in *BroadwayWorld*, above.

20. *Memoir*, 275.

21. John Kander in *BroadwayWorld*, above.

22. At eight minutes the song-and-dance sequence was too long and a bit repetitive; trimmed to four minutes, it would have fulfilled its aim of varying the pace and tone, with the black comedy of a fast-paced vaudeville-style routine.

23. Chris Jones, 'The Visit': Chita Rivera Stars in Broadway Musical About Revenge', *Chicago Tribune*, 23 March 2015, https://www.chicagotribune.com/entertainment/theater/sc-the-visit-broadway-review-20150423-column.html, accessed 15 June 2023.

24. David Rooney, *The Hollywood Reporter*, May 2015, https://www.hollywoodreporter.com/news/general-news/chita-rivera-visit-theater-review-791063/, accessed 15 June 2023.

25. Chris Jones, 'The Visit', above.

26. The great majority of the lyrics in *Curtains* are by Ebb, although Kander wrote lyrics for a thinly disguised autobiographical song called 'I Miss My Friend'.

Conclusion

The Kander and Ebb legacy

Kander and Ebb occupy a unique position in the history of the Broadway musical. Their joint career (1962–2004) remains the longest songwriting partnership in Broadway history. Also remarkable is the way John Kander has completed and supervised the staging of all the works almost finished before Ebb's death, effectively extending that career by almost twenty years. Although the recent Broadway musical, *New York, New York* (2023) closed after a brief run, a national tour was announced for 2025. The films of *Cabaret* and *Chicago* were both highly profitable and the most critically lauded of all film musicals since *The Sound of Music* (1965), giving them worldwide recognition. *Cabaret* may well be the most often revived Broadway musical internationally, while the 1996 revival of *Chicago* has made it the longest-running American musical in New York and London. On one hand, they have attempted work of high artistic ambition in a quasi-operatic style (*The Visit* is comparable in this respect to Sondheim's *Passion*); on the other, they have succeeded more often in a commercial arena than any other 'serious' musical theatre writers. Their daring conjunction of high art and popular music has produced masterpieces such as *Cabaret, The Kiss of the Spider Woman* and *The Scottsboro Boys*, while they have on occasion created delightful pieces of sheer entertainment (*Curtains* and *Liza with a Z*).

Ebb had, with various degrees of input from his partner, written the television specials, *Liza* (1970), *Liza with a Z* (1973), *Ol' Blue Eyes Is Back* (1973) for Frank Sinatra, *Gypsy in My Soul* (1976) for Shirley MacLaine, *Baryshnikov on Broadway* (1980), *Goldie and Liza Together* (1980), *An Evening With Liza Minnelli* (1980), *Liza in London* (1986), *Liza Live at Radio City Music Hall* (1992). Ebb also wrote the stage concert *Liza at the Winter Garden* (1974) and *Minnelli on Minnelli* (1999). The duo supplied two songs for *Lucky Lady* (1975), two for *A Matter of Time* (1976), the title number for *Stepping Out* (1991) and soundtrack music for several TV movies.

The pair's two most famous songs are internationally popular: 'Cabaret' (made famous by Minnelli and Louis Armstrong, and covered by scores of popular vocalists) and 'The Theme from *New York, New York*', introduced by Minnelli and made into a chart hit by Sinatra; the latter number is regularly used as a kind of anthem by New York baseball and football teams, in particular the New York Yankees. After the terrorist attacks of 9/11, it became the unofficial anthem of New York City. Songs like 'My Coloring Book', 'I Don't Care Much', 'A Quiet Thing' and 'Maybe This Time' have been introduced by Streisand or Minnelli and covered by many others, while 'All That Jazz' is ubiquitous.

Although their first completed musical, *Golden Gate* (1962), has never been performed, Kander and Ebb now have seventeen produced stage musicals to their credit. After Ebb's death, Kander continued his solo career by co-writing a triptych of three one-act musicals, *The Landing* (2013) as well as *Kid Victory* (2015) with playwright Greg Pierce. In addition, he wrote music for a 'dance play' based on a Henry James novella, *The Beast in the Jungle* (2018), which was choreographed by Susan Stroman. In 2023, the 96-year-old Kander collaborated with Lin-Manuel Miranda (lyrics), David Thompson and Sharon Washington (book) to create the latest 'Kander and Ebb' musical, *New York, New York*, directed and choreographed by Susan Stroman.

Re-purposing a number of the team's songs – 'One of the Smart Ones' from the unproduced *Golden Gate*; 'Wine and Peaches', a song cut from *The Rink* before its opening; 'I Love Music' from the incomplete score of *Wait for Me, World*; 'I'm What's Happening Now', originally intended for *The Rink*; a snatch of 'Happy Endings' from the film *New York, New York*; 'Let's Hear It for Me' from *Funny Lady*; 'Marry Me' from *The Rink*; 'A Quiet Thing' from *Flora, the Red Menace*; 'Sorry I Asked' written for Minnelli's concert season at Radio City Music Hall (1991), as well as the ubiquitous 'And the World Goes Round' and 'New York, New York' from the movie. 'They're Cheering for Me Now' (2017) was written by Kander and Miranda as part of the *Hamildrops* series.

The duo's ability to create songs in their own distinctive voice is manifest in several shows, while their mastery of a number of approaches to pastiche in their work is astonishing. From *Cabaret*'s Berlin jazz of the late 1920s to the Greek folk music of *Zorba*, their styles have included 1940s American jazz, Latin American popular music, 1930s big-band swing, 1950s 'golden age' musical theatre, 1920s American jazz and vaudeville, ragtime and African American spirituals and minstrel music. They have utilized source material as diverse as novels by Lester Atwell, the Argentinian Manuel Puig and the Canadian Robert Fontaine, the stories of Christopher Isherwood, modern classic dramas by Thornton Wilder and Durrenmatt, as well as original material.

The overwhelming majority of their musicals are epistemologically complex, using techniques of meta-theatre, pastiche and parody to layer their work with the kind of self-reflexivity that confronts audiences with the unavoidable tension between brute reality and its manifold means of representation. Many of their musicals manifest the aesthetic of the *mise en abyme*, the effect of a 'hall of mirrors' representing itself to infinity. While such an approach marks the distinctiveness of much of their output, the true reason their work is so admired may be because the quality of craft skills evinced throughout their oeuvre is unrivalled by any songwriters in the period with the exception of Stephen Sondheim, commonly regarded as a genius. Characterized by an ironically adult perspective on dying, desire, love, racism, ageing, show business, capitalist exploitation, sexuality, revenge and crime, their work has nevertheless been highly accessible while subliminally maintaining a faint thread of optimism that 'out of the darkness [. . .] there's going to be a happy ending'.

Bibliography

Applin Warner, Rebecca, *The Musical Theatre Composer as Dramatist: A Handbook for Collaboration*, London: Methuen, 2023.

Babb, Kent, *The Washington Post,* 9 June 2014.

The Barbra Archives', https://www.barbra-archives.info/funny_lady_ overview. (Accessed 30 July 2022).

Barnes, Clive, Review, *70 Girls, 70*, *New York Times*, 5 April 1971.

Benedict, David, *Variety*, 13 December 2021, https://variety.com/ 2021/ legit/ reviews/cabaret-revi ew-eddie-redmayne-1235131905/. (Accessed 14 December 2021).

Block, Geoffrey, *Enchanted Evenings,* New York: Oxford University Press, 2009.

Brantley, Ben, *New York Times*, 23 March 2007, Section E, 1.

British Theatre.com, https://britishtheatre.com/review-curtains-wyndhams-theatre-london/. (Accessed August 2022).

Carpenter, Humphrey, *W.H. Auden: The Biography*, London: Faber and Faber, 2010.

Childs, Kirsten, Interview with John Kander, How Music Shapes Us, https://www.youtube.com/ watch?v=HmJ3gMEVkXE. (Accessed 30 July 2022).

Clarke, Kevin, http://operetta-research-center.org/berliner-ensemble dreigroschenoper/. (Accessed 3 August, 2023).

Coe, Richard L., 'A Tough Act to Follow', *The Washington Post*, 31 October 1977, https://www .washingtonpost.com/archive/lifestyle/1977/10/31/a-tough-act-to-follow/48d53450-5692 -4536-9bbf-6e2b4d1fba30. (Accessed September 2023).

Corry, John, 'If You're Just Wild about Eubie, This Is for You', *New York Times*, 12 May 1978.

Crompton, Sarah, *Whatsonstage*, 12 December 2021, https://www. whatsonstage. com/news/c abaret-review-eddie-redmayne-and-jessie-buckley-lead-shattering-west-end-revival_55529/. (Accessed 14 December 2021).

Deutsch, Didier C., 'A Look Back', liner notes for *Chicago: A Musical Vaudeville*, CD reissue, Arista, 07822-18952-2, 1996.

The Drama Teacher, https://thedramateacher.com/chicago-bertolt-brecht/. (Accessed 12 October, 2022).

Engel, Lehman, *The Making of a Musical: Creating Songs for the Musical Theatre,* New York: Scribner, 1977.

Everett, William and Laird, Paul eds., *The Cambridge Companion to the Musical,* 3rd edition, Cambridge: Cambridge University Press, 2017.

Furth, George, John Kander and Fred Ebb, *The Act,* New York: Samuel French.

Gaertner, Belva, https://scandalsandsweets.com/belva-gaertner-the-real-velma-kelly-2. (Accessed 2 December 2023).

Gallagher, Stephen, 'Goodbye Berlin, Hello Broadway', https://www. Guide to musicaltheatre.com /shows_c/cabaret_berlin.htm. (Accessed 16 December 2021).

Garebian, Keith, *The Making of Cabaret*, New York: Oxford University Press, 2011.

Gilvey, John, *Before the Parade Passes By*, New York: St Martin's Press, 2005.

Goldman, William, *The Season: A Candid Look at Broadway,* New York: Limelight, 1969.

Gordon, Robert (ed.), *The Oxford Handbook of Sondheim Studies,* Oxford: Oxford University Press, 2014.

Gordon, Terri J., 'Film in the Second Degree: *Cabaret* and the Dark Side of Laughter', *Proceedings of the American Philosophical Society*, Vol. 152, No. 4 (2008).

Gottfried, Martin, *All His Jazz: the Life and Times of Bob Fosse,* New York: Da Capo Press, 2003.

Green, Jesse, *Vulture*, online journal, May 2015, https://www.vulture.com/movies/. (Accessed 9 July 2021).

Hirsch, Foster, *Harold Prince and the American Musical Theatre*, Cambridge: Cambridge University Press, 1989.

Kael, Pauline, 'The Current Cinema', *The New Yorker,* 17 March 1975.

Kael, Pauline, *Deeper into Movies*, London: Calder and Boyars, 1975.

Kammen, Michael, *Mystic Chords of Memory,* New York: Vintage, 1993.

Kander, John and Fred Ebb, *The Songwriters: An Evening with Kander and Ebb*, https://www .youtube.com/ watch?v=UtW9IBH3GtY. (Accessed 11 July 2022).

Kander, John, Interview with Rob Berman in *Playbill*, May 2015, https:// playbill.com/article/caba ret-just-closed-the-visit-just-opened-and-zorbas-at-city-center-the-summer-of-john-kander- com-348164. (Accessed 2 June 2015).

Kander, John and Fred Ebb, with Greg Lawrence, *Colored Lights,* New York: Faber, 2003.

Kander , John and Fred Ebb, *Great Performances,* https://www.youtube.com/watch?v= vDl RejHmwy. (Accessed 4 March 2022).

Kerr, Walter, *New York Sunday Times*, 11 April 1971.

Knapp, Raymond, *The American Musical and the Formation of National Identity,* Princeton: Princeton University Press, 2006.

Knapp, Raymond, *The American Musical and the Performance of Personal Identity,* Princeton: Princeton University Press, 2009.

Kobel, Peter and Shaner, Timothy (ed.), *Chicago, the Movie and Lyrics*, New York: Newmarket Press, 2002.

Lawson-Peebles, Robert (ed.), *Approaches to the American Musical*, Exeter: University of Exeter Press, 1996.

Leve, James, *Kander and Ebb,* New Haven: Yale University Press, 2009.

Levine, Suzanne Jill, *Manuel Puig and the Spider Woman: His Life and Fictions,* New York: Faber, 2000.

Marmion, Patrick, *The Daily Mail*, 13 December 2021, https://www.dailymail.co.uk/tvshowbiz/ article-10302945/At-Eddies-Cabaret-sets-wunderbar-PATRICK-MARMION-reviews-Cabaret .html. (Accessed 16 December 2021).

Mast, Gerald, *Can't Help Singin'*, New York: Overlook Press, 1987.

Masteroff, Joe, John Kander and Fred Ebb, *Cabaret*, New York: Newmarket Press, 1967.

Masteroff, Joe, John Kander and Fred Ebb, *Cabaret: The Illustrated Book and Lyrics*, New York: Newmarket Press, 1999.

McLaughlin, Robert, *Stephen Sondheim and the Reinvention of the Broadway Musical*, Jackson: University of Mississippi Press, 2018.

McNally, Kander and Fred Ebb, *The Kiss of the Spiderwoman,* New York: Samuel French, 2011.

McNally, Kander and Fred Ebb, *The Rink,* New York: Samuel French, 1985.

Miller, Scott, *Deconstructing Harold Hill*, New York: Heinemann, 1999.

Miller, Scott, http://www.newlinetheatre.com/chicagochapter.htmlfile:/kanderebb/. (Accessed 3 April 2022).

Minnelli, Liza, John Kander and Fred Ebb, The Creative Process, file:/kanderebb/TheCreativeProce
s:LizaMinnelli,JohnKander&FredEbb(1974),You Tube. (Accessed 27 August 2022).

Mordden, Ethan, *All That Jazz: the Life and Times of the Musical Chicago*, New York: Oxford
University Press, 2018.

Nash, N. Richard, John Kander and Fred Ebb, *The Happy Time*, New York: Samuel French, 1968.

O'Donovan, Ryan, *Queer Approaches in Musical Theatre*, London: Methuen, 2023.

Prince, Harold, *Contradictions,* New York: Dodd, Mead and Co., 1974.

Prince, Harold, *Sense of Occasion*, Milwaukee: Applause Books, 2017.

Puig, Manuel, *Kiss of the Spider Woman,* trans. Thomas Colchie, New York: Vintage Books, 1979.

Reinking, Ann, 2017, https://www.brainyquote.com/authors/ann-reinking-quotes/. (Accessed
September 2022).

Rich, Frank, *New York Times*, 30 March 1981, https://www.nytimes.com/1981/03/30/theater/
stage-lauren-bacall-in-woman-of-year.html. (Accessed 19 September 2022).

Rogers, Bradley, *The Song Is You*, Iowa City: University of Iowa Press, 2020.

Rosenfeld, Bill, CD liner notes, *Flora the Red Menace*, RCA, B000003F51.

Schechter, Scott, *The Liza Minnelli Scrapbook*, Kensington: Citadel Press, 2004.

Smith, Patricia Juliana (ed.), *The Queer Sixties*, New York: Routledge, 1999.

Stein, Joseph, John Kander and Fred Ebb, *Zorba*, New York: Random House, 1969.

Stempel, Larry, *Showtime,* New York: W.W. Norton, 2010.

Stone, Peter, John Kander and Fred Ebb, *Woman of the Year*, New York: Samuel French, 1984.

Swain, Joseph, *The Broadway Musical: A Critical and Musical Survey,* Oxford: Oxford University
Press, 1990.

Thompson, David, John Kander and Fred Ebb, *Flora, the Red Menace,* New York: Samuel
French, 2012.

Thompson, David, John Kander and Fred Ebb, *The Scottsboro Boys*, https://www.nypl.org/sites/
default/files/scottsboro_boys_final.pdf. (Accessed March 2020).

Thompson, David, John Kander and Fred Ebb, *Steel Pier,* New York: Samuel French, 1998.

Wasson, Sam, *Fosse*, Boston and New York: Houghton Mifflin Harcourt, 2013.

Wilder, Thornton, *The Skin of Our Teeth*, in *Our Town and Other Plays*, Harmondsworth: Penguin
Classics, 2000.

Winkler, Henry, *Big Deal*, New York: Oxford University Press, 2018.

Wolf, Matt, *Sam Mendes at the Donmar*, New York: Limelight, 2002.

Wolf, Matt, *The Arts Desk*, 18 December 2019, https://theartsdesk.com/ theatre/curtains-wyn
dhams-theatre-review-unexpectedly-giddy-fun. (Accessed September 2022).

Wolf, Stacy, *Changed for Good,* Oxford: Oxford University Press, 2011.

Zacharek, Stephanie, Essay on *The Woman of the Year*, Criterion Collection, 2017, https://
www.criterion.com/current/posts/4514-woman-of-the-year-a-womans-place. (Accessed
September 2021).